THE PSYCHODYNAMICS OF WORK
AND ORGANIZATIONS

THE PSYCHODYNAMICS OF WORK AND ORGANIZATIONS
Theory and Application

WILLIAM M. CZANDER

GUILFORD PRESS
New York   London

© 1993 The Guilford Press
A Division of Guilford Publications, Inc.
72 Spring Street, New York, NY 10012

Printed in the United States of America

This book is printed on acid-free paper.

Last digit is print number: 9 8 7 6 5 4 3 2 1

Library of Congress Cataloging-in-Publication Data

Czander, William M.
    The psychodynamics of work and organizations : theory and application / by William M. Czander.
        p.   cm.
    Includes bibliographical references and index.
    ISBN 0-89862-284-0
    1. Work—Psychological aspects.   2. Organizational behavior.
3. Psychoanalysis.   I. Title
BF481.C93   1993
158.7—dc20   93-13405
                                                                  CIP

Acknowledgments

I would first like to thank all those who assisted in this project: graduate and undergraduate students who gave me much needed insight into the world of work; patients who helped me understand the basis of our connection to work; managers, employees, and consultees, who labor in the trenches, who willingly let me snoop around and learn.

I would especially like to thank Ms. Donna Wolf and Ms. Orin Kennedy Greene for helping with the editing and Ms. Wray for her help in a case analysis.

I am most grateful for the Louis Capalbo Fund and the School of Business at Manhattan College for their generous support which allowed me the time and resources to search the literature and write the book.

I would also like to thank the faculty and my colleagues at the Psychoanalytic Institute of the Postgraduate Center for Mental Health for their insight and criticism and David Lasky of The Guilford Press for his help. In addition, I would like to thank Sidney Furst for his strong encouragement.

Above all, I would like to thank Alicia, Eliza, and Giovanna for their patience, support, and willingness to sacrifice during this project.

Contents

Introduction

Following the great migrations and industrialization of the nineteenth century, the population of the United States tended to concentrate in the great metropolitan regions. These fluid collective aggregates have spawned the development of large, complex institutions: church, government, educational, and corporate. In addition, the closed societal caste system that provided fixed status was no longer acceptable and began to dissipate in the late nineteenth century. These large, complex institutions provided unfettered freedom of mobility for both the individual and the family. On the other hand, the creation of large-scale institutions resulted in large-scale hierarchies which created a new caste system. The caste system was no longer based on social class or economic and inherited status; it was based on position in the hierarchy. As these large-scale hierarchies expanded in size, complexity, and heterogeneity, they also extended horizontally, consuming more and more territory and social space.

Although one must gaze in wonderment at the accomplishments of these hierarchical modern organizations and the improvements they have made in the world, one hopes perhaps there could be a "better way." Theorists and teachers of business are constantly responding to this hope, and they do so by continuously proposing new and exciting organizational structures, procedures, technologies, programs, and processes to make the organization more effective and efficient and at the same time to increase commitment and esprit. Invariably they come up short. Perhaps the reason is their lack of understanding of the conscious and unconscious forces that bind people together and stimulate motivations for work and achievement, or perhaps they do not adequately understand the "dark" forces that underlie human behavior, or they fail to understand what Fromm (1970) refers to as "system man." System man is the person who goes

1

to work in these large complex bureaucratic organizations. The system man is poorly understood. He/she is given more criticism than understanding, especially by social theorists. He/she is typically viewed as unhappy, and is characterized as alienated, a victim of a consumer-oriented society, a person "hell-bent" on filling up an empty life with material goods, a self-less person who will assume any shape required by his/her superiors, and a person unable to assume a shape of his/her own. Such harsh treatment stems from a lack of understanding of this "man."

Careful examination of system man is lacking. Theorists tend to focus on his/her behavior. If system man's motives are examined they are typically general and glib constructs devoted to developing a picture of a person who is eager to be shaped, manipulated, and controlled in some paternalistic manner. System man's motives seem to be more for the benefit of those who are seeking to control rather than for the "man" himself. Is it any wonder that system man is viewed as empty. Fromm (1970) supports this when he says:

> Perhaps it started with Spinoza. It was greatly advanced by Freud. To be sure, it still is only a crude model of a system, but I believe that only to the extent that managers or, in general, people who try to understand . . . a large enterprise, take the System Man as seriously as they take the system economics, the system technology, and so on, can they meaningfully talk about human ends in relations to the aims and ends of the managerial process. (p. 169)

This statement stimulates a question: Why is system man viewed in such a colorless manner? Why has he/she not been taken seriously? The answer may be found in the prevailing attitude that exists toward the organization and work in general. Corporate leaders and their consulting experts have been seeking utopia through organizational integration, which is what they generally have in mind when they speak of modernizing, updating, rationalizing, transforming, or planning for the organization (Roszak, 1969). In their attempts to seek efficiency, social security, large-scale coordination, and higher levels of affluence, they develop what is referred to as a "bureaucratic attitude." This attitude maintains that the function of management is to control passion. Robert S. McNamara (1968) typifies this attitude and he claims the following:

> Some critics today worry that our democratic, free societies are becoming overmanaged. I would argue that the opposite is true. As paradoxical as it may sound, the real threat to democracy comes, not from overmanagement, but from undermanagement. To undermanage reality is not to

keep free. It is simply to let some force other than reason shape reality. That force may be unbridled emotion; it may be greed; it may be aggressiveness; it may be hatred; it may be ignorance; it may be inertia; it may be anything other than reason. (pp. 109–110)

The work of overmanagement, according to McNamara, is to "shape reality." This is the thrust of those who hold the bureaucratic attitude. They suggest a rational view of the organization as optimally an instrument of efficiency. Following Gouldner (1954), they see the organization as a "structure of manipulative parts, each of which is separately modifiable with a view to enhancing the efficiency as a whole" (p. 56). Along with this view is one of the worker as an object to be managed in much the same way. Theorists proposing a rational model of the organization, and holding beliefs that it is the job of management to structure the organization in a manner that will increase control of passions, suggest a dim view of human nature. They profess a belief that these "shadowy forces" contained in the minds of employees must be controlled and "managed." This view leaves little room for understanding the complex forces that motivate system man. It also presents an interesting paradox: it generates the belief that only through the control of passion will reason prevail, and it dismisses any notion that suggests that reason can only prevail through an understanding of this complex and dynamic figure, system man.

Much of the criticism today against U.S. corporations is lodged against management, and those institutes of higher education that educate them. Hayes and Abernathy (1980) have blamed management for failing to establish the structures and cultures conducive to innovation and increased productivity. Others look at the Japanese success and claim that U.S. management has failed because they hold motives antagonistic to innovation (Bowles, Gordon, & Weisskopf, 1983). The university is condemned for educating elitists who are intent to enter the corporate caverns to enhance themselves in a narcissistic manner. In addition, those who teach are accused of being intellectually bankrupt; of relying on outmoded theories generated from industrial corporations that no longer exist; of being content with the theories of Etzioni, Argyris, McGregor, Selznick, Perrow, March and Simon, and Roethlisberger and Dickson, who wrote between 1933 and 1964. However, one can take heart. There is a growing interest in trying to understand system man and the forces that impinge on him/her. This movement is led by those who wish to see the organization as a more cooperative enterprise, functioning in harmony with less control and more shared responsibility. They no longer see the organization as a rational system but instead as a system filled with intangibles that are complex sets of social relations. Also, they see the organization as an historical entity, continuously undergoing evolution. They are convinced that statistical correlations tell us nothing useful about the organization. They reject any notion of a grand theory of the organization, but instead are content to flow back and forth between theory and case analysis. And, finally, they are no longer content to see system man in a simplified manner. They are not intellectually timid of the "black box" and they believe that to understand system man requires an understanding of his/her unconscious motives. Psychoanalytic theory now enters the world of organizational theory as a method to understand system man.

THE PSYCHOANALYTIC PERSPECTIVE

The traditional view of system man is that he/she is motivated by economic matters and must be managed. The psychoanalytic perspective suggests a different point of view. It suggests that the desire to seek and obtain things is not motivated by the need for material goods; it rejects the economic view. Furthermore, the psychoanalytic perspective suggests that the motivation to control passion and perhaps the wish to manage or to be managed may be the function of a neurotic condition; that is, nothing more than an attempt to blunt the more "shadowy" wishes and motivations for human relatedness and the fears associated with the creative drive to master and accomplish.

It is the work of psychoanalytically inclined social scientists to challenge and change this bureaucratic attitude, and in doing so to bring into the workplace those things that contribute to making work a meaningful experience that will contribute to rather than detract from mental health.

EDUCATING STUDENTS OF MANAGEMENT

Any book on organizations is really a book about hierarchies, about the social order of organizational life and the influence hierarchies have on this social order. As with any hierarchical system, there are iatrogenic consequences, and this is especially apparent in bureaucratic systems that are structured to rule behavior, control resources, and establish dominance of one over another.

This book is the culmination of 16 years of consulting to organizations, working with patients, training in psychoanalysis, and teaching employed managers who are pursuing their MBA degree. The writing of a book in which psychoanalytic theory is exclusively applied to work and the organization has evolved out of these experiences. Of particular significance has been my work with graduate students, who have convinced me of the need for an in-depth way to think about and study work and organizations. It is apparent that the more general theories associated with work and organization have little relevance to employed graduate students. Students feel that contemporary organizational/behavioral theory does not answer their most basic and meaningful questions. When they think about work they want to know why things do not work out as expected, why superiors behave in certain ways, and why the workplace contains feelings and emotions that sometimes make work a good experience but often make it a mediocre and sometimes a bad experience. They want to learn about themselves and their relationship to work and the organization and their career, and they want to understand the relationship between career satisfaction and satisfaction outside the career. Students love to talk about their experiences at work, their successes and failures, their aspirations and dreams, and the blocks that often appear from time to time, which stifle aspirations and cause hardship and sometimes depression and rage. They want to understand their experiences in a personal way, and they believe that if they can do this, they will be able to engage with the world of work with an increased capacity.

THE FOCUS OF A PSYCHOANALYTIC THEORY OF WORK

The focus of this book is the development of a psychoanalytic understanding of work in the organization. In the past, the psychoanalytic exploration of work has focused on the individual engaged in a creative act. The most prominently explored areas of work are those of the artist, writer, and actor. This creative work is rarely viewed within its social context, and the worker is not often portrayed as the struggling employee or entrepreneur working to obtain success within a competitive business environment. Instead, the employee is seen as an isolate, struggling with intrapsychic conflicts and trying to overcome these blockages to gain freer expression. Historically, psychoanalysts have investigated great leaders, politicians, and to a lesser degree, societal deviants like the assassin and the criminal; however, these efforts have focused on an analysis of the individual. They have tended to explain success or failure by exploring the connections between the subject's childhood and the events that occurred later in life. They have ignored exploration of the psychodynamics associated with the person at work in large, complex, and formal organizations, and the dynamics found within the situations where most people go every day to seek success and fulfillment.

When studying a person within the formal organization, many problems are apparent. For example, should the focus of study be the person, the group, the intergroup, or some larger system? In the formal organization, a psychoanalysis of the individual is problematic, in part because most work-related activities take place in groups, but primarily because most who work within or consult to organizations tend to see the organization as an ideal, as a rational decision-making body. They prefer to believe that by using technological thoroughness they can orchestrate a harmonic endeavor; that is, they can guide behaviors toward a single coordinated effort. So they respond likewise, by establishing a complex array of structures, rules, roles, and interactions. This response makes the application of psychoanalytic theory problematic, because theorists have to comprehend exceedingly complex situations and such an analysis increases the risk of becoming reductionistic (see Chapter 5). The key issue in writing a text such as this is to apply theory to specifics, not to general psychological constructs such as motivation, learning, commitment, perception, and so forth, but more to organizationally relevant issues such as authority, work roles, autonomy and dependency, and the interpersonal issues that arise at work.

Work in formal organizations is time-consuming and emotionally overwhelming. Consider that an employee spends on average 50 weeks a year, 40 hours a week, 5 days a week at work, and when travel and preparation time and the work of worry about work are included, the time devoted to work is most likely 70 to 80 hours a week. But all this time is not spent working. Estimates are that an employee spends only 2 to 4 hours a day engaged in actual work; the rest of the time is spent on work-related activities, or as one employee said, "I'm like a fireman at work, on call." What happens during these other hours, the hours on call, is perhaps more important than the actual work an employee does. These work-related activities contribute greatly to the employee's sense of satisfaction and hold great potential in offering to the employee an existence in a "psychological community." Organizational theorists maintain that it is some combination of participation in the formal and informal systems that provides for a psychological attachment to work.

From a psychoanalytic perspective, attachment to work is considered the result of the gratification of conscious and unconscious fantasies associated with occupational and career aspirations. It is the content of these fantasies and their analysis that presents insight into how the organization can change, and increases the probability of gratification associated with work. However, in most instances the organization comes up woefully short in its capacity to gratify an employee's conscious and unconscious wishes. The reasons for this are found in the nature of the organization, its general pyramid shape. Given the organization's structure, not all employees will be able to reach the heights to which they aspire, and this will precipitate narcissistic wounds and behavioral reactions. It is for this reason that the gratifications associated with an employee's wish are rarely attained, simply because employees unconsciously seek from the organization the love they never received from their family of origin but nevertheless still try to obtain. At the same time, the organization uses employees to perform tasks and sometimes causes them to suffer deprivation by demanding conformity to stated and implied requirements.

This book suggests that working in a formal organization will precipitate psychic conflict. How this conflict is handled, either by the employee or by the organization, will determine whether the employee is able to sustain the absence of psychic gratifications and is capable of either seeking alternative gratifications or utilizing defenses.

The book is segmented into two parts: the first part is theoretical; the second part is an application of theory to specific cases. In the first part, I present the three major theories of psychoanalysis as they relate to work and the organization: Freud and classical psychoanalytic theory, object relations theory, and self psychology theory. Each of these theories is assessed in terms of what it contributes to our understanding of work. Also included in this section is a chapter exploring the relationship between psychic structure and organizational structure and the variables that promote and detract from a psychic connection to work and the organization. This chapter is followed by one devoted to the method or the way in which a psychoanalyst thinks; that is, how he sees the organization, what he looks for, and the way he interprets data. The activity of applying psychoanalytic theory to problems at work requires knowledge of the theory as well as an ability to "think analytically." Chapter Five examines the cognitive processes involved in thinking in this manner, where one focuses on themes and metaphors. The content of communication is the aim of psychoanalytic consulting, that is, to go beyond that which is overt and to focus on the organization's covert life. If nothing else, it is hoped that this text will help the reader appreciate these covert processes in the organization and their power in influencing decisions, efficiency, effectiveness, and behavior at work.

The second half of the book begins with an exploration of how consultants consult to organizations by identifying nine methods of organizational consultation. A new model is added, psychoanalytic consulting, and the guideposts used in this model are identified. Each of these guideposts is applied to a specific problem in an organization. The problem is assessed from a psychoanalytic perspective and a case analysis is presented and discussed.

PART I

THEORY

CHAPTER 1

Freud and Work

Love is a relationship we have with one or very few others.
Work is the embodiment of our relations to our whole culture,
past, present and future.
—EDMOND WEIL (1959, p. 124)

Except for several forays into the psychodynamics of creativity and numerous psychohistorical studies of personalities who achieved greatness, the literature on the psychoanalysis of work is meager. This disappointing fact is especially apparent in the psychoanalysis of work in formal organizations. The paucity of psychoanalytic literature is troubling considering the amount of time one spends "working for a living." Forty to 60 hours a week spent at work is common for most people, and for most people, work is the single most time-consuming activity in their adult life. Given the pervasiveness of work in the life of the modern adult, one would expect work to be given significant status as a subject for study in psychoanalytic circles; however, this is not the case. As a result, we do not have a psychoanalytic theory of work.

Freud wrote very little about work; no paper is devoted to the subject, and his thoughts about work appear as antidotal observations, often confined to footnotes. When one considers the meaning of work during the period in which Freud developed his theories, his lack of attention, and perhaps lack of clarity, can be explained. The Victorian middle class, especially Freud's patients, did not work and were members of the "leisure class." If they did work, it was an economic necessity deriving from some type of family tragedy. During this period it was considered offensive to have employment, that is, to be in the employment of another. Members of Viennese society were not corporate employees in the contemporary sense, and the so-called managerial class was small in numbers.

11

The sparseness of Freud's writings on the subject of work have presented contemporary psychoanalytic writers with what seems to be confusion about his thoughts. Freud is accused by a number of writers (Neff, 1977; Hendrik, 1944a; Erikson, 1950; Lantos, 1952; Menninger, 1942; Oberndorf, 1951; Jahoda, 1966) of making contradictory statements about work and of being ambivalent about the subject.

To begin to understand Freud's view of work requires a discussion of these accusations. For example, Freud (1930/1961) says, "[O]n one hand work is one of the two great pleasures of human activity, [and on the other, it is] not as a pleasurable activity to be sought, but as a painful burden to be endured" (p. 111). Neff (1977) and others use this quote to reinforce their argument that Freud is contradictory.

These arguments are false and demonstrate an inadequate understanding of Freud's writing. Stating that work can be both a painful burden and a pleasurable activity is not necessarily a contradiction. Freud is suggesting that the creativity and effort required to accomplish work-related tasks are painful, and the pleasure is associated only with outcome and achievement. In this sense, work is a pathway to pleasure and happiness. Put another way, Freud saw work as a road to pleasure, but concluded that this road may be painful. This position brings about his lament that "it is unfortunate that people do not value work as a path to happiness" (Gay, 1988, p. 545). Freud tries to answer the following questions: Why is work experienced as a painful activity to be avoided, and why is pleasure obtained from it? The answers can be found in his three psychic requirements of work: (1) work requires a renunciation of the instincts; (2) it means giving up the pleasures associated with play and childhood and entering into a life ruled by the reality principle rather than the pleasure principle; and (3) it means giving up the freedoms associated with childhood. Freud suggests that if these requirements are not met through work, work will be too painful and avoided altogether. Consequently, the worker will never have an opportunity to gain the pleasure associated with accomplishment because he/she cannot delay gratification or endure the necessary suffering.

WORK AS A RENUNCIATION OF THE INSTINCTS

Freud believed that the capacity to obtain pleasure through work can come only when one has been able to adequately curb his/her instincts. This position evolves from Freud's materialistic and deterministic position concerning the role of instinctual drives as a motive underlying all human behavior, especially work. According to Freud, all humans are confronted by drives that are produced by physiologically based instincts. At the base of these drives is the pleasure principle, the chief principle or motivator of all psychic activity. This principle holds that we all have urges to discharge instinctual tension, namely, sexual or aggressive instincts, in a manner that will bring about maximum pleasure.

Although Freud believed that these instincts lie at the basis of all human behavior and function as fundamental motivators, he did not presume that they could be shaped into specified behaviors in any particular way. Consequently, he emphasized that which was instinctual rather than the instincts themselves. Therefore, any form or type of behavior is driven or motivated by an underlying instinct—including work, which Freud saw as a complex activity capable of gratifying many drives and thwarting others.

Freud believed that the mature adult has a responsibility to society. To be responsible and to work the person must accept the limitations demanded by society of these sexual and aggressive instincts. Freud suggests that if allowed to run rampant, these instincts would destroy society; similarly, if these instincts could be curbed, society would flourish. The basis of Freud's theory concerning the relationship between the employee and his/her work and the organization centers around the employee's capacity to curb these instincts. This capacity is a necessary condition for the employee not only to be able to work and experience pleasure, but to make a contribution to society by producing things. To develop Freud's theory, Hall (1954) points to the utility of defenses and how they serve to curb the instincts and thereby contribute to an increase in the employee's capacity to work. This capacity is developed in the following manner:

> First the child must relinquish a sense of omnipotence, fed by the womb and early nurturance; he must renounce partial sexual drives, the oedipal objects, and later excessive family attachments, thus acquiring his first mode of judgement and independence. His curiosity must be cultivated, and education must be tactfully reinforced, and biological instincts curbed by setting limits but not overdrawn. The mature adult must learn how to know the nature of his own drives so that they can be accepted or rejected, according to a moral standard which Freud left unexamined, as "self evident." Reclaimed from the unconscious and from an unrealistic sense of guilt, the strengthened and mature adult can most effectively maximize real satisfaction, discharge social responsibility and achieve reasonable pleasure in work. . . . (p. 31)

The key to working is the capacity of the employee to use the "reality principle" to modify the "pleasure principle." The reality principle motivates one to postpone or renounce "pleasure" according to the perception of social reality. Pleasure, then, can be obtained in adult life only when the reality principle supersedes the pleasure principle. Given the nature of contemporary bureaucracy, this view suggests that the reality principle is ultimately defined by the organization, or by the nature of one's work (i.e., one's occupational role). To psychically accept this principle at the expense of the pleasure principle is to accept the conditions established by the work environment, which consist of the role, structure, and informal relations established at work. Work becomes enjoyable when the employee is able to accept or internalize the organization's definition of pleasure. In this sense, work may resemble play. However, Freud would most likely disagree with this view. He maintains in his writings that work and play have little in common psychically. This position forces him to have a dim or harsh view of the psychic realities associated with work.

PLAY AND ITS ROLE IN THE PREPARATION FOR WORK

Freud differentiates work and play by suggesting that what play is for the child, work is for the adult. However, for the adult work is a necessity and it means a life ruled by the reality principle rather than the pleasures and freedoms associated with play and the pleasure principle. Freud suggests that success in work life is a function of an employee's acceptance of the frustrations associated with scarcity. The struggles and conflicts experienced in adult life center around scarcity, and mastery of these struggles associated with scarcity begins in childhood through the activities associated with play. Freud (1920/ 1955) describes play as an attempt in childhood to gain this mastery, which is vital if the child is to come to terms with the constraints experienced during the oedipal period, when parents, as the child's first authorities, attempt to constrain freedoms. Acceptance of parental constraints along with the experiences of mastery prepares the child for work.

Avoidance of work in adult life is seen as a continuation of oedipal struggles for freedom against the oppression of authority, the parents, who are experienced as a constraining force. People who cannot work are not able to identify with these early authority figures. Consequently, Freud sees the unemployable as not able to invest his/her aggression against authority into his/her superego,[1] and there-

---

[1]In *Totem and Taboo* (1912–1913/1953), we find Freud's first formulation of the role of the ego ideal (later to be called the superego). Freud saw the ego ideal as a condition of repression which has important implications sustaining the employee's self-regard and his capacity to achieve the fantasies contained in the ego ideal, as well as the ability to love other people. As we shall see in Chapter 3, the ego ideal is an agency that plays a significant role in the psychical relationship to work. The superego has an important connection to work in its characterization as an internal code or conscience. This entity, in Freud's tripartite model of the psyche, is formed in response to rewards and punishments from parental figures, which result in an internalization of moral codes.

fore unable to fully internalize authority. These employees are against authority and are constantly engaged in conflict and reparation. At work, the lack of internalization of authority makes an employee's relations with authority (those who have the power to frustrate wishes and create scarcity in reality and in fantasy) problematic; consequently, the employee experiences authority and authority structures, namely, bureaucracies, as confining and constraining.

According to Freud, to be able to work with joy and satisfaction means accepting the position that one must give up freedoms. However, this process is far more complex than merely internalizing authority or accepting societal or organizational constraints.

WORK AND GIVING UP FREEDOMS

Freud suggests that total instinctual gratification of impulses is only found among primitives and infants. To restrain or postpone instinctual gratification is the price one must pay to love and work in a civilized society (Freud, 1930/1961). To Freud, absolute instinctual gratification is impossible; that is, paradise is unobtainable. Furthermore, Freud suggests that culture cannot be developed as long as one remains in paradise. This position underlies Freud's efforts to define how culture is derived from both restraining and postponing instinctual gratification. While Freud suggests that giving up freedoms associated with the postponement of drive impulses is unpleasurable, he holds that to remain in "paradise" portends a greater degree of suffering. To avoid the souring of "paradise" as one approaches adulthood, one must leave it and enter the world of work. It is here, in the world of work, that one will experience the greatest potential for psychic pleasure. Pleasure can be obtained by working through the suffering associated with restraint and accepting the defensive functions associated with work. If an employee is unable to accomplish this, he/she will be inhibited at work and will avoid altogether the potential pleasure that may be experienced in or derived from work. This is made clear in Freud's (1926/1959) brief foray into work:

> In inhibition in work . . . the subject feels a decrease in his pleasure in it or becomes less able to do it well; or he has certain reactions to it, like fatigue, giddiness or sickness, if he is obliged to go on with it. (p. 89)

The organization, like society, confronts the person with a major dose of external reality. This is the burden that one must pass through on the way to pleasure. Consider Freud's (1930/1961) following statement:

No other technique for the conduct of life attaches the individual so firmly to reality as laying emphasis on work; for his work at least gives him a secure place in a portion of reality, in the human community. The possibility it offers of displacing a large amount of libidinal components, whether narcissistic human relations connected with it lends it a value by no means second to what it enjoys as something indispensable to the preservation and justification of existence in society. (p. 80)

According to Freud, to live within or work within the constraints of the organization, one must internalize its values, norms, and standards and make it part of one's mental life. If this internalization occurs, the organization, like society, offers opportunities for psychic gratification.

THE CAPACITY TO WORK

To be able to work and to be connected to work in a psychically gratifying manner require that an employee have the following capacities:

1. The capacity to turn the libido[2] outward, away from narcissism[3];
2. The capacity to desexualize, sublimate, and deaggressivize the libido and aggression,[4] respectively;
3. The capacity to create and maintain strong identifications with a leader (Gabriel, 1982); and
4. The capacity to enter and become a member of a group.

Each of these psychic capacities will be examined.

[2]Libido is the second of Freud's two instincts, aggression the other. Like aggression, libido is a hypothesized energy located in the id and Freud initially viewed it as sexual in nature. But later on it took on a meaning closer to "life force" or "life energy"; however, it still contains sexual, erotic, and pleasurable connotations.

[3]Narcissism has come to mean many things in the field of psychoanalysis. In the classical sense it is considered an early stage of development when the libido is invested in the self or ego, that is, love of self. In normal development this investment is turned outward toward others. In neurosis it remains fixed on the self.

[4]Freud introduced the concept of aggression as a "separate and independent striving" (1905/1953, p. 52) and he saw its origin as the "impulse to master" (1905/1953, p. 53). He claims that aggression as an impulse is instinctual and can only be inhibited by shame and sympathy. In *Beyond the Pleasure Principle* (Freud, 1920/1955) he returns to the problem of aggression and the compulsion to repeat unpleasant experiences (repetition compulsion). In this paper he articulates the death instinct and views aggression toward others as an example of the death instinct deflected outward. In *Instincts and Their Vicissitudes* (1915/1957), Freud asserts that hate must precede love in the development of one's relation to other people. "The relation of hate is older than that of love" (p. 139).

Turning the Libido Away from Narcissism

Along with Freud, contemporary psychoanalytic theorists (Erikson, 1950; Menninger, 1942; Oberndorf, 1951; Bieber, 1970; Jaques, 1951; Lantos, 1952; Deutscher, 1968; Jahoda, 1966; Rohrlich, 1980), support the psychic value of work and reject those who see work as offering little in the way of psychic fulfillment (Chisholm, 1946/1967; Marcuse, 1955). They all maintain that work provides the opportunity to form libidinal ties. These ties are formed not only with one's task at hand, but with others in the work environment. Freud gave equal psychic value to forming libidinal ties with others and performing one's work by producing things and achieving goals. The attainment of libidinal gratification with others at work includes being part of a larger culture, a community in a psychological sense, and making a contribution to this group, and perhaps society in general, by collectively working on a specific task.

This is confirmed in *Civilization and Its Discontents* (1930/1961), where Freud states:

After primal man had discovered that it lay in his own hands, literally to improve his lot on earth by working, it cannot have been a matter of indifference to him whether another man worked with him or against him. The other man acquired the value for him of a fellow worker, with whom it was useful to live together. (p. 99)

Here Freud claims that when pleasure or displeasure is associated with work it is a function of the quality of the sense of community the employee experiences at work. When Freud says that work is a force that binds people together, he is referring to this sense of community. This is in agreement with his claim that work, along with love (ananke and eros), is the basis for communal life. Work has value by providing an opportunity for the creation of communal life.

According to Freud, love is an evolutionary relation; it is initially narcissistic; that is, the first object one loves is oneself. Hate comes first because external objects are perceived as impinging upon primary narcissism and consequently these objects are hated. If these objects give pleasure (this is a developmentally later period), they are introjected to become part of the self. Freud says that all infantile forms of love are fused with hate and only at a later stage, the genital stage, can love and hate become antithetical. However, if development is arrested at one of the stages prior to the genital, one's relations to others in adult life will be characterized by the more primitive love–hate relations and the adult will vacillate between introjects of love and projections of hatred toward the same object at different points in time.

The creation of community serves as binding function. This binding function can be assessed by understanding the function of the social context associated with work. Thus the social context associated with work provides the context for the creation of a sense of a psychological community which provides a binding function. Employees who experience this sense of community have constructed opportunities for psychic discharge that may or may not be available within the actual task system.

If the organization fails to provide opportunities for libidinal attachment, or the creation of a psychological sense of community, employees will experience unpleasure resulting from psychic deprivations. Under these conditions, object choice is then focused on narcissistic concerns, or, in some instances, the employee responds with sadistic, aggressive forms of acting out. Acting out evolves from the experience of frustration, where the employee displaces sadistic or degrading feelings onto minority members in the organization. It can also lead to other problem behaviors such as sexual acting out, high absenteeism, alcoholism, and conflicts with authority. If these libidinal ties cannot be provided within the task system, it is the responsibility of management to provide opportunities for psychic gratification within a context adjacent to the task system. This is generally referred to as the establishment of an informal system.

It is also the task of management to operationalize Freud's basic idea concerning the attainment of pleasure associated with work: that the employee must be able to experience himself as contributing to or playing an important part in civilized life.

Neutralizing and Sublimating the Sex and Aggressive Instincts

Only through sublimation[5] is an employee able to find gratification through work. Through sublimation the employee is able to redirect libidinous instincts toward new and refined behaviors. In *Civilization and Its Discontents* (1930/1961), Freud says that "sublimation of instincts is an especially conspicuous feature of cultural evolution; thus it is sublimation that makes it possible for higher mental operation, scientific, artistic, ideological activities to play such an important part in civilized life" (p. 97).

[5]The concept of sublimation of the instincts as it relates to work was not fully developed by Freud. Ilan (1963) suggests that while sublimation has been used frequently by Freud and others in the psychoanalytic literature, it has not yet been uniformly defined or fully elucidated. The most commonly used definition suggests that sublimation is the deflection of instinctual drives to aims that are more susceptible to the ego and superego.

The capacity to attain gratification through task-related activities occurs not only because the instinctual drives are directly gratified, but because derivatives that are highly socialized deflections of early primitive impulses are gratified. Gratification can be attained through the sublimation of early primitive drives through work activities. For example, how does one who works within a bureaucracy shuffling papers all day long sublimate his/her sexual and aggressive drives? It may seem that this employee has significantly fewer opportunities to do so than, let's say, a football player, a prizefighter, or a police officer. But if we examine what this so-called paper shuffler actually does all day long, we may see that there are indeed ample opportunities for the gratification of these impulses. Anyone who works in an office is aware that social interactions play a significant role in permitting cathexis of drive-related impulses. Impulses of a sexual or aggressive nature can be gratified through intimate contact, competition, discussion, meetings, or sadistic pranks against fellow employees and superiors. This type of gratification is apparent even in the stodgiest work environment. On the surface, it appears that employees must constrain behaviors associated with regressive impulses. However, under the surface employees find an abundance of outlets for gratification of the most primitive impulses. Consider a bank teller who must demonstrate appropriate behaviors in the face of unseemly and suspicious customers who place their money in the teller's hands. A public smile, good manners, and a customer-is-always-right attitude must prevail as tellers interact with clients. However, the behaviors that go on in the "backroom" serve a cathartic function and essentially allow a psychological arrangement where "public displays" can be maintained. In the backroom, employees can regress and allow their resentment, rage, and libidinal affects to emerge full force while in the company of other employees. This is also apparent in a teachers' lounge, where teachers can take "time off" and allow themselves to experience a therapeutic catharsis that will enable them to return to their "onstage" performance. In one public elementary school, for example, the principal claimed that his teachers were unhappy. They were frequently absent, appeared to be angry with students, and had actually engaged in verbal fights with parents. He went on to say that due to overcrowding, he had turned the teachers' lounge into a classroom. He was unaware of the impact of taking away this important area. The teachers now had no place in which they could regress. Work was experienced as a constraining activity, with no opportunities for the cathexis of impulses. Consequently, these impulses emerged on the job in destructive ways. Managers must be aware of the need for areas that permit regression, an issue fully explored in Chapter 9.

The need for such an arena is especially important for those who work in bureaucratic organizations where opportunities for the sublimation of sexual and aggressive impulses are rare. This is why many organizations encourage their employees to participate in sports activities after work, or install a workout room to promote physical exercise.

It may be that one reason for the so-called Japanese miracle is their frequent use of excercise and mass physical activities. Matsushita Corporation is a prime example: Each year some 7,000 managers gather each New Year's day. Every day Matsushita's 200,000 employees attend "morning meetings" where the Matsushita company song, along with its creed, principles, and spirits, is recited aloud. During "relaxation exercises," each person massages and pounds the back of another person, and then turns around to give and receive similar benefits. During the day, while at workstations, the exercise routine is repeated for 5 minutes at the end of each hour and for 10 to 15 minutes midmorning and afternoon. Matsushita claims that it is good for the workers and increases productivity. What it actually does is allow the employees to discharge instinctual energy prior to or during work stoppage so that they can obtain increased tolerance for the lack of or scarcity of opportunities on the job. In the United States we also see a rise in these mass activities, as corporations seek to emulate the Japanese.

Identifying with the Leader

Freud first struggled with the issue of leadership in *Totem and Taboo* (1912–1913/1953). In this important work Freud explores the mechanisms of projection and identification, which he considers to be vital in understanding the connections between leaders and their followers.

The concept of identification is central to Freud's topographical model of the psyche. In both *The Ego and the Id* (1923/1961) and *The Dissolution of the Oedipus Complex* (1924/1961) Freud suggests that it is through the passing of the Oedipus complex that the child's object cathexis (the investment of psychic energy in an object) is replaced by identification with parental authority. Identification with parental authority is also important in the formation of the superego. "The ego is formed to a great extent out of identification which takes the place of abandoned cathexis by the id" (1923/1961, p. 38). Once established, the ego forms the superego.

Identification with parental authority is significant to the understanding of the employee's relationship to work. The capacity to work and to use work as a sublimative activity is a function of an employee's ability to have successfully passed through the process of relinquishing oedipal object cathexis and substituting identification with parental authority. Identification with parental authority forms the basis not only for the development of the superego but also for an array of psychic investments in work-related objects.

The process of identification is also significant in explaining the employee's attachment to work for another reason: Freud maintained that the mechanism of identification lies at the basis of all relations between the leader and the group. Relations are established through identification of the follower's ego with the leader (the object). This process involves the introjection of the leader or some admired or loved aspect of the leader which is incorporated into the follower's ego ideal. Freud maintains that cohesion is found in a group when all members introject the same object into their ego ideal and then identify with each other. Leadership is (then) established when each member of the group places part of his/her own ego with the leader or some aspect of the leader. For example, in superior–subordinate relationsips, subordinates unquestioningly follow orders when they have replaced a part of their ego, the ego ideal, by introjecting the leader or some admiring attribute of the leader into their ego as an ideal. This phenomenon explains why soldiers willingly give up their thinking capacity and blindly follow orders from their leader. They have introjected a part object into their ego ideal, in this case the leader's admired thinking capacity. The soldiers as a group become a cohesive unit because they have all identified with each other in this unique capacity, the ability to give up their own thinking capacity. From this point on the leader will think for the group. Just how the process works is explained in *Civilization and Its Discontents* (1930/ 1961). In the context of identification and aggressive impulses, Freud says:

> A considerable amount of aggressiveness must be developed in the child against the authority which prevents him from having his first, but nonetheless, his most important satisfactions, whatever the kind of instinctual deprivation may be; but he is obliged to renounce the satisfaction of his revengeful aggressiveness (provoked by the original frustration). . . . By means of identification he takes the unattackable authority into himself. The authority now turns into his super-ego and enters into possession of all the aggressiveness which a child would have liked to exercise against it . . . we may assert truly that in the beginning conscience arises through suppression of an aggressive impulse, and that it is subsequently reinforced by fresh suppressions of the same. (pp. 76–77)

The chief motivation for renouncing revengeful aggression is castration anxiety,[6] and Freud maintains that out of the fear of castration a conscience is born (the superego). In leader–follower relations the aggressiveness of the subordinates is renounced. This renunciation is accomplished when the subordinates identify with the leader and introject the leader's characteristics to reduce their own aggressive affects.

In *Group Psychology and the Analysis of the Ego* (1921/1955), Freud's most explicit attempt to relate interpersonal behavior and intrapsychic structure, he began a conceptualization of leader–follower relations by stating: "In the individual's mental life someone else is invariably involved, as a model, as an object, as a helper, as an opponent . . ." (p. 82). The most obvious link in understanding leadership, as put forth by Freud, is once again the process of identification, which leads to a change in the ego—a differentiation and idealization of a part of the ego into the ego ideal. Freud asserts that leadership can be assessed from two perspectives. First, membership and bonding in a group is based on the substitution by the members of an actual person, the leader, for the internal ego ideal. Thus all the members share the same ideal, the same goals, the same critical agency insofar as the members have substituted this leader for their internal ego ideal. Second, in discussing the "herd instinct," Freud points to another factor that explains leader–follower relations. This factor is derived from the concept of envy: All members desire to be the favored son of the idealized father. Here identification is seen by Freud (1912–1913/ 1953) as a cannibalistic fantasy combining admiration and hostility: "The violent primal father had doubtless been the feared and envied model of each one of the company of brothers: and in the act of devouring him they accomplished their identification" (p. 142). A reaction to fear and envy is to avoid this expression, to repress it and instead utilize the defense called reaction formation. This defense takes the form of creating the norm of egalitarianism to avoid the affects associated with envy and jealousy.

The process of leadership, the taking in or introjecting attributes of an admiring object (another person), is always undertaken with a degree of ambivalence. The genesis of this ambivalence is stated in

---

[6]According to Schafer (1968), Freud's idea of castration anxiety associated with the oedipal complex as the chief incentive for identification to take place, and for creating what constitutes superego functioning, is problematic. Castration anxiety places boys/ men into a punitive mode of superego formation; that is, they identify with authority out of a sense of fear and nothing else. Also, for girls/women the consequences are worse; castration anxiety places them into a passive–reactive mode, with deficient superego functioning. This view has special implications for understanding the sex differences found in the acceptance of authority by followers in organizations.

Instincts and Their Vicissitudes (1915/1957), where Freud asserts that hate must precede love in the development of one's relation to others. "The relation of hate is older than that of love" (p. 139). Love is described as being originally narcissistic—the first object one loves is oneself: At first all external objects are felt to be impinging upon the primary narcissism and are hated. Later, to the extent that they give pleasure, external objects are introjected and felt to be part of the self. But this relation is itself ambivalent—"a type of love compatible with abolition of any separate existence on the part of the object" (1915/ 1957, p. 133)—as is the later and sadistic impulse to mastery "in which injury or annihilation of the object is a matter of indifference" (1915/1957, p. 127). All these preliminary (infantile) forms of love are fused with hate, combinations of loving, and frustrations, and it is only when the genital stage has been reached that love and hate become antithetical. To the extent that development is arrested at one of the preliminary stages, one's relationship to a leader will be characterized by these more primitive love–hate relations.

This leads to the other significant factor suggested by Freud in his attempt to explain leader–follower relations—projection. Freud says that this defense stems from ambivalence toward loved ones who have died:

> It is quite possible that the whole concept of demons was derived from the important relation of the living to the dead. The ambivalence in that relation was expressed in the subsequent course of human development by the fact that from the same root, it gave rise to two completely opposed psychical structures: on one hand fear of demons and ghosts and on the other hand veneration of ancestors. (1912–1913/1953, p. 65)

This subject of demons and totemic animals proves important as Freud attempts to grapple with the notion of leader–follower relations, because it is through demons and totemic animals that children relate intrapsychic processes and conflicts with their real parents (the first authority) to fantasized personifications. Freud says: "Spirits and demons . . . are only projections of man's own emotional impulse. He turns his emotional cathexes into persons, he peoples the world with them and meets his internal mental processes again outside himself" (1912–1913/1953, p. 91). The projection of emotional impulses onto real and fantasized demons or monsters allows children to use the external object, the monster, to offer control. This control is accomplished through an identification process and helps to explain the relationship between leader and follower later in one's life. This process serves to increase an understanding of the projection of idealized fantasies onto the leader as an object that serves to protect the subordinate from constructed demons.

Durkin (1984), building on the work of Anna Freud, proposes another mechanism to explain leader–follower relations. She suggests that "identification with the aggressor," together with projection, allows the subordinate to defend against the masochistic, submissive position by projecting aggressive fantasies onto the superior and then identifying with the leader as an aggressor. She then suggests that the subordinate "introjects the authority to whose criticism it is exposed, and incorporates them in the super ego. It is then able to project its prohibited impulses outward, then the subordinate is able to identify with the leader" (p. 91).

In *Libidinal Types* (1931), Freud made his final attempt to study leadership. Here he develops a topology of leadership and suggests that an employee's relationship to the leader as an object is a function of the relations between two or more intrapsychic agencies. He explores three types of leaders. One is the erotic type, an individual concerned with being loved, who dreads any loss of love, and who is typically dependent on his/her objects. Another is the obsessional type, who is controlled by his/her superego, dreads "anxiety of conscience" (guilt) more than loss of love, and is more dependent on his/her inner ideals than on other people. The third is the narcissistic type, who is described mainly in negative terms. This individual is not overly dependent on others, nor does he/she feel much conflict between his/her ego (sense of self) and superego (internalized ideal). Freud suggests that leaders are often of the narcissistic type, and they function as leaders because of their capacities for charisma, aggressiveness and independence. Freud goes on to say that there are few examples of a pure type to be found, and he outlines characteristics of various combinations—erotic, obsessive, erotic–narcissistic. He suggests that the ideal leader would be a blend of all three: in harmony with himself (and with various aspects of himself), capable of loving and being loved, and still guided by his/her values. To the extent that one type of leader arises over another, it is because one mode has been emphasized or exaggerated at the cost of others.

Entering and Becoming a Member of a Group

Of particular importance in understanding organizational dynamics is Freud's contribution to the study of group psychology. While he did not directly explore how a "group psychology" can be applied to an organization, his theory does help to develop a fuller explanation of the dynamics of leader–follower relations and group cohesion. For example, Freud claims that working with others in a social environment provides the greatest opportunity for psychic gratification, and this gratification is obtained through membership in a group. The stage for obtaining gratification in social groups is set in early childhood, through the process of identification with parents. Parents can facilitate this process by instilling in the child functional models of behavior, values and ideals, and the capacity for empathy. The social group as a binding force occurs later on in childhood, where it provides an avenue to escape the misery begun in childhood, which is associated with the renunciation of the instincts. Work then can be conceptualized as associated with two distinct but overlapping psychic functions: providing a task to be performed and providing opportunities for working together with others. We will explore both of these functions: the psychic connection to work through group membership and the gratification associated with task performance and obtained through the symbolic representation of an employee's trade.

FREUD'S ANALYSIS OF GROUPS AND THE PROCESS OF IDENTIFICATION

Freud sought to answer the following questions: How do groups form and how do groups bond together to engage in group-related activities? In his analysis of group formation and cohesion he discovered that dynamics evolve from psychological factors as opposed to instinctual drives. In his seminal effort in this area, Freud (1921/1955) hypothesizes that a natural continuity exists between the dynamics of individuals and those groups, and he advances a theory to explain the psychology of groups on the basis of changes in the psyche of the individual mind. He develops the position that the degree to which a person is emotionally bonded to a group is a function of the degree to which the individual is psychically altered. The key to understanding this phenomenon of bonding is found, once again, in the mechanism of identification, which Freud refers to as the earliest expression of an emotional tie with another person and a basic force of group life.

Freud suggests that cohesion in groups is based on substitution by members of an actual person, the leader, for the internal ego ideal. This concept, fully discussed in the section on leadership, is most apparent in Freud's (1917/1957) analysis of group cohesion. Here he tells of an Assyrian tribe that takes flight on learning that the leader has had his head cut off by Judith. In this case, not only has the commonly shared external object (figurehead) binding them together been lost, but the leader having lost his head, every follower, every soldier has lost his head, and they then behave as such. This is apparent in all groups and organizations where the leader is suddenly terminated, resulting in chaos.

In *Civilization and Its Discontents* (1930/1961), Freud postulates that the conflict between civilization and the person represents in part a conflict between Eros (forces of unification and combination on which civilization is based) and the Death Instinct (forces that tend to break down structures into their separate parts deflected outward as aggression, toward others). Freud suggests, as do many social psychologists following Freud, that if society or the group is to maintain cohesiveness and avoid anarchy, aggression must be directed outward, perhaps at alien groups (demons). However, this process is only one way a group can deal with its own internal aggressiveness or aggressive impulses. Internal aggression is also kept in check by the process of identification. But above all, Freud maintains that the foremost method of dealing with internal aggression is to invest it in the superego, which then functions as a system of internal authority(s) who then possesses the power to frustrate instinctual wishes. He says, "Every piece of aggression whose satisfaction the subject gives up, is taken over by the superego and increases the latter aggression (against the ego)" (1930/1961, p. 76). Freud goes on to say that aggressive impulses are the most significant force responsible for the severity of the superego, more so than actual parents.

In *Totem and Taboo* (1912–1913/1953), Freud makes his first explicit suggestion of what may be considered a relationship between the person and the organization. He suggests that morality, religion, and social organization originate from reactions to the primal murder of the father. This position is drawn from both clinical evidence and his anthropological studies. It was written at a time when he was interested in the issue of repression of unconscious instincts and symptom formation from the perspective of id psychology. Later, when Freud's attention shifted to concerns of the ego, as found in *The Ego and the Id* (1923/1961) and *Inhibitions, Symptoms and Anxiety* (1926/1959), he did not apply the processes of ego functioning to problems of social organization and work. The ego was not used in a formulation of the psychodynamics of work, except in its capacity to function as a servant of the id and the superego.

THE SYMBOLIC VALUE OF TASK PERFORMANCE AS A SUBLIMATING ACTIVITY

While the classical psychoanalysts maintain that displeasure is reduced through the symbolic activities and values that work represents, it is the reality principle, the principle established by the world of work, that serves as an external influence on the id and its tendencies and endeavors. The reality principle may offer harsh renunciation or more subtle opportunities for sublimation. Thus work becomes one of the main devices whereby the healthy ego can accomplish its primary task, to influence the instincts (Ginsberg, 1951). However, connection to an occupation is not exclusively tied to drive reduction. If drive reduction is not accomplished through work-related behaviors, it can be accomplished through the psychic processes involved in work-related ideation and fantasies. The idea that work is related to unconscious fantasies moves a psychoanalytic theory of work into the interpersonal realm. This has special significance for the study of work in organizations. A contemporary psychoanalytic theory of work must consider the person within the "world at work" and how the work environment influences conscious and unconscious fantasies. Freud approaches this topic when he explores leadership and the psychodynamics associated with leader–follower relations. Most workers are employed in hierarchical organizational structures where superior–subordinate relations prevail. To work essentially means to follow orders, and gratifications obtained from work are often a function of the employee's ability not only to follow orders but to develop a relationship with the superior. Freud explores the psychic mechanisms involved in these unique relationships, and he explains how the subordinate accepts the role of being a follower. Being a follower and the psychic acceptance of this role have implications for how the employee both renunciates and gratifies instinctual wishes and their derivatives.

Freud maintains that work serves two psychic functions: (1) it provides a context for discharge of the libidinal and aggressive instincts (Holmes, 1965), and (2) it binds men together (libidinal ties). The binding function of work occurs in the actual task system (where one performs work) either through the blunting of impulses and their "aim-inhibited affection" or through sublimation of impulses. It is hoped that the occupation one chooses will have the capacity to stimulate interests and offer activities that can function as outlets for instinctual discharge. This discharge may be found through the activities and the tools associated with one's work, but it also is found in ties formed with others at work.

The classical psychoanalytic position maintains that one is tied to one's work only if it offers instinctual gratifications. The two-function model of work suggested by Freud allows for observation of the symbolic meaning associated with employment. Work takes on a symbolic function psychically, when instincts and their derivatives obtain gratification. This gratification generally occurs through work roles and work activities. The binding function of task performance is most likely the result not of an internalization of activities themselves, but of the symbolic importance these activities take on, over time, and how they serve as defenses against instinctual impulses.

Of critical importance are the opportunities to displace and compromise psychic wishes of drives by using one's role. It is the activities performed within this role, performed over and over again in a predictable fashion, that hold the greatest potential for blunting or discharging psychic impulses. The predictability of these activities performed within a role become gratifying because over time they become part of the ego and take on an ego-functioning capacity. In this sense the ego is able to fuse the instincts and then synthesize them through work activities. Work then becomes a condensation vehicle or an outlet for instinctual impulses.

When assessing the relationship between a particular job and its psychic value it would be a mistake to assume that a particular job is gratifying because it gratifies a particular instinct. It is much more complex. Freud (1915/1957) maintains that to account for the behavior of an adult requires an analysis of the interactions and functions of not only the instincts and the id, but the ego and the superego. An adult learns from experience that instinctual tension can be reduced by engaging in complex behaviors or ideas (Hall, 1954). Additionally, instincts and their derivatives can undergo an infinite number of displacements and compromises over time as one searches for and clutches the interests, ideas, habits, objects, etc., with which he/she comes into contact during the waking day. Work and its activities fit into this mode, in a symbolic manner, as an instinctual tension reducer.

Sachs (1933) was the first to assess the symbolic or condensation function of a worker's tools. He suggests the following:

> We have long known that the tools which enable man to accomplish his work more successfully . . . without achieving independent and automotive existence of their own are mostly phallic symbols. Their employment is . . . a substitute for the sexual act. (p. 405)

Following Sachs, Roheim (1943) explores the psychic value of occupations: He sees the soldier as reenacting his body destruction fantasies and engaged in oedipal fantasies; a lawyer engaged in an endopsychical struggle between the superego and ego; a scientist engaged in voyeurism by prying into the secrets of the primal scene; a painter playing with feces; and so forth.

Menninger (1942) suggests that of all methods available for absorbing or sublimating aggression, it is the energies used in work that are most valuable. We see evidence of this when psychic tension is reduced through the symbolic value that work represents. Consider the psychic pleasure that can be derived from an occupation that represents a fight or an attack on the environment, as expressed in farming, butchering, surgery, etc. Or consider how oral aggression may be gratified through teaching, speaking, singing, etc.; or how anal gratification may be obtained through the work of banking, garbage collecting, etc. All occupations are aimed at reducing conflict and gratifying drive derivatives, and the success of any occupational choice is found in its functional utility in servicing unconscious gratifications. It is not only the tools associated with work that allow for the discharge and gratification of drives, but the activities associated with work, the requirements of the role, the nature, status, and gratifications associated with being in a profession or occupation, and the symbolism associated with the organization one works in.

Brenner (1982) suggests that all occupational choices are the result of the compromise formations. The choice of an occupation is found in the ability of the occupation to reduce conflicts over childhood drive derivatives that give rise to anxiety, depressive affect, or genetic conflicts. Thus, he sees occupational choice as a mixture of a wish fulfillment (gratification of drive derivatives), tension aroused by drive derivatives in the form of anxiety and depressive affect, and defenses aimed at reducing or eliminating displeasure. The function of all occupations, like compromise formations, is not to eliminate psychic conflict but to offer gratification by altering its derivatives.

PROBLEMS AT WORK

The psychoanalytic explorations devoted exclusively to problems of work begin with Ferenczi (1918/1950). Ferenczi's paper, as well as others that followed, focuses on how engaging in work activities wards off the instincts and how engaging in work prevents neurotic disturbances. Ferenczi claims that neurotics, in particular, are those who excessively rely on work to serve a defensive function and that "when such a person is faced with inactivity by illness or accident, the outbreak of a neurosis, or getting worse of an existing one, is not infrequently the consequence" (p. 174). Similarly, Pederson-Krag (1955) states that when sublimation is blocked, regression results, and the person either enters into schizoid withdrawal or begins to exhibit sexual or aggressive drives in the form of symptoms. Also, Menninger (1942) considers drudgery in work as not allowing for the fusion of aggressive and libidinal instincts, which does not give the work a conscious form of satisfaction.

Pruyser (1980) confirms Menninger's position and adds that regression results when work does not absorb the energies of the aggressive and libidinal instincts. It is only after the energy of the instincts is absorbed through work that work becomes an object of gratification. When this occurs, the activities of work do not impinge upon or become an enemy of the instincts but an object of drive satisfaction. Work then, when viewed as an object for drive discharge and satisfaction, will significantly reduce pull in opposite directions of the reality and pleasure principles. Thus, work functions as a primary means of tension reduction (Freud, 1930/1961). Viewed in this manner, the paradox often attributed to Freud is understood: Work can be both an energizer and an energy reducer.

The classical psychoanalytic position also maintains that at work, the worker forms libidinal ties to work. These ties can only occur when work activities offer opportunities to reduce drive tension. Being libidinally tied and bound to reality means being tied to work and all that work implies, and this occurs, as Freud (1930/1961) claims, "only when work is capable of providing every considerable discharge of component impulses, narcissistic, aggressive and erotic" (p. 80). Weil (1959) supports this view by suggesting that work is a safety valve in intrapsychic life, in that it placates the superego. Consequently, the absence of work, as well as the nature of one's work, has the potential to lead to the most serious psychic disturbances. The contributions by Jahoda (1966) concerning the psychic problems that arise in the absence of work are also relevant. She says, "If work is man's strongest tie to reality, then the absence of work should leave him less solidly in touch with reality" (p. 630). In essence Jahoda confirms Freud's position that given the absence of work as an object of drive tension, one is overwhelmed with the intensity of drives seeking gratification, and regression results.

Being unable to work limits opportunities for sublimation and the ability to win recognition by producing things (Erikson, 1950), and according to Ginsburg (1956), severance from work results in two types of behaviors: (1) severance increases efforts to assert feelings of sexual adequacy, and (2) it precipitates a retreat into a resigned, passive, dependent attitude. Both of these responses are the result of the "castrating blow" of being unemployed, which increases the conscious feeling of worthlessness and the unconscious experience of guilt. The guilt associated with being unemployed results from one's incapacity to fulfill the wishes contained in the ego ideal; that is, one no longer has an opportunity to use work to placate the superego. When this occurs, one will release the aggressive instinct, by projecting onto the frustrating object; in this case the frustrating object is the object that denies employment, which may be a company, the state, a person, or the self. Ultimately aggressive instincts cease to be projected outward and are turned against the self, leading to depression—a common occurrence among the long-term unemployed. Freud (1917/1957) says that "the striking feature of the melancholic is the manifestation of the dread of poverty . . . loss of a job increases the affect associated with this fear" (p. 245).

Being unemployed or underemployed leads to depression because the ego ideal is left depleted. In *Totem and Taboo* (1912–1913/ 1953) some of Freud's first formulations of the role of the ego ideal (later called the superego, which is later integrated into his work on oedipal development) are developed. The ego ideal is discussed as a critical, censorial agency within the ego, the formation of which "would be a condition of repression" (1914/1957, p. 74). The concept of repression of object cathexes,[7] in turn, has important implications for the relationship between self-regard, the extent to which one achieves one's ego ideal, and the capacity to love other people. If object cathexis is ego syntonic,[8] one feels lowered self-esteem when separated from the loved object, but the feeling of being loved raises one to new heights once again. If the object cathexes is repressed, any love given to an object is felt as a depletion of the ego: "satisfaction . . . is impossible and the re-enrichment of the ego can be effected only by withdrawal of the libido from its objects" (Freud, 1914/1957, p. 80). The realization of one's inability to love, and for that matter to work, "has an exceedingly lowering effect upon self-regard" (Freud, 1914/ 1957, p. 78).

The thrust of this argument, that to be unemployed is psychically damaging, is not meant to suggest that merely being employed is, in and of itself, psychically valuable. To believe that work has the capacity to promote sublimation is very different from the assumption that a particular job will actually offer opportunities for sublimation. Just as the pleasure–unpleasure aspects of work are hierarchical, the functions of work may be considered in a similar manner; that is, the reality binding function of work is necessary if work is to function as an avenue of escape from the societal indifference associated with the pleasure principle. Ideally, work allows for the expression of sublima-

[7]Object cathexis is the investing of libidinal energy into an object (person, thing, or activity).

[8]Ego syntonic refers to values, ideas and affective states that feel like "it belongs" and is consistent or part of one's ego.

tion of libidinal motives and aggressive instincts, and it is the activity of work and the relations with others at work that allow the employee to move away from narcissistic concerns and more toward a psychic attachment with the leader and the community, which is psychically gratifying. However, work in contemporary organizations is far from ideal. Most occupations in bureaucracies fail to bind the person to reality because they fail to perform these psychic functions. Consider those jobs that demand monotony and routine and provide for very little in the sense of "being in" a psychological community. Many writers on work problems (Jaques, 1951, 1971; Menzies, 1960; Kernberg, 1975, 1980) agree that merely engaging in work does not add to sublimation, and they suggest that in many cases being at work in the organization may in fact precipitate increased regression. Additionally, some writers on work and work-related problems go further and maintain that there are many types of work, in many kinds of organizations, that contribute to various forms of psychopathology (see Marcuse, 1955; Chisholm, 1967).

FREUD AND CHANGE

As a clinician and theorist Freud was ultimately interested in change. As a clinician his work entailed bringing about curative change in his patients. As a theoretician and "archeologist of the mind," he was interested in the explanation of phenomena as they evolved over time in their historical context. As Freud's theory of the mind matured, so did his view of the process of change. He developed four models of change: developmental change, affective change, cognitive change, and interpersonal change. These models are not exclusively tied to clinical work with patients; they can play a role in understanding all aspects of the change process, especially with groups and individuals who are not in treatment (Samberg & Frances, 1987). These models can help increase knowledge about the organizational change process and they are examined with this purpose in mind.

Developmental Change

The developmental model of psychological growth is considered one of Freud's greatest contributions. Freud and theorists who followed suggest that the infant and later the child moves through developmental stages of psychological growth. Later this view was extrapolated to all living systems and to adult development. As children move through these stages of development they can become fixated or experience what is considered today to be developmental arrest. This means that people, or for that matter all living systems, have the potential to become developmentally arrested at a particular point in time. When arrested they resist any attempts to move them forward to another stage of development. This view also suggests that under certain conditions, generally conditions charged with anxiety, people will regress to certain stages only to seek the comforts associated with that stage. In psychoanalytic treatment, when faced with the prospects of change, the patient often regresses. When this regression occurs, it allows the analyst to rework or resolve conflicts that had occurred at that particular stage. If these conflicts are resolved, the patient is able to move onto the next stage in a more conflict-free fashion.

Developmental growth as a concept by which to study humans over time has been applied to organizations by theorists who study organizational life cycles and the developmental stages of groups and organizations. These theorists suggest that organizations also move through predictable stages of growth over time, and that certain events can occur that impede development or precipitate a return to an early stage of functioning. Organizations have the capacity to remain fixated at a particular stage of growth. They can hold on to behaviors unique to a particular stage and seek comfort in the activities associated with that stage in spite of the demands for forward movement and growth. This is most apparent when organizations undergo change, especially technological change. When anxiety-producing events occur, employees may consciously regress to an earlier stage of development. This regression often takes the form of employees calling out for the "good old days," to return to a stage where a work environment existed that was experienced, in reality or fantasy, as being more comforting. This type of regression presents special problems for organizational consulting. This phenomenon will be explored in Chapter 9.

Freud saw changes that resulted from psychosexual developmental as a natural evolutionary process occurring gradually over time. However, he also put forth other theories of change that were purposeful and not based in nature.

Affective Change

Affective change is associated with Freud's early writings and evolved from his so-called cathartic method of treatment. This type of change occurs when there is a release of anxiety or tension that was previously held in check through repression of memories, affects, or wishes. Freud maintained that insight was not the way to bring about change. He viewed insight as an intellectual activity that was of little value because it failed to produce deep structural change. On the other hand, the release of tension would "open the dam" and allow for greater possibilities of restructuring the mind psychically. The release of emotional tension was thought to be a method of treatment for people who suffered from trauma, stress reactions, grief, mourning, physical injury, job loss, and so forth. It was used to counteract defenses that are commonly used to defend against or repress the powerful emotions connected to stressful events and the eventual mumbling, denial, or depressive responses that eventually evolve.

Cognitive Change

When Freud states that the aim of psychoanalysis is to "make the unconscious conscious," he is suggesting cognitive change. Bringing unconscious material or its derivatives to the conscious level of word representation is the basis of cognitive change. Often the psychoanalytic consultant in the role of being a detective/educator typically brings about this type of change by establishing a greater degree of understanding of the dynamic forces that underlie a particular symptom.

Cognitive change is typically thought of as an attempt to create change by imparting information to the client with the intent to clear up distortions, erroneous premises, or assumptions and to promote more realistic alternatives to previous ways of functioning. This is an important aspect of organizational consulting, and most consulting falls under this model. However, Freud eventually gave up this model as well as the affective model. He discovered that change is never completely influenced by imparting information or cathecting emotions because the client will most likely resist. Freud's discovery of the importance of resistance to change ranks as one of his greatest contributions to the field of psychology. He maintains that often clients resist change consciously and, most troubling, unconsciously. This led him to the fourth model of change.

Interpersonal Change

In Freud's work with patients he noticed that they had a reaction to him which he called a "mysterious element." This mysterious element emanates from the role of doctor. Later on he referred to it as a "transference reaction." The process of change evolves from an analysis of transference reactions, the reaction the patient has to the doctor. Freud (1912/1958) identified these reactions and determined that their analysis was a critical part of the process of change. Change could occur when the patient transferred feelings, thoughts, and wishes onto the doctor. These feelings were often wrought with conflicts stemming from the patient's early relationships, especially with parents. The course of the entire change process is a function of these transference reactions and they can move in either a positive or a negative direction.

Rarely if ever is any relationship free from these reactions. This is certainly true of the consultant–consultee relationship. The capacity of the consultant to understand these reactions will influence the nature of the consultation work: its diagnosis, intervention, and eventual outcome.

In psychoanalysis, the analyst as a change agent offers him/herself up to the patient and becomes the recipient of these transference reactions. Change occurs through the process of allowing patients to use the situation to repeat past dysfunctional or pathological interpersonal transactions. Through identification and clarification of these repetitions the patient and change agent collaborate in reaching a new understanding of the nature of their relationship. If the analysis is successful, the work is based less on distortion. The capacity to reduce distortion in treatment will have beneficial results outside the treatment, where the patient will have increased introspective capacities.

In consulting work the capacity to analyze a transference reaction and bring about change is highly unlikely or impossible. However, an awareness of the ubiquitous nature of transference reactions is important, especially if the consultant wishes to understand the dynamics underlying resistance to change. Also, awareness is important because precipitating factors that lead to organizational dysfunctions may be the result of the particular manner in which an employee experiences and responds to problems and others at work, especially those in authority (in Chapter 10 these reactions are discussed).

Transference reactions trigger a propensity to change on the part of the client in two ways. First, change may occur because the consultant is a symbol of hope that things will now get better or that change is coming. This type of reaction is a positive transference reaction and often increases the likelihood of change. Second, the reverse is true. The consultant can be seen as an extension of an "evil" program or leader. This negative reaction increases resistance to change and makes the consultant's work problematic.

PROBLEMS IN THE APPLICATION OF CLASSICAL PSYCHOANALYSIS TO THE ORGANIZATION AND WORK

Classical psychoanalysis, or Freudian psychoanalysis, while providing enormous insight into human nature, presents a major obstacle when applied to work in organizations. A major debate within the academic work of psychoanalysis beginning in the 1960s centered around the value of Freud's instinct and biologically based motivational theory as a determinant of human behavior. This controversy fits nicely into the nature–nurture debate of the present.

Many contemporary theorists suggest that acceptance of the Freudian view that human nature is driven by biological forces, forming the foundation of libido as a force or drive structure, presents a restricted view if applied to work and the organization. For example, to rely on instincts as the only way an employee can derive pleasure from his work means that pleasure can only be derived from some of the instinctual components of the behavior associated with work (Neff, 1977). Ferber and Kent (1976) suggests the following:

> [B]y reducing all social and personal phenomena to a biological basis . . . all objects, relations, and events are nothing more than manifestations of instinctual striving, and if these striving are unconscious then all human experiences must be suspect and all objects, relations and events nothing more then disguised, displaced or sublimated expressions of instinct. Additionally, it means that all we experience is an illusion and we are nothing more than a product of assorted conflicts and defense mechanisms. (p. 444)

Additionally, applying Freud's theory to work and the organization presents a view of intrapsychic life that is distinct from organizational life. If it is true that all motivation is tied to biology, why should the organization matter at all?

Furthermore, nowhere in Freud's work does he suggest that the ego is involved in the motivation to work. Even though Freud gave the ego increased importance later in his writings, he did not give it autonomous functions. Consequently, all work activities are derivatives of the instincts and can only be understood in terms of the id, the superego, and repercussions of social reality. He assigned to the ego the task of maintaining harmony between opposing forces, the demands of instincts, the superego, and external reality. The ego is not given adaptive functions; it can only gain gratification through defensive processes. Therefore all work activities are defensive in nature.

Some followers of Freud attempt to integrate instincts into the capacity to work by expanding their nature and by giving instincts special capacities, like the instinct to work (Hendrick, 1943), or the instinct to achieve (Lantos, 1943).

However, as long as Freud and his followers remained tied to instincts and the biological basis of drives and gratification, their view of external reality and its relationship to psychic life occupies a less than significant place when applied to work and the organization.

We now turn to the ego psychologists, who gave the ego adaptive functions and thus drew closer to the creation of a psychoanalysis of work.

EGO PSYCHOLOGISTS

The ego psychologists have reacted against the determinism of instinct by lessening its importance. This case is made by Loewald (1971), where he says: "In the course of ontogenetic development then, instincts, while also remaining active as such, become transmuted into higher forms of that psychic excitation which we described as motivation, such as for instance, 'will' " (p. 104).

Loewald goes on to say that instinct is a psychoanalytical psychological concept, and he suggests that it should be kept free of biological and ethological connotations. He considers instinct not as a physiological stimulus, but only as a psychic representation of a physiological stimulus.

Loewald's (1960a and 1970) efforts bring the field of ego psychology away from those who sought to hold on to instinct and move the study of the person more into the realm of the external world. For example, Loewald (1960) maintains that while Hartmann (1958) made great contributions to the development of ego psychology, he did not solve the instinct problem but faithfully adhered to it. While Hartmann suggested that the ego had strengths and capacities, he also maintained that if environmental pressures were too great the ego was capable of collapsing into regression. This view contributed greatly to bringing into perspective the relationship between psychic life and external reality, and Hartmann, among others, provided a clearer look at the interplay between ego and reality. Following Hartmann, the ego psychologists saw the ego not as a separate entity responding to external reality as an impingement that precipitates defensive reactions but as a mediator, unifier, and integrator. According to Loewald (1960a), the essence of the ego is to maintain increasingly complex levels of differentiation and objectivation of reality. This view of the ego permits a fuller understanding of how a person adapts to the world of work and adapts to an ever-changing environment. The ego psychologists counter Freud's (1940/1964) rather secondary view of the ego as a "servant of the id and superego" (p. 166). They move the Freudian ego to a higher plane with more powers than it was previously given. Following Hartmann (1958) they generated the view of an autonomous ego whose functions were no longer considered born from the struggles between instincts pushing forth and reality forbidding them.

According to Hartmann (1958), the ego is used in classical psychoanalysis in an ambiguous manner. Hartmann (1984) attempts to clarify the concept of the ego by demonstrating concern not so much for what the ego is but for what it is not. For example, it is not synonymous with "personality," it does not coincide with the "subject" as opposed to "object" of experience, and it is not exclusively "awareness" or "feelings." Hartmann suggests, as Blanck and Blanck (1974) and others have suggested, that the ego can only be defined by its functions.

EGO FUNCTIONS

To complete his conceptualization and its awesome responsibilities, Hartmann (1958) stripped the id of its power as a source of all psychic energy by giving the ego energy of its own. By placing energy in the ego, Hartmann could then view it as having the power to neutralize the libidinal and aggressive energy contained in the id. But more significantly, the ego now had energy to perform its own functions and engage with its environment in a conflict-free sphere. The functions of the ego center around the relationship between the person and social reality. The ego is considered an organization of adjustment; it controls mobility and perception, tests the reality of the present, and anticipates the future. It also functions as a mediator among the properties, requirements, and demands of the internal psychic apparatus (Hartmann & Lowenstein, 1962). The ego is composed of multiple substructures and capacities, an array of apparatuses that reflect defense and cognition.

Gratification plays a key role in the formation of the ego. The ego is formed when a child can delay gratification, and according to Hartmann (1958), the ability to delay can only be tolerable if the child knows that deprivation is short-lived, and indulgence will arrive. Thus, the ego is viewed not only as playing a role in controlling drives but as adapting to its environment. The ego is now considered an executive of the body system or soma and is responsible for all human behaviors and interactions.

In addition to the main function of the ego, its capacity to organize and control motility and perception (which includes perception of external reality as well as the self system), it also serves as a protective barrier against excessive external stimuli, and in a somewhat different sense against internal stimuli. Hartmann (1958) goes on to say that "the ego can be described as [engaging] in detour activities, they promote a more specific and safer form of adjustment" (p. 115). This significant function of the ego is its inhibiting nature, which is its ability to utilize defenses. Another significant function of the ego is its synthetic function, or organizing functions, and its regulation of internal realities. Thus the ego is seen as having two functions: inhibiting and organizing.

Prior to Hartmann, Nunberg (1933) developed a list of ego functions that are necessary if a person is to adapt to work. He sees the ego as having the following functions: (1) synthetic—the integrative functioning of external and internal realities, thought and perception; (2) differentiation—the ability to differentiate internal from external reality; (3) reality testing—the capacity to distinguish perception from ideation; (4) anticipative—the capacity to orient one's actions in light of the future and to defend against possible danger; (5) rational action—the capacity to think and reflect as opposed to act; and (6) ego interest—the capacity to center oneself and establish relationships with the external world. These ego functions and their capacities are all necessary if a person is to engage in gratifying relationships at work. The significance of multiple functions of the ego is found in their ability to explain the relationships between ego capacities and work activities. Occupations vary regarding the degree to which a specific ego capacity is required. For example, the differential function of the ego is particularly useful in managing boundaries or functioning in the role of gatekeeper in an organization, a role that requires an ability to determine who gets in and who does not. The capacity of ego interests has specific utility in the area of role definition or in a role that requires curiosity, like performing research. Any role or occupation draws on specific ego capacities, and the ability of a person to function within a given role is a function of the development or the strength of that ego capacity. If an employee is deficient in a certain ego capacity, he/she will not be able to gratify what Hartmann calls the need for mastery, another ego capacity, and perhaps other capacities as well, and self-esteem will be lowered. When this occurs, the employee may try to alter the role to utilize more well-developed capacities, or he/she will withdraw into a self-protective state of isolation, avoiding experiences associated with failure and shame.

Hartmann suggests that certain types of work can precipitate pathological reactions, and that in some cases these pathological reactions can lead to successful work adaptation. Regression of certain ego capacities may be part of the requirements for successful adaptation at work. For example, in some jobs the most significant role requirement is the capacity to think; in other jobs it may be the capacity to act; in others the capacity to watch, and so forth. Hartmann maintains that these capacities require regressive ego conditions and that some jobs require greater degrees of regression than others. Regression of ego capacities can also be found in specific occupations (e.g., acting, singing, or dancing on stage, which requires regression of the capacity to preserve the dignity of the ego, or sports activities, which require regression of the ability to hold aggressive urges in check). Hartmann (1958) says:

> The term progressive adaptation is self-explanatory; it is an adaption whose direction coincides with that of development. But there are successful ones, which use paths of regression. I do not refer only to the well known fact that genetic roots of even rational and adapted behaviors are irrational, but rather to those highly adapted purposeful achievements of healthy people which . . . require a detour through regression. (p. 36)

WORK AND THE EGO

Working is now considered to be a function of the capacity of the ego. To optimally engage in work-related activities requires that the energies directed toward work be contained within the conflict-free ego sphere. Working is no longer exclusively considered born from the struggles between instincts and reality.

Hartmann (1958) with the conflict-free ego sphere suggests that action that can have a rational base. In Freud's theory a rational base for action is not possible, but for Hartmann it is possible and is based on the conscious and preconscious weighing of goals, means, and effects of a possible course of action (Meissner, 1975). For Hartmann, rational action will be adaptive if it gratifies the drives and superego and simultaneously gratifies the interest of the ego within a given social context. On the other hand, irrationality remains based in primitive preconscious and unconscious ideation; it is "governed by principles derived from an emotional or drive-dependent base" (Hartmann, 1958).

According to Hartmann and the ego psychologists, ego interest and gratification of the ego at work are adaptive if the energy of the drive is lowered and the ego can create a balance among the various psychic systems and between these systems and the environment. However, rational action and rational responses to environmental conditions may impair adaptation to other environmental conditions. Also, what may appear as successful adaptation to the work environment may merely be compliance. According to Meissner (1984), compliance induces psychic conflict if the action of adaptation required by the ego places excessive demands on other systems.

The capacity of the ego to be related to work in an effective and adaptive manner "is related to the stability of the ego's internal state of equilibrium" (Meissner, 1984, p. 503). Hartmann sees internal disturbances as causing distortions in relation to reality and reality as a precipitator of internal disturbances. This is defined by Hartmann as regressive, and regression is not only a disturbance of an internal state, but it also as serves an adaptive purpose. For example, fantasy prepares the individual for interaction with external reality by making connections between the past, the present, and the future and creating soothing affects. Also, play is considered an aspect of regression, and it serves an adaptive purpose by giving the ego renewed energies through reducing the internal disturbances associated with internal and external realities.

PLEASURE AND WORK

Hartmann sees pleasure derived from work as exclusively an ego reaction. According to Hartmann (1958), Freud's position that pleasure derived from working flows from the libidinal aspects associated with work activities does not adequately explain the impact of social and cultural determinants on work gratification. Furthermore, instincts do not explain how the parent–child relationship shapes the nature of the psychic relationship with work that the child will eventually have as an adult. Assuming that most forms of gratification in adulthood must be either delayed or gratified indirectly, Hartmann says that they must be worked for. This is accomplished when the original energy once available for instinctual acts "floats" into the ego and then becomes desexualized and deaggressivized (i.e., neutralized) (Hartmann, 1958). Hartmann goes on to say that the gratification of libidinal instincts through defenses, like sublimation, is not a primary characteristic of work. He sees sublimation as a deflection of instinctual drives with the aim of making them more acceptable to the ego and the superego. He sees work and the capacity to work as representative of the ability of the ego to engage in a coherent pattern of adaptive behaviors which may be a function of conflicting needs. However, through work people are able to develop new adaptive structures. To be able to increase their capacity to work, they must give up their old structures of gratification and become involved in new structures. The original energy contained within the old structure is gratified when a person is able to engage in self-preserving activities in these new structures. However, it is the interaction of these new structures with external reality, the organization and work, that can precipitate a psychological force impinging on a person, offering little gratification and precipitating a pathological reaction or producing satisfaction and a sense of well-being. As Jahoda (1966) suggests, we now can consider work "an external reality," an environmental force capable of shaping the ego.

CHAPTER 2

Object Relations Theory and Work

Work is play, and even when I'm composing a score and I'm at
it 12 hours a day, 7 days a week on end—it's play.
—LEONARD BERNSTEIN (1990)

Having been shown the limita-
tions of the instinct model, one is left with an inadequacy of totality,
that is, a failure to understand the full range of possible relationships
formed in the organization. It is here that the object relations school
of psychoanalytic thought enters. What makes the object relations
school attractive as a model for contributing to an understanding of
work and the organization is its lack of emphasis on instinct.

Object relations theory provides a distinct interpersonal basis for
understanding work in organizations. As such, the theory suggests a
view of the person as object seeking, as opposed to the classical view
which sees the person as pleasure seeking. In addition, the theory
explains behavioral dynamics from both a conflict defense model and
a two-person interactional model. Also, the socalled middle school of
object relations permits a clear inclusion of environmental or cultural
factors in a systemic theory that up to this point psychanalytic theory
would not allow.

The main thrust of the object relations school is its primary
emphasis on the analysis of the person and his objects. Object relations theorists believe that, over time, the person acquires the psychological capacity to relate to objects. This belief opposes that of the
classical school, which maintains that the person is born related to an
object. Also, while the classical theorists maintain a constitutional basis

of adaptation to the environment, the object relations theorists maintain that adaptation is a learned (reluctantly) process. And finally, the classical theorists maintain that the value of an object lies in its capacity to give instinctual pleasure, whereas the object relations theorists claim that the value of pleasure lies in the capacity to enrich the relationship. The relationship gives pleasure, not instinctual gratification.

The object relations theorists emphasize the environment. The parents create and are the child's environment, and as such, if they are "good enough," they are able to buffer the child from the dangers in the external world. Additionally, the parents mediate between the child and his/her own internal world by providing a constant, reliable, and empathic environment.

The differences between classical theory and object relations theory are even more apparent when one explores elements of work. The classical theorists would argue that work can be understood as a defensive activity (Menninger, 1942; Oberndorf, 1951). Following Freud's dual instinct theory, they conclude that as an adult activity, work is designed to satisfy sexual and aggressive impulses. Gratification is obtained primarily through the defensive processes of sublimation, which involves two aspects: (1) a desexualization and de-aggressivization of ego components, and (2) a merger with the person's instinctual world. The object relations theorists take an entirely different perspective. They maintain that the capacity to work evolves from a child's relationships with his/her parents, relationships that begin from feedings with mother and the strong, protective experiences with both mother and father. Relationships, if positive, lead to an idealized image of a united parent, which, according to Bowlby (1973), Winnicott (1965), and Stern (1985), lead to elements in the capacity to work: attachment, competence–mastery, and curiosity.

The object relations school places primary emphasis on the importance of an individual's relations with actual (external) and fantasized (internal) objects. The term *object* is used, rather than *person,* mainly because the object of a relation is not always a person; it can be an organization, a group, an idea, a symbol, and, particularly in infancy, parts of the body. Herein lies one of the main features of object relations theory that makes it an important contribution to a psychoanalytic theory of work and organization. As stated previously, the person is seen as object seeking. The libido as object seeking allows the object relations theorists to make a clear separation from drive theory, for now sex and aggression are no longer viewed as innate drives. Rather, they are viewed as one of the many ways the person responds to the need to be attached, related, and connected to other objects such as people, work, and the organization.

Melanie Klein's work with children led her to develop theories and concepts of behavior that split the psychoanalytic society in England and led to the development of the object relations school. While still holding on to the instinct theory of her predecessors, in particular the aggression instinct, she clearly moved psychoanalysis into the interpersonal world.

THE WORK OF MELANIE KLEIN

Klein emphasized that to understand the effect of experience on the person, one must first understand the internal state (i.e., the anxieties to which one is susceptible) and the types of external impingements that are likely at a particular point in the person's development to cause pain or pleasure. This seems self-evident. To be hungry for 2 hours must be an extremely different experience for a 10-month-old infant than it is for a 30-year-old adult.

The most significant aspect of Kleinian theory is her conceptualization of how one perceives. She suggests that one sees the outside world in terms of internal concerns, and one's experiences in the world reinforce some anxieties and diminish others. This has special implications for the person at work in the organization, because it suggests that the organization, as an external reality, will have a significant impact on the psychodynamic processes of the employee. Klein sees interaction with external reality as a mode of controlling or enduring in one's internal life. At work in the organization, an employee can project or displace internal conflicts onto work activities or objects and therefore control internal anxiety and bring internal conflicts to a happy ending. Consequently, work is viewed as an attempt to master internal conflicts and their resulting anxiety.

KLEIN AND WORK

Klein stresses the extent to which anxiety resulting from internal conflicts motivates the person to focus more closely on external reality. She maintains that defenses can be functional and that projection[1] and displacement[2] of internal conflicts onto the external world have several advantages for the person. In the first place, projection and

[1]Projection from a Kleinian perspective is considered a normal part of development, not necessarily neurotic, where the person ascribes higher affects and wishes to another.

[2]This is the transference of affect or wishes from their original object to another object.

displacement allow an internal conflict that was passively endured to be actively controlled and mastered. For example, through work one can displace an internal conflict onto aspects of the job and the interpersonal relations that go with it, and consequently better control the conflict. In adulthood, one follows principles that are born in child's play, and one works toward the mastery of anxiety through one's satisfactory creations.

Kurt Vonnegut, Jr., once said that he was afraid he would go crazy if he did not write. Writing keeps at least some of the conflicts outside himself and under control. So for Klein, engaging in work serves an important psychic function by allowing the person greater control and mastery of anxiety. This function requires a reciprocal relationship between the person, his/her fantasy object(s), and the external environment. In this instance, work provides a vehicle for a kind of feedback loop. At the base of this loop are two psychic constellations which evolve from two types of anxiety. Klein refers to these two types of anxieties as persecutory anxiety and depressive anxiety.

PERSECUTORY ANXIETY

Persecutory anxiety is found in what Klein calls the paranoid schizoid position. It is of a paranoid nature and is characterized by the processes associated with a phenomenon called splitting, which Klein refers to as schizoid. Persecutory anxiety is a primitive anxiety and it is associated with the fear of annihilation. Persecutory anxiety occurs when objects in the environment get inside the ego and overwhelm and annihilate the ideal object and the self (Segal, 1967), triggering anxiety and conscious fears such as paranoia. To manage these fears, the person will utilize an array of defenses. The first defenses are introjection and projection, which are used simultaneously through the process of splitting. This process can take two forms. First, the object is split into good and bad parts. The person splits by projecting good objects outward to prevent the experience of badness, worthlessness, and guilt. Now in order to maintain this experience the person may introject external persecutors and then identify with them. It is as if the person is saying unconsciously, "They are correct, I am bad"; however, if the person is unconsciously defending against the experience of "badness" he/she will defend by projecting the badness out and then introjecting the "good." This defensive process begins at the onset of anxiety, and the function of splitting of good and bad objects is to keep the persecutory (fearful) objects from damaging the idealized objects contained within the ego. The thrust of the defensive process is to protect the idealized object, even if this means using the defense of denial, which is an expression of the inability to differentiate between good and bad objects.

If persecutory anxiety is excessive, the defense of introjection will be inhibited, leading to difficulties in establishing a secure sense of possessing or holding on to idealized internal objects. In other words, as a result of excessive anxiety all objects are felt to be persecutors and the person will have difficulties establishing relationships at work. In addition, if persecutory anxiety is intolerable, development remains fixated at the paranoid level, increasing the probability that people will be related to as part-objects rather than as whole persons; that is, the person will be unable to differentiate and the process of projection will intensify.

Klein considers inadequate ego functioning as the inability to differentiate, to see the object as having both good and bad qualities. Typically, under conditions of frustration, external objects are experienced as bad, but when, at the same time, the employee wishes to see the object as good he/she will experience intolerable ambivalence. It is this intense ambivalence that precipitates splitting. Splitting is used to preserve the idealized good object. The badness of that object is displaced onto another object so that the employee may maintain the experience of a good object and consequently preserve the ego by reducing tension. Similarly, disappointment or failure at work is often experienced as a narcissistic injury, an injury to the self system. As a way of preserving the internalized good object representation in the face of narcissistic injury, the employee utilizes splitting by displacing the experience of rage and contempt and projecting it outward and away from the self. Splitting results from regression to the stage of the grandiose self, a move that protects the vulnerable self from injury (Doroff, 1974). The employee may say, "I don't need you, I don't need this place." This reaction is to the narcissistic wound and will result in a withdrawal of the narcissistic cathexis. Here, splitting protects the employee; it preserves the grandiose self through the projection of internal bad object onto the boss, other employees, the organization, and so on. The employee may say, for example, "I am not bad, you are." The loss associated with the disappointment is denied by maintaining the fantasy that one still has contained within the self all the necessary attributes that are experienced as residing within the other.

Splitting, projective identification, and idealization are vital to the understanding of the psychodynamics of the relationships between superiors and subordinates, especially negative affects. Consider the following: A superior is insensitive and upsets a subordinate who then feels the emotion of outrage. These affects are a frequent occurrence at work when one feels slighted, left out, injured, and so forth. In response to these affects, the subordinate splits off parts of the self and projects them onto the superior. In turn, the superior is now perceived as an external persecutor par excellence, since the superior now possesses not only the real frustrating aspects for which he/she is actually responsible, but all the sadism and hateful projections. As a frustrating figure the superior becomes all the more terrifying, and the subordinate's persecutory anxiety spirals upward.

On the other hand, when good feelings and good parts are projected onto the object, the object is idealized. This process of idealization is important in the development of superior–subordinate relations because it is an integrative element in that it promotes bonding in the organization. In addition, Klein considers this process an important aspect of normal development. Idealization is important in Kleinian theory because it is through this process that the ego maintains an alliance with good objects, which are vital to preserve internal security. However, if this process is excessive, one might feel that all the good aspects of the self lie outside the self. If this occurs, even the occupationally successful executive will feel emptiness and excessive dependence on idealized external objects that are endowed with the good aspects of the self.

The phenomenon of splitting is important to the understanding of groups and systems. Just as excessive splitting reduces the synthesizing function of the ego, in social systems excessive splitting causes similar results, often leading to a state where one feels lonely, without internal support, and persecuted by internal and external bad objects. Narcissistic injuries and other types of disappointment at work precipitate regression. Under conditions of regression, splitting results. In normal development, splitting states are transitory and are abandoned when one feels gratified by the good object. Real gratification reduces the level of frustration, reinforces the relation to the good object, and reinforces the force of synthesis and unification.

The other significant aspects of Kleinian theory that have relevance for understanding the person at work are the processes of envy and reparation.

ENVY

Klein places envy in a dominant position in her theory, and in doing so enhances the interpersonal nature of her theory.

The organization is an arena in which the experience of envy is played out in a continuous fashion. Conflict is inevitable given the inequitable nature of the organization, its reward system, various levels of the capacity to use discretion, status, and power differentials, and the allocation of scarce resources. Underlying conflict are the affects associated with envy. Whether conscious or unconscious, envy may lay at the base of all organizational conflict.

In *Envy and Gratitude* Klein (1975), says that envy is one of the most primitive emotions. It evolves from dyadic interpersonal relationships in which one person envies the other (object) for some quality that the first person wants or admires. Envy is most problematic when persecutory anxiety is experienced. In this state, the process of splitting cannot occur and the idealized object cannot be maintained, because identification with the idealized object is destroyed as a result of the powerful feeling of envy. If the object cannot be idealized it becomes persecutory and feared, and the rage toward the object precipitates guilt. Consider the following example: A chief executive officer (CEO) decides to offer himself as a mentor to a young MBA who has recently joined the company. The MBA withdraws from the CEO, and in the process projects feelings of guilt into the CEO. What is projected into the CEO are feelings that the CEO has too much power, status, money, etcetera. The CEO feels the projected guilt, and in a reparative attempt moves closer to the young recruit, who once again withdraws. The CEO responds by inviting the young recruit to his home for a weekend visit. The young man experiences rage and confronts the CEO and says, "You are intentionally trying to make me feel inferior and this invitation is the last straw." The young man rejects the invitation and in a rage begins to tell other employees that the CEO is greedy and a manipulator. Examining the issue of envy helps to explain the young recruit's reaction. His envy toward the CEO would not allow for an introjection or identification of the CEO as a figure to be idealized; thus the basis of the mentoring relationship was destroyed. The young recruit's envy triggers a splitting phenomenon where he projects persecutory fantasies onto the CEO. The young recruit's rage increases to the point where he attempts to destroy the CEO, who represents a combination of a powerful and a persecutory figure. This persecutory figure cannot be introjected. The rumors the young recruit spreads about the CEO serve two purposes: they allow the young recruit to destroy the object and they allow him to project his own bad parts, parts associated with greed, power, and envy and his wish to take power from the CEO. If the CEO has these attributes, the young recruit is absolved. While the MBA recruit consciously wishes for success and power, and sees this relationship as vital to that end, his unconscious envy paralyzes his attempts. As Klein suggests, the aim of envy is to spoil, but in this case spoiling is a defense used by the young recruit because a spoiled object does not arouse envy (Segal, 1967). Another defense against envy is rigid idealization; however, this creates a vicious cycle: the more intense the idealization, the greater the envy. This vicious cycle often occurs when a young recruit is at the beginning of a potential mentoring relationship and is in awe of his/her superior; however, the fact that the superior may value the young recruit unleashes intolerable anxiety. The anxiety produces one of two defensive responses: (1) the subordinate may devalue the superior or (2) the subordinate, believing that that which he/she envies may someday be his, may hold on to and preserve the good idealized object with such intensity as to thwart any attempt by anyone in the organization to devalue the superior. This rigid idealization is a defense against the subordinate's intense envious feelings and the underlying fear that those qualities that are envied may never be attained: the power, status, or position of his/her idealized superior. These two reactions are most often observed in mentoring relationships where young subordinates react to their feelings of envy in many ways, most of which provoke intense anticipatory anxiety in their superior.

According to Klein, integrating persecutors and idealized objects will lead to stronger ego functioning. If people can contain the idealized object, they will be less afraid of their own aggression and will experience less anxiety; thus the ego will be less likely to split and will be more able to differentiate, that is, to see the object as having both good and bad qualities. If this occurs, the person will be able to move on to what Klein refers to as a higher-order position, the depressive position. However, before exploring the depressive position it is necessary to discuss reparation, an important concept for developing a psychoanalytic understanding of motivation in the organization.

REPARATION

The bases of Kleinian theory are the instincts of hate and sadism, which have the real potential to cause injury. Klein claims that children are born with voracious oral sadism, which is projected onto the mother. This sadism is eventually translated into persecutory anxiety (i.e., fear of the mother who becomes a retaliatory object). Klein says that anxiety evolves from these destructive instincts, and the person's relations with external objects in the future will become attempts to master this early destructiveness in a manner similar to the way in which it was mastered with the mother.

With aggression at the base of one's intrapsychic existence, these internal destructive impulses are directed outward against objects to maintain an internal state that is relatively tension free. If the person, in infancy, is unable to negotiate these impulses, the external world becomes a dangerous place, a place of terror where one is continuously threatened by persecutors. It is only through the act of reparation that the person develops an awareness that his/her hate and sadism can cause injury.

Klein (1940) articulates this view in *Mourning and Its Relation to Manic–Depressive States*. She sees the depressive position as similar to the process of mourning, which occurs when ever one must overcome the pain of an unhappy experience. Klein suggests that every advance in the process of mourning involves a deepening of the person's relationships to his inner objects, the happiness of regaining them after they were felt to be lost, and increased trust in them and love for them because they proved to be good and helpful after all. Klein emphasizes that painful and anxiety-provoking experiences can lead to a new sense of strength and mastery if they are not so excessive as to be overwhelming. In adulthood, grief resulting from the death of a loved one is the extreme form of promoting a reawakening of the pain felt in infancy. On the job, numerous experiences have similar results, although they may not be as powerful. A successful resolution of entry into the organization, termination from employment, job transfer, and even promotion will depend on the rediscovery of the good internal objects of one's childhood.

Reparation is the primary mechanism in Klein's theories by which the person learns to reduce depressive anxiety or guilt. Here the person relates to objects (mainly part-objects) in terms of his/her satisfaction or frustration. The reparative act results from an awareness by the person that his/her greed, sadism, and wishes have caused or may cause injury. This is largely the result of omnipotent fantasies that the object will be destroyed or used up. The resultant motivation is to heal these imaginary injuries and to make reparation; according to Klein (1940) this is accomplished through projection. The process of reparation begins when these fantasies are projected outward. Once this is accomplished, one is able to reduce depressive anxiety (guilt), and according to Klein, one can then negotiate destructive affects or feelings and can gain the experience of being connected to the world and to work.

DEPRESSIVE ANXIETY

The depressive position has been described as one of Klein's greatest achievements, and it occupies a central position in the development of her theory of psychic structure and the person's relations with external reality. Her theory of the depressive position, like most of Klein's work, evolved from her work with children.

The relational aspects of this model are applicable to work because even though the theory is based on childhood observation, the characterological methods used in adult life have changed very little. This is certainly true for the depressive position, because depressive anxiety is never eliminated; it is never fully worked through. Therefore, at work, given the abundance of affects associated with ambivalence, anger, guilt, and so forth, the experiences of the early depressive position are reawakened. Greenberg and Mitchell (1983) confirm this when they state: "[T]he fact of one's objects in the face of one's own conflictual feelings remain a central concern throughout life. All loss is experienced as a result of one's own destructiveness and as a retaliation for past hatefulness and injuries" (p. 127).

The main characteristic of the position is that anxiety is associated with the fear that one's destructive impulses will destroy the loved and dependent object. Anger and rage at the good object, which inevitably occur, bring forth both mourning and guilt. Depression is the result of the experience that the good object will be lost. As a result, the person mourns and experiences the loss of the good object through his/her own destructiveness. This destructiveness precipitates guilt and attempts at reparation. According to Segal (1967), the pain of mourning experienced in the depressive position and the reparative efforts used to restore the loved internal and external object lie at the basis of all creativity and sublimation, and form the basis for one's attachment to work.

If one's early experiences in the depressive position have been successfully worked through, one is able to engage in relations with good objects, both internally and externally, and loss later in life will not be experienced as debilitating. The inability to work through depressive affects may cause the person, when faced with rage, guilt, and object loss, to utilize the defense of splitting. The person may then regress and become flooded with constant anxiety, which becomes a major impediment to the capacity to work. Internal conflicts will then control the person's internal life and relations with external reality will be pathological; that is, internal balance will be lost and the person will be unable to use external reality to promote internal security. This person, at work, demonstrates the dread of boredom or deadness. In this case, the employee will be prone to use the organization and its structure, policies, rules, and standards to promote security and reduce psychic tension. Bion (1961), Mann and Hoffman (1960), and Hirschhorn (1988), like Klein, see work as a way of reconciling these conflicting tendencies and establishing a coherent pattern of adaptive behaviors that have the potential to satisfy needs. Hirschhorn (1988) bases his theory of work in the organization on the processes of reparation. He sees the motivation to do "good" as a healing process.

To follow Klein is to see work as an attempt to master the anxiety associated with the experiences of aggression and loss. Therefore, the key to achieving the necessary balance, and to being able to work, is not, as Freud claims, in satisfying the sexual and aggressive demands but in developing the assurance that one can accept hostile affect and use reparation or, as Klein (1964) says, "the assurance that one can be assertive or aggressive toward the object . . . by knowing, harm can be tempered by restitution should it occur."

Mourning and loss bring forth affects associated with the depressive position. Life in the organization involves a considerable amount of loss. Consider change, which is a frequent occurrence on the job. Each time an employee changes jobs, social groups, departments, and so forth, a loss is experienced and a mourning process results. With every change the employee must alter his/her motivational state to adapt to the requirements of the new situation. It also means giving up the real and fantasized gratifications associated with the old job. It is this giving up that precipitates the mourning process.

Successful mourning requires the employee to come to terms with the loss associated with the change. This loss may entail angry and depressive affects associated with the disappointments of the lost objects. The affects may be unconscious. For example, when an employee is given a promotion, he/she may demonstrate behaviors of elation, but these behaviors may be short-lived, and the employee may slip into a depressive state where he/she is overcome with conscious feelings of worthlessness or finds fault with the new job. These are all expressions of depressive affect associated with the mourning process.

Given the frequency of change and instability in the modern organization, mild forms of depression are prevalent. As a result, employees react and are often observed to be oblivious to important issues; they seem aloof and disinterested in their work or in their relations with customers. What may appear on the surface to be a function of apathy or low esprit are attempts by employees to avoid the experience of the affects associated with loss.

When employees occupy a depressive position they project their inner state onto the organization and in so doing claim that the organization no longer cares. In the depressive position, employees may retreat from the work environment into a schizoid position. Employees do so because they are preoccupied with concerns over separation from, loss of, and harm to significant objects in their environment, especially those objects that communicate with the employees' unconscious (Ashbach & Schermer, 1987). Employees use the organization as an object to receive the products of these affects which must be disavowed if they are to reduce tension. The key defense at play here is projective identification.

PROJECTIVE IDENTIFICATION

There is considerable controversy concerning whether projective identification evolves from the internal experience of a dangerous impulse, as Klein suggests, or whether it begins with the experience of frustration, as a reaction to a dangerous external object. However, if we are to make the best use of projective identification in understanding organizational behavior, it makes the most sense to see the process as interpersonal in nature. This is confirmed by Knapp (1989), who offers the following definition: "[It is] an interactive process where the projector [and projectee] both consciously attempt to delegate or induce a particular role, or set of feelings in another for the purpose of reducing his own anxiety" (p. 56).

In spite of Klein's position that projective identification is an internal defense, it must be considered an interpersonal phenomenon, primarily because it is concerned with the psychic reaction to an external, frustrating figure. The interactive nature of projective identification is further enhanced when Klein suggests that parts of the self are split off and projected onto an external object. This is hardly a one-person psychology, for it requires an object, a recipient to receive the projected dangerous impulse. Segal (1967), in her review of Klein's theories, confirms this view: "[I]n this process parts of the self and internal objects are split off and projected into an external object which then becomes a container of the projections. The projector then controls and identifies with the projected parts" (p. 27). In projective identification, the person tries not only to enter the object but to control it by controlling the object's reaction and behavior.

This defensive process holds a crucial place in organizational analysis because it helps to explain an array of "emotional" reactions that arise when people work together. Emotions, like primitive aggression and their derivatives such as competence, power, achievement, and the wish for dominance, are all understood from the perspective of projective identification. The critical issue in trying to understand projective identification is its excessive nature. The greater the affect of aggression and its derivatives, the more the person will engage in splitting and the process of projective identification, (Kernberg, 1980).

Maintaining the interpersonal context of projective identification, Bion (1948/1962) says that most people project back and forth, and when they exchange bad objects there is a tendency to fend off these objects and look only for good objects; that is, they seek only to become a container for good objects. This may explain to a degree why some employees seek roles that have been historically viewed by others as containers for good objects. Ogden (1982) also maintains that projective identification is interpersonal. He calls it a group of fantasies and accompanying object relations having to do with ridding the self of unwanted objects (aspects of the self) and then disposing of these unwanted aspects of the self by projecting them onto another person. The person who projected then discovers what was extruded when the recipient responds. Ogden goes on to suggest that the goal of projective identification is different from the Freudian defense of projection:

> In projection we put parts of the self onto another and then distance ourselves from the object. In projective identification we put parts of ourselves into the other, and we feel close to (at one with) the object, and we then get the object to behave in accordance with our projections. (1982, p. 138)

Consequently, Knapp (1989), Bion (1948/1962), Ogden (1982), Balint (1937), and others see projective identification as a method of communication. It is a form of communication because it requires a capacity on the part of the person projecting to assess the nature of the recipient, and his/her readiness to receive; second, the projector must have the capacity to induce a feeling in the recipient. A critical question that has been unexplored concerns the issue of congruence between projector and recipient, and how congruent feelings are induced. The issue worthy of exploration is how one gets the object to behave in accordance with the projection. It may be that in the organization, inducement occurs as a result of environmental reinforcers such as roles, culture, and behaviors and experiences that are communicated over time and created by the projector and others, all pressing to promote the required feelings and behaviors in the recipient. Additionally, projective identification requires unconscious collusion, that is, a willingness on the part of the recipient of the projections. We see some evidence of this at meetings at which a superior, in an attempt to get his/her way, communicates a set of feelings to subordinates, and then uses the subordinates as a container for angry, aggressive projections that render them passive and compliant to the superior's wishes. A number of writers suggest that employees bring to the organization certain predispositions or valences where they may become receptacles for certain types of disturbing emotions. Even when occupying a specific role required by the organization, employees may unconsciously seek to receive projections from others in informal groups or work groups (Bion, 1961; Ringwald, 1974; Gibbard, 1974; Lieberman, Yalom, & Miles, 1973).

According to Langs (1980), projective identification can be an interpersonal phenomenon and not exclusively intraphysic. Simultaneous mutual unconscious projective identifications can exist where employees place their own mental contents onto the others, while consciously setting the stage for these projections. In many organizations, projective identification is either a role requirement or a requirement for membership in a department or an informal social group. From this perspective, the process is more than a defense. It may be functional or, as Ashbach and Schermer (1987) suggest, normative and adaptive. Ashbach and Schermer indicate that projective identification is an ongoing developmental process and can be understood as an intrapsychic process, a process of interpersonal interaction, and a group process where the group functions as a container. In addition, projective identification may be viewed as (1) a defense, where people can distance themselves unconsciously from unwanted parts of the self and at the same time keep these parts alive in another; (2) a mode of communication, where persons can make themselves understood by exerting pressure on another person to experience a set of feelings similar to their own, (3) a type of relatedness, where the person who projects, experiences the other as a receptacle of his/her affects, and (4) a pathway to psychological change.

Knapp (1989) suggests that environmental conditions increase the likelihood that a type of regression will occur that will precipitate projective identifications. While she does not identify the mechanisms involved that bring forth projective identifications, she does suggest that environment influences the process. For example, she says that strange, new, and coercive environments, where an employee's sense of identity is not well delineated or has been compromised, contribute to projective identifications. Knapp (1989) refers to these situations where "persistent projections by important others become internalized part-objects that can then affect the sense of identity for the object of the projection" (p. 54). Knapp goes on to say that the intensity of the interaction and the status and power of the projector will influence the extent to which projections become accepted as an aspect of one's identity. Additionally, she says that the person most susceptible to projections will be the person most dependent or needy, or least differentiated.

Bowers (1984) confirms this when he asserts that the degree to which a person has a sense of self determines the extent to which he/she receives projections from others. At work this is especially problematic; typically, organizations recruit employees because of their capacity to receive projections from others, generally their superiors. In some instances CEOs are brought into an organization with the unconscious intention of causing lower-level executives to project onto the newcomer hateful affects. Also, departments within organizations can function as containers for projections from others (departments). Some departments seem to get the blame for all that goes wrong in the organization, and the other departments then feel absolved from wrongdoing and responsibility. All organizations use employees and departments for projective purposes, and it is these projections and the unconscious structure that is created that make change and innovation problematic.

In addition to status differentials, two other organizational factors are most likely to precipitate projective identifications: (1) the experience of narcissistic wound and (2) entry into a new and strange work situation.

NARCISSISTIC INJURY AT WORK

An employee receives a reprimand from his/her superior and as a result feels incompetent, worthless, enraged, and embarrassed. The reality of the situation as perceived by the employee is essentially insignificant because it cannot modulate the affects the employee experiences. Consequently, the employee's internal objects assume the full emotional impact of the charge and the employee feels the full range of emotions. At the moment the employee experiences rage, the injury may trigger the unconscious construction of a relationship to the superior based on continuous projective identifications. In addition, these projective identifications are probably not new; they are generally a function of the history of the relationship between the superior and the subordinate and the type of relationship expected as a function of the organization's culture. For example, the employee may project unconscious angry impulses onto the superior, and the superior will experience or carry the anger projected onto him. These projective identifications may be a replication of the employee's earlier child–parent interactions, which contained frequent states of rage where the bad object was experienced as an intrusion and the good object was experienced as a loss.

In projective identifications the employee attempts to keep out the intrusive bad object (parent) by separation and withdrawal, which allow him/her to hold on to the good object. These experiences, and the sense of disappointment the employee feels, may actually be a construction motivated by an unconscious wish to see the superior as an idealized parent who will gratify all desires. When this wish fails and rage results, the guilt associated with the rage may be projected. The employee, using projective identification, induces guilt in his superior by telling the superior, "You hate me, I know it." This is an attempt by the subordinate to control the superior and project onto him the rage the subordinate experiences and at the same time to communicate to the superior that he/she is the source of all the subordinate's frustration and thus should feel guilt. According to Levinson (1984), many superiors respond to the guilt projected onto them by their superiors by engaging in some type of reparative act. This act may be an offering of a gift, like a promotion or a salary increase.

ENTRY INTO THE ORGANIZATION

The experience of a new and strange situation also precipitates projective identification. Upon entering an organization employees experience regression as a method to reduce anxiety. The organization requires formation of object relationships so that employees can learn the duties associated with their task, but the secondary purpose of the object relationship is to reduce conscious and unconscious anxiety. If an employee is unable to establish object relationships to reduce anxiety, he/she will continue to regress. The regressive experience during entry is a matter of degree, and the greater the regression the more primitive is one's connections to objects.

Under these conditions, projective identifications are used by the entrant as a form of relatedness or attachment to the organization and its objects within. In this regressed state, employees project affects associated with primitive persecutory objects onto their superior and colleagues. These projections can be verbal or nonverbal. During communication these affects precipitate an array of affects in the superior. The employee begins to feel related to or attached when he/she experiences the superior's response to that which is projected. For example, while the employee is demonstrating independence and verbally says to the superior, "Yes, I know how to do it, I'm fine now," the superior may say to him/herself, "That's not true, the newcomer is unsure and too anxious to work alone." The employee may respond with annoyance and rage, causing the superior to withdraw, feeling punished by the employee. The thrust of this interaction begins when the employee, in a regressed state, unconsciously establishes an interactive process where he/she can project this rage at being helpless and dependent onto the superior. Then the entrant controls the feelings contained in the superior. Now the employee has the superior in the dependent mode, racked with guilt and seeking forgiveness. This process is unconscious, and the entrant, experiencing helplessness and dependency, unconsciously projects the affects associated with this experience onto the superior, which then allows the employee to identify with these projected parts of the self as they are contained within the superior.

PROJECTIVE IDENTIFICATION AND LEADERSHIP

Both the interactive nature and the power of projective identification are clearly demonstrated in the relationships between leader and follower. Projective identification not only promotes leader–follower relations but provides a way in which organizational members can psychically regress and experience a sense of bonding and cohesion. Freud (1917/1957) suggests that identification with the leader is the glue that cements this relationship. He uses the process of identification as a link that leads to a change in the ego; that is, the idealization part of the ego changes into the ego ideal. Freud further asserts that this identification is inherently ambivalent since it is a mechanism based on oral incorporation.

Freud's example of the panic and flight of the Assyrian soldiers on learning that their leader has lost his head in conflict with Judith (Chapter 1) helps to explain projective identification. When the leader loses his head, the commonly shared external object (figurehead) that bound the soldiers together was lost, and all the soldiers behaved as if they had lost their head. According to Freud, this event occurred because each soldier identified his ego with the leader as an external object. While Freud considered this a process of identification, he left out an important step, the beginning of the process, when the soldiers first project part of themselves. This example, if considered in its totality, is one of projective identification. All soldiers go through a socialization process on the way to becoming a soldier, and boot camp is an example of this process. During this socialization process, soldiers are uprooted from family and friends and thrown into a highly disciplined anxiety-producing situation. Their ego and usual defense processes are altered. Under the stressful conditions of military training, soldiers are considered successful when they are convinced that their "thinking capacity" is an unwanted part of the self; that is, in combat it may get them killed. Under these regressive conditions soldiers project their thinking capacity outward onto an ambivalent leader (both benevolent and feared). Soldiers then identify with this part of the self that is now contained in the leader. In this situation, two conditions result: (1) dependency, when each soldier has given up part of himself, his thinking capacity, and (2) bonding or cohesion is achieved among the soldiers, when they have collectively projected a common aspect of their ego.

Klein (1946–1963) confirms Freud's description as in fact projective identification by suggesting that when followers take a leader for their ego ideal they are engaged in projective identification. In the case of the Assyrian soldiers, the defense of projective identification, which has bonded them, broke down when their leader lost his head. The head (the thinking capacity) bonded them together, and when the head was lost, they were lost and panic resulted. The socialization process and the anxiety of combat precipitated regression, and the defense of projective identification kept them in this regressed state. As Waelder (1951) states, "[R]egression in the ego occurs when one attributes greater power to the protector than he/she actually has, as children we do this with our parents" (p. 170). However, under conditions of extreme anxiety regression serves a significant function: The group feels protected by the leader from both real and fantasized dangers.

LEADERSHIP AND THE OEDIPUS COMPLEX

All struggles between superiors and subordinates are essentially oedipal struggles. Although psychoanalytic writers have placed the oedipal complex firmly in childhood, Loewald (1960A) has suggested that this complex will reappear in later periods of life, in both normals as well as neurotics. During the course of life, oedipal conflicts repeatedly require repression, internalization, transformation, sublimation, and some level of mastery. However, the reappearance of these early conflicts is a function of the person's changing levels of experience and maturity. Consequently, reality-based issues may precipitate regression and a return to this early oedipal period.

The organization and work are particularly significant in reawakening oedipal conflicts. Because the organization is a hierarchical system, it closely resembles the family structure, and the competitive nature of work requires that one continuously move up or ahead and achieve the top position. Psychodynamically, all employees want to be the favored child of the idealized leader, and all want to take the leader's place. Jealousy of the leader's power, perks, and position often precipitates an array of affects, most of which are prohibited and not expressed. Instead, a reaction formation develops and with it the norm of equalitarianism, which permits the defense against envy, rivalry, and murder. According to Loewald (1960a), the dominant features of the Oedipus Complex are parricide, guilt, responsibility, and atonement. The critical event during this period is the wish to murder the parent; however, this wish can also be represented as a wish to murder a symbolic parent, or anyone who stands for parental authority.

In superior–subordinate relationships, wishes for ascendancy, assertion of responsibility, and ambition are all symbolic representations of the wish to murder the parent and take his/her place on the altar of authority and power. As a result of these wishes, strong feelings of guilt are aroused. It is the reaction to the experience of guilt that stimulates behaviors that can be observed in the organization. For example, it is all too common for an adversarial relationship to be developed so that the guilt experienced by the subordinate can be reduced, or at least displaced. For younger employees, guilt associated with ambition, assuming responsibility, and even autonomy seeking are all symbolic representations of murdering the parent (i.e., taking over). This wish arouses fear and anxiety associated with the retaliative fear of castration; consequently, atonement and reparation are attempts to make up for the wish and to reduce the anxiety associated with the fear of retaliation. The guilt associated with the wish and atonement is played out when the employee seeks employment in a bureaucratic organization with regimentation and rigidity, or the employee undermines his/her chances for advancement. This occurs if atonement is not reduced by mourning and reparation. The employee then seeks punishment, and this wish for punishment becomes inexhaustible and follows a clearly repetitious pattern. Punishment, whether by others or by oneself, is inflicted in the service of guilt.

An example of the Oedipus Complex at work occurred in a management succession program created to prepare young employees for management positions. After a period of one year in operation, the executive constellation of the organization realized that this program was failing. To change the program the executives hired a consultant. The consultant was a retired executive from the same company, and he had many friends of long standing among the executives. The consultant was hired as an unconscious representation of the executives' wish to keep the program from succeeding in its stated purpose, and to use the program to essentially eliminate any threat from the younger employees. After reviewing the program and making changes, the consultant met with the executives and announced, "I don't know what's wrong with these young people, they just don't have what it takes to move up."

The consultant was unconsciously colluding with the wishes of the executives to create a program that would render the young employees incompetent and would symbolically castrate them. The actual program was structured to force the young employees to compete with each other, and it took a heavy toll, as the young employees acted out the wish of their superiors and destroyed themselves. These executives used the program unconsciously to protect themselves from the "young bucks." The activation of competition in the program intensified themes of an oedipal nature, and the unconscious affects associated with incest, hostility, and guilt proved overwhelming for the trainees, who engaged in the defense of reaction formation and withdrew into passivity or fled from the program, and in some cases from the organization.

The executives had unconsciously avoided designing a program in which the trainees could master the guilt associated with oedipal wishes. The executives failed to provide the necessary constancy, nurturance, and acceptance that would have enabled the trainees to reconcile their ambitions with the unconscious wish of parricide.

THE WORK OF W. R. D. FAIRBAIRN

W. R. D. Fairbairn took psychoanalytic understanding into an exclusively relational area, and in doing so he made a significant contribution to understanding work and the organization. Fairbairn represents the most radical departure from the classical position of psychoanalysis. He completely rejects the idea that the ego exists in a unifying form from birth. This allows him to develop a theory of motivation that is devoid of instincts and dependent on relations.

Additionally, Fairbairn argues that energy is integrated into the ego structure and not a separate part outside the structure. In claiming that the ego structure contains energy, and not the id, he completely rejects the idea that structure is established to deal with or channel directionless energy. The rejection of the instincts and the development of an ego containing energy are important for understanding work. First, Fairbairn's views allow one to see more clearly what underlies the motivation for work. It is not the gratification of impulses. The motivation to work is seen as an attempt to obtain and maintain relatedness to objects in one's environment. Thus the motivation to work can be viewed as a function of the search for and the maintenance of contact with others (Greenberg & Mitchell, 1983). Consequently, work is not considered a defensive activity, as the classical theorists maintain, and pleasure derived from work is not obtained through the process of sublimation and the disguised gratification of the instincts of sex and aggression. The gratifications the person seeks in work are now viewed as a function of having obtained satisfactory relations with others, and gratification is a function of the person's ego capacity, as well as the organization's ability to provide a context.

In suggesting a relational model, Fairbairn proposes a model of psychic structure quite different from Freud's tripartite model. He proposes a model of the mind in terms of stable dynamic patterns of thought, fantasy, and behavior, and he uses the terminology of a "functional structure" without inherent energy. In Fairbairn's structure, two important characteristics prevail: (1) an important dynamic of intraphysic structure is the occurrence of splits in the ego, followed by repression of one part of the ego by another; and (2) the primary object of repression is not the repression of unacceptable impulses, but rather the repression of intolerably bad object relations. He sees conflicts as created by projecting one's impulses, particularly oral–sadistic impulses, onto others. Conflicts and the splitting of the ego exist to some extent in all individuals, but they are most apparent in what Fairbairn describes as schizoid individuals; that is, people whose lives are characterized by a profound sense of isolation and detachment from others, a preoccupation with an inner reality, to the exclusion of external reality, and an attitude of omnipotence.

Central to Fairbairn's conception of intraphysic structure is the notion that one part of the ego is capable of repressing another part. The ego is composed of three parts. The first is the libido, which is the object-seeking part. The libido attempts to develop relations with objects in the external world. Another part of the ego is the anti-libidinal ego. This part is motivated to lacerate or sabotage object relations. It is also referred to as the internal saboteur and is similar to Freud's superego. According to Mitchell and Greenberg (1983):

> The antilibido is the part of the ego that becomes the repository for all the hatred and destructiveness which accumulates as a consequence of the frustration of libidinal longings. . . . It is attached to and identifies with the rejecting object. . . . Much of the rage [is] . . . directed toward the exciting object [and] the promises and enticements of mother. (p. 166)

Employees carry within their antilibidinal ego the experience that they are unloved, that their love for mother is not wanted by her, or that their love drove away mother because they demanded to much of her. When an employee experiences failure at work, the affects associated with these experiences are repeated and the employee responds by withdrawing from all of the object relations connected to work. The employee then experiences him/herself as alone, unloved, and perhaps self-righteous. In some instances this wish to repeat is so great that the employee unconsciously creates the failure situation so that he/she can repeat or experience the early affects associated with failure. These earlier experiences also precipitate aggressive responses, especially when the employee experiences frustration with the job or career.

The antilibidinal ego also focuses its rage at the libidinal ego. According to Mitchell and Greenberg (1983), "[T]he antilibidinal ego hates the libidinal ego for its hope, for continuing to perpetuate the belief that the promises of mother may yet be fulfilled" (p. 166). This internal conflict explains self-destructive acts. When one engages in self-destructive behavior, the antilibidinal ego undermines any and all attempts to obtain a gratifying, meaningful relationship with others through work or love. "It hates and punishes the libidinal ego for any attempts to get something from the other . . ." (Mitchell & Greeberg, 1983, p. 166). Additionally, this part of the ego is aligned with the rejecting object. It directs aggression that is felt as a consequence of frustrating relationships toward the self and internal objects.

The third part of the ego is the central ego. This is the part of the ego that if left untouched by splitting and repression, is capable of maintaining satisfying object relations.

Fairbairn makes the important point that the integrity of the sense of self is inevitably compromised by one's inability to maintain object relatedness in the world. The inability to love compromises one's sense of efficacy, and one's inability to relate to these needs in the face of frustration causes a substitution of an internal conflict for what seems an intolerable external situation. An unloving object invariably leads not only to the regression of the frustrating aspects of the object, but also to the rejection of aspects of the self that become lost to the central ego. Consequently, the conscious and accepted sense of self is lost.

The employee seeks gratification of wishes contained within the central ego. The central ego is critical in our understanding of failure at work, because this part of the ego strives to live up to the ideals of an internalized ideal object. The central ego assumes that "if these ideals are met, relatedness and contact will be forthcoming" (Mitchell & Greenberg, 1983, p. 165). This central ego strives for perfection, and in this striving it avoids bad internal objects in the repressed subsidiary ego. If the central ego fails, the bad internal objects in the antilibido are cathected and the self system is then preoccupied with bad objects. When this occurs the employee is preoccupied and loses contact with people and work is diminished. This is especially apparent in organizations in which group participation is vital to the work. Withdrawal from work or social groupings will have pronounced effects on both work productivity and career success.

FAILURE AT WORK

Fairbairn rejects the notion that conflicts are internally determined and claims that it is the frustrating aspect of external relationships that evolves as a source of conflict. This view suggests that all interaction and activities associated with work are attempts to create or maintain object relations, both internally and externally, with the ultimate goal of obtaining gratifications and avoiding frustration. However, avoiding frustration is an impossible task. Over time, one will experience impingements upon the self, which will activate the contents of the repressed affects contained within ego splits by threatening the very survival of the central ego (Ashbach & Schermer, 1987; Greenberg & Mitchell, 1983). Under conditions where impingements exist, the central ego can actively work to alter the environment; however, in organizations, especially bureaucratic organizations, the options to alter one's environment are severely limited. Fairbairn (1952), maintains that under these conditions, the person will respond by adopting the schizoid position.

The schizoid position is adopted initially in infancy where the infant, unable to alter environmental impingement, such as deprivation, defends against the affect of anger and destruction by becoming detached and withdrawing into a fantasy world. Through withdrawal the infant can control the object internally and survive. For the adult, under conditions that precipitate anxiety, the same will occur—a withdrawal from social interaction and entry into intense involvement in fantasy life. This process allows an employee to hold on to the good aspects of the object and the belief that the object will someday provide gratification. By withdrawing and fantasizing, one can keep the central ego intact and protect it from the depriving and threatening world.

As mentioned before, schizoid withdrawal is utilized if one is unable to change the object environment. At work, when faced with frustrating and depriving objects, an employee may seek entry into an informal group and seek refuge in this group as a defense against the frustration and resulting affects. Often this group maintains a persecutory mode or a depressive position vis-à-vis the frustrating object. The group will come to be seen as a good and nurturing object capable of protecting the self from the frustrating object, which becomes a persecutor. Under these conditions, involvement in work is seen as secondary, and the motivation to work is lost as employees huddle together, engaging in fantasized supportive behaviors. In some cases, the group will regress to a primitive level of object relatedness where the members become fully devoted to maintenance of and allegiance to internal objects.

According to Fairbairn (1952), under these conditions of regression the structural characteristics of the organization are established. Even though the aim of developing a structure is motivated by the wish to establish object relatedness, it cannot be accomplished because the employee is preoccupied with internal object representations. Therefore, the established structure becomes nothing more than a representation of the employee's internal state. When this occurs, other employees react to the proposed structure as if it is incomprehensible. The most primitive regressed states are apparent when an organizational structure is designed as a representation of a projection of internal objects; that is, as a wish for a blissful union with the all-giving maternal object. However, often the most apparent motivation for designing a structure is to protect the self and avoid the experience of vulnerability and deprivation.

All employees expect the creation of a new structure to provide for adequate object relations. When this does not occur, frustration is experienced, which precipitates aggression. Fairbairn does not consider aggression to be a drive or an instinct; he sees it as an interpersonal response to frustration and not as a primary factor in promoting relations with people.

THE "GOOD ENOUGH" ENVIRONMENT

Object relations theorists assume that parents both create the child's environment and, if they are "good enough," buffer the child from the dangers associated with the external world and his/her own internal reality. From this perspective, the organization and its authority structure can be viewed as nothing more than a symbolic recreation, or representation, of aspects of the early parent–child relation.

As a symbolic parent, the organization must be good enough if it is to buffer its employees from the dangers associated with power, authority, termination, loss, deprivation, and the employees' own internal conflicts. To do this, the organization must be constant, reliable, noncritical, and empathic and at the same time show patience and set limits. However, in the organization this is almost an impossible task for two reasons: First, the ideal or experience of being good enough is relative, and the experience will vary dramatically from employee to employee, leading to the potential of creating a single experience that is good enough for one employee and "bad" for another. Second, given the nature of the tasks of the organization and its constituent units, the work itself will lead to conflicting levels of gratification, deprivation, and constraints that may be distributed inequitably, with economic imbalance due to scarcity. There are three reasons for this. First, structurally the organization is an inequitable system, with a scarcity of resources that promote competitiveness. Second, work is based on an exchange theory where one is compensated for one's efforts. Ideally, organizations are structured to eliminate human passion. The third and perhaps most significant reason why good enough is not possible is that employees seek to join an organization and obtain from it those gratifications and love they never obtained in their primary family.

Is it any wonder then that most employees see the organization as a source of frustration and deprivation. Frustration and deprivation are most apparent for employees at the point of entry into the organization, when the new entrant is perceived as a person who may threaten the balance of gratifications or acquire "too much," and may be perceived as a sibling.

If the organization is unable to provide good enough parenting, the ego of the employee is weakened. When the employee's ego can no longer approximate the ego ideal, or wished for self-image (see Chapter 3), the employee's defenses, which have previously helped to explain earlier incongruities, fail. Consequently, the employee's ego can no longer sustain an object relationship with the organization. The organization is experienced as a lost object, which results in a loss of confidence, a loss of interest, and the reexperiencing of affects associated with anger and aggression.

Aggression, in particular, is important because it is a way in which one can bring the object (organization) close to experience and capture a union. In this instance, aggression or hostility against the organization and the boss, who were once admired objects, replaces the previously wished for infantile magical attempt at a union with the object. The union is experienced as an introject where the employee in fantasy can merge with the once powerful and gratifying object and gratify distancing needs as well. In this instance, the employee moves to a position where he/she withdraws from the emotional life of the organization and functions more or less in a "robotic" manner on the job. This process is closely aligned with what is described by Doroff (1974) as the phenomenon of object splitting. According to Doroff, when employees are faced with conditions of frustration they will experience the object (organization or boss) in a way that preserves it in an idealized state. This is accomplished either through distortion of reality or through feeling betrayed by the organization and its leadership, because they have failed to function as all-giving objects. When this betrayal is experienced by the employee, the response is to withdraw and react with rage.

MOTIVATION TO WORK

Bowlby (1973) and Winnicott (1965) conceptualize the motivation to join an organization and engage in work in terms of attachment, competence–mastery, and curiosity.

The motivation to work is a delicate psychic issue and it is formed, heightened, limited, or destroyed during the early stages of entry into the organization. This process of entry offers considerable insight into the utility of object relations theory in understanding behavior at work. When one enters the organization for the first time, object relations are not yet formed, the requirements of the role the employee must occupy have to be learned, and, consequently, the entrant experiences a considerable amount of anxiety. Under conditions of anxiety during this process the employee will regress, that is, retreat backwards in search of protection and security from this new and strange situation. If entrants cannot physically retreat or cannot locate security, they will create a fantasized safety net within their psychic world, which is split off from reality. The entrant will cope with reality by making a compromise, by living half in and half out of object relations.

Fantasized safety is healthy if it consists of preparation (i.e., mental rehearsal). However, the entrant knows very little about the organization (i.e., the world he/she is facing). All the entrant can hope to do is call on experiences in similar situations and hope that they approximate the new reality. The entrant tests out these old experiences and if they are congruent with the new reality, his/her anxiety is reduced, but if not, his/her anxiety will most likely increase. Under these conditions the entrant will, in desperation, seek any object and utilize this object in a transitional way to reduce anxiety. When there is no object available to buffer the entrant's anxiety, the entrant is in danger of withdrawal from reality and total involvement with his/her inner objects, which leaves the ego with little capacity to handle reality. Under these conditions the entrant will appear awkward, tense, "spaced out," and unable to hear instructions, and he/she will "get lost" and respond inappropriately to reality demands.

An extreme example of this is an employee's withdrawal within him/herself. According to Guntrip (1969), this person may produce a superficial attitude of being superior to others. The employee may say, when instructed to operate a machine, "I can do that, no problem," when the employee knows inside that he/she is helplessly lost. The omnipotence is merely a defense against feeling inferior. The superiority is characterological and it is established to master the anxiety associated with the new frightening reality.

Entry is a particularly difficult problem for a person who has schizoid difficulties. A person with little capacity to feel emotional warmth and connectedness with objects will find meeting new people and getting to know a new environment problematic. This person may appear, on the surface, to be indifferent to these new objects; he/she may even appear cold or in an awkward manner gregarious and willing, but this is nothing more than a characterological style the person has developed over the years to deal with internal anxiety. The characterological style in essence allows the person to escape from what is experienced as an intolerable situation. This escape is accomplished by the establishment of a "false self."

FALSE SELF

According to Winnicott, environmental failure, lack of attunement, and impingements result in fragmentation, a split between the "true self" and the "false self." The true self, the source of spontaneous needs, images, and gesture, becomes detached and atrophied (Greenberg & Mitchell, 1983). The false self then comes forth to assume the caretaking function lacking in the environment.

The false self arises because genuine wishes and needs are not attended to. To withdraw is too painful; therefore the child adapts him/herself to the emotionality of the mother. It is as if the child says, "Tell me what to be and I'll be it." The child develops a self that has no shape of its own; rather, it takes its shape exclusively from its environment. This is similar to what Lifton (1968) calls the "protean self," Reisman, Glazer, and Denney (1950) call the "other directed personality" or the "malleable personality," and some call the "bureaucratic personality."

According to Mitchell (1988):

> Theorists like Winnicott, Sullivan, and Farber, assume a powerful primary need for interpersonal connectiveness which makes it necessary for the child to change himself to the parents vision of him; to present himself/herself in a way that is both visible and palatable; to become, in Sullivans terms, the parent's definition of "good me." (p. 106)

Mitchell (1988) goes on to quote Farber (1976), who characterizes the false self as a process of "promiscuity," a tendency to feel driven ". . . as though they would be everything to everyone" (Mitchell, pp. 195–196).

The false self provides an illusion of personal existence, and it protects the true self by complying to environmental demands (Greenberg & Mitchell, 1983). When an employee operates under conditions of the false self, he/she engages in a detached schizoid fashion, constantly ruminating about work-related activities with the intention of maintaining self-esteem. The employee actively engages in behavior to avoid what he/she experiences as annihilation of the self. The employee loses all spontaneity of the self, and he/she does not respond to others as real objects but as objects to be used in an overly adaptive way to protect the integrity of the true self. The false self evolves out of the person's experience in the work environment. If the work environment is not experienced as "ego supportive," the employee is not able to experience work activities as containing "transitional objects" (Winnicott, 1958).

THE TRANSITIONAL OBJECT

Winnicott (1958) suggests that the transitional object is an instrument the entrant uses to cope with the depressive affects invoked during entry. One of the emotionally troubling aspects of entering an organization is that it evokes separation–individuation issues from childhood. Consequently, at entry employees experience a repetition of affects associated with early separation experienced in their relationship with mother. Winnicott (1958) developed the theory of transitional objects as a way to explain how the child moves from dependence and symbiotic attachment to individuation and autonomy. For the child this object may be a blanket, a teddy bear, and so on. The object plays a role in reducing anxiety in situations that are new, strange, and different.

There is considerable controversy in the field as to whether transitional phenomena are normal or pathological and whether they are carried into adulthood. With regard to the existence of transitional phenomena in adulthood and at work, Winnicott suggests a link between transitional and cultural phenomena.

Eagle (1981) sees transitional phenomena as:

the need to develop symbolic supportive substitutes for early sources of security and safety. In a sense, they represent internalized home bases to which one must periodically return before setting out again. . . . This is sure close to what Winnicott has in mind when he referred to certain cultural activities (e.g. music, poetry) as periodic therapeutic regression and as similar to transitional phenomena. (p. 544)

Hirschhorn (1988) and Morgan (1988), suggest that transitional phenomena can be applied to work situations and maintain that products of work can function as transitional objects. Greenberg and Mitchell (1983) agree:

Transitional experience is rooted in the capacity of the child to play; in adult form it is experienced as a capacity to play with one's fantasies, ideas, and the world's possibilities in a way that continually allows for the surprising, the original, and the new. (p. 196)

Morgan (1988) claims that transitional phenomena and associated areas of illusions and fantasies explain how we engage in work, construct organizational reality, and cope with organizational change. He says that at work:

Just as a child may rely on the presence of his or her doll or teddy bear as a means of reaffirming who and where they are, managers and workers may rely on equivalent phenomena. . . .

He continues by suggesting that:

when engineers were faced with the prospect of having to give up slide rules and use computers instead they resisted. They could not give up the symbolic object and move towards the new object because the transitional object is lacking. (p. 221)

Technological change, as with any type of change, requires a transitional object if the change is to occur with limited anxiety. For the engineers in Morgan's example, resistance is centered around what the computer symbolically represents. On one level the computer symbolically represents a new object to be mastered, controlled, and fed. This, according to Farber (1976), is the unconscious equivalent of early experiences in which the failure to master and control precipitated trauma. He says, "[A]ccording to Francis Broucek (1979) the infant undergoes 'trauma' when he is merely 'unable to influence' an 'event' he expected 'to be able to control' " (p. 207). The machine represents to the engineers the unknown, a terrifying monster, and results in the feeling of powerlessness. Just as a child clutches a blanket to tolerate the darkness of the bedroom, the engineers require a transitional object to face their fears of the new machine. When the organization fails to provide this object, and at the same time demands abandonment of the old object (slide rule), the workers resist. Morgan (1988) reports that the company went bankrupt.

On the other hand, there are those who see the computer as a transitional object, and these people are often referred to as "computer addicts." According to Ingber (1981), these people cannot be away from their machines, and even when they are separated, they sleep for a few hours, and then return to engage in an object relationship with the object. This attachment is found among those who keep a computer terminal in their bedroom or close by and travel with their "laptop" computer, which is immediately hooked up when they arrive at their destination. In this instance the computer assumes the role of an object capable of performing Bion's (1970) "containing" function and Winnicott's (1958) "holding" function. The computer is able to receive the operator's projections and functions as a container for the operators projective identifications. These projective identifications result in a machine that performs the same psychic function as a teddy bear, which gives the operator a sense of comfort and security.

Of course, this is true in all aspects of work. When one works, one seeks work that represents an ability to reconcile internal conflicting tendencies and their resulting anxiety by creating a coherent pattern of adaptive behaviors to ratify these conflicting needs. At work one attempts to repeat behaviors that have worked successfully in the past. However, this repetition rarely works to the employee's satisfaction, and at work one must reluctantly give up old satisfactions and seek new sources of satisfaction. This requires that the employee, from the very beginning of employment, push to develop the necessary structures to attain gratification. Of course, the organization pushes back, and this often results in conflict. The inability of either party to reconcile this conflict will result in the lowering of efficiency and effectiveness at work.

CHAPTER 3

Self Psychology

Self Psychology can come to the defense of analysis applied
outside the clinical setting by pointing out that the scrutiny of
an unrolling life if viewed as the struggles of a self to realize its
basic patterns can furnish data that may be as significant and as
reliable as those obtained during therapeutic analysis.
                                     —HEINZ KOHUT (1985, p. 82)

Kohut, blending the theories of
Winnicott, Fairbairn, Hartmann, and Jacobson, presents perhaps the
clearest explanation of a theory of the psychoanalysis of work. Kohut
proposes a self psychology where the self system is conceptualized as
being the recipient of all relationships and the foci of all attempts to
maintain relatedness, in particular, ambitions, ideals, and creative acts
(Stark, 1989). Self psychology's strength as an applicative theory of
work lies in its definition of what constitutes mental health. Work
occupies a central position in this definition. A mentally healthy
person is a person with a firm or secure self system, motivated by a
striving for power, a realization of basic idealized goals, and an ability
to tap basic talents and skills that are consistent and capable of forming an arc between the person's ambitions and ideals.

Self psychology goes beyond the classical school of psychoanalysis
by focusing not on the ego or its component parts but on the self as a
system and how this system compensates for early deficits as it struggles to achieve a healthy state. It can be considered a psychology
concerned with deficits that result from attempts to create self-
objects, early in life, through the interaction and internalization of the
psychic structures of mother and/or father which form the basis of the
person's nuclear self later in life.

Both normal and pathological development of the self system result from what Kohut calls transmuting internalization,[1] which is the parent's empathic responses to the infant's creative and developmental efforts. These early internalizations form the basis of the person's connection to work, and whether work is experienced as a joyful, creative, and fulfilling activity or a drudgery and coerced form of employment, a job. According to Kohut, these early experiences require positive empathic responses from parents if the child will later in life be able to take the necessary risks to strive for idealized goals. If the parents can be responsive to the child's exhibitionistic striving, then the "basic structure of the nuclear self relating to creative ambition results" (Gruneberger, 1971, p. 563). The employee's experience of work later in life is the result of early exhibitionistic striving (the child's wish to be observed, to be the center of attention).

According to Kohut, the self develops out of the child's relationship with parent(s). He calls these relationships self-object relationships. There are two self-object functions presented to the infant by the parents: (1) mirroring[2] of the child's spontaneity (i.e., the parents' responsiveness to the child), and (2) the child's idealization of the parents. These two self-object relationships are referred to as the bipolar self and they relate to work in several ways.

Mirroring brings about ambition and work effectiveness (the basic striving for power and success) which is accomplished when the parents respond to and confirm the child's sense of vigor, greatness, and perfection. Mirroring promotes the child's relatedness to work when the parents are attuned and responsive to the child's developmental accomplishments, and later on to the child's needs for warmth and recognition. Consider the following example: A child returns home from kindergarten and, as most children do, presents to mother his/her work for the day. The work represents the child's efforts and he/she expects from mother a mirroring response. This response is considered mirroring if it is consistent with the child's wish. Let's say the child wishes for praise, and the mother responds to this wish by saying, "Oh, this is terrific, you are a great little artist, you do such good work," and she promptly places the work on the re-

[1]Transmuting internalization is similar to Jacobson's (1964) idea of selective identification where the infant attempts to gain a likeness of the admired object, who then becomes the equivalent of an admired hero.

[2]The concept of mirroring is similar to the notion of mothering which is a reflection of the influence of early parenting on infant development. It is an imitative/interactive experience between mother and infant (Pine, 1985), and if successful it will elicit active responses and engagement on the part of the infant for the purposes of obtaining the reward from mother, which ranges from smiles to verbal expressions of joy at seeing the infant's productions.

frigerator with the child's other efforts. Contrast this response to that of a mother who does not mirror. The child enters wishing praise but the mother is busy and off in her own world. She says "Not now," or "Can't you see I'm busy?" and she does not respond. The question is, Do experiences like this have an effect in later life on one's connection to work and ambition? Kohut says that they do.

The second pole of self-object functioning is the idealizing parental image. This develops when the child can merge with the image of the parent as an object capable of providing calmness, infallibility, and omnipotence. When this idealized image of the parent is merged with the child's self, the child is capable of developing a sense of ideals, values, and the need to identify with admired others he/she will meet later in life. From these two experiences Kohut suggests that the child's self develops; children experience themselves as being seen as perfect by the admiring parent, and the parent is seen as perfect and then linked to the admiring child. When this occurs, a tension arc between the two poles is activated, which in turn activates the basic talents and skills of the child (Milrod, 1982). Over time, as a function of these experiences, children will exhibit a more developed sense of self[3] as a valuable and competent person in the world.

CAREER CHOICE

Self psychology attempts to answer questions related to career choice by analyzing the relationship between fantasy and work. Fine and Wolf (1987) suggest that career choice is a function of the life plan, a program of actions that evolves from the following: the nuclear self, the self system's self-object needs, and what is called a search for optimizing self-object experiences.

Occupational choice and the satisfaction obtained within one's occupation are associated with two needs. The first is for gratification of the search for the fulfillment of a wish. This wish evolves from the

[3]In the literature we do not have a clear definition of self. The notion of self is essentially symbolic in that the idea of "my" self is communicated to others through personally meaningful representations. This is evidenced by the many ways in which the concept of self is used to communicate. A few examples are the true self, the fragmented self, finding oneself, the private versus the public self, or self-experience. The idea of self is defined as the experience of a "self-feeling," that is, how one feels about him/herself. This feeling about "me" is a function of a number of symbolic characteristics; for example, the "sense of self" as it relates to work would be related to the employee's experience of his/her capacity to "do," to have an impact on the environment, to be a "self-initiator" as opposed to a passive "receptor"; this is one among many factors related to these "feelings about self."

need for an empathic response to the basic grandiose exhibitionistic striving experienced in childhood. The second is the need to avoid real and potential fragmentation of cohesion of the self system. This avoidance is associated with the need to experience a sense of safety and comfort within an occupational role and the activities associated with this role. Underlying all motivations associated with the choice of an occupation is the search for the fulfillment of a wish. Occupational choice can be considered a function of the defensive functions of the occupation and its related activities, the self-object experiences the occupation provides, and the gratification of exhibitionistic and grandiose strivings.

Viewing occupational choice as serving a defensive function is consistent with the classical and object relations views of the nature of work. Self psychologists view work somewhat differently. While they see work as serving a defensive function, they see the defense activity as restorative in the sense that work is a way of avoiding fragmentation of the self system. For self psychologists, occupational choice and its related activities have a restorative potential. For example, consider the person who is diagnosed as having pathological disturbances. At the same time this person has a highly successful and productive career. Here work may serve to protect a weak ego or self system from fragmentation. Consequently, it is the work that is restorative.

Some authors add that creativity itself may evolve from intrapsychic conflict (Kubie, 1961; May, 1975; Stark, 1989). In many occupations the insanity of famous people has been well documented and has contributed to the creation of mythologies that suggest that in some occupations, insanity may be a prerequisite for success. For example, in bureaucratic organizations employees with narcissistic character disorders[4] tend to climb the corporate ladder with a high degree of success. Narcissistic characters are able to succeed for two reasons: (1) they are better able to use the organization and its people in a manner that will gratify their needs for achievement and self-aggrandizement and (2) they are able to promote idealization. Typically, bureaucratic organizations offer an environment that is depersonalized and one in which the idealization of others is based on the value of image, as opposed to substance. Under these circum-

---

[4]The narcissistic character disorder is generally marked by a pervasive pattern of grandiosity either in fantasy or in behavior. Narcissists demonstrate a lack of empathy in their relations with others and are usually bent on using others to advance their own needs (exploitative). They have a strong desire to be noticed and singled out as being special, often without appropriate achievements. They have a powerful sense of entitlement. They have a need for constant attention and admiration and tend to be exceedingly jealous of others and often downgrade the achievements of others.

stances, those with narcissistic character pathology are able to thrive. Thus, for this type of employee, work provides opportunities for cohesion of the self by gratifying exhibitionistic and grandiose wishes. It is the organization that provides avenues where the employee can both compensate for deficits of the self and accommodate this defective self system to a functional role.

Occupational choice is associated with an unconscious wish aimed at the gratification of early exhibitionistic strivings. This view shifts the focus of an analysis of the forces that leads to a particular choice and how the child's environment influences choice.

OCCUPATIONAL CHOICE
AND EXHIBITIONISTIC STRIVING

While it is suggested that a relationship exists between occupational choice and grandiose exhibitionistic strivings, it is unclear how these strivings are actually at the base of a choice. It would seem that the manner in which these early strivings were actually met and gratified would have consequences for the later development of ambition. However, although ambition is a motive necessary for a particular choice, it is not sufficient to explain why a person chooses one occupation over another.

The parental response to these strivings may steer the child in a certain career direction. For example, as the child seeks gratification, how the parent responds, the degree of exuberance or disdain shown, will influence choice. Consider children who are praised for their art, writing, speaking, memorization, physical prowess, and so forth. Each of these responses may form the underpinnings for a particular choice. Later on in the childrens' development, in early adolescence, exhibitionistic strivings are operationalized in two ways: (1) "in the use of others to obtain admiring or mirroring of grandiosity without acknowledging others own attributes and needs" (Stark, 1989, p. 146), and (2) through the use of others, especially an occupational figure, as idealized objects.

Gratification of exhibitionistic strivings is apparent in adult life. The adult's choice of an occupation and eventual satisfaction in a career evolves from the search for an admiring object. Gratification is obtained either through the role provided by the occupation and the status it offers or through a relationship with an idealized role model who psychically assumes the parental position of an admiring object. This admiring or idealized object comes close to the concept of mentoring which has a profound influence on an employee's capacity to function effectively and achieve success. Understanding the motivation for occupational choice seems to center exclusively on the nature of interpersonal relationships, but what of innate skills, psychomotor and cognitive functioning? These capacities may lay dormant or rise to the fore depending on the nature of the relationships and their reinforcing tendencies on these grandiose fantasies.

OCCUPATIONAL CHOICE AND CHARACTEROLOGICAL STYLE

Perhaps another way of thinking about occupational choice from a self-psychological perspective is to consider characterological style as providing a linkage between grandiose exhibitionistic strivings and environmental options. Characterological style refers not only to how the person imagines him/herself, but also to a set of qualities or characteristics that the person presents to the world. In Kohut (1971) and Kohut and Wolf (1978), five characterological styles are presented. The first are mirror-hungry personality types. Mirror-hungry personalities are those who seek attention, admiration, and recognition from others to compensate for the inner experience of worthlessness. Second are the ideal-hungry personalities, who are constantly seeking a relationship with another person or institution that contains beauty, power, prestige, money, and so forth, so that they can feel good about themselves. They constantly search for objects they can admire and use these others to compensate for underlying emptiness. Third are the alter-ego-hungry personalities, who constantly need a relationship with another to serve as a twin to confirm and sustain their self system. Fourth are the merger-hungry personalities, who seek attachments to another to be able to fuse their identity with that person because they fear the threat of separation. And finally there are the contact-shunning personalities, who avoid contact with others to avoid the experience of rejection and the deeper fear associated with being engulfed.

Kohut and Wolf (1978) explore other characterological styles. These styles refer to how people express their innermost self to the world. First is the understimulated self, who is characterized by the inner experience of being boring, who lacks vitality, and who seeks overstimulation to ward off the inner experience of deadness. Second is the fragmented self, who expresses his/her lack of an inner sense of cohesion by appearing disorganized and expressing hypochondriacal concerns. Third is the overstimulated self, who is frightened of his/

her grandiose and exhibitionistic fantasies and responds by withdrawing from success and events where he/she could become the center of
attention. Fourth is the overburdened self, who feels the world is a
dangerous place and responds by always being ready for attack, by
being suspicious, hypervigilant, and paranoid.

These characterological styles are representative of fixed ways of
interacting and negotiating relationships with objects in the world.
Occupational choice is gratifying only when it is suitable to the individual's characterological style. Characterological style consists of
traits and mannerisms adopted as a response to anxiety. If an occupation suits one's characterological style, it means that the occupation
provides avenues for self-expression, anxiety will be reduced and a
degree of comfort will be attained. These styles are self-protective in
that they protect against anxiety but also protect the employee's
fantasy life from real and imagined psychological injuries.

WORK, FANTASY, AND THE SELF

Work and occupational choice are significantly influenced by fantasy.
Contained within fantasies associated with work are sets of wishes or
ideals of a professional nature. These fantasies contain not only the
achievement of some types of career successes but also all the contents
of fantasies related to the wealth, power, and love that success will
bring.

In psychoanalytic theory, the relationship between mental life
and fantasy occupies a central position. The expression of unconscious fantasies, especially those fantasies that contain wishes, are
considered by classical psychoanalysts to form the basis for all symptoms, dreams, and character formation (Arlow, 1969). Fantasies
associated with work activities are pervasive in one's waking life, and
they probably exceed in number those fantasies associated with play,
sex, and love. In dreams there is also ample evidence that work plays a
significant role and occupies a central position as a theme. Of the 25
dreams reported by Freud, (1900/1953) in *The Interpretation of Dreams,*
17 were concerned with work-related issues.

Social psychologists represent an interesting example of the pervasiveness of fantasy and work, and they suggest that a general belief
exists that everyone wishes to increase their socioeconomic status
(SES). As a rule, this is achieved through work, that is, through active
engagement in an effort to "make one's dream come true." It is
generally considered dysfunctional for one to expect that "dreams"
will come true if one maintains a passive position, such as wishing for

good luck or for another to save or rescue oneself. On the other hand, an active fantasy is associated with engaging in efforts and achievement and working toward a goal. Fantasies can generally be divided into categories, such as active or passive, dominating or submissive, aggressive or libidinal; however, for the purposes of creating an understanding of the relationships between the person and work, it may be helpful to separate fantasies into the categories of conscious fantasies and unconscious or primitive fantasies. These fantasies are contained within a mental agency referred to as the ego ideal.

WORK AND THE EGO IDEAL

Historically, psychoanalysis has neglected the development of the ego ideal and its relationship to work. Initially, Freud (1914/1957) viewed the ego ideal as derived from the superego, as the conveyor of retaliatory responses from the superego to aggressive and libidinal wishes. Although Freud (1921/1955) made no direct mention of the relationship of the ego ideal to work in *Group Psychology and the Analysis of the Ego,* he altered the ego ideal in a way that made it consistent with work. Essentially he defined two functions of the ego ideal: (1) a "self observation, moral conscience" function, which is similar to his 1914 description; and (2) an agency function, which holds the fantasies associated with work. Freud (1921/1955) says:

> [I]t is heir to the original narcissism in which the childish ego enjoyed self-sufficiency; it gradually gathers up from the influences of the environment the demands which that environment makes upon the ego and which the ego cannot always rise to; so that man, when he cannot be satisfied with his ego itself, may nonetheless be able to find satisfaction in his ego ideal. . . . (p. 130)

Freud not only describes an important agency of the ego ideal but states its function as primarily protective, which has profound significance to work. The fantasies associated with work are directed consciously and unconsciously toward gratification. When gratification is not obtained, for whatever reasons, the fantasy is not given up but safely tucked away in the ego ideal. The capacity to keep the fantasy allows one to continue to work in spite of the numerous narcissistic injuries experienced.

This idea that the ego ideal is related to work and ambition is described by Grotstein (1983), who suggests that ideals and ambitions are contained in a self-object unit which resides in the superego and the ego ideal. He refers to this as the "self-object of destiny" and says that it "is the guarantor of ambition" (p. 189). Piers and Singer (1952) also claim that a relationship between the ego ideal and work exists; they see the ego ideal as goal setting and maintain that it has four attributes: (1) the core of narcissistic omnipotence, (2) the sum of positive identifications with parental images, (3) layers of later identifications, and (4) goals connected to the need for mastery. However, it was Reich who made the most significant contribution to an understanding of the relationship between work and the ego ideal. She places the psychic connection to work in the ego ideal and gives this agency a psychic structure that allows for a greater understanding of work. Initially, Reich (1954) claimed that the ego ideal is formed prior to the development of the superego, and she says that it is an early narcissistic formation that is removed from the superego.

Later, Reich (1960) described the ego ideal in terms that closely resemble Kohut's grandiose self, a self that functions as a container for the child's narcissism. She explains that the ego ideal contains the fantasy that the person is an admired, omnipotent, and idealized object, which she refers to as the wished for self-image, and it contains a fusion of both self and object representation. This is similar to Kohut's bipolar self, which he describes as a process where the person wishes to be "his own ego ideal."

In a fashion similar to Kohut, Reich suggests that work evolves from fantasies associated with the idealizing parental image, and these fantasies are contained within the ego ideal. These idealized images are nothing more than "identification with parental figures seen in a glorified light" (Sandler, Holder, & Meers, 1963).

Placing fantasies associated with work in the ego ideal and completely separating the ego ideal from the superego allow for greater understanding of the complexities associated with work and career choice. Such a separation permits a view of work different from the notion held by classical psychoanalysts, that work is merely an activity used to sublimate the instincts and their derivatives. Also, removing the ego ideal from the superego leaves open a conceptualization of a psychic attachment to work as an attempt to obtain early narcissistic gratifications. This is in opposition to the classical view, which suggests that the superego influences work and conceptualizes work as a behavior motivated by fear of punishment (Nunberg, 1933). In addition, separating the ego ideal from the superego and then placing the psychic connection to work in this agency minimizes the defensive functions of work. It lessens the significance of the classical position by seeing work as more goal directed and as being toward the object, as opposed to being against the object. Such a separation also allows fantasies associated with work to have a soothing function, with the potential of activities associated with work becoming good objects as opposed to a fearful objects.

Perhaps another way of seeing the relationship between fantasy and its association to work is to suggest that these fantasies can be lodged in either of these agencies, the ego ideal or the superego. This view suggests that the response to work and career choice is a function of the agency in which the fantasies are located. If the fantasies are located in the ego ideal, one's connection to work is that of being connected to a soothing and good object. On the other hand, if the connection is contained within the superego, the object (work) is that of a harsh, punitive, and fearful object. This connection has special implications for understanding an employee's relationships not only to career choice but to other aspects of working such as authority, membership in a social grouping, the capacity to delay gratification, work inhibitions, and so forth.

Additionally, whether one experiences guilt or shame may be a function of the agency in which the fantasy is located. Hirschhorn (1988) says that this emphasis on guilt over shame comes as no surprise because psychoanalytic writers have failed to differentiate the superego from the ego ideal. The failure to differentiate between the superego and ego ideal is a response to living in an alienated, industrialized society. Hirschhorn continues:

> In this context of sinfulness and guilt there was a tendency for people to measure their triumphs, their victories over sin, chance, and other people. But the feeling of triumph represents what Klein believed to be an extreme reaction to the depressive position [see Chapter 2]. It embodies the fantasy that one is ultimately good because others are bad and terrible. It is the emotional cul-de-sac of splitting. (p. 235)

This may explain the unconscious motivations for either the creation of or response to bureaucratic systems. Consider the nature of competition in organizations, the pyramid-shaped structures, grading students on a curve, and so forth. All of these imply that if one succeeds, it is only because someone else has failed. Therefore, organizations become systems in which guilt predominates over shame. Evidence suggests that in organizations where shame prevails, competition is less apparent and individualism is devalued. This is true of Japanese corporations.

CAPACITIES OF THE EGO IDEAL

Most psychoanalytic writers about the capacity to work focus on ego capacities. However, a full understanding of the motivation to work requires an assessment of the capacities of the ego ideal. In a pragmatic view of the ego ideal, Novey (1955), Lampl-de Groot (1962), and Hartmann and Lowenstein (1962) see the ego ideal as containing goal- or aim-directed fantasies that serve a positive and soothing function.

Beginning with Jacobson (1954), it is generally assumed that the ego ideal evolves from early preoedipal wishes. These wishes are formed to protect the child from anxiety associated with narcissistic injury and they play an important role in the creation of a self-image. This self-image contained in the ego ideal is a configuration of unconscious wishes. These wishes contain affects and derivatives associated with early object relations and drive gratifications. Along these lines, and bringing this idea of the importance of the ego ideal closer to the classical psychoanalytic position, Sandler, Holder, and Meers (1963) hold that instinctual drives might be reconceptualized as "the wished for response of the object" (p.143), and Emde (1991) believes that drive manifestations serve more of a useful purpose when they are thought of as "wishes" in the context of interpersonal relationships and affective needs.

It is suggested that the ego ideal contains the psychic base for the person's connection to work, and a significant aspect of this connection is the associated grandiose fantasy, which is an expression of the wish to be admired and omnipotent. Thus, the ego ideal is a self-protecting psychic agency. It contains the longing to be the object of love in a falsified world filled with idealized others. The ego ideal protects these fantasies, these wishes, dreams, and hopes, from the danger of disillusionment. The fantasy in which lies the expressed wish for career success, greatness, and achievement is used for soothing or comforting purposes. Or, as Smith (1977) suggests, "it is the wish to have all of one's needs met in a relationship hallowed by perfection" (p. 311). Jacobson (1954), like Reich, refers to these fantasies as the "wished for" or idealized self-image, which she defines as what the person wants to become, made up of admirable qualities associated with important figures in the person's life. She sees the idealized self-image as a stable structure established in infancy. Over time, this structure contains what Fine and Wolf (1987) call the life plan, which becomes a constellation of the person's nuclear self, self-object relations, and grandiose exhibitionistic strivings.

IDEALIZATION FANTASIES AND WORK

An image is an inner picture or mental representation of the self. According to Kohut, mental representations are the equivalent of ideas about the self. Goldberg (1980), in reviewing Jacobson's efforts, suggests that these images are similar to "temporary printouts or readouts of very complex configurations, much as the computer delivers a reading that is but a minute reflection of an internal network of activity" (p. 6). Considered from this perspective the idealized self is a "printout" or mental representation of the "type of person I wish or want to be." However, this printout is quite vulnerable; it is sensitive to injury. Throughout the life cycle one experiences impingements upon the idealized self. Criticism, rejection, and failures are commonplace in everyday life, especially in work. Thus, the following question emerges: How does the idealized self remain intact when faced with such environmental onslaughts? One response, and perhaps the most frequent, is withdrawal. The idealized self seeks refuge from danger by locating itself in the ego ideal, which becomes a fortress intent on protecting the idealized fantasies from an insecure and dangerous world.

Seeking refuge and hiding in the ego ideal present special problems for a person engaged in work. At work, one is expected to take risks and operationalize the idealized self by attempting to achieve goals and accomplish tasks. If an employee is intent on protecting the idealized self, he/she will withdraw from having ambition and in the process will assume a stilted, detached relationship with the work environment. Protecting the fantasy may become so involved and filled with feelings of insecurities that the employee may withdraw from work altogether.

When a person engages in work it does not mean that he/she places idealized self at the fore and allows fantasies to be exposed to injury. In order to work one must be able to alter the fantasies within the idealized self in such a manner that they become ideals. It seems that the idealized self is particularly vulnerable at work when it does not have ideal representations to enact the fantasies with a sense of safety. According to Antonovsky (1991), Freud claims that one continuously uses work (namely, creativity) to overcome narcissistic fixation. She suggests that this fixation is self-love, or an idealization of the self. One overcomes narcissistic fixations through love and work. To be fixated narcissistically is to be frozen in a state of habitual self-love. To be in this state precipitates illness. The capacity to work requires the capacity to move out, away from the narcissistic home base, toward others (objects). From this perspective, working becomes an attempt to avoid the illness associated with narcissistic fixation. Work then provides a vehicle that allows one to move away from self-love, or away from idealization of the self (Antonovsky, 1991). However, this position holds true for the person in an occupation in which creativity is apparent or where one feels the love of community of professionals. What about the employee in a corporation in which opportunities for creativity are scarce and the hierarchy promotes competition? After many decades of experimentation it seems that contemporary organizational theorists may have inadvertently found a solution.

As a result of the tremendous economic gains Japanese and German corporations have made by competing in the global marketplace, writers are now maintaining that if corporations are to remain innovative and competitive they must create a participatory, risk-taking culture, a culture that maximizes collectivism and a powerful sense of commitment to the corporation. To work in such a corporation requires giving up self-love. The idea is that only love for others, the corporation, is acceptable. Love for one's profession or career is considered narcissistic. In the new corporation, the leader or the executive constellation are the only ones who are permitted to keep their self-love intact, not the followers. Those who are permitted self-love can do so as a function of their position. This may be one reason why, in these typically hierarchical corporations, employees aspire to the top position. It also provides insight into why the prevailing character disorder found among executives is the narcissistic disorder.

To fully understand this phenomenon it is necessary to explore the motivation for destruction of the professional ego ideal, which is problematic for the employee but necessary if an organization is to attain the ideal culture. Current thinking concerning an ideal culture suggests that commitment and loyalty can be best attained when employees identify with the corporation as opposed to an occupation or a career. To attain this ideal culture requires giving up one's professional ego ideal. When one gives up the professional ego ideal, one in effect gives up self-love.

Contemporary leaders are expected to manage the culture of the corporation. The leader functions primarily as a salesman for the organization and its culture. The corporate leader is not expected to engage in demonstrations of love for others. Instead, the leader's job becomes one in which he/she exposes and communicates to employees how the corporation dispenses love to its loyal and commited followers. In other words, the leader's job is to sell the love of the corporation to its employees.

The leader does this by representing the corporation as an ideal family. Self-love, that which is typically found in the professional ego ideal, is replaced by love for the corporation. Gratification is found when the corporation returns this love. This gratification occurs only when employees imagine that they are obtaining the equivalent of what they give; for example, their wages are equivalent to their work. But this is an illusion, maintained by the idea of a fair exchange, which is nothing more than an exchange of affection.

Freud (1920/1955) says that it is the erotic libido that maintains this illusion. It is in the erotic libido where exchange and reciprocity are contained (consider sex). Narcissism holds the greatest danger for this illusion. To experience inequity is to initially experience narcissistic injury. In these powerful corporate cultures, the ideal is sought. For an employee to seek more or to attempt to reduce an inequity is considered to be engaging in behaviors destructive to the team. This employee becomes a bad object, one who is motivated by narcissistic concerns, and he/she is often accused of behaving against the corporation. The function of the corporate culture is to withdraw the employee from these narcissistic preoccupations, to the equivalent of a state of mind the Japanese call self-less. When self-love is given up and replaced by corporate love, the ideal is attained and dependency results.

Inhibitions in work result when work is perceived as having the capacity to damage narcissism fixation. Inhibition occurs because the employee has not been able to turn idealization as an expression of narcissism into an investment of ideals. In opposition to this position, Schafer (1968) claims that to transform idealizations into an ideal creates a falsehood that the ideal has been attained. He claims that when idealized fantasies are contained in the ego ideal, the person believes that his/her aspirations have been fulfilled when, in fact, they have not. However, what Schafer is describing is a narcissistic fixation. To believe that fantasies have been fulfilled when they have not is the same as protecting idealization from threat.

Falsification of ideals is a way to hold on to the original narcissism. This is the basis for a narcissistic character disorder and it is also the underpinnings of what the new corporation unintentionally creates by demanding such high commitment, loyalty, and love for the corporation. Ideals can be falsified or they can be perceived in a manner close to reality. This can be explained by understanding how the holding of ideals evolves from idealization. The holding of ideals evolves from the children's experience of disillusionment with themselves and their parents. According to Antonovsky (1991), the child's capacity to move from narcissistic fixation, idealization of the self, to an investment in ideals is a function of the following:

> the strength of early object ties, which lives on in our relationship to our ego ideal and keeps us trying to become one with the ego ideal as a way to unite with the love object; the degree of ego maturity achieved; and the basic balance of libidinal and aggressive inclinations. (p. 395)

Idealizations can be transformed into ideals in two ways: (1) they can be falsifications or pseudoideals, that is, a way of believing things are perfect when they are not, or (2) they can be representations of the person's aspirations or goals of perfections (Morrison, 1984). Ideal representations function as vehicles by which the fantasies contained in the idealized self can be negotiated and gratified in the world of work. Ideal representations also allow an employee to engage in work while holding on to the fantasies of the idealized self in the ego ideal.

To keep the ego intact and functional, the process of gratifying fantasies contained in the idealized self requires a person becomes tied closely to reality and work. When elements of the idealized self are gratified, the soothing effects are reinforced by integrating the fantasies into the person's self-representation. It is as if the person says, "I've made it, this is who I am." Consequently, work and occupational choice and their gratifications are obtained through a repetition of patterns that have been reinforced since infancy. These patterns are the way in which the person seeks his/her ideal, and they become part of that person's characterological style. According to Kohut (1977), the person knows no other way of obtaining goals.

When faced with criticism and "bad" parenting, the child does not simply give up the idealized self-image or idealization. It is tucked away and preserved in the ego ideal, away from an insecure and dagerous world. Thus the idealized self remains in its primitive form and the child is unable to develop an ideal representation; that is, the child is unable to develop ideals. In adulthood, this child is ruled by a life devoted to protecting the idealized self-image. A life ruled by ideals is perceived as threatening to this image. The question must be answered: How does this relate to work? The ideal self as described by Schafer (1960), Hartmann and Lowenstein (1962), Jacobson (1964), and Schecter (1979) is a self represented by ideals. Given the subjective and lofty nature of the aspirations contained within the ideal self, it seems that holding an "ideal" is holding a set of wishes or perhaps fantasies associated with an ideal mental image.

The issue about what is reflected in this image is debated within psychoanalytic circles. Also, what is wished for and the motivations for the wish are exceedingly complex. Nevertheless, idealization and an investment in ideals are important aspects of a person's relationship to work, and they underlie not only the choice of occupation but also the gratifications obtained from working. The nature of what is represented in the image and the motivation for the wish is explored below.

GRANDIOSE FANTASIES, THE IDEALIZED SELF, AND WORK

Milrod (1982) equates the idea of a wished-for self-image with the idealized self. He says that the idealized self does not contain Kohut's grandiose self, and he goes on to suggest that fantasies associated with the grandiose self must be curbed to a significant degree in order for the wished-for self-image to be formed. Milrod seems to misunderstand the utility of the grandiose self as a motivating force in occupational choice and motivation to achieve. The issue is not curbing the grandiose self but rather, as Kohut suggests, expressing it in a functional gratifying manner, through work or career.

The idealized self can be traced to primitive, archaic grandiose and exhibitionistic strivings and also a derivative of an early wish for the infant–mother bond (Mitchell, 1988). This position is similar to Klein's, where she suggests that this wish is eventually expressed throughout the life cycle as the wish to be cared for. In adult life and at work, this wish is experienced and gratified through symbolization. In agreement, Mahler (1972) suggests that the idealized self, like other self-images, may be an expression of a symbolic wish, a longing for fusion with mother and an escape from the dangers associated with being autonomous, which is perceived as surrender. Smith (1977) concurs by suggesting that this fantasy is a magical wished-for closeness, and likewise, she claims that the gratification contained within this fantasy brings relief from painful yearnings associated with the fear of abandonment through separation. These yearnings are reduced through the wish for symbiotic attachment. In addition, Klingerman (1980) confirms the significance of the early wish and its relationship to work. He says that there are at least three main currents in the creative drive:

1. An innate intrinsic joy in creating, relating to what has been termed *functional* pleasure. This is perhaps the most important factor in an employee's connection to work, but one we have the least knowledge about.
2. The exhibitionistic grandiose ecstasy of being regarded as the acme of beauty and perfection, and the nearly insatiable need to repeat and confirm this feeling.
3. The need to regain a lost paradise—the original bliss of perfection—to overcome the empty feeling of self-depletion and to recover self-esteem. In the metapsychology of the self this would amount to healing a threatened fragmentation of the self that occurs frequently at work by restoring self-cohesion capacities through a merger with a self-object and a gratification of the wish for mirroring needs of approval, recognition, and love.

How these fantasies are used to connect one with work is explained below.

As stated earlier, over time archaic grandiose strivings become organized into the idealized self. The organizational process begins during the rapprochement subphase of the separation–individuation process (Mahler, 1965), where the presence of mother plays a vital part in the organization of pleasurable experience. According to Pine (1985), "a child in the second year of life, busily at play (work) and seeming to be absorbed with inanimate objects and with his own motor activities and vocalizations, may immediately lose all pleasure when mother leaves the room" (p. 97). Consequently, for the idealized self to become invested in ideals, these ideals must be able to function as a hub whereby the ego can connect unconscious grandiose strivings to social reality. In addition, the attachment to the object (mother), the illusory symbiotic union, must be contained within the ideal.

If the grandiose self and exhibitionistic strivings are to function as components capable of being gratified, these fantasies will contain the motivation for work and will have the capacity for object relatedness through work and career success. If this object relatedness is to be possible, these archaic fantasies must contain the capacity for differentiation. In addition, if the conscious content of having ideals is an ego structure of what the person wishes to be, an analysis of the unconscious content underlying the conscious wish will provide an analysis of not only the motivation for occupational choice, but also the capacities for work. This is structurally understood in the following way; The idealized self specifies not only the type of fantasy organization that will lead to specific gratification but also the degree of motivation necessary for attainment of that gratification. Like a child at play, a person will construct over time a certain image of him/herself that will ensure that gratification is obtained. Therefore, contained within this image is the wish for an illusionary symbiotic union with mother. Exhibitionistic strivings then become one method among many to gratify this wish, but an important one.

All work activities, including choice of occupation, involve the fantasy of total incorporation or a kind of refusion of the initial lost merged self-object representation, that of mother. It is suggested that this total incorporation underlies the idealized self-image, and that this image is the connecting point between a person's unconscious life and work. To suggest, as Milrod (1982) has, that this self-image evolves from a stable ego structure, which is possible only after the separation–individuation phase, contradicts the position maintained by Kohut and others. Kohut claims that this wish contains archaic grandiose merger strivings and evolves from self-object representations in the early infantile symbiotic phase. By placing this wish at the beginning of the individuation phase, Milrod leaves out the wish for magical fusion, primitive affective identifications, and early playful imitation, which are important unconscious functions related to occupational choice and work gratification. By placing the wish at the differentiation phase, one obtains a totally different picture. Work can now be understood as a threat, as a symbolic representation that is perceived by the self as containing elements that will potentially result in fragmentation of the self or annihilation of the self.

THE FANTASY OF PERFECTION AND ITS CONNECTION TO WORK

Kohut (1977) suggests that exhibitionistic strivings influence ego structure as well as an ambition constellation that connects the person to work in a gratifying way. Exhibitionistic strivings are essentially a repetition of early wishes to be seen, observed, admired, and valued. At the base of this wish is the wish to be perfect, a narcissistic wish. According to Rothstein (1980), the wish for "narcissistic perfection is a defensive distortion of reality—an affectionately labeled fantasy based on the originally perfect self-object bliss of the symbiotic phase" (p. 22). Rothstein (1980) and Mahler (1972) maintain that this wish, like others, propels an eternal longing which is carried on over the course of one's entire life cycle.

When Kohut describes needs, what he is really describing are wishes (Eagle, 1990), and this wish to be mirrored is nothing more than a wish to be merged with an idealized image, mother. The search is to attain that blissful symbiotic state with mother, a state of well-being. Rothstein (1980) views the wish as a wish for narcissistic perfection, and he sees this wish as ubiquitous and as being neither healthy nor pathological. However, whether it eventually becomes pathological or not depends on the capacity of the ego and its ability to integrate this wish into an occupation in a gratifying manner. Rothstein (1980) suggests that "a healthy ego integrates its pursuit of narcissistic perfection in a manner that is in harmony with its endowments and [searches] for gratifications available in reality" (p. 24).

The key issue in maintaining a healthy outlook as one invests in this search is the capacity of the ego to delay, to demonstrate patience. The ego can delay if it is able to avoid the experience of imperfection, which is experienced as an injury. As employees pursue the wish for perfection, they must be able to defend against the dread and experience associated with imperfection. The state of imperfection contains that which is the opposite of perfection: death, rage, castration, abandonment, and so on. Consequently, when an employee is criticized, rejected, or terminated, the experience of this narcissistic injury is not so much the loss of self-esteem, face, shame, and so forth, but a blow against the search, a discouraging setback against the wish, and an unconscious feeling that the employee will never attain nirvana, that he/she is indeed imperfect.

According to Greenberg and Mitchell (1983), this situation arises when the superior is unable to tone down the employee's wish to merge the grandiose self-image with the mirroring self-object, ("I am perfect, and you admire me"), or when the superior does not function in a capacity where he can allow the employee to fuse with the idealized self-object ("You are perfect, and I am part of you"). The devaluation of the employee by the superior severs this connection. By not being able to fuse with the idealized self-object, the grandiose self-image is vulnerable to slights, and it is as if this self-image stands alone.

Klingerman (1980) confirms this when he says:

> Kohut has explained in great detail the . . . oscillation between the grandiose self and idealized object—how when inadequate or unempathic mirroring leads to traumatic loss of self-esteem the child regains his cohesion by merging with the admired idealized selfobject. (p. 388)

In applying this to the world of work, Kohut (1980) says:

The maxim that the self requires a milieu of empathically responding self-objects in order to function, indeed in order to survive, applies not only in the instances of selves who because of unusual talents and skills are able to express their pattern in a form that has broad social consequences, it is even more valid in the case of anonymous Everyman. (p. 454)

When the idealized self-object is not available, the capacity of the self to delay is incapacitated and the employee then demonstrates "more rigid, compulsive pursuit of narcissistic perfection . . . in a form that is unattainable, isolating and maladaptive . . ." (Rothstein, 1980, p. 24).

Gratification of grandiose strivings is necessary if the idealized self and the holding of ideals are to remain intact. Without gratification the image is shattered and the self system may fragment. For organizational theorists this raises major questions: What type of leader serves as the idealizing object for employees? What organizational characteristics make such demands on employees that their self-cohesion is weakened to such a point that they are particularly vulnerable to specific idealizing self-object needs? Lang (1984) suggests that these idealizing needs are more pronounced in men than in women, and he suggests that for women, mirroring seems to have a predominant function. If this is the case, mirroring needs may have application in answering questions concerning differences between men and women at work.

PROBLEMS WITH WORK

Kohut (1977) links problems with work as reflecting underlying disorders of the self. These disorders are directly related to employees' experiences with their respective parents, and their parents' disorders. For example, if the parent was unable to serve as an empathic, care-giving, or mirroring self-object, that is, the parents were involved in their own fixations and obsessions, then they were unavailable and nonresponsive to the child's search for a self-object. Under these conditions, the child's only choice is to respond to whatever is available, even to a disturbed parent. This parent, and for that matter any parent, will serve as a self-object.[5] If the parent is disturbed, he/she

---

[5]Kohut's concept of self is not considered a psychic structure as the id, ego, and superego would be. But he sees the "self" as a structure in itself, cathected with instinctual energy and a continuity in time. For normal development to occur the parent must function as an idealized self-object that will be internalized or taken in, to become a self-regulating part of the psychic structure.

will serve as a pathological self-object. When this occurs, the child develops a deficit of the self system, and the child enters the adult world of work with a disorder of the self. According to Grunebaum's (1989) review of Kohut's deficit model:

> Disturbance in the development of the structure of the self occur when faulty responses by self-objects, maternal and paternal, occur which do not permit or which interfere with transmuting internalization that are necessary to adequately promote integration and cohesion of the self. This leads to a variety of behavioral disturbances and pathological functioning. . . . Defective or frustrating lack of response by the maternal and paternal self-object prevents or can be damaging to the development of the basic nuclear structures of the self and lead to defects and "feebleness" of the self that in turn cause fear of disintegration of the self and impaired functioning of the self. (p. 563)

The employee, in an attempt to compensate for these early deficit self-objects, seeks adequate self-object relationships and these relationships become important because they are excessively relied on to generate ambition and ideals. When the self-object is experienced as adequate, connectedness to an object is capable of being formed with a superior and esprit, commmitment, and loyalty dramatically increase. Kohut (1980) confirms this when he says:

> The infant is psychologically complete so long as it breathes the psychological oxygen provided by the contact with empathically responsive selfobjects . . . , it is no different for the adult who is complete, independent and strong as long as he feels responded to. (pp. 480–481)

If this statement is true, it has special significance for management. Management is always concerned with improving esprit, commitment, and loyalty. The question that needs to be answered is: What is this self-object and how are these self-object ties formed?

At work an employee encounters various self-objects which can be divided into two major categories. First, there are objects that respond to and confirm the employee's sense of vigor and perfection. These objects function as a mirroring self-object. According to Kohut, mirroring affects ambition by gratifying the employee's grandiose fantasies such as the wish to be seen as perfect, competent, powerful, and so on. The second object is the idealized leader who functions in the parent's image. Ideally the superior presents an image with which the employee can merge. When this merger occurs, the employee experiences a sense of calmness and omnipotence. At work, if the superior is able to function as an idealizing self-object, that is, the superior is able to gratify the employee's idealized fantasies, the employee will be able to generate his own self-motivation, provided early damage to the self has not been too severe or traumatic.

In cases where damage to the self has been severe, the employee may respond to the idealized self-object with mistrust or become so helplessly attached to the superior that he/she will give up all attempts at autonomous functioning. Some evidence of this is presented in Chapter 10. When damage to early self-object relatedness has been severe, later self-object relationships serve little positive function, and relationships at work will periodically precipitate fragmentation, which fosters pleasure-seeking activities combined with periodic rage. When they feel responded to by their superior, fellow employees and subordinates will provide much needed "mirroring acceptance, the merger with ideals, [and] the sustaining presence of others . . ." (Kohut, 1980, pp. 494–495). Consequently, work impairment is not the result of the interplay between drive, defenses, and conflicts but a threat that work imposes to the organization and cohesion of the self.

Self-fragmentation is perhaps greatest when the employee enters the organization for the first time. The process of entering an organization precipitates a considerable amount of anxiety. The fantasies associated with the "new job" cause a regression when early issues related to wishes associated with grandiosity and idealization are awakened. These issues are awakened because of the annihilation fear and the wish that the new organization will serve as a parent imago. In a voracious manner, the entrant seeks mirroring of grandiose fantasies; however, rarely is mirroring available. The entrant also seeks an "idealizing object to shore up feelings of identity, hope and power . . ." (Stark, 1989, p. 146).

When an employee enters an organization, he/she makes an increased investment in the self system. This investment takes the form of an intense focus on self-consciousness, as the entrant tries to hide narcissistic concerns. During entry, it is as if the entrant sees him/herself through a mirror image which is used to practice integrating the self system that is fragmented as a result of the anxiety associated with being in a strange and frightening place.

If the entrant brings to the organization an already fragmented self system, the entry process may become so overwhelming that the entrant's self-representation is projected outward to a point where the organization and its facilitates, coworkers, and superiors are considered worthless and devalued. This process is a defense that protects the entrant's idealized self-image from being destroyed by the feelings associated with the unacceptable self. This is accomplished by getting rid of psychically, or projecting outward, those unacceptable parts of the self.

During the interview, the entrant is typically overwhelmed with self-doubt, a heightened sense of self-consciousness, and an increasingly fragmented self. The interviewee may be greeted with coldness and indifference, which will increase his/her feelings of inadequacy. The entrant will respond to this situation with an array of affects ranging from inferiority and self-condemnation, to over-confidence. The entrant is excessively concerned with what the interviewer thinks of him/her and seeks kernels of support; this can be in the form of a smile, a nod, or a friendly or encouraging word. It is as if the entrant is saying, "Do you think I can succeed?" "Am I valued?" "Do you want me?" Sometimes an entrant will embrace a job offer, even though he has major doubts about the company, to compensate for feelings of inferiority initially projected into him/her by the interviewer. It is vital during this period that the entrant see his/her coworkers and superiors as empathic objects. If this is possible, self-fragmentation will be reduced by providing continuity to the entrant's idealized self-image. In addition, the fantasies containing hope that relate to the idealized self-image will be exceedingly vulnerable during this period. Even the most inconsequential slight is experienced as a major narcissistic blow.

The organization's leaders can reduce potential fragmentation by placing an empathic net over the entrant during this period. Over time, this empathic net comes to be symbolized as a new self-object and will combat the tendency for the entrant to experience a tarnishing of the idealized self-image. Attempting to capture a self-object in a strange and terrifying environment is fraught with anxiety, and the empathic net reduces this tension.

PROBLEMS WITH CAREER SUCCESS

Success in one's career is not the panacea for emotional health. Often career success causes an explosion of destructive forces that had been repressed and dormant. All employees respond to success with unconscious fears. These fears are associated with attainment or gratification of an unconscious fantasy. Fears associated with success can be placed into two broad categories, preoedipal and oedipal. Preoedipal fears associated with success evolve from early fears of loss of love, separation anxieties, and abandonment. Oedipal fears are associated with castration anxiety and conflicts with the opposite sex parent.

Unconsciously, success means that a wish may be gratified. If this wish is a merger with the gratifying object, the employee may unconsciously undermine or withdraw from the success out of the fear that the object will consume him/her, just as an overbearing mother may consume the infant. Thus the gratification of the unconscious fantasy may precipitate fears of engulfment.

Viewed from another perspective, the wish for union embedded in the fantasy may be threatened by career success if the success is experienced as a separation from the object contained in the wish. For example, success as a gratification of the wish is unconsciously undermined if the affects associated with the gratification (e.g., excitement and joy) are experienced as a repetition of earlier affects associated with the attachment to mother. It may be that the excitement associated with success brings affects similar to those experienced with the expectation that the nurturing, good mother will appear. If these affects are associated with disappointment, the mother does not appear and success and the affects of joy and excitement are extinguished. By unconsciously rejecting success, the employee avoids disappointment. If this experience (success) is not consummated, no attachment was obtained and the employee avoids the anticipatory affects of sadness and loss. Consequently, when the employee begins to experience joy in some career success, the success is ruined because joy unconsciously is associated with rejection and depression. Success may also bring depression because the employee unconsciously feels he/she is a failure, that he/she invariably falls short of the expectations embodied in the fantasy. In other words, success may be an admission that the fantasy cannot be realized (Smith, 1977), and when this occurs success will be undermined to protect the primitive grandiose fantasy and the wish that total fulfillment will someday be obtained. Thus, failure is a way of holding on to the fantasy that says, "My day will come."

FAILURE AT WORK

When a person experiences failure at work, a gulf is created between the idealized self-image and self-representation. The employee attempts to repair this schism in a number of ways:

1. The employee may deny personal involvement in his/her failure and project rage onto the evaluator (authority figure). However, this projection may compound fragmentation if the evaluator is a much-needed idealizing self-object.

2. If the employee accepts that he/she indeed has limitations, he/she will treat the idealized self-image as if it were a self-representation and respond by assuming the equivalent of Winnicott's (1965) false self. The employee will structure a schizoid existence at work, the equivalent of a psychic withdrawal.

3. The employee can avoid self-fragmentation after he/she has received a narcissistic injury through temporary withdrawal. This type of withdrawal from work may allow the employee to recharge the idealized self-image. According to Stark (1989), "[It] makes sense to see the striving after perfection as compatible with inertia or work inhibition . . ." (p. 154); avoidance allows the employee to capture a "tension-free state," where he/she can recharge by merging with the maternal self-object and once the recharging is complete return to battle.

4. The employee may close this gulf by libidinalizing it. When this occurs, the ego can draw on the libidinal energies to maintain a level of self-regard and to fuel the ego and its choices (Mitchell, 1988).

Failure at work is generally viewed as a precipitator of depression, however, a number of defensive reactions can occur. According to Milrod (1982), when failure occurs, what was once shameful now becomes a "venture and source of pride." The employee experiences pride and great value in "being different," in being a "deviant," and may project onto others those defective parts of him/herself, while emphasizing characteristics that exemplify his/her being different. On the other hand, the opposite behavior may result; the employee may take pride in his/her failure, boasting about the calamities he/she has created. The employee may show an addictive devotion to self-ennobling behavior, or the employee may become preoccupied with his/her limitations. The employee may react to any encounter in which his/her limitations are tested by publicly devaluing him/herself and then politely escaping in an ingratiating manner. These feelings of shame and self-debasement are similar to the narcissistic conflict described by Rubins (1983), where the employee demonstrates a conflict between his/her behavior and the expectations contained in the ego ideal. If the employee feels he/she has done something wrong, the employee will defend against the experience of shame by becoming excessively grandiose or, as Jacobson (1964) suggests, becoming excessively reliant on an aggrandized idealized self-image.

A helpful way to understand the nature of the fears associated with work is to explore Anna Freud's (1966) connection between repressed masturbatory fantasies and conscious masochistic fantasies. This connection explains two important psychic phenomena: (1) how an unconscious fantasy influences a conscious fantasy, and the relationship between unconscious and conscious fantasy and the idealized self-image, and (2) how the fantasy associated with a behavior symbolically precipitates annihilation fears.

In the first phenomenon, if repressed masturbatory fantasies contribute to conscious masochistic fantasies, it is the masochistic fantasy that contributes significantly to the creation of the idealized self-image. The image, in this case, would contribute to a passive fantasy where the employee fantasizes a victim role that contains a structure to allow him/her to obtain a wish, the wish to become a victim and work for a harsh sadistic superior, or the wish to become a victim by being employed in a dangerous occupation. In this case, exhibitionistic strivings are condemned by early self-object relationships and the employee can only repeat an archaic gratification through the experience of being in the role of a victim. It is as if the pleasure associated with ambition must also include pain and humiliation. Victimization then becomes the royal road to obtaining the wish.

In the second example, pleasure associated with masturbation is contained in the erotized fantasy. The erotized fantasy incorporates an object. It is the object of the fantasy that precipitates anxiety. If the object is frightening, it may be repressed, bringing about masturbatory fantasies devoid of the object, or the entire fantasy may be repressed. If masturbation as an activity continues under these conditions, it is devoid of pleasure because it no longer contains the fantasy or the significant object in the fantasy, and under these conditions the act becomes routine, rote, or a compulsion. It is the symbolic representation of the object within the fantasy that precipitates annihilation anxiety, and it is the pleasure derived from mergence with that object that becomes prohibited. In the first part of this connection between fantasy and masochism the employee still pursues the object but can only do so in a masochistic manner; in the second, all pleasure is removed, the employee responds to the object in schizoid isolation, and spontaneity is deadened. At work, if the fantasy or fantasy object associated with the idealized self-image becomes eroticized, the employees' involvement with work will become mechanistic and empty.

SUMMARY

The unconscious wish will have an array of influences on work. Below are ways in which unconscious wishes function:

1. The wish may function as a rebellion against the need to renounce instinctual gratification (classical position).

2. The content of the wish is a catharsis of unconscious mental content (Sharpe, 1950). Therefore, the wish serves a soothing function.

3. The effects associated with the wish affect ego functioning by altering one's perception of work and the quality of one's efforts. This function is consistent with Arlow's position regarding the relationship between the fantasy and the ego. Arlow (1969) says that under the pressure of the fantasy, the ego will "scan . . . and select discriminately from data perception those elements that demonstrate some consonance or correspondence with the . . . fantasies" (p. 8).

4. The relationship between work activities and fantasy will be reciprocal; that is, work will stimulate fantasy and fantasy will stimulate work.

5. The wish will condense or replace memories, and vice versa.

6. The content of the wish is reassuring and it may be, as Arlow (1969) suggests, a defense against anxiety precipitated by work activities. For example, contained within the fantasy may be an identification with the aggressor, and occupational choice may take the form of penetrating and destroying, like an occupation that requires cutting, drilling, melting, or killing.

7. Self-representations are organized into the wish, and the wish can integrate self-representations. For example, the wish will serve a narcissistic function if it is able to contribute to the maintenance of self-representation, structural cohesion, and temporal and spatial stability.

8. The wish will influence an employee's perception of work. The employee's capacity to take reality into account in construction and maintenance of the wish will be an indication of the degree of work pathology (Sandler, 1981).

9. The idealized self-image is considered an attempt to gain intimacy and provide for self-esteem regulation (Reich, 1960).

10. The idealized self-image contains a wish for gratification and a magical wished-for closeness as a relief from painful yearnings associated with the fear of abandonment (Jacobson, 1954).

CHAPTER 4

The Relationship between Intrapsychic Structure and Organizational Structure

> . . . every social organization produces those character
> structures which it needs to exist.
> —WILHELM REICH (1928, p. 122)

ORGANIZATIONAL STRUCTURE

Organizational structure is most often thought of as it is portrayed on the organizational chart: hierarchy, reporting relationships, area of responsibility, status, area of discretion, and so on. Structure often reflects what the organization can and cannot do, its capacities, how tasks will be accomplished, and who will accomplish them. Structure reflects these things by revealing the dynamic elements associated with how people interact and who they interact with. For example, structure often influences the physical design of the organization, qualities of space use, and proximity associated with task relations (i.e., how and why people are grouped together and their functional relations). Also, the culture of the organization is reflected in its structure (Lincoln, Hanada, & McBride, 1986) and in how, and the degree to which, the organization manifests control, its degree of centralization, its required formality, and its communication networks.

Most executives and many organizational theorists believe that organizational structures are developed with rational motives in mind, and they point to a number of constructs (e.g., organizational size, goals, environmental constraints and technology used in determining how to structure. Those who see the creation of structure as a function of environmental factors generally point to marketing conditions, product competition, and customer relations; they typically suggest that the structure they propose is designed to follow a particular strategy. Others suggest a less deterministic view and maintain that structures evolve over time, and that the primary motive for structural change is to adapt to a changing environment (Miller & Rice, 1967). Furthermore, they suggest that the structure of the organization is a configuration that defines authority, creates communications channels, and clarifies employee movement "up the ladder," and finally, that structure establishes a context within which the organization can accomplish its short- and long-term goals.

Much of the literature on the evolution of structure assumes that structure should and often does have a rational[1] base, and if the structure fails or is maladaptive, it is because management has failed to carefully assess reality. These theorists fail to entertain the possibility that organizational structures may be created for reasons that are other than rational. They fail to entertain the assumption that these structures may evolve from sets of psychodynamic issues that have very little to do with the goals of the enterprise—issues that may in fact constrain the efficiency and effectiveness of the enterprise.

DiTomasi (1984) refutes the assumption that structures are created with rational motives in mind. She suggests that structures are often established as a response to some covert conflicts in the organization. She believes that in bureaucracies, all too often organizational theorists fail to interpret the meaning underlying the decision to develop a particular type of structure. Generally, in an analysis of the decision to develop a particular structure, theorists tend to focus on the suitability of the structure as it fits within a given theory. Covert motivations associated with the decision to structure are usually left unanalyzed.

Organizational theorists continue to force their designs of a structure to fit theory, in spite of the ambiguity of the theory or the results of a given structure. For example, DiTomasi says that when an organization makes a decision to decentralize a structure, theorists assume that this decision is made to reduce managerial control and

---

[1]The term *rational* is presented here as it applies to the decision-making process that uses numerics and statistical analysis, as a method of reasoning based on a careful assessment of stated factors generally devoid of introspection. Rational when used as a term for sane as opposed to insane does not necessarily fit. A rational decision does not take into account those conscious and unconscious forces that may influence a decision but are not included in the analysis.

share power, but this is a faulty assumption. The decision to decentralize, like many other organizational decisions, is subject to contingencies and constraints in both purpose and meaning. Di Tomasi (1984) presents an example to support the view that decisions to decentralize an organization do not always follow the prevalent belief that it is accomplished to decrease management control and promote autonomy. In her analysis of the U.S. Department of Labor's decision to decentralize, she says that the decision was not motivated by management's desire to decrease control. In fact, the decision was motivated by the desire to increase management's control and dominance. She concludes that the motivation to decentralize occurs when subordinates press for power. Management then decentralizes to fragment the subordinates' power and to enhance their own power. The organization's leadership designs a structure to broaden its power base, often at the expense of subordinates.

It is relatively recent that theorists have suggested that organizational structure may be designed and developed through a set of motivations that may be other than rational. The current trend in organizational research is to assess the nature of these motivations (Kets de Vries & Miller, 1984). Some studies now suggest that the motivation to structure is a function of the personality types or styles of the executive constellation, or the culture of the organization or other covert processes (Miller, Kets de Vries, & Toulouse, 1988; Jaques, 1951, 1971; Kernberg, 1978; Kets de Vries, 1980, 1984; Maccoby, 1976; Zaleznik & Kets de Vries, 1984; Merry & Brown, 1987; Harvey & Albertson, 1971; Mintzberg, 1988).

In particular, Kets de Vries (1984) and Kernberg (1976) isolate behavioral patterns and personality styles and relate them to the type of organizational structures they are most likely to create. Consider what Kernberg (1976) says: "Top executives may create shared fantasies that underlie a dominant organizational adaptive style" (p. 422). These theorists suggest that organizational structures are created to reflect the unconscious fantasies associated with the wishes and needs of executives. These unconscious fantasies may be associated with the wish for power, idealization, order, security, and domination, as well as fear of loss and castration. Attempting to assess the relationship between these covert processes and organizational structure is indeed difficult. For example, Progogine and Stendger (1984) suggest that executives may establish a structure to cover a chaotic system underneath, and at the same time, a structure that appears on the surface to be chaotic may be a cover for a fresh, orderly, and adequate system functioning underneath. I suggest that a structure that appears disorderly may serve a covert function, such as protecting certain employees or departments from certain types of anxieties (Czander, 1983).

If structures are established to gratify or avoid certain anxieties, it is vital that those responsible for establishing a structure have a clear understanding of their own motives. Avoiding such an analysis, or avoiding the issue by assuming that one has a rational base for one's thinking, increases the probability that the structure will fail to accomplish its stated purpose by inviting resistance from others.

A critical issue facing those who seek to analyze a relationship between the covert or intrapsychic life of the employee and the organization's structure is how to make this grand "leap of faith" between an unconscious motivation and the establishment of a structure. Considering the enormous variance between the personalities of employees and these external structures, how can such a relationship be conjectured? A key is found in the investigation of the commonalities and purposes of the two structures, namely, intrapsychic structure and organizational structure. For example, they have one significant commonality: Ideally both structures have the potential to permit opportunities to engage in harmonious interactions with objects and other structures in the person's immediate environment over time. An examination of the nature of intrapsychic structure will assist in investigating this relationship.

INTRAPSYCHIC STRUCTURE

A considerable amount of confusion exists about what constitutes psychic structure. There are nine conceptualizations of what psychic structure actually is: Beginning with Freud (1940/1964), structure is defined as a set of laws governing processes of mentation; Rycroft (1956) defines structures as pathways of discharge; Hartmann (1958) as forms of energy; Gill (1976) as modes of organizing; Noy (1968) as modes of perception; Holt (1967) as structures to conceptualize primary processes; Miller and Rice as processes to establish boundaries; Rogers (1980) as processes to conceptualize information; and Rapaport and Gill (1959) as configurations of a slow rate of change.

The general view is that psychic structure provides the person with the conscious and unconscious ability to sort out and separate the self from the external world. According to Rogers (1980), structure provides for a polarity of pleasure–pain clusters that have been internalized during early years and are condensed so that the person, as an adult, is able to establish a set of psychological boundaries. Intrapsychic structure is not static; it continuously changes and develops over time. However, most psychoanalytic theorists suggest that intrapsychic structure is malleable in the beginning years of life and becomes less malleable as one gets older. Psychoanalytic theorists conclude that by the time the person enters the world of work, the intrapsychic structure is set and will alter very little. Given the lack of malleability of intrapsychic structure, the goals facing employees are twofold: (1) to adapt to the organization and (2) to alter the organization to meet the requirements of the employee's own psychic structure, or as Kets de Vries would suggest, "to suit his/her personality."

In the first case, the employee reacts to the structural characteristics of the organization in an adaptive fashion. The employee uses his/her psychic structure to defend against the demands of the organization when they are experienced as psychic impingements. This view is consistent with the Freudian or classical position in psychoanalysis which suggests that ideally, organizational structure is internalized by employees to serve a binding function and to help them defend against primitive anxieties. Another view suggests that subordinates will accept a given structure as long as they see the leader of the structure as an ideal, heroic, awesome, or powerful figure and their organization as equally powerful. Acceptance of structure from this perspective can be considered a masochistic quest for a benevolent duplication of parental power and a continuation of the sadomasochistic power struggle witnessed in the family (Wolberg, 1975).

The second adaptive response to organizational structure is essentially active. Here the employee seeks to alter his/her job domain, and in some cases the entire structure of the organization, to gratify intrapsychic needs and wishes. This response is closely aligned with the object relations school of psychoanalysis. Both of these modes of operating within structures are examined here.

CLASSICAL VIEWS OF THE DEVELOPMENT OF STRUCTURE

Early studies of groups by Lebon (1985), McDougall (1973), and Freud (1921/1955) state that without structure, nihilism would prevail, and en masse groups would move from one emotional state to another with no sanctions or moral codes. They maintain that the very dread of anarchy is the primary motivation for developing structure. However, to create a psychoanalysis of the relationship between intrapsychic and external structure, and the motivation for developing a structure, one must assume that there is more at play than the dread of anarchy or the fear of primitive anxiety.

Management creates the structure of the organization. The rational view suggests that structure is established to provide roles, superior–subordinate relations (authority), work groups, and what amounts to a division of labor. However, these are not the unconscious motivators for creating a given structure but rather the outcomes. The classical position maintains that structures are unconsciously protective decisions. Following a Kleinian position, environmental impingements and work requirements precipitate unconscious reactions both individually and collectively. The behaviors that employees demonstrate in response to these impingements are a function of unconscious defenses against libidinal and aggressive wishes and the anxiety associated with these wishes. Employees defend against the anxiety associated with these unconscious wishes by utilizing defenses such as denial, projective identification, splitting, and projection. Borrowing from the psychoanalytically oriented cultural anthropologists, it is maintained that organizational structure is established to defend against the primitive anxieties associated with libidinal and aggressive wishes that are aroused within the context of work. Furthermore, they maintain that the organization's structure itself is established to function as a defense. Thus structure is established first to reduce the anxiety associated with the primitive wishes that are aroused, and then to defend against the greatest dread—conditions of anarchy and the absence of structure. While these theorists maintain that structure is established to defend against the dread of structurelessness, others maintain that structures are established in response to the arousal precipitated by a given structure (work activities). Perhaps this explains why organizations so frequently reorganize.

Field (1974) claims that it is valuable for organizational theorists to assess the similarities between what is known about organizational structures and what Freud says about psychic structure. Field says that an analogy can be made between the tripartite model of psychic structure[2] and a classical model of organizational structure. He sees the CEO as performing ego-related functions and he sees the equivalent of the superego as being embedded in the culture or value system of the collective organization. The id contains those irrational forces that come into play as employees compete for resources to gratify their basic wishes. Field goes on to suggest that repression is a

---

[2]The tripartite model of the mind proposed by Freud is composed of the the id, the ego, and the superego.

powerful defense used by an organization to deny aspects of its history that are found to be intolerable or connected to unethical behaviors.

The classical psychoanalytic position, the drive model, when applied to a theory of motivation for creation of a structure, suggests that organizational structure is designed to control and repress. This model of the structure is consistent with the view prevalent among classical organizational theorists, beginning with F. W. Taylor, often called the father of scientific management, who says: "Under scientific management initiative . . . control is obtained with absolute uniformity. This is the job of management to establish rules, laws, formulas, to define the tasks to be performed and the means to be used in doing the work" (1939, p. 70).

In Taylor's view, management does all the thinking. If labor is allowed to think, management will lose control and chaos will result as labor seeks to avoid the adult responsibilities associated with productivity. Consequently, management must specify what is to be done, how, and the exact time allowed for doing it. Applying this to the Freudian position, we see that the function of the ego (management) is to control the internal world of the organization, which takes on qualities of the id, a system of "darkness" primarily motivated to obtain pleasure without limits or sanctions. Therefore, management's unconscious motivation for creating a particular structure is to repress and keep this "dark side" from emerging.

Carrying this analogy further, the organization imports external reality into its structure through the use of objects that serve as introjects. These objects bring into the system varying degrees of civilization, moral codes, and values, but also varying degrees of a willingness to punish those who violate the internal moral codes. This is similar to Freud's idea of the superego, a "dominant mass of ideas" (Greenberg & Mitchell, 1983), ideas that function as the underpinnings for a system of control and regulation. Therefore, internal structure is created to impose authority on employees— authority that has been introjected by the organization, mediated by its executive constellation, and internalized by the staff.

Freud, in his later writings, gave the ego heightened influence as a mediator between the internal world of the id and external reality. This allowed Miller and Rice (1967) to draw analogies between psychic structure and organizational structure. They say that the ego, like a CEO, acts as a boundary manager of the system, as the one who is responsible for determining not only what gets into the system but what exits. If sublimation is the chief defense used in determining the capacity to work, then work becomes possible only after the ego is capable of functioning relatively free of the oppressive demands of the drives. Then the ego is able to react to its own and the organization's aims. If the drives contained within the organization and members are antisocial in nature and have the potential to destroy the capacity to work, then it is the responsibility of management, the organization's ego, to provide the necessary structure and to direct drive aims from their original purpose to ones that are more appropriately geared toward socially acceptable reality, such as work effectiveness and efficiency.

All organizational structures provide a schemata to the employee for reliable and prudent patterns of action. The organization requires discipline and this can only be accomplished if the following occurs.

1. Ideal patterns of behavior and requirements of discipline are buttressed by the employee's strong connection and devotion to work, profession or organization.
2. The employee is able to internalize the moral codes of the organization/profession into his/her professional ego ideal. Internalization is not possible when the authority structure of the organization prohibits autonomous functioning. In these organizations, where authority refuses to give up the wish to control and regulate, the identification process will fail and the professional ego ideal will fail to develop in a mature manner. Consequently, the internal mechanisms of morality, the professional ego ideal, will remain weak and employees will increasingly rely on the authority structure of the organization to function as an ego and a superego surrogate. Over-reliance on the external structure of the organization to nurture the work ego will increase dependency, stifle innovation and risk taking, and increase the potential for conflict and regression.

The major criticism of the classical or drive-dominated model is that it sees structure as evolving from id demands and the motivation to control impulses of an essentially sexual and aggressive nature. This view suggests that structures are predetermined and essentially defensive, as continuously "moving against" primitive anxieties. The overdetermined view leaves little room for a view of development of structures as "moving toward." Here is where the object relations school of psychology enters. This school suggests that structures are created with interpersonal motives in mind.

OBJECT RELATIONS VIEW OF THE DEVELOPMENT OF ORGANIZATIONAL STRUCTURE

Winnicott (1965) suggests that ideally, the relationship between the person and his/her environment should lead to (1) a deeper more gratifying inner self, the true self, (2) a greater degree of spontaneity, creativity, and the experience of being alive, and (3) the capacity for empathy for others (Ashbach & Schermer, 1987). When we apply this theory to the world of work, we find that the attainment of these lofty outcomes is rare. As a matter of fact, many organizational theorists using the object relations model suggest that given the nature of work, its tasks, and the relationships with others, the employee will experience rejections, disappointments, and psychic injuries.

Just as the dread of anarchy and the release of primitive anxiety lie at the foundation of the classical position, the object relations theorists see the creation of structure not necessarily for defensive purposes but primarily to obtain the gratification associated with relational wishes. Organizational structure is psychically created to facilitate a holding, nurturing environment. However, one cannot create the ideal relational environment at work for two reasons: (1) there is competition for scarce resources, and (2) given the hierarchical nature of the organization, some employees have more status, authority, and greater opportunities for gratification than do others. The organization is not a democratic system. As a matter of fact, the organization more often resembles a parent–child situation, a situation that precipitates conflict, and often structures are created to ensure psychic survival.

ORGANIZATIONAL STRUCTURE AS A DEFENSE

According to Menzies (1960), as a result of anxiety associated with work, the employee develops "socially structured defense mechanisms" (p. 401). These defenses are the result of externalization where characteristics of the employee's psychic defense organization are made part of the relationship with the external environment. Menzies (1960) says that social defenses are developed over time as a result of collective interaction—a type of unconscious agreement among the organization's members results. This position raises a number of questions, and if these questions are adequately answered, a theory can be created that will explain how organizational structure is developed and perhaps the relationship between psychic structure and organizational structure as well. Before this theory can be fully developed, the following questions must be answered:

1. What are socially constructed defenses?
2. How are they different from psychic defenses?
3. What are the mechanisms involved where psychic defenses become social defenses?

The general position is that social defenses are nothing more than a collectively agreed upon process, similar to shared beliefs and values; however, defenses are assumed to be unconscious. How then is agreement attained? The precondition for the development of a social defense is the collective experience of anxiety. Under these conditions, one member articulates a way or process that can be used by everyone to reduce the experience of anxiety. This one member externalizes the defense in behavioral terms. Thus, a social defense must be considered an expression of an unconscious defense in behavioral terms. The group accepts the behavior; that is, the members identify with the wish underlying the behavior only if they feel the identification will reduce their anxiety. This is accomplished through the interplay of conscious and unconscious affect, that is, a collusion where members unconsciously internalize the potential of the defense in reducing anxiety. When the articulated defense is not experienced as having the potential to reduce anxiety, a conscious compromise may result where the behavioral activities of the defense may be altered. Thus, a social defense is the operationalization of a psychic defense and is a result of a conscious compromise that is based on unconscious ideation.

In Menzies's (1960) case analysis of nurses, this process is apparent where the nurses consciously agree to engage in the behaviors associated with the defense of depersonalization. The conscious compromise is internalized and contributes to reducing anxiety by becoming part of the behavioral repertoire of the nurses. Menzies claims that this defense is used to reduce the anxiety associated with libidinal and aggressive wishes which are evoked when the nurses are required to perform tasks in a certain manner. Consequently, role requirements, when they precipitate anxiety, will bring forth defenses in response. These defenses may be used by small groups of employees, as in the Menzies case, or they can be utilized to construct an entire organizational structure. As Menzies suggests, social defenses are necessary. They allow employees to work on their respective tasks and to make this work tolerable.

Travelbee (1974), in agreement with Menzies, concludes that an internal, irrevocable, and profound change occurs when one enters the nursing profession. He suggests that the young person, in most cases a woman, is confronted with her own sense of vulnerability. Nurses are exposed to illness, suffering, and death, which precipitate a number of behavioral responses to anxiety, and they may become indifferent, detached, or facetious. Of significance in defending against the anxiety is the ability of the nurse to locate and utilize a supportive environment either through primary group membership or through a relationship with a supportive, experienced leader/manager.

Jaques (1971) spells out the nature of this supportive environment when he states, "[A]ll institutions are unconsciously used by their members as mechanisms of defense against psychotic anxieties" (p. 477).

While social defenses and the structure these defenses create are used to reduce anxiety, it is suggested that excessive reliance on defenses and structure may contribute to dysfunctional forms of ego functioning and even to pathological conditions. Consider the following example of the entry into the organization of a new employee. Often, entering employees are quite dismayed when after a brief period of time on the job they see their colleagues as immature and regressive and displaying sadistic and aggressive behaviors with supervisors, customers, and others. From a psychoanalytic perspective, these types of behaviors are social defenses against primitive anxieties associated with a task, and are the creation of a structure that is dysfunctional and actually contributes to regression. The entering employee observes these behaviors and, when confronted with the new and strange role and structure, his/her anxiety increases even more. This contributes to a psychic crisis and a regressed state. Typically the entrant in the regressed state will resort to earlier modes of internalizing (Hanlon, 1990). Therefore, to reduce this crisis he/she will seek entry into a supportive container (an informal group), and his/her professional ego ideal will undergo an alteration by internalizing both the social defenses and the dysfunctional structure. If the entrant refuses either of these, he/she will take on the role of a social isolate, who then becomes the container for hostile, sadistic, and persecuting projections. This may contribute to a further increase in anxiety, rage, or schizoid withdrawal.

If the entrant capitulates to the pressure from the group and engages in the behaviors expected in a dysfunctional organization, he/she may find these required behaviors inconsistent with his professional ego ideal. The function of the professional ego ideal is to protect the person from anxiety associated with the tasks of a given role, and internalization of a professional role generally occurs prior to entry. Therefore, a key issue for the entrant is whether the role at work is congruent with the entrant's professional ego ideal.

An incongruity will precipitate anxiety and promote regression. If the professional ego ideal breaks down, the employee will exhibit a schizoid withdrawal. Work will be entered into with limited esprit and the employee will vacillate between the affects of guilt and rage. He/she will begin to question his/her career choice, and the organization will be experienced as a bad object. Work can only be tolerated then if the employee utilizes social defenses that are congruent with his/her professional ego ideal. Disillusionment and depression are frequent responses if the employee continues to engage in work behaviors associated with a dysfunctional structure, and is not able to utilize social defenses. For this employee, when behaviors are not utilized to reduce anxiety, anxiety is increased because they conflict with the professional ego ideal. Menzies (1960) agrees and says:

> If social defenses are forced on the employee they perpetuate pathologi-
> cal anxiety. . . . These defenses are oriented to the violent, terrifying
> situations of infancy, and rely heavily on violent splitting which pre-
> cipitates the anxiety. By permitting the individual to avoid the experience
> of anxiety, they effectively protect the individual from confronting it.
> Thus, the individual cannot bring the content of the phantasy anxiety
> situation into contact with reality, therefore, anxiety tends to remain
> permanently at a level determined more by phantasies than by reality. . . .
> Consequently, this . . . interferes with and . . . inhibits the capacity for
> creative symbolic thought, for abstract thought, and for conceptualiza-
> tion. They inhibit the full development of the individual's understand-
> ing, knowledge, and skills that enable reality to be handled effectively
> and pathological anxiety to be mastered. Thus the individual feels help-
> less in the face of new and strange tasks or problems. (p. 427)

Menzies, although clearly articulating the problems with social defenses, fails to clarify how "forced internalization of social defenses" occurs. She suggests that when employees enter the organization, they are faced with an existing system of social defenses, but how they introject these defenses is unclear. Jaques (1971) offers insight when he states the following:

> [O]rganizations . . . provide institutionalized roles whose occupants are
> sanctioned, or required to take into themselves (force), the projected
> objects or impulses of other members. The occupant of such roles may

absorb the objects and impulses—take them into themselves and become either good or bad objects with corresponding impulses—put them into an externally perceived ally; or enemy, who is them loved, or attached. The gain for the individual in projecting objects and impulses and introjecting their careers in the external world, lies in the unconscious cooperation with other members of the institution or group who are using similar projective mechanisms. Introjective identification then allows more than the return of projected objects and impulses. The other members are also taken inside, and legitimized and reinforced attacks upon internal persecutor, or support manic idealization of love objects, thereby be reinforcing the denial of destructive impulses against them. (p. 477)

Jaques implies that the characteristics of the role coupled with group pressures may force acceptance of social defenses. The chief mechanism for forced internalization is projective identification. The entrant who is already experiencing anxiety and deprivation is an "easy" target for projections that have to do with bad objects associated with colleagues, supervisors, machinery, and so forth. When the entrant responds with affects associated with anxiety, helplessness, and primitive wishes to be saved from these "persecutors," the entrant is then capable of being freed from the constraints of his/her professional ego ideal and can internalize the social defenses to ward off these affects. The social defenses are internalized by the entrant, when they are capable of overpowering the already weakened professional ego ideal through affects precipitated by the experiences of the entry and the pressure of colleagues. The defense used here is referred to by Jaques as introjective identification and by Meissner (1972) as identification with the introject. Jaques (1971) suggests that this defense is a process of construction of the self-organization according to a pattern provided by the introject. Meissner (1972) elaborates:

> Since it derives from a relatively autonomous base . . . it is governed by more autonomous ego interests and secondary process patterns of organization. The identification therefore tends to be selective, adaptive, ordered to integration with the pre-existing patterns of ego structure and defensive organization. (p. 241)

Meissner considers identification with the introject as having little basis in infantile development or adult psychopathology. He removes it from drive consideration and departs from Jaques and Menzies. Meissner also suggests that identification with the introjected succeeds only when consistent with preexisting psychic structures. This clearly makes the defense adaptive; that is, the process may be used to reduce primitive anxiety precipitated by work, or as Jaques and Menzies have claimed, it may be used as a vehicle to allow the employee to integrate the work tasks with his/her ego structures. Viewed from this perspective the following question emerges: Are organizational structures merely externalized social defenses, or are they replications of preexisting ego structures? Put another way, are organizational structures replications of ego structures that are shared by a collectivity, the organization's employees, and composed of defenses and an array of ego functions and capacities?

As stated before, social defenses are a way of structuring external reality to avoid the anxiety evoked in work. Menzies and Jaques, who suggest that social defenses have pathological consequences, see the employee in a no-win situation. If employees attempt to escape from the organization's constructed social defenses, and later on if they attempt to confront reality, their anxiety will dramatically increase and psychic decompensation or regression to a primitive mode of functioning may result. It seems that in order for an employee to confront organizational reality, he/she must work through the anxiety without the use of social defenses. To accomplish this successfully would require one to work in an organizational context capable of providing the necessary support, nurturance, and transitional objects. Experience dictates that this kind of organizational context is exceedingly rare. It is most common for employees to be left alone with their anxiety, with their peers and social defenses embedded in the organization's structure as the only means with which to protect themselves from these environmental impingements. In addition, if social defenses are already embedded in the organization's structure and these defenses are not consistent or congruent with the employee's preexisting patterns of ego structure and defensive organization, anxiety will result. On the other hand, organizational structures can be quite malleable and at certain periods of time susceptible to influence. Under these circumstances, employees can impose their preexisting ego structure and defense organization onto the organization's structure, thereby creating a structure that is psychically gratifying. And finally, if a match between the employee's intrapsychic structure and the organizational structure fails, the employee will not be able to adequately confront the organization's reality. Under these circumstances the employee will experience unnecessary anxiety and will be encumbered with unconscious regressive pulls into primitive modes of functioning as a feeble attempt to restore ego balance and reduce anxiety. These regressive pulls may, over time, become part of the organization's structure and culture. This is why some organizations appear to outside observers as pathological, where behaviors like aggression, schizoid detachment, and narcissistic preoccupations prevail. But to the insiders (the employees) the organization is comforting.

ORGANIZATIONAL STRUCTURE AND CONTROL

Models of mentation or mental activity assume a dualistic existence of thought processes. The mind is structured in a way to guide or provide pathways for thinking. Considered in this manner, it is similar to thinking of an organizational structure as being established for the purpose of creating and maintaining pathways to communication. Structures of organization are viewed in a number of ways: as decision-making systems, control systems, political systems, and information systems, and all these views are founded on cybernetic principles. Structure then becomes the skeleton for providing necessary order for the processing of information for the purpose of achieving defined goals. The question facing the psychoanalyst is: If this structure is established for the purpose of communication, what is the nature of that which is communicated?

Globus (1974) suggests that three types of communicative processes move through these structural systems. He calls them process one (P1), the realized unconscious or preconscious—that information which can be recalled; process two (P2), the secondary process—information that is in our immediate consciousness; and process three (P3), information that is unattainable and beyond the reach of consciousness. P3 is seen by Neisser (1967) as the primary motivational information processing framework or structure. According to Neisser (1967, p. 3), the unconscious is "a multiple activity," somewhat analogous to parallel processing in computers, which constructs "crudely formed thoughts or ideas on the basis of stored information" (Rogers, 1980, p. 304). This stored information is repressed, beyond the person's, or in this case the organization's, awareness. Nevertheless, this stored information influences or motivates all that goes on in P1 and P2. P2 is "serial in character." This process is constructed by "ideas and images which are determined partly by stored information, partly by preliminary organization of primary processes and partly by wished and expectations" (Rogers, 1980, p. 304). It is these wishes and expectations that are motivated by P3 and in many instances denied or deflected by P1 amd P2. Using this framework, we can conceptualize the organizational structure as being developed by an interplay of these three processes, but always motivated in varying degrees by P3. Neisser (1967) claims that the primary element of control found in structures is contained in secondary process thinking which is similar to the executive routine of a computer. It is P1 and P2 that manifest the motivation for control.

This view raises a number of issues for understanding the characteristics of decision making, control, and cooperation. For example, the mechanistic organization relies on secondary process thinking in decision making, but is the motivation or method of control contained within P1 or P2? If the method for control were contained in P2, the motivation for control would be established in the service of P3; that is, this structure is primarily created to ameliorate or defend against information beyond the organization's awareness. This organization would then establish control and a structure without knowing why it behaves as it does, and its explanations would be nothing more than rationalizations.

On the other hand, if the motivation for establishing control within a given structure were a function of the method established in P1, motivation would be more closely tied to reality or the organization's perception of reality. Why is this the case? In P1, there is greater access to information, the process uses or retrieves more information, and the information used is closer to P3, the real source of motivation. P2 uses less information and is further removed from P3; therefore an organization that relied on P2 to create a structure would emphasize control at the expense of cooperation and would have a vertical authority structure requiring repression. Employees in an organization that relied on P2 would utilize communication processes that manifest secondary process thinking, with heightened repression and the wish for vertical authority relationships emphasizing external forms of control. Information that was beyond secondary process thought would be viewed as either unimportant or threatening and the system would create barriers and greater degrees of control. On the other hand, an innovative, entrepreneurial organization emphasizing a horizontal structure would possess capabilities of primary process thinking.

Assuming that organizations create structures to provide a necessary order for the processing of information (mental material), the function of creating a structure is to reduce or defend against environmental dangers and internal anxieties. The method of processing information is more than just a structure—it is essentially how the organization communicates. Organizations rely on an array of methods, modes, and mediums to communicate mental material. Some are verbal and written, but most are in the area of representational symbolisms, such as architecture, use of space, events, stories, and how the workday is ordered.

By returning to the position that organizations structure to reduce or defend themselves from environmental dangers, the very
nature of this process from a psychoanalytic perspective is now ex-
plainable. Chief among environmental dangers are dangers associated with separation and loss. Fear of the environment for the employee means that it is a dangerous place and has the power to destroy
or damage. These fears are associated with infantile fears of separation from the primary object, the mother. Fears of this type are
replicated in organizational life and they are often founded in the
experience that something will occur to destroy the organization:
employees will leave, they will be seduced away by other organizations, the organization will be injured causing people to be terminated
(symbolic death), the organization will be taken over (by some symbolic monster waiting in the closet), and so on. These experiences are
often the result of some environmental impingement upon the organization, reminding the organization that it is vulnerable and such
dangers exist. This fear is pointed out in Chapter 9, where the nurses
in the intensive care unit experience increased anxiety when their
leader's (symbolic mother) car does not appear in the parking lot.
It is also pointed out in Chapter 12, in the discussion of intergroup
relations. Often these fears are repressed and lodged within
the P3 communicative structure. This structure will influence the
decision-making efforts and all communication processes in P1
and P2. The communicative process will then be influenced by defenses of denial and projection to cope with the affects emanating
from P3.

Both danger and anxiety tend to diminish when a structure is
established that is free of denial and projection and the motivation for
establishing a given structure is not based on unconscious wishes. The
establishment of a structure, for the purposes of defining a communicative process to promote object relatedness, is the equivalent of
creating an organization capable of mature ego functioning. To reach
this level, those designing the structure must be able to analyze and
isolate those factors or forces around which the structure of the
organization is organized. The following are some questions that
must be asked when engaging in an analysis of structure:

1. Is the structure organized to prohibit or defend against latent
   demons from making their appearance, that is, to repress
   (Freud or the classical school), or is the structure organized around the vicissitudes of early object-seeking wishes,
   to promote optimal human relatedness (the object relations
   school)?

2. Is the structure organized around certain types of methods used in the past to deal with anxiety (the object relations school), and do these methods manifest themselves as a compulsion to repeat (Freud or the classical school)?
3. Is the structure organized around the aims to achieve stable goals and ideals, to chart a course through a real or fantasized future (self psychology), or is the structure organized around deficits in the organization caused by some type of trauma in the organization's past?

STRUCTURAL VARIATION AND ITS IMPACT ON EMPLOYEES

A critical issue concerning organizational theorists is how to understand the relationship between differing structures and the effect on employees. An organization has an infinite variety of structures from which to choose. A number of theorists have attempted to develop topologies of structures, and according to Mintzberg (1988), there seem to be five to eight structural configurations.

What prompts an organization to adopt a particular type of structure? Most theorists suggest that factors such as the age of the organization, the organization's technology, its size, and the nature of its environment will influence the type of structure an organization adopts. According to Mintzberg (1988), not one of these factors alone determines why a structure is chosen, and he goes on to suggest that "organizations can select their situations in accordance with their structural designs just as much as they can select their designs in accordance with their situations" (p. 277). To follow the traditional view of developing structures is to assume that the organization responds in a passive manner to situational pressures and then structures accordingly. On the other hand, the psychoanalytic position suggests that while these external situations may play a role and may actually be powerful in influencing structural development, it is the unconscious motivation of the employees that will ultimately determine the structure.

Organizations can be classified according to a concept used by Freud to differentiate between psychosis and neurosis. In psychosis, the person uses the defenses of denial and disavowal; that is, the person distorts or denies certain activities and perceptions of external reality. In neurosis, the ego responds to intolerable drive demands by making use of the defense of repression. In the organization, as well as in all social groupings, the function of a hierarchical structure is to establish repression, maintain order, and allow the executive to function without having to respond to the demands of the subordinate staff. This structure presumably permits the executive the freedom to attend to external reality, the organization's environment (boundary management), in a less conflicted or nonconflicted manner. Consequently, the function of the vertical structure is to maximize control by repressing troublesome ideation internally in the organization. If the executive constellation must continuously attend to the impulses of the internal organization, it will be unable to attend to the demands of its environment and the entire system will be exposed to misperception and misdirected energy which will increase the organization's vulnerability. Consider the vertical structure, sometimes called the hierarchical or bureaucratic structure, and no doubt the most common of all organizational structures.

VERTICAL STRUCTURE

The vertical structural configuration is centered around the maintenance of control. This is what is typically referred to as the bureaucracy; it is a metaphor that signals red tape, closeness of supervision, clear and rigid rules and regulations, routine activities, offices, or roles, each with clearly defined rights and privileges. Rewards and punishments are used as motivational instruments and are supposed to be based on "objective" evaluations of performance. However, this process is rarely objective; instead it is political, which precipitates conflict and adversarial relations between superior and subordinate. According to Morgan (1988), in this system "they [employees] have an incentive to engage in various forms of deception to protect themselves" (p. 165). According to Gouldner (1954), the conflict perpetuated by this reward and punishment system is cyclical; as employees seek to evade control and management responds by increasing its control, the system goes on becoming more and more bureaucratic. The defensive nature of this type of structure, with its emphasis on reward and punishment, creates conservativeness, and over time management will attempt to reduce all uncertainty through the use of categories, rigidity, and obsessively defined duties for protective purposes. It is not the nature of the task that precipitates anxiety and dread but the structure itself.

The bureaucratic system ends up promoting a structure that rewards conservative efforts. Efforts that are innovative, different, or risky are viewed as deviant. Management defends itself against complexity in the work and withdraws from tasks that are undefined and may lead to punishment. Interpretations of complex problems, if they cannot be handed over to specialists, are rationalized and made to appear simple or are dismissed outright. When problems do persist they become dramatized and the reactions to problems take on hysterical proportions. An extreme of this type of reaction is defined as a psychic contagion reaction where employees experience contagious somatic reactions to some unknown substance (see Chapter 9 for more on this reaction). Mild reactions may take the form of scapegoating an employee or department by displacing the anxiety associated with the lack of clarity of the problem onto another: It is as if the problem can be located in another, it can be dealt with. Also, in this system problems and uncertainty are passed around like "hot potatoes" as employees avoid negative evaluations or episodes that may endanger their career. This tends to create a climate of falseness or gamesmanship, and for an employee to thrive in this type of environment requires a certain type of character structure.

The acceptance of a vertical structure psychically occurs through the process of regression of superego functioning, where internal autonomous regulatory activity is reduced and its place is taken by an object that assumes a regulatory role. The structure assumes regulatory authority over the subordinate only when the subordinate assumes a submissive position. The regulatory authority takes over the superego functions, such as conscious ideals, morality, equality, self-observation, and the reality testing of the ego. The regulatory authority is external; it is embedded in the structure and is, under certain conditions, incorporated by employees over time through participation in organizational activities, rituals, myths, ceremonies, and tasks. These activities are designed not only to promote incorporation of the regulatory authority of structure but to punish deviators or those who do not join in. Punishment serves to promote intrapsychic defenses against conflict associated with submission or the wish to overthrow the authority and seek liberation. When an employee finally submits to the authority structure, his internal aggression is displaced onto deviants who are unconsciously perceived as psychic threats.

Conflicts between the demands of the authority structure and the requirements of the employee's professional ego ideal will produce symptoms of a narcissistic type. Defenses such as denial and projective identification will predominate and regression to a less differentiated phase of development will result. To stop regression employees unconsciously wish for greater degrees of control. For example, in an environment in which control and regulation already prevail, employees will use the organization's structure in a sadomasochistic way to punish and monitor themselves and others. Where control and regulation do not exist, employees will "act out" in a manner that brings about an increase in control from management.

The critical factor in working and finding "comfort" within a bureaucracy is the externalization of control. It is as if the organization takes on the responsibilities of internal psychic agencies. According to Horkheimer (1949), "social repression is concomitant with the internal repression of impulses" (p. 78). The authority structure of the organization provides a psychic function; it serves as an externalized superego.[3] This phenomenon somewhat contradicts the psychoanalytic theory, which suggests that superego development begins at the preoedipal period and is complete at the end of the oedipal period. If this is true, why would the internalization of the external superego regulation still occur for a person employed in an organization as an adult? The partial answer is that the superego development that occurred during the oedipal period is never completed or arrested; it merely continues to develop and alter throughout adult life. If identification is considered a defense utilized by the superego to build its structure, then what is observed in the person's relations at work are products of that process.

Consider the employee's motivation to take pleasure in being subordinate, and in the experience of obedience. When the employee places him/herself in this position, aim-inhibiting and regulatory functions of the superego are now externalized and become a function of the organization's structure. Regulatory functions are turned over to the organization, such as self-esteem regulation, the regulation of libidinal and aggressive energies, and the affects associated with object relations. When an employee remarks, "It's a good thing I get evaluated every few months, I know where I stand," he/she is not only associating pleasure with obedience but confirming the need for externalized regulatory functions. It is as if the employee is saying, "If they do not tell me how I am doing, I will not know, for I have no internal mechanism to conduct such an evaluation; I have a general feeling, but I can never be certain."

What is apparent in this type of response is the tragedy of emptiness that is born from the depletion of internalized object relations, which leaves an inadequate superego structure. For this em-

---

[3]The superego is not regarded here as some internalized code. The view of the superego expressed is similar to Chein's (1972) position. He states that there are two major facets of the superego: "(1) the acceptance of an external authority as the arbiter of what one may and should properly do and (2) the concept (in enormous measure implicit) of what the authority requires" (p. 234). He considers these two kinds of morality that exist side by side, but the second as containing the power to influence the first. The superego, in introjecting what the authority requires, is not, as some psychoanalysts would suggest, a moral code; it is the image of authority.

ployee, the need to please others and to be seen as pleasing is an overriding concern, but it is what this concern represents that forms the basis for the motivation to work within a structure that requires such rigid obedience. Most psychoanalytic explanations of rigid obedience and oversolicitude consider them to be surface responses to the underlying and often unconscious affects associated with aggression, hatred, envy, and competition. The employee may actually seek pleasure in the experience of being obedient when his/her behavior and feelings can function as a defense against the fearful affects of aggression. The employee's defensive structure[4] is reinforced when the employee obtains praise from a superior for obedience. Consequently, the employee continuously seeks praise or a favorable evaluation to keep this defense mobilized.

Ideally, organizational structure should not be established to fortify pathological defenses. It should be established with the view in mind that structures are nothing more than technical instruments for mobilizing human energies and then directing these human energies toward set aims (Selznick, 1988). Structures should be designed not only to use the talents of employees but to increase the potential to tap into and expand on the inhibited potential of all employees in ways that are respectful of and empathetic to their sense of self-worth and dignity.

---

[4]Within the field of psychoanalysis there are three major motivations for the establishment of a defense structure. The first, closely aligned with the classical position, suggests that the defense is to oppose some internal or unconscious drive. The second, the defensive structure, is established to avoid or preserve some type of relationship that would otherwise precipitate anxiety. The third, motivation, is to preserve some wish associated with the enhancement of psychological development.

CHAPTER 5

Understanding Work and the Organization from the Psychoanalytic Perspective

> The most value ladened areas to study are mental states and social institutions; to study them together forces the researcher into the abyss of the subjective world.
>
> —WILLIAM M. CZANDER

This chapter explores the nature of psychoanalytic thinking, namely, the methodology and cognitive capacities used in assessing and interpreting organizational phenomena. To fully understand work and the organization from a psychoanalytic perspective requires education and training in two disciplines: psychoanalysis and organizational theory, and more specifically, knowledge of clinical practice, intrapsychic theory, and the social psychology of group behavior, plus knowledge of organizational theory and the practice of management.

The first obstacle faced in joining the two disciplines of organizational theory/behavior and psychoanalysis is the antipathy each has for the other. These two disciplines are far apart in their respective views of what constitutes "good" explanation. On the organizational behavior side, theorists and practitioners rely on a mode of explanation that is referred to as the behavioral/causal mode. On the other hand, the psychoanalytic consultant relies on the analytic-inference mode of explanation. The incompatibility of these modes of explanation precipitates a divergence between the disciplines and makes their integration problematic. This divergence is explored below, in an

attempt to bring psychoanalytic theory into the realm of organizational theory/behavior.

THE BEHAVIORAL/CAUSAL MODE OF EXPLANATION

The behavioral/causal mode of explanation is the most frequently
used method used to explain organizational phenomena. Those organizational theorists who seek to explain relationships in the organization by using this mode present two problems to psychoanalytically
oriented theorists. First, they pretend that what they disregard does
not exist, namely, mentation, cognition, and the unconscious. Second,
they suggest that covert processes of mentation are not the proper
concern for the scientific enterprise. These two positions, especially
the second, are most apparent in organizational theory and behavioral textbooks. The behavioral mode maintains the position that
good science is the only valid method to explain the nature of people
at work. Organizational theorists further maintain that problems with
the field of organizational theory and behavior are a function of the
tendency of scholars to foster theories or viewpoints that purport to
explain some organizational phenomena without both empirical evidence and empirical validation. Furthermore, they state that good
science is objective science, and that objectivity can only be maintained
through rigid adherence to experimental design and statistical analysis. Following from the rigidity of experimental design, these theorists
seek out impelling factors that either contribute to or cause behaviors.
A review of modes of explanation that appear in organizational
theory and behavioral textbooks (Czander, 1990)[1] suggests that the
type of theory that predominates in the literature borrows heavily
from laboratory research. Consequently, it is de rigueur for organizational theorists to be devoted to the application of learning theory,
perception, motivation or attribution theory, and the other sub-
disciplines of psychology that rely on the type of laboratory experimentation that demands large numbers of subjects, control
groups, and statistical analysis.
    When this methodology is applied to the organization, a picture
evolves that suggests that the organization is nothing more than a
rational system, with a homeostatic control structure containing fac-

---

[1]A review of 32 organizational behavior/psychology textbooks revealed that only 3
included any mention of Freud, psychoanalysis, or the unconscious. All devoted at least
one paragraph to behavior modification and 12 devoted a full chapter to the subject.
The absence of the unconscious is representative of the field of organizational psychology and its preoccupation with applying behavioral engineering and technology, rather
than understanding why behavioral dysfunctions exist at work.

tors, episodes, events, and so on, that do nothing more than trigger responses.

When applying experimental laboratory research to the organization, researchers assume that a factor or a set of factors will precipitate a set of behaviors, and the only acceptable or plausible explanation is scientific causation or correlated relationships. Furthermore, these researchers maintain that once factors are isolated in the laboratory that contribute to a given behavior or set of behaviors, these same factors will have the same influence on behaviors in other settings. Those who try to extrapolate experimental findings from one setting to another fail to accept the position that behaviors can only be understood and explained in relation to the context within which they occur. Consequently, assuming that what goes on in the laboratory can be directly applied to people at work is a mistake. To do so is to assume that people will behave the same no matter where they are. To believe this would be to believe that one who knows the experimental results associated with learning, perception, attitudes, obedience, group behavior, and so forth, thereby knows how to lead an organization effectively. Behavior is relative, and failing to accept this fact can lead the researcher to believe, for example, that a 40-year-old man who tells a dirty joke at a meeting at work, tells dirty jokes in other places.

Over the past several years, followers of the behavioral/causal mode of explanation have moved into the consultancy field in increasing numbers. Adherents use the same type of experimental manipulation that they use in the laboratory, mainly in the area of technology of behavior modification. These consultants have moved into organizations when unwanted dysfunctional or maladaptive behavior, as detected by management, is to be eliminated. One reason for their apparent popularity is that the technology they use can be easily understood by management. It is relatively simple to explain, and it operates under the rubric of being a science, which is exceedingly appealing to the technologically minded managers who prefer to see human behavior in terms of feedback loops, binary-coded routed information systems, and correct-state outputs (responses) generated by some antecedent inputs (stimuli).

Levy-Leboyer (1988), exploring the problems associated with applying psychological theory, suggests that a major problem with the application of the behavioral/causal mode is that its proponents are seen as "expert," as technologists who possess a bag of techniques and social gadgets ready to apply to any type of organizational problem, in any type of organizational setting. The behavioral/causal mode of explanation is easily "packaged" and bought by corporate management. Behavioral/causal mode consultants disregard the fact that problems and situations may be unique, and they fail to recognize that what may prove to be scientifically sound in one situation will most likely fail in another. They sell to management a "promise," that is, the hope that the "package" will provide an immediate solution to the organization's perceived difficulties.

It is evident that even under the auspices of normal science, as the behavioral/causal mode consultants see themselves, these consultants often fail to pay attention to the operational aspects of their results, be they generalized theory or numerical output. In the application process, the critical question of the validity of research *begins* and does not, as some would suggest, *end*. If these consultants consider themselves applied scientists, they are in the business of actualizing values, and as Solomon (1971) suggests, their mission is to aid the actualization of either "desired" or "desirable" values, just as the clinician does in therapeutic practice. Behavior/causal consultants would deny this and claim that they represent value-free science. Consequently, they often operate without a firm theoretical and philosophical valuation base, and rarely do they engage in the required self-reflection that is vital when one engages in research, where results are generalized and applied.

RELIANCE ON CAUSALITY

The behavioral/causal mode relies on cause in its explanatory process. Even those theorists who recognize the simultaneous operation of a plurality of causative factors still maintain a tendency to think in terms of single causes. The impact that this type of thinking has had on the field of organizational theory is perhaps most apparent in the Hawthorne study, completed by Rothlinsberger and Dickson (1939). This study is considered by many to be the most significant factor leading to the development of the human relations movement in organizational and management theory. It was the beginning of a school of research that attempted to establish relationships between the attitudes of workers about their work situation (dependent variables) and certain aspects of work performance (independent variables).

A volume of research on work satisfaction followed this study, and for the past 50 years, researchers have developed an array of measures to assess satisfaction. Satisfaction indices have been related to practically everything that can be quantified in the world of work, from profitability to absenteeism. These researchers, in applying the behavioral/causal mode of explanation, attempt to understand or explain organizational phenomena by searching for the motive of a particular behavioral act. They observe behavior and then search for the motive for that behavior; in so doing, they seek the cause of that behavior. However, the deterministic thinking used in this mode contains problems. As these researchers look for a particular motive, they invariably come up with a motivational state. Finding a motivational state may well tell us something about cause and effect, but it is far from deterministic. All the researcher can say about the results is that the motivational state is located and that this state may in some cases elicit behavioral effects (deCharm, 1968). Neff (1977) further expands on the deficiencies of the behavioral/causal mode when he says:

> Assuming the reliable measure of job satisfaction can be devised and assuming further that reliable indices of work efficiency are readily obtainable, there is still no reason to expect that any very clear or close relationship exists. . . . Even a minimal analysis of the manner in which work is organized in contemporary society suggests the operation of a great many intervening variables. First, there is the problem of the occupational level of the workers under study. The conditions which influence work behaviors and the degree to which job satisfaction can be a significant variable are manifestly very different in the several cases of unskilled workers, foremen, middle-line executives, and self-employed professionals. Among many intervening variables which operate with different force in different conditions are: (a) the degree to which output is under the control of the individual worker; (b) the enormous differences in the nature and kinds of interpersonal relationships which the differing occupations entail; (c) the relative amounts of horizontal and vertical mobility which are realistically possible; (d) the very wide differences in standards of performance; (e) the highly different weights placed on such norms and values as achievement and ambition. (p. 163)

If one includes among these variables a second set of intervening variables such as labor policies, technological differences, unionization, geographical and cultural differences in the labor force, and inter- and intrapersonality differences, one can see how the simple cause-and-effect mode of explanation can be exceedingly incomplete. Thus, it is not surprising that in the abundance of research devoted to job satisfaction, inconsistent findings tend to be the rule rather than the exception (cf. Herzberg, Mauser, & Snyderman, 1959).

As suggested above, the behavioral/causal mode of explanation is conducive to faulty thinking. This view is confirmed by what Chein

(1947) refers to as the "ahistorical form" prevalent in its research methodology, referring to the fact that these theories have no past or future. Also, studies indicate that the behavioral/causal mode tends to lose sight of individual workers. Because this mode tends to be exclusively psychometric,[2] with interest focused on statistical relationships, one can assume quite reasonably that different employees could get the same "score" on a measure for quite different reasons (Neff, 1977). This type of inadequate explanation is common with the use of any performance appraisal instrument.

According to Jahoda (1982), experimental social scientists have helped uncover how some parts of us operate, (e.g., memory and perception), but as long as they try to emulate the *physical* sciences they will inadequately explain human behavior. Rigid adherence to the behavioral/causal mode of explanation rules out social dimensions and much about people's experience. These experimenters have yet to create an experimental study that examines the whole person, as well as the dynamic processes that underlie behaviors, making the person alive, active, and unique. By excluding the unconscious processes of mentation, the experiences that form the foundation for all behaviors are excluded. Unconscious processes are the center from which one can study and develop a general theory about the relationship between the person and his/her environment. To be able to engage in this type of investigation requires a different paradigm of thinking, conceptualizing, and perceiving.

We can now move on to the mode of explanation used by the psychoanalytic consultant, which is similar to the "conditional" mode (Lewin, 1947), the "conditional-genetic" mode (Chein, 1947), and the "clinical-inference" mode (Klein, 1976). This mode, which borrows heavily from the others, is referred to as the "analytic-inference" mode, because of its differences and the fact that it is primarily created to engage in the work of consulting to organizations.

ANALYTIC INFERENCE

In this mode, events are explained in terms of their coexisting conditions. A condition refers to those circumstances that determine the occurrence or nonoccurrence of events, as well as the manner of their occurrence. To see this more clearly, it is helpful to return to the issue of job satisfaction. Earlier we saw how the behavioral/causal mode of

[2]Psychometrics refers to the measurement of mental capacities such as personality assessment, evaluation of intelligence, aptitude testing, and employment testing.

explanation helped to investigate job satisfaction. Here we will see how job satisfaction can be explored and explained using analysis and inference.[3]

When one considers job satisfaction, one begins with the acknowledgement that work arouses feelings and emotions, as well as requiring aptitudes and skills. To understand job satisfaction from this mode requires an understanding of the events that preceded the assessment of job satisfaction. The historical background of the employee may reveal conditions that led to a particular job satisfaction measure. Suppose an employee has parents who were both highly respected professionals. This employee did not complete his schooling and accepted employment considered by his parents as a sign of academic and career failure.

If one were to measure job satisfaction based on job characteristics, one would obtain a false reading because of the antecedent conditions of this particular employee. It is reasonable to assume that issues related to professional identity, self-esteem, authority, mutual respect, and personality variables would have a significant impact on any job satisfaction score.

As a psychoanalytic construct, job satisfaction does not spring forth instantaneously as a fully developed subject for testing. It is the end result of a developmental process and life experiences. Consequently, the analytic-inference mode maintains the view that the past functions in the present. The study of job satisfaction must follow the premise that past occurrences establish something about the very nature of the present employment situation. The past is understood in two ways. First, the past pertains to "expectations," that have been engendered in the employee in the course of his life experiences, perhaps as a set of expectations. These expectations are themselves end results of the progressive modification that the employee has experienced over time through his/her "normal" or "traumatic" developmental processes.

Second, while these expectations perpetuate the past, they derive their meaning only in relation to present-day realities (job satisfaction). Therefore, they operate as present, not as past, but it is the expectations rather than the situations from the past from which they are derived that are dramatically effective in conditioning present behaviors and attitudes toward the job. For example, to see low

[3]A word of caution: The major complaint against the analytic-inference mode is that it tends to be reductionistic. Later on the value of the utility of reductionism within this mode is explained. For present purposes, assume that reductionism is embedded within this mode, and it is the very nature of reductionism that facilitates clarity of the phenomena being explored.

morale, absenteeism, worker unrest, and even sabotage as being pertinent only to the past is to miss their dynamic role in the present. To assume that an employee is depressed or happy because of some job characteristic is to miss the person's dynamic past.

Those who use the paradigm of the behavioral/causal mode, reject this way of studying job satisfaction. They claim that to engage in such a "clinical" investigation places the meaning of the data in the hands of the investigator. The major problem here is that the investigator is "loaded up" with values. Additionally, these researchers claim that the power of the behavioral/causal mode lies in its value-free methodology, or at the very least, strong attempts in that direction. On the other hand, they claim that the analytic-inference mode moves in the opposite direction, and that the analytic-inference mode uses a small number of subjects, often using only a single case or subject (an N of one). This is further evidence of its "unscientific" nature.

Researchers base their complaints against analytic inference on the philosophy of logical positivism. They are against analytic inferences because of the lack of empirical evidence and the use of the sometimes ambiguous logic and the unclear universal language in their analysis of phenomena. Furthermore, they claim that their science is neutral, value-free, and containing universal language, and argue that only their mode of explanation is confirmable because their statements correspond to facts, and that only these facts, obtained by using the behavioral/causal mode, can be compatible or incompatible with generalization (Edelson, 1984). However, when studying something as complex as the employee in the organization, to hold to the methodological truths as defined by those who propose the behavioral/causal mode assumes that a general theory does in fact exist. But no such theory exists. Without a general theory of the person at work, or the workplace, neutrality, value-free research, and rigid methodology will actually be constraining factors in the development of a theory. As stated before, the behaviorist, sociologist, anthropologist, political scientist, and psychoanalyst will look at the workplace and will all report different findings. They all see the workplace and the employee within it from their own theoretical orientation. Kuhn comes close to suggesting that the so-called progressive accumulation of truth that the scientific community holds so dear may, in itself, be something of an illusion, and the so-called scientific method may be a myth (Roszak, 1969).

How one sees things is not only a function of the discipline adhered to, or the mode of explanation adopted; it is a function of one's cognitive structures. Kuhn (1965) called them paradigms, Husserl (1965) called them referential structures, and Kohut (1971) called them idiosyncratic thematic templates. All agree that these structures or paradigms are the preconditions for determining how to make sense of what we see. From this perspective, analytic inference is a way of seeing.

Analytic inference is similar to Sherwood's (1969) concept of "separate domain." He says that explanations of human behavior belong to a domain of explanation separate from the explanation of "nonhuman phenomena." This position has been stated by contemporary psychoanalytic theorists such as Grunbaum (1977), Klein (1976), Schafer (1976), and Holt (1976), among others. They collectively claim that analytic inference is concerned not with the question *how*, but with the question *why*, and in asking this question, analytic inference seeks an explanation of behavior in terms of its meaning and intention. It is suggested that analtyic inference not be judged by the dictates of "normal science" but by the precision [with] which it is defined, its systematic relevance, and by the quality of issues it raises for future thought and investigation.

THE WORK OF ANALYTIC INFERENCE IN CONSULTING TO THE ORGANIZATION

In analytic inference, the structure used for analysis is a cognitive set that integrates psychoanalytic theory, organizational/management theory, and self-knowledge to gain a complete understanding of the setting and the individual's relationship to it. The following is a brief review of this mode of explanation as it is applied to consulting practice.

Similar to the clinical setting, when engaging in the analysis of the organization, the psychoanalyst uses not only knowledge of the theory and practice from other disciplines but knowledge experienced from within. This requires an intuitive understanding of the organization and the events within it. This intuitive knowledge is what Polanyi (1958) calls "tacit knowing," that which the analyst feels, which can never be fully articulated but which is crucial to a thorough psychoanalytic investigation. This method of investigation is just as crucial to "scientific" knowledge as are facts and laws. To put this aspect of analytic inference into a simpler conceptual form, it is nothing more than drawing from that vast reservoir of material all that one knows but cannot tell. This is precisely why it is not an easy task and it is usually avoided, for one is often constrained by one's own inhibitions, biases, and defenses which limit the ability to see or feel. In addition, one often does not trust what is seen or felt, and thus relies on others and so-called more objective things to help deal comfortably with the unknown.

It is argued that to follow the dictates of personal knowledge is far superior to following the methodologies of "normal science." In applied research such as consulting, the results, the prescription, or the intervention is the result of a dynamic process between the consultant and the consultee(s). To be in a position to adequately offer a helping service that is intent on obtaining a knowledge of the other (the consultee(s) and the organization) requires sufficient indwelling, tacit knowing, and personal knowledge. Furthermore, to enter the domain of another's life space, another living system (the organization), requires a degree of personal involvement that demands that the consultant make an effort to experience values, empathy, freedoms, democracy, dignity, and self-worth as they relate to oneself and all human beings. In essence, this is the polarity between those who adhere to a behavioral/causal mode of explanation and those who adopt analytic inference. Tomkins (1965) describes this polarity when he suggests:

> Let us now briefly examine some general features of what I regard as the basic ideological polarity in Western thought. In the foundations of law, or math, or science, or art, or child rearing, theorists who address themselves to one another of these domains appear polarized on the same issues. The issue constitutes a polarity from the extreme left through a middle of the road position to the extreme right wing position. The issues are simple enough. Is man the measure, an end in himself, an active, creative, thinking, desiring, loving force in nature. Or must man realize himself, attain full status only through struggles toward, participation in, conformity to a norm, a measure, an ideal essence basically prior to and independent of man? . . . When man has thought about man he has either glorified himself or derogated himself. He has judged himself to be inherently good or basically evil, to be the source of all values or to be worthless. (p. 79)

Analytic inference, while relying on data, does not try to "objectify" the investigator, and the psychoanalyst as an investigator applies psychoanalytic theory by becoming an instrument by which to see and assess the social reality of the workplace. This is accomplished by basing the psychoanalytic work on a model of research and intervention that assumes the existence of an experiencing "ego." This "ego" sphere contains the structure for perceiving social reality, and this structure provides all the conceivable perceptions of an external object by performing a mental synthesis. But the ego does not function as a camera that focuses on an object. It is guided by perception, remembering, and imaging, along with knowledge and experience. Of critical importance is the use of imaging, especially given the complexities of organizational life.

Under exceedingly complex conditions, such as the organization, where variables that influence behavior can be multiple and continuously change over time, the use of imaging can be helpful in defining the nature of what is to be studied and how situational conditions create an influence.

THE PROCESS OF IMAGING

Imaging is considered by Freud and others to be that region between hallucination and perception, dreaming, and reasoning. It is within this region that the psychoanalyst attempts to decipher the story or events that form the basis for a particular set of behaviors. It is here where the psychoanalyst begins the process of collecting data for verification of a variety of hunches and/or assumptions about the organization, and starts to formulate a conceptualization of the change process. Perceptually, things are imagined and a word is attached. Imaging is a primary process that relies on associations or connections that are guided by affects. These affects or feelings are the cornerstone of the complicated process that the psychoanalyst seeks to unfold. This process is accomplished by the cognitive evolution of the unconscious processes that underlie and influence all affects that are touched on when associations are triggered by a thought or perception. The ego, in its perception of external reality, is influenced by unconscious processes that respond to the associations that perceptions trigger. The ego then defends against or provides avenues for perception that will satisfy affects contained within the ego state. Modes of imaging result from the interplay between the ego (the self system) and affects. Thus the ego balances and maintains a state of affects by gratifying unconscious wishes as well as the demands of social reality.

Wolhiem (1974), using the following example, presents a model of perception that explains the essence of the analytic-inference mode. The analyst is examining the relationship between a superior and a subordinate. The analyst finds that his/her perception of their relationship is guided by his/her experience of two affective states that are triggered: empathy and sympathy. The analyst discovers from introspection that when he/she experiences the affect of empathy in others, it is a function of the anxiety observed in the relationship. When the superior fears, the subordinate fears, or perhaps when the superior is courageous, the subordinate is courageous. On the other hand, when the analyst experiences the affect of sympathy, he/she is influenced by the following observations: When the superior fears, the subordinate pities, or when the superior is courageous, the subordinate admires. It follows that the affects experienced by the consultant and the images he/she creates alter the perception of what is observed. The ego, which contains these affective states, may shift over time to affects ranging from pity to envy, from admiration to disgust, from lust to rage, and so on, and these modes of affect are influenced by the perceiver's internal state (the unconscious).

The ability to introspect, to attach a word to an affect, is the beginning of the investigation of the full nature of whether the person is perceiving or misperceiving reality; that is, whether one's internal state is influencing one's perceptions. Engaging in reflection then allows one to move on to the next stage, where one's perceptions will either be confirmed or disconfirmed by gathering additional data. Consequently, when obtaining data through the analytic-inference mode, the psychoanalytic consultant is primarily concerned with how data impinge upon his/her emotional and mental state. The following is an example of how one engages in this form of analysis.

At a meeting, we experience emotional pain. We begin to feel that the meeting is a dreadful place and our mind begins to wander. We are having an unpleasant experience, but this mere fact is an unproductive explanation unless we link it with other facts. That is, we need to explore why we are having an unpleasant experience. We may begin the process of exploration by asking questions: Is the room too hot? Is the leader degrading or belligerent? Are the other people in the room hostile or competitive? Essentially, to begin this process we ask the question, What is the nature of my unpleasantness? Am I anxious, am I needy, and if so what am I in need of? We begin to make connections, and if we can engage in the analysis with uninhibited perception, we may be able to ferret out the nature of our discomfort.

If a correct and satisfying analysis is to take place, two things must occur. First, one must stabilize the meaning of one's pain by taking it out of the context of subjective experience through the establishment of the vicissitudes of feeling pain. Second, must seek logical connections between the concept of the group meeting contributing to the pain and other concepts outside the group meeting that could also possibly contribute to one's present state. Once this is accomplished, one begins the process of "operationalizing" the relationship or connection between one's feeling state and the activities within and without the group meeting. As suggested above, accomplishment of this task can occur only through an analysis or a search for deep-seated meaning, which can be obtained through both analysis and interpretation of historical data. From this analysis and interpretation one creates a hypothesis of unconscious motives contributing to one's pain.

To conceptualize this work of the psychoanalytic consultant another way, the consultant relies on the nonrepresentational domain to see and understand behavior. In the nonrepresentational domain, representational data are utilized, but they are used in a different manner. First, meaning is attributed to data by using the self as an instrument, and second, from what is observed, inferences are made about characteristics of the person in the organization.

Rogers (1980) makes a distinction between the representational and the nonrepresentational domain with the following example. When a cat meows in a way that means something such as, "I want you to give me milk," the expression is representational, but if one considers that the cat may be expressing the relationship of dependency, the cat may be saying, "mama, mama," the expression becomes nonrepresentational or symbolic. To understand the meaning of behaviors within the nonrepresentational domain requires interpretative skills and interpretative effort.

According to Edleson (1984), a psychoanalytic interpretation is a hypothesis about the situation under investigation. Interpretation in the field of consulting follows the accumulation of facts (data and reports from participants) used in conjunction with what is symbolically represented in the organization. Symbolic representation would be those words, actions, ceremonies, or artifacts that are used by the organization and its members as a shared experience. The use of symbol as metaphor in psychoanalytic investigation allows the investigator to interpret that which bonds or stabilizes a group or a collective goal-directed effort. If change is to occur, the consultant must be able to understand the dynamic forces that hold the employees to their work. Beginning with an interpretation of the metaphor or symbol allows the consultant greater access to these dynamics and any resistance that occurs as the process of change evolves. Of significance in this process is the ability of the consultant to interpret metaphor.

INTERPRETATION OF METAPHOR

In the organization, the metaphor is frequently used to create a sense of community or to rally this community around some issue or goal.

The metaphor is a method of communication that only has power if its meaning is shared. Metaphors, or for that matter, all organization-al symbols either expressed as images or words, are a way of connect-ing the person with the experience of being in the group. According to Wilson and Weinstein (in press), at the juncture of language and thought is the concept of word meaning, a key concept in conducting an analysis of the mind. From this perspective, the metaphor provides rich figurative data to analyze conscious ideas and unconscious dy-namics which are stressed or suppressed through their use and organizing utility. This view is emphasized by Lakoff and Johnson (1980), who suggest that one's engagement and interaction with the world are inherently metaphoric and who explain how levels of ubiquitous metaphoric construction support the capacity to order, grasp, and make sense of reality.

Sharpe (1950) considers the activity of interpreting metaphor as requiring characteristics associated with poetic diction, and following Milton's view, she suggests that interpretation of metaphor should be "simple, sensuous, and passionate for the poet's task is to com-municate experience, which includes sound along with the power of imagery which springs from unconscious sources" (p. 168). According to Sharpe (1950), the simplest of all poetic devices used in interpreta-tion is the simile. This is the equation of two dissimilar things by means of a common attribute. She puts forth the following as an example of how a metaphor is formed: "[T]he plough turns up the land as the ship furrows the sea." When the words "like" or "as" are omitted, the simile becomes a metaphor and it is read, "The ship ploughs the sea."

Consider the following connection of the phrase most associated with IBM, "big blue." The word "big" is an expression of a wish embedded in the early philosophy of the founder, Thomas Watson, to be big, to grow. This wish is also captured in its name, beginning with the word "international." The name "big blue" thus becomes an expression of the wish to be as big as the sky. However, another view is included that is related to the nature of the relationship between the organization and its customers. This relationship is defined as one based on trust and a shared sense of values, beliefs, and expectations. "Blue" is now seen as associated with bigness, as is the sky, and with trust, as in "true blue." The color "blue" stimulates a number of additional association, such as "elitism," associated with "bluebloods," and "clean," associated with "clear blue water." These associations, which have different meanings to each person, culminate in the form of a collective image that is the basis for a "shared meaning," and if one places these associations together, one obtains a view of IBM, a picture of the company that was created by its founder and passed along to others. Thomas J. Watson Jr. (1963/1984), son of the founder of IBM, and one-time chairman of the board, describes this image in the following statement:

> The basic philosophy, spirit, and drive of an organization have far more to do with its relative achievements than do technological or economic resources, organizational structure, innovation, and timing. All things weigh heavily on success, but they are transcended by how people in the organization believe in its basic precepts and faithfully they carry them out. (p. 13)

Another system of beliefs is communicated through simple phrases by IBM such as "IBM means business." According to Deal and Kennedy (1982), this statement expresses quality, and it also lends credibility to the less formal metaphor of "big blue" by suggesting that IBM really means it. Change IBM to "I," and it becomes "I mean business." In organizations, the ability to create a culture for work and collaboration is a function of the organization's ability to use metaphors in a manner that will create a shared sense of meaning. Many theorists (e.g., Edelman, 1977; Hirsch, 1980/1984; Pondy, 1978, Ouchi, 1981b) suggest that the core values of the organization are communicated and understood through metaphors. As Siehl and Martin (1984) state:

> These core values define the basic philosophy or mission of the company. Sometimes the core values concern technical issues such as one which Ken Olson, the founder and president of Digital Equipment Corporation expresses as: "Our job is to make a good product. Growth is not our primary goal. After making good products, growth is the natural occurrence" (*Fortune,* April 23, 1979). Or they can be financial in nature, as is reflected in an underlying values of Data General: "We're in this business to make money. It just so happens that the computer business is the best way to do that. But if we could make more money selling rye bread, we would consider doing that" (Herb Richman in *Fortune,* April 23, 1979). Oftentimes the core values are humanistic and emphasize the people and customers of the organization. Values of this type include Dana Corporation's "Productivity through people," IBM's "IBM means service" and "Respect for the individual," DuPont's "Better things for better living through chemistry," and GE's "Progress is our most important product." (p. 228)

These metaphors convey an underlying belief system that binds employees together and often is a motivational force in determining why an employee joins a particular organization or departs after a period of unhappiness. Management generally proposes and popularizes a particular metaphor, and the employee's capacity to accept or reject a metaphor is generally a function of how "in step" or "out of step" this manager is with the values and beliefs of the employees; that is, the attitudes and values of a manager are expressed in his/her use of metaphors.

In everyday language, metaphors are frequently used to describe wishes and anxieties (affects) that are not understood and are beyond one's cognitive and perceptual threshold. These metaphors are referred to as "implied metaphors" and are used to describe the experiential world. The metaphor is a response to an internal state and helps to bind anxiety and discharge affects. This is accomplished when the metaphor establishes a relationship between internal experience and those things that are familiar and less complex. For example, words expressing mental and moral states are usually based on an analogy drawn between mind and body. Examples are "in my heart," "a striking thought," "up yours," "a wealth of knowledge," "food for thought," "a spotless character," "hot temper," "complete ass," or "real prick."

According to Sharpe (1950), these metaphors carry meanings of a secondary and primary nature. For example, a person says, "That boss is a real bitch." The secondary meaning, the meaning with the greatest universal appeal, focuses on the content of the message, that the boss is doing things to make the person unhappy. The primary meaning focuses on the content of the words used to describe the affective state, which would be found in the interpretation associated with the prohibited definition of the word "bitch," in this case having to do with its sexual nature. Bitch is associated with a female dog, capable of pregnancy, as one who has sinned and produces children in a careless manner, which is the result of impulsiveness. Returning to this boss, now he can be seen as impulsive, careless, and insensitive. Through an analysis of the metaphor, a clearer picture of the nature of the complaint emerges.

Frequently, the social context or social structure will define the parameters within which a metaphor may be used and understood. For example, in organizations, sports and machine metaphors are common. The function of the sports metaphor is to communicate affects associated with teamwork, aggression, and competition, as well as to articulate win–loss situations. However, if one considers the primary processes associated with sports metaphors, one finds that they are commonly used in connection with the wish to be loved and admired, to expose the phallus and thereby exclude women, as a way of gratifying unconscious homosexual wishes, or as an expression of some oedipal conflict. When the organization is described using the metaphor of a machine, on a secondary or concrete level it is an expression of the organization as a place that is well lubricated, efficient, passionless, and a human-less object. However, the primary processes suggest an experience of being an appendage to the machine, an expression of feelings associated with being controlled and dependent. The affects associated with this metaphor create an analogy to that of Harlow's (1972) monkey, who was raised in a cage with a "mother" constructed of wire.

Consider slogans and sayings attributed to professions. For example, in a New York City public school the following is carved in granite above a doorway, "Teachers Are Born Not Made." This statement suggests an occupation with a higher calling and employees who wish to see themselves as very different from others. The slogan serves to create a shared experience, that all who teach have a gift, they are special and "blessed." From this perspective, the slogan is an expression of the wish to be protected by this "higher authority," as one engages in an occupation where failure is high and must be rationalized if one is to continue.

To analyze a metaphor requires reaching into the primary meaning of the words and symbols used, and the context in which they are used. The primary meaning is considered an expression of a collective wish, the organization's "storehouse" of experiences, myths, values, and beliefs. In addition to expressing a wish, these metaphors are used to establish a framework for containing anxiety associated with events in the past, present, and future. The metaphor or symbol condenses these events. For example, one phrase can capture several mental images. While these images may vary from employee to employee, over time they become institutionalized, as employees find utility in the form of a shared experience. Team spirit may be aroused if a chosen metaphor expresses secondary and primary mental processes. These metaphors are most effective if they are able to express primary processes associated with our very existence, namely, our bodies, life, death, and procreation. Of particular relevance is the expression of power, life force, and conquest through the use of metaphors and symbols representing sexual content. The indirect expression of sexual metaphors and symbols is apparent in organizations in which the nature of the task involves libidinal arousal.

Symbols have long been associated with work. Consider the anvil sign for the blacksmith, the shoe for the cobbler, and the balanced scales for the attorney. Almost all organizations have symbols, often called logos, that convey to the outside world, through the processes of condensation and displacement, the covert mental life of their collective efforts. The symbol is effective if it is experienced as an accurate representation of the members' attachment to the organization on an unconscious level. If the symbol is accurate, it will convey the meaning associated with the members' shared experience, and result in increased cohesion. Trice and Beyer (1984) confirm this view when they state:

> The consolidation and interdependence of cultural forms is particularly evident in rites and ceremonial which combine various forms of cultural expression within coherent cultural events with well-demarcated beginnings and ends. In performing the activities of a rite or ceremonial, people make use of other cultural forms—certain customary language, gestures, ritualized behaviors, artifacts . . . symbols, and settings—to heighten the expression of shared meanings appropriate to the occasion. . . . (p. 654)

An analysis of the events and their contents provides interpretation of the strength of the shared meaning, the dominant values in the organization, and the dynamics that represent unconscious processes.

Another method of analyzing the organization is through interpretation of the stories that are reported by the organization's members and its customers. Martin, Feldman, Hatch, and Sitkin (1983) have identified several themes from an analysis of organizational stories:

1. What happens when a superior breaks a rule and is caught by a subordinate;
2. How a "small person" climbs to the "top";
3. Incidents that confirm whether a superior is "human" or "inhuman";
4. Treatment of an employee who was fired or disposed of in some fashion;
5. How a superior responds when a subordinate makes an error;
6. How a superior deals with hindrances; and
7. How a company helps or fails to assist employees who are in trouble.

Within the activities associated with work, or within the structure of a formal organization, repression of unconscious wishes and motivations is required. The metaphor, symbol, or story has utility in that it allows for the release of that which is repressed in an indirect and socially acceptable manner, as derivatives. Or the metaphor or story may serve a defensive purpose in helping the employee and the group cope with some of the fears and anxieties associated with the work.

INTERPRETATION AND CHANGE

The analytic-inference mode of explanation is above all else the explanation of motives or motivation. According to Chein (1972), "A motive is any directed act that requires a subordinate expediting act to be included in it" (p. 79). (It is the subordinate expediting act that underlies the motive. These are impelling conditions, a conscious or unconscious wish or desire and are of concern to the psychoanalyst.) To carry this further, for every behavior there must be at least one unconscious or preconscious behavior. A motive (a wish, desire, anger, love, sex) is not a unidimensional concept. It is multidimensional, and this is true even for the simplest motive. To gain access to knowledge of a motive requires an identification of one's motivational state and the associations connected to this motivational state, namely, that which influences it. This requires the detection of bits of information.

For example, a consultant reported what he considered to be a major failure in his attempts to intervene in a small organization that was experiencing conflict. During the initial consultation with 20 staff members, resistance toward the intervention was apparent. Staff members arrived late for meetings and during the meetings appeared disinterested. The consultant interpreted their resistance by offering the following statement, "You don't want to be here because you feel that I'm here to make or force you to be friends and to like each other. This is not my intention. I don't feel that you need to be friends at the place you work, and I don't even know if I feel that likability is necessary for a group of people to work together." The staff laughed and their anxiety was immediately reduced.

This interpretation provided insight, knowledge, and another way of thinking about work, relationships, and the organization. But most important, it reduced the potential of the consultant's becoming the target of massive projections and displacements having to do with the staff's fear and anxiety. The interpretation was directed at those defenses employed to restrict experience. The interpretation, as all interpretations must do if they are to precipitate change, altered an aspect of the consultee's perceptual frame; that is, it altered the organized entities of the experiencing structure of the consultee's mind. This reorganizing of experience eventually creates new structures, which then will alter the perceptual structure. When this occurs, the consultee's way of perceiving reality will be changed in the sense that he/she will never perceive it exactly as he/she once did.

There is one question that must be raised and answered at this point: Can an intervention in an organization change psychic structure? If one assumes that a person's actions are a function of his/her experience, then all one can say is that experience has changed. However, if one assumes that the contents of experience are generated by its representational structure (Schwartz, 1989), one may not need to answer the question whether the contents of structure have been changed. However, one can conclude that the attitudes toward these contents have changed, that they have become more realistic and mature. Interpretation ought to reduce defenses and open the possibility to a new way of thinking and feeling or judging experience, actions, and needs. This type of intervention is detailed in the consultation described in Chapter 11.

The key aspect of change that differentiates psychoanalytic consulting from other types of consulting is that through interpretation and the attainment of insight, "structural change" results. The structure that changes is psychic structure. Psychic structure, as are all structures of mentation, is a conceptual term. Intellectually, structure is a post hoc explanatory concept. It is not directly observed but inferred. How to make inferences about structure is a much debated issue, almost as hotly debated as the issue of what a structure actually is. Rangell (1955), in his examination of structures, offers Freud's (1923/1961) definition of psychic structure as clusters of functions. To follow this definition allows the psychoanalytic consultant to believe that all human structures can be investigated, including organizational structures. Additionally, Rangell (1955) refers to the definition of Rapaport and Gill (1959), that structures are "configurations that allow a slow rate of change" (p. 803). Following this definition, the consultant sees psychic structure as in a continuous flux process, and inferences are then made about the process and rate of change of structure.

If structures are defined in these two ways, one can then make distinctions about the types of structures that exist in the organization. As stated previously, it is commonly understood that organizations have two major categories of structures: formal and informal. Formal structures are characterized by the organizational chart, including policies, rules, specializations, configurations, departments, and structures within departments. Those who focus on informal structures focus on relationships, culture, and sociopsychological attributes. All these structures have at their base a psychic structure that forms the foundation for the structure and its character.

When making inferences about psychic structure, Rapaport and Gill (1959) maintain that the psychic structure is significantly different from other structures because it resists change and employs defensive measures to maintain its steady state. In disagreement with

Rapaport and Gill, it is not a question of either/or; it is a matter of degree. When compared to other structures, the psychic structure has a significantly stronger degree of resistance and defense against change. Change will then occur when these defenses and resistances, once established to protect, are no longer needed to the same degree, and the employees can now function with a greater degree of choice. They are no longer constricted by old and dysfunctional defenses.

To put it another way, behavior can be modified only through an alteration in the cluster of functions. Thus psychoanalytic change in the activity of organizational consulting is thought of as an enlargement of conscious memories of the past where (1) the history of the organization is understood in the context of the history of the symptom under investigation, (2) the members of the organization experience less anxiety about their work and their relationships and their destiny, (3) the members of the organization take collective responsibility for the problem(s) and work toward resolution in a manner that optimizes the organization's efficiency and effectiveness, and finally (4) those who are collectively involved in the work improve their self-esteem through a clearer understanding of the boundaries between the self and environment. Psychoanalytic change occurs as a result of an improved differentiation between self and others, an increased capacity to function autonomously, the experience of less anxiety when faced with ambiguity, and an increased capacity to move away from the oppression of judgment, evaluation, and subordination, which will eventually permit employees to make decisions with a greater sense of dignity and freedom.

PART II

APPLICATION

CHAPTER 6

Review of Current Methods of Consultation

What everybody echoes or in silence passes by as true today, may turn out to be a falsehood tomorrow, mere smoke of opinion, which some had trusted for a cloud that would sprinkle fertilizing rain on their fields.

—HENRY DAVID THOREAU

In this chapter, existing consultation methods have been isolated. Articulating these methods has presented problems in differentiation; for example, some methods articulate the entire consultative process with clarity, while others leave large gaps when explaining what they actually do. Still others only vaguely present their techniques, philosophy, interventions, and the nature of the consultant–consultee relationship.

WHY REVIEW METHODS?

It is important to discuss why a review of current methods of consultation is necessary. For the purposes of this book, consultation is defined as the activity of one or more persons from outside the organization who are called in to change or add to the efficiency or effectiveness of the client's system. This activity may include changing the organization's structure, goals, and personnel and/or the behavioral patterns of its employees. Consulting is considered an interpersonal event; that is, it is two systems meeting to accomplish a given task. The ability to accomplish this task is a function of the nature of the relationship established between these two systems. Consultants approach this relationship in varied ways. Thus, a review of methods used by consultation theorists and practitioners permits a comparative analysis and increases understanding of the entire consultative process.

A model of consultation, similar to models of planned change, offers the change agent a framework or an outline to follow. A consultant engaging in a consultation activity may be entering an unfamiliar and complex system of formal and informal social arrangements. Because of the complexity of the system, and perhaps naivete about the focal organization, the consultant is often at a disadvantage when attempting to understand the presenting problem, or to overcome the resistance that occurs when the potential or actual change process is begun. The consultant faces many different questions and issues at the onset of a consultation. For example, why was the consultation requested? Whose interests will the consultation serve? What is the task of the consultation? What will be the primary focus of the consultation? With whom will the consultant meet? When? Where? How long? What will be the nature of the contract be? With whom, and with whose approval? Should the consultant do this consultation under these conditions and within this situation? Finally, when the consultant considers the social, psychological, economic, and political factors that may have influenced the request for a consultant, the complexity of these questions increases and a number of other questions emerge. Consider the process of entering the organization.

CROSSING THE BOUNDARY INTO THE ORGANIZATION

Many of the behavioral patterns and dysfunctions already established in the organization will be "played out" or replicated as the consultant enters. At this point the subjective state of the consultant becomes valuable in determining just how the system is responding, and how the system will respond at a later time to the consultant's work. In addition, the consultant, as an object entering the system, is able to make subjective observations according to how he/she is treated as an intervening object. From his/her internal or introspective perception, the consultant will see how the system manages its boundaries, and how it treats other objects as they cross the boundaries. The entry process is crucial for another reason. It is during this period that the consultant can begin to answer the following questions. Does this situation actually merit a consultation? Can the consultant be effective in this situation? Are the reasons given by management for requesting a consultation accurate? Is management using the consultant for some purpose that is beyond the consultant's immediate awareness? The critical issue facing the entering consultant is how to think about this complicated social system called an organization, with its complex and often hidden problems. The consultant finds refuge in the acquisition of a methodology for doing the work. To acquire an accurate perception of the relevant issues, the consultant constructs a role as a device to reduce "noise." Just as the research scientist develops and follows a method of inquiry, and the clinician develops or follows a method of diagnosis and treatment, the consultant uses a method for understanding the problems, gathering data, making a diagnosis, and conducting an intervention. For this reason, the student of organizational consultation should be able to study and then compare and contrast existing methods.

There is an additional reason for presenting various consultative methods. If these methods and their unique comparative elements can be isolated, they may then be contrasted, quantified, and evaluated.

What follows is an attempt to glean from the existing literature the major methodologies used in current practice. From this review, the reader should obtain adequate knowledge of the conceptual and theoretical underpinnings that help to guide experienced consultants.

METHODS OF CONSULTATION

Nine methods of consultation are discussed: organizational development consultation, mental health consultation, consulcube, process consultation, technical consultation, feedback consultation, organizing consultation, management consultation, and transformation consultation. Other methods of consultation may exist, and it is possible that the nine methods discussed here do not totally encompass the methods most commonly used by practitioners. Further complicating the issue is that experienced consultants claim that they often use their own individual methods. Furthermore, they use what works, never relying on any one method.

DEVELOPMENT OF MODELS OF CONSULTATION

Before discussing the actual methods defined, it is important to clarify the thinking used in the development of these models, and the differentiating characteristics used to distinguish one model from another.

For our purposes, a model is defined as the creation of a set of constructs that represents a somewhat simplified version to the viewer of a system. The intention of these models is to facilitate comprehension of a consultative style by limiting the amount of extraneous variables found within the entire consultative process.

Models are essentially viewed as closed logical systems with defining parameters that can be specified a priori. Specifications of models are composed of postulates and axioms concerning the global consultative process. This process has the disadvantage of increasing the risk of overlapping between methods, which increases the possibility that some models may contain characteristics found in others and vice versa. Therefore, the models can be viewed as devices whereby sources of variation within each are reduced by fitting the global or abstract dimensions into a simplified set of postulates or axioms.

The following characteristics were chosen not only because they assisted in model structuring, but also because they facilitated a more complete differentiation. They were chosen on the basis of three criteria: (1) the significance attributed to them by consultants and writers about the field of organizational consultation, (2) their significance in facilitating a delineation among models of consultation, and (3) their power in isolating unique aspects and common patterns among models.

CHARACTERISTICS USED IN DIFFERENTIATING MODELS

Defining characteristics begins by asking the following question: What is the main thrust of the consultative effort? Given that the consultant is actively engaged in a complex project, what will the consultant tend to concentrate on? What will the consultant see as important? Seven characteristics are used to differentiate models, and each of these characteristics identifies what is unique about the method under study.

Focus

What population or setting is most appropriate for this model of consultation? Does the model emphasize one setting with a single population or is it available to many differing settings and populations? Either the emphasis of a target can be defined explicitly through the stated focus or definition of apparent successes or implicitly through the language used, the techniques or training, and the expertise required of the consultant.

Definition of Consultation

Most models of consultation present an explicit definition of consultation. This definition indicates in a general manner the mission of the consultative enterprise, its expected outcomes, and the consultant's view of him/herself as a change agent.

Assumptions Underlying the Effort

Where, or with whom, in the organization is the consultant most interested in working? What are the theoretical and philosophical beliefs that make up the underpinnings of the thinking the consultant brings to the enterprise?

Roles

Models can be differentiated according to the consultant's self-perception as a change agent. The consultant's professional identity is a significant factor that contributes to the definition of other roles. In addition, "colleagueship" (i.e., relationships with other groups and associations) also facilitates role definition. Role definition is important because it can assist the consultant in the choice of an appropriate model of consultation based on prior training, education, and experience.

The client is also required to assume a role during the consultative process. The kind of role expected of a client differs depending on the model of consultation.

Objectives

This area differentiates models with respect to their intent, that is, what the intervention is expected to achieve.

Entry

This characteristic is vital in differentiating models. The amount of attention paid to the entry process varies among models, as does the style of negotiating one's entry.

Key Intervention Techniques

The type of methodology the consultant follows is helpful in differentiating intervention techniques. The techniques used also include the nature and the quantity of units of subsystems the consultant prefers to work with, as well as how the consultant actually brings about that change.

ORGANIZATIONAL DEVELOPMENT CONSULTATION

Organizational development consultation (ODC) is the most popular model of consulting used today. It is a type of consultation proposed by Steele (1969a), Argyris (1964, 1970), and others associated with National Training Labs (NTL). The aim of ODC is to improve the internal climate of the organization. This is accomplished by increasing the staff's ability to solve problems and make decisions by concentrating on the human variables that both impede and facilitate problem solving, decision making, and most important, change. In addition, ODC diagnoses structural patterns in the organization and applies social psychological principles to identify covert resistance to change.

Organizational development (OD) consultants define consultation as a complex educational strategy intended to change beliefs, task definitions, attitudes, values, and structure of the organization so that the organization will be able to adapt to change with minimal stress.

OD consulting is viewed as a total organizational effort, but sometimes specific groups or subgroups within the organization can be targeted. Entry into the organization requires a strong commitment from management, because the consultant needs access to power points in the client's system (Argryis, 1970). These points of entry and receptiveness to change are the key to the eventual resolution of the client's difficulties.

OD consulting is a diffuse model, and it is rare to find two OD consultants who agree. The techniques and methods used in the consultation vary considerably. OD consultants employ techniques for diagnosis and interaction developed by individually and technologically oriented strategies of social intervention. These include T-groups, team training, grid lab, receiving feedback, one-to-one coaching, action research, confrontation, group meetings (Bechland, 1971), and reformulation of job descriptions (Hornstein, Bunk, Burke, Gindes, & Lewicki, 1971). In general, the most commonly used techniques are similar to those described by Rosenblum (1970) in his discussion of the training methods of consultation.

Under this model, the consultant meets regularly with employees of the organization in a group. He/she may approach the work as a case seminar, where each group member presents case material for discussion by the group, or he/she may follow a sensitivity group

(T-group) format where feelings concerning a particular case or fellow workers can be explored and understood. The intention of both of these very different approaches is to heighten sensitivity to the nature of the problem, consider a course of action, and obtain consensus on the nature of the problem. By focusing on the processes, dynamics, and issues that inhibit communications, the consultant hopes to open channels of communication and bring about an improvement in decision making, morale, interpersonal relations, job performance, and role definition.

OD consulting requires that the consultee in effect be trained. If the client is trained properly, an appropriate degree of openness will follow, which will maximize creativity and learning.

The OD consultant is generally a behavioral scientist or someone with human relations training, and his/her role during the consultation varies considerably.

The consultant's evaluation of a consultation effort is based on multiple criteria that include the quality of the effort as well as the speed of task accomplishment. In addition, an evaluation also considers both client satisfaction and consultant satisfaction in its analysis. Specific criteria for evaluation are lacking in this type of consultation and the evaluation is strongly pinned to the initial diagnosis and presenting problems.

OD consulting closely follows the position that change can occur only if two conditions are met. First, following the work of Kurt Lewin, a certain degree of tension is necessary before change can occur; that is, tension is required to promote a willingness among the employees to change. This is referred to as the unfreezing process. Second, change will only occur after a careful diagnosis is obtained. In establishing preconsultative work or preconditions for change, the OD consultant demonstrates to the employee that he/she appreciates the complexity of change. For example, the consultant recognizes that even if the "problem" is isolated, and general agreement exists that change is necessary, there will be several different ways to approach change or problem resolution (Dyer, 1982). This view and the potential problems associated with the change are openly communicated to the employees.

The OD consultant follows a matrix of two dimensions. One dimension is the unit of focus, which is the individual, the unit or department, or the intergroup or total organization. The second dimension is the location of intervention. This can be viewed as a systemwide issue, a technical issue, an administrative issue, or an external issue. The purpose of locating the intervention on both axes of the matrix is to reduce the complexity of the intervention and to isolate both the unit of change and the method employed in bringing about the desired change.

Of equal importance to the total consultative effort is the process of entering the organization. OD consultants generally negotiate entry through top management. They consider a strong commitment by top management to the consultative endeavor an essential ingredient if the consultant is faced with resistance to interventions (Lawrence & Lorsch, 1969).

An organizational development consultation's (ODC) attempt to bring about cognitive and attitudinal changes in employees. Identifying the type of change is the essential initial step in bringing about a change in the climate of the organization and helping the organization to better adapt itself to its environment and alter the behavioral patterns of its employees (Dalton & Lawrence, 1970).

Basically, clients are viewed by the OD consultant as holders of facts. The client is an active participant in the consultative endeavor and is expected to fulfill the role of student. This is especially true in the sensitivity training or group-oriented change approaches. In this role, clients are expected to learn new ways of thinking about and approaching problems, and it is hoped to change their entire cognitive process or conceptual framework regarding the change process.

The consultative method is an attempt to alter the client's way of solving problems by using the step-by-step process of information gathering, diagnosis, intervention, experimentation of new ways of working, and eventual reinforcement evolving from observing positive results (Lewin, 1947; Dalton & Lawrence, 1970; Tannenbaum, Kavcic, Rosner, Vianello, & Weisner, 1968). This is accomplished when the attitudes of key members of the organization are changed.

Change leaders are selected from the organization. Typically they are management personnel, but they can be lower-level employees, union leaders, and so on. The work of ODC is then to change the attitudes of these key members, who are expected to return to their organizations and in turn influence their peers.

Change in the key members is generally accomplished through their participation in a group experience led by the consultant. Diagnosis of the organization is an important part of the process, and diagnosis generally follows research and knowledge found in the social science literature. In the group experience, the key members are expected to present data, and these data are critically examined by all, including the consultant. Over time, firmly held assumptions are "given up" and constructive action is eventually taken. The consultant's aim is to clarify the organization's functioning and its problems through a combination of self-diagnosis, in the group, and organizational diagnosis using information obtained from meetings prior to the group and data presented during the group. The change evolves from the group experience where members, through intensive experiential group work, discuss their respective values, beliefs, and feelings about the organization, its problems, and the process of change.

Another method of the change process and intervention technique is proposed by Steele (1969). According to Steele (1969), the consultant may assume many roles to facilitate the change process. Steele (1969) identifies nine roles the consultant may assume. He suggests that the consultant is expected to have the flexibility and diagnostic knowledge to define which role is necessary to facilitate the desired change in the organization.

The rationale for this type of consultation is that organizational dysfunctions are believed to be caused by some internal or external tensions in the system, and that the system expends significant amounts of energy and resources to either reduce or defend against the tensions. The change consultant alters the system so that it can adequately respond to tensions and at the same time maintain the necessary resources to work on the task(s) of the organization.

Summary of Characteristics

Definition of Consultation

The ODC is a complex educational strategy intended to change beliefs, attitudes, values, and structures of the organization so the organization can better adapt to environmental turbulence and change.

Focus

The ODC concentrates on people-oriented variables within the organization.

Assumptions Underlying the Effort

The ODC is viewed as a process to unfreeze certain structures (Figure 6.1).

Roles

The consultant's role is to bring about change in the employees' cognitive and attitudinal system through learning and experiential

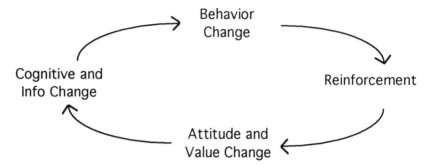

FIGURE 6.1. Model of organization interacting with its environment.

efforts. The client's role is to become a student or learner in structured anxiety-producing situations.

Objective

The objective of the ODC is to alter the dysfunctional behavioral patterns of employees.

Entry

The OD consultant's entry into the organization is negotiated through top management and requires strong management commitment.

Key Intervention Techniques

Intensive experiential involvement in groups led by consultants, as well as individual consultations, is the key intervention technique of ODCs.

MENTAL HEALTH CONSULTATION

A minor area in the field of consultation was pioneered by Caplan (1964, 1970) and his associates at Harvard University. Their approach focuses on the mental health of the individual by working with professionals in disciplines other than those generally associated with problems of mental health and mental illness. The objective is to increase the skills of non–mental health professionals in the diagnosis and treatment of disorders.

Any person or member of a group or profession that performs important "caretaking" services in a community is a proper target for mental health consultation, including pediatricians, nurses, social workers, teachers, physicians, police officers, and clergy (Spielberger, 1974). The consultative activity can be with individuals or with groups of people.

Mental health consultation may be defined as a process of interaction between specialist and client. The consultant assumes no direct responsibility for action based on his/her findings. The only responsibility the consultant has is to inform his/her clients. Rieman (1963) defines mental health consultation as "a helping process, an educational process and a growth process achieved through interpersonal relationships" (p. 85). Caplan's approach to mental health consultation assumes that the caretakers working within the community have initial contact with the clients experiencing stress or crises. Therefore, the thrust of consultation is to help the caretaker utilize mental health principles more effectively. This is expected to have an ameliorating effect on the numbers of clients who develop serious mental disorders.

The consultant is typically a specialist in the area of mental health and mental illness and is generally affiliated with a local group practice, hospital or university. Increased visibility heightens the probability that a consultant will be called on if a consultee needs assistance with a client. Professionals inside the realm of psychology, psychiatry, social work, and psychiatric nursing generally occupy the position of consultant.

This method of consultation suggests some ambiguity about who the client actually is. The consultative effort is centered on three areas of interaction: the person with the presenting problem, who is called the client, the third party (or caretaker), and the consultant. The client presents the problem to the caretaker and the caretaker presents the problem to the consultant, and this, according to Caplan (1970), places the caretaker in the role of consultee. It therefore seems reasonable to assume that the caretaker becomes the consultant's client.

The consultee is typically an active participant in the consultation process. Information, techniques, and knowledge are obtained by the consultee's clients. The consultee assumes the role of a student in the consultant–consultee relationship, and authority is defined by the nature of the work, which gives a specialized role to the consultant. The objective of mental health consultation is to bring about change or a situation that can facilitate treatment and/or prevent emotional problems or psychiatric disorders. This objective is accomplished by a variety of intervention techniques or approaches: consultee centered, individual-case oriented, and group-case or program oriented.

Using an orthopsychiatric model, the focus of mental health consultation is on primary prevention, to spot and correct those factors that contribute to emotional dysfunctioning. According to Caplan (1964), the goal of the mental health consultation is to reduce the number or rate of new cases of "disorder" or adjustment failure by focusing on a specified target person or population. This goal is accomplished by identifying and eventually offsetting disruptive conditions in the organization prior to the onset of actual dysfunctions. Bringing about change in the chosen target will, in turn, prevent dysfunctions in the larger group or system.

Prien, Jones, Miller, Gulkin, and Sutherland (1979) see the work of mental health consulting as operating under a psychological and psychiatric clinical model and offering the following services to organizations and their employees:

1. An appraisal of factors in the employee's personality that bear directly on the employee's fitness or unfitness for work. This appraisal is a part of both the employment interviewer's and the physician's preplacement examinations.
2. Recognition of neuropsychiatric conditions in their earliest manifestations, not only in applicants for work but also as these conditions appear any time after employment.
3. Evaluation of neuropsychiatric factors in posttraumatic conditions covered by worker's compensation.
4. Consultation on the placement, transfer, promotion, or progress of employees.
5. Assessment of undesirable job behaviors such as absenteeism, tardiness, drug and alcohol use, theft, sabotage, and so on.

The mental health consultant in the organization functions as therapist, mediator, researcher, and educator. In addition, the mental health consultant is expected to have knowledge of OD strategies, especially organizational diagnostic skills to equip the consultant to access the nature of a "destructive" organizational environment (Prien, Jones, Miller, Gulkin, & Sutherland, 1979).

Summary of Characterstics

Definition of Consultation

The mental health consultant adds to the knowledge of the consultee in areas of mental health. The consultant assumes no direct responsibility for action but contributes to an understanding of isolated mental health problems.

Focus

Mental health consultants interact with professionals in groups or individually.

Assumptions Underlying the Effort

The mental health consultation assists professionals to deal more effectively with individuals who manifest problems.

Roles

The consultant's role is one of a mental health professional trained in consultation techniques. The client is generally a professional who has opportunities for early detection of mental illness in non–mental health arenas.

Objectives

The objectives of the mental health consultation are to assist the client in diagnosing emotional problems and to bring about a change that will facilitate either treatment or prevention of emotional problems.

Entry

The mental health consultant's entry into the organization is sanctioned and invited and can be short or long term. Minimal effort is required in contract negotiation.

Key Intervention Techniques

The key interventions in mental health consultations are individual-case oriented, group-case and organizational oriented, and consultee centered to improve mental health. Diagnostic and referral techniques are also used.

CONSULCUBE

Consulcube methodology is of special interest to the beginning consultant. Of all the methods discussed, this one provides clear parameters for the consultation. Blake and Mouton (1976) have developed and patented a cube, called the consulcube, that gives the consultant an opportunity to isolate what he/she is to do, the issues in need of resolution, who to target for change, and the type of change desired. The consulcube is of considerable help to the student consulting for the first time as well as to the experienced consultant who feels unable to see a situation clearly because of either the complexity of the presenting problem or a consultee who makes issues ambiguous for the consultant.

Of the three ways in which a consultant can intervene, identifying the units of change is perhaps the most helpful. Often consultants fail to assess which unit of change will have the greatest impact on the organization. Identifying the units of change—individual, group, intergroup, organization, and larger social system—gives the consultant an opportunity to step back and assess who the consultee should be.

An integral part of Blake and Mouton's consulcube is their grid (1964). The grid utilizes a six-phase approach which contains the consulcube's theoretical basis. The first phase demonstrates how concern for the individual interacts with concern for production and a particular type of management style. The next four phases apply organizational development principles to work settings, and the final phase evaluates the first five phases as well as establishing new objectives. According to Blake and Mouton (1964), the grid not only focuses on making work relationships more effective but it helps give the manager a language system for describing his/her current managerial preferences.

The consulcube is not without its problems. It is based on the assumption that dysfunctions in the organization are cyclical and repeat themselves. While this may or may not be true, there is ample evidence to suggest that dysfunctions over time may take many different shapes and forms and may be acted out in a variety of ways. Attempting to diagnose these complex issues, and furthermore to categorize them into one of four focal-issue categories, is a major weakness of the consulcube. Even if one were to categorize an issue, it would be presumptuous to imply that the reasons for a given dysfunction lie exclusively within one category. For example, one can think of many morale/cohesion issues that are related to authority/power issues, which are related to unclear goals and objectives.

Summary of Characteristics

Definition of Consultation

The consulcube is designed to assist the client in solving problems that are believed to occur in cycles.

Focus

The consulcube is used mainly by business organizations but can be applied to service organizations.

Assumptions Underlying the Effort

Problems occur in organizations in repetitive ways. The consulcube consultation is expected to break the cycle.

Roles

The consulcube consultant's role varies from active to passive–receptive. The consulcube consultant client is usually a professional with human relations training.

Objectives

The consulcube method investigates cycles of behaviors. The aim of the consulcube method is to break the isolated cycle(s).

Entry

The consulcube consultant is always invited by top management, but it is unclear how initial contact is made.

Key Intervention Techniques

The consulcube method has five types of intervention techniques, four types of focal issues to be consulted to, and five units that can be changed.

PROCESS CONSULTATION

Process consultation (PC) works toward a joint diagnosis of a problem within a system by the consultant and client. PC, as developed by Schein (1969) and Bennis (1962, 1965), gives a psychological orientation to the consultative activity. They define PC as a set of activities on the part of the consultant that will facilitate the client's perception of, understanding of, and sensitivity to events that occur in the client's environment. The consultation focuses on developing a management appreciation for, and an ability to articulate, what is needed from the consultant. A major assumption of PC is that management has considerable difficulty in knowing what is wrong within a system. The objectives of the consultation are to assist management in seeing the problem, participating in the diagnosis, and generating a remedy so that eventually management will be able to identify problems and gain new insight into the operation of the organization.

The processes within a system that are typically identified by PC are work flow, interpersonal relations, and intergroup relations.

PC can be used for business, human services groups, and organizations. The consultant is invited by the system's leadership into the group or organization. However, entry procedures are unclear. The consultant enters a system without a clear sense of mission or need but does so with caution and openness to issues related to unclarity of objectives. The objectives of the consultation and the needs of the client become clear through discussion and joint diagnosis.

The key to PC lies not in finding a remedy to the system's ills but in sharpening the client's ability to assess difficulties within the system. PC assumes that no organization is perfect and that the best result a consultant can achieve is to help the organization diagnose its own problems. An expectation implicit in PC is that the client is the source of the answer or remedy for the diagnosed problems. Thus the consultant is generally a behavioral scientist skilled in interpersonal relations who can understand individual as well as system defenses, and who can promote an atmosphere of trust and openness in which difficulties can be explored.

In this model, the consultative process is in many ways similar to insight-oriented psychotherapy. Insight develops as a function of thorough mutual exploration of the consultant–client relationship, as in the work a therapist might engage in with a patient.

The client assumes an active role in the consultation. After discussing difficulties and alternative solutions, the client is expected to make the ultimate decision if one is necessary.

PC assumes that a successful consultation will increase the system's effectiveness in problem isolation and resolution. This depends on the client's ability to learn diagnostic skills. Given this assumption, an evaluation of the effectiveness of PC is concerned *not* with an increase in the system's effectiveness but with the client's ability to assess system problems. Client satisfaction is valued in PC, but client satisfaction may be a dubious evaluation factor because if the ability to assess a problem is of value rather than the resolution of that problem, then it is possible for the consultation to be a success and the problems still to persist. What is lacking in PC are definable intervention techniques for resolving system problems. The problems facing PC are similar to those facing insight-oriented psychotherapy, where the ultimate objective is not clearly defined symptom relief.

Bennis (1962, 1965) and Schein (1969) make no mention of a method for an evaluation of PC and discuss little concerning which characteristics or criteria determine a successful consultation. Schein describes PC as "a set of activities on the part of the consultant which helps the client to perceive, understand and act upon the process events which occur in the clients environment" (p. 147). Schein identifies process from six perspectives of major concern within the consultative endeavor: communication, roles and functions of work groups, group problem solving, group norms and growth, leadership and authority, and intergroup cooperation.

The process consultant may become involved in the problem-solving aspects of the consultation by offering suggestions, but more often the process consultant will work with the consultee in a manner that facilitates autonomous solutions. From this perspective, the process consultant enters the consultation with no preconceived ideas or plan of action. The consultee is expected to articulate the issues and work toward solutions with the consultant, assisting in a reflective or insight-orientated and nondirected role.

Summary of Characteristics

Definition of Consultation

The PC helps the client to perceive, understand and act on events that occur in the client's environment through the use of educational and clinical techniques.

Focus

The PC focuses on business and helping professionals in groups and organizations.

Assumptions Underlying the Effort

Managers need help in articulating a diagnosis and needs. The process consultant helps the organization diagnose itself. The client is expected to see problems and share in the diagnosis and in generating a remedy.

Roles

The process consultant is a behavioral scientist, expert in relationship development. He/she is able to remove defenses and promote trust.

The PC is similar to insight therapy. The client is active and involved and ultimately makes choices.

Objectives

The goals of PC are to identify processes (work flow, interpersonal, and intergroup relations) and increase effectiveness in problem finding by increasing diagnostic skills.

Entry

The process consultant enters through the top and is invited. He/she enters without a clear mission and proceeds with openness.

Key Intervention Techniques

PC promotes joint diagnosis and assessment and assists in sharpening the diagnostic skills of the client and in finding a remedy.

TECHNICAL CONSULTATION

This is a method of consultation concerned with the delivery of technical services. It is questionable as to whether these services can accurately be called consultations because they have one factor in common that differentiates them from the other methods described here. They provide a service that is related to the actual task of the organization itself; that is, they provide an explicit technical-assistance service for the purpose of filling a void in the organization. The intention of technical-service consultations is not to mobilize the resources of the organization with the aim of increasing efficiency and effectiveness but to become an actual resource. These services, which are explicitly task-oriented, include legal, engineering, accounting, market research, maintenance, data analysis, and medical.

The delivery of a technical service to an organization may have a significant impact and may precipitate significant change. The consequences of bringing this type of specific expertise into a system has not been studied, and it appears to be of little concern to the technical consultant. Recently, however, technical consultants have been paying attention to the acceptability level of the organization and the resistance likely to evolve when new technology is introduced into a system. While technological consultants have, in increasing numbers, claimed to be taking what they refer to as a holistic approach to technical implementation, the objectivity of their analysis is colored because of their desire to sell their equipment or services. In fact, many technological consultants and their companies are more concerned with the marketing aspects of their work than with conducting a careful and objective analysis of their impact on the organization.

Technical consultants generally provide a direct service to an organization. This service may be continual over time, such as maintenance (daily) or auditing (once a year); otherwise technical consultants may enter for a brief period to train employees to use the technology (e.g. word processing or computer utilization).

A key factor that differentiates the technical consultation from others is that it is primarily concerned with implementation. The consultant who trains staff in the use of equipment is rarely concerned with an assessment of the equipment's economic, social, and political impact on a given system.

Summary of Characteristics

Definition of Consultation

The technical consultation assists the organization by providing expertise to employees where it is lacking due to incompetence, lack of time, or unwillingness to perform.

Focus

The focus of a technical consultation is on the individual, the group, or the entire system.

Assumptions Underlying the Effort

Given the enormity of change in the areas of technology, taxation, regulations, and so on, organizations lack the resources to do the work. Or, an organization may find it financially expedient to use another firm for periodic services.

Roles

The technical consultant performs a service for the organization in a specifically defined area and generally for a specified period of time.

The client may assume the role of a learner, but often the client allows the consultant to work undisturbed and later meets to discuss the progress and provide new information.

Objectives

The goal of the technical consultant is to fill a void in the organization by providing manpower and/or expertise that the organization lacks. Neither the consultant nor the organization sees as its intention the mobilization of the organization's resources to do the work.

Entry

The technical consultant generally enters the organization through top management, although others can be authorized to recruit help. The duties of the consultant are clear.

Key Intervention Techniques

The technical consultant offers expertise in a specified area. The consultant is usually attached to a base firm that offers expert services (e.g., legal, accounting, computer, marketing, and maintenance). Many consultants operate independently.

FEEDBACK CONSULTATION

Feedback consultants are generally planners, team leaders or researchers who function primarily as data collectors who will return the data to the organization either in raw form or after an analysis. However, on some occasions, when requested, the analyzed data may take the form of a prescription or recommendation for system improvement.

The consultant focuses on the entire system or subsystems. The research generally falls under the category of operation research or survey research. Due to the development of computer capability, feedback consultation has the potential for producing an ecological analysis of the organization's functioning through computer simulations and model-building programs. However, the major thrust of feedback consultation is its naturalistic observation method of research which has a strong potential to increase knowledge about the organization.

The consultant's work assumes an educative function; that is, the consultee receives the reported results of a given project. The results of the project are intended to increase the system's awareness of the functioning of the various subsystems and their interrelationships, especially in the areas of resource utilization and productivity.

There is little authoritative work in the area of feedback consultation as a method used to improve organizational functioning. Little is known of the methodology used in improving the organization's functioning except that it is left in the hands of the management of the organization. The consultation ends when the project is presented, and often if the results are to be accepted by the organization, they must be congruent with the values and assumptions held by management. By not taking an active role in the resolution of resistance to the change process, considerable room is left for misinterpretation and failure on the part of the organization to introduce the results or recommendations into its operations.

Summary of Characteristics

Definition of Consultation

Feedback consultation facilitates the decision-making process in the organization by increasing the availability of information and by going through enormous amounts of existing data and looking for clues that may be of assistance to the consultees.

Focus

The feedback consultation focuses on the entire system of subsystems and on the systems environment.

Assumptions Underlying the Effort

The organization's leadership requires information to make accurate decisions, and the feedback consultant is hired to gather data and sometimes to analyze the data and make recommendations in the form of a report.

Roles

Feedback consultants are researchers working for management. They have no involvement in the resolution of the problem or in the actual change process.

The client states the nature of the problem to the consultant and receives the complete report.

Objectives

The goal of the feedback consultation is to enhance the decision-making abilities of management through the presentation of raw data, analyzed results, or recommendation. Data are analyzed for their implications to organizational growth, product development, investment opportunities, and so on.

Entry

Feedback consultants are invited by management, generally with a written contract and a request that a report be submitted.

Key Intervention Techniques

The feedback consultant assists in the resolution of problems and increases decision-making abilities by providing feedback in a report to a person or group with the responsibility and authority to change the system.

ORGANIZING CONSULTATION

Consultation to communities, community groups, and union organizing, with the intent to build an organization, was initially outlined by Alinsky (1959). This type of consultation assumes that the client is oppressed by powerful individuals, groups, or institutions and that the only response on the part of the powerless community workers is to develop a powerful counteractive force among themselves. The consultant organizes the community or workers to oppose those in power and to bring about a desired change.

Professional organizers are most likely to consult within communities that are economically or politically impoverished or are in a crisis initiated by a maladaptation or malfunctioning of either the community, the institution, or larger society.

A professional organizing consultant can enter a community and begin organizing at will or with an invitation. The consultant assumes that some communities and groups of workers in need of consultation do not have the organizing expertise to collectively recognize what they need or to recruit assistance from the outside. In addition, a powerless community or worker population may be too fearful to enlist the aid of an outsider.

The organizing consultation initially focuses on three areas:

1. Data collection and assessment are required in the problem areas identified by the consultant, as well as an examination of the self-interests of the residents and identification of the leaders.

2. The consultant must develop a climate of credibility and trust with the clients.
3. The consultant must assess the method to be used to unify various groups and factions in order to create a power base.
4. The consultant is viewed as the chief strategist who will suggest or implement a variety of techniques to gain legitimacy, power, and authority for the community or workers and the work group within.

The organizing consultant is generally a person who has had experience in community organization practice—either as an organizer or as an apprentice to an organizer. Although the client is viewed as the community or group, the consultant accepts the task of training selected participants to become organizers.

The evaluation of an organizing consultant consists of an assessment of the changes the community and workers were able to bring about.

Summary of Characteristics

Definition of Consultation

The organizing consultation helps workers or communities to develop a power base to counteract oppressive forces that have initiated a crisis. The consultant formulates a strategy and techniques to be used in what is viewed as a struggle.

Focus

The emphasis of the organizing consultation is to oppressed workers or communities. The focus is on groups and individuals. Organizing consultants train participants to become organizers.

Assumptions Underlying the Effort

Workers and others are oppressed by powerful organizations that exploit and pollute. The only response is to develop a powerful counteraction.

Roles

The organizing consultant functions as organizer and chief strategist. The organizing consultant's clients are workers, groups, and communities in a state of disorganization.

Objectives

The objectives of the organizing consultant are to collect data, set goals, and organize. Goals are expected to coincide with overcoming basic unmet human needs.

Entry

The organizing consultant's entry is either invited or uninvited. The consultant can enter any system deemed in need of services.

Key Intervention Techniques

Through data collection, the self-interests of the powerful and powerless are examined. Leaders among the oppressed are identified and efforts are unified to create a power base.

MANAGEMENT CONSULTATION

This form of consultation integrates research in the behavioral sciences utilizing many disciplines and relies on managerial and organizational psychology. Behavioral science research is applied to organizations by developing and packaging specific techniques.

Usually after a period of diagnosing or assessing the organization in question, the management consultant assumes the role of educator. Typically, workshops are designed where techniques are explained to the consultees and their application is attempted either in actual situations or in simulations. Staff members assume the role of students and are invited to participate in an assessment of the application procedures and process. The assessment takes place in workshops to ensure that the dilemmas and resistance are understood.

Management consultation often maintains a molecular position with respect to improving organizational functioning; that is, while the consultant may have insight into organizational problems of a general nature, the consultant finds greater utility in focusing on smaller, more clearly defined areas of work–task situations.

The consultation rarely attempts an in-depth analysis of the dynamics and underlying inter- and intrapersonal causes of a problem. The management consultant maintains that if the staff can do things differently, or if new methods are learned, the functioning of the organization can be modified to the degree that effectiveness will increase and previous dysfunctions will be subordinated.

Because the consultant may only utilize a limited number of techniques, which contain low flexibility, the ability of the consultation to produce a long-term correction in the system is often lacking. The popularity of the techniques used is probably explained by their relative simplicity and their promising nature. The lack of effectiveness of these techniques is indicated by their inability to endure over time. For example, years ago, program evaluation review technique and management by objective were in vogue. Later it was leadership and group training; now we see quality of work life, zero-balance budgeting, and total quality management.

Management consultation is often used by formal consulting firms, although its use by private entrepreneurs has increased. Consultants do not need training in the understanding of the theory and practice of management, marketing, organization, and so on. They are known primarily for their ability to verbally present material and conduct a workshop or module. Often consulting firms have subsystems that specialize in marketing workshops or training modules. The initial aim of the consulting firm is to sell a programmer project to a company and then bring in its team of experts. Often these experts offer training without prior knowledge of the organization or the consultees (the working members). Thus, the consultation takes the form of sending consultees to school to learn some new skills, and the extraneous benefits from this type of venture are rarely explored or understood.

Summary of Characteristics

Definition of Consultation

The management consultation delivers new and alternative ways or methods of managing sales, marketing, personnel, and so forth. The consultant is an expert in a specified area of management and he/she instructs consultees who then put the technique or method into practice.

Focus

The emphasis of the management consultation is generally on a small subsystem or group of employees within a subsystem.

Assumptions Underlying the Effort

The organization gets into a rut and new techniques and methods are needed to create enthusiasm and provide alternatives to the "old" and often ineffective methods.

Roles

Initially the management consultant functions as a salesperson who sells the technique, workshop, or training module to the company. Then the consultant assumes the role of trainer or instructor. The client or company assumes the role of consumer and student who is expected to learn and then apply the new techniques.

Objectives

The management consultant aims to bring to the staff up-to-date information and training in the latest techniques, information, and strategies, with the purpose of reducing problems and providing alternatives to existing procedures and styles. It is expected that the new knowledge will improve system functioning.

Entry

Management consultants enter an organization only through top management.

Key Intervention Techniques

Staff are trained using educational modules that can include workshops, conferences, lectures, films, simulations, and tests. Management consultants use programs to teach areas such as MBO, Theory Z, stress reduction, and other techniques to avoid burnout, etc.

TRANSFORMATION CONSULTATION

Transformation consultation evolves from the field of management consulting. This method sees the entire organization as the focus of change, not localized issues within the organization. Strongly influenced by the management efforts and organizational cultures that exist in Japanese and German corporations, this consultative effort seeks to change the organization by transforming its culture and structure. Methods are used to make the corporation more innovative, participative, consumer oriented, and, it is hoped, more competitive in the international marketplace.

Generally modeled after Japanese industrial corporations, transformation consultants propose to transform the so-called traditional organization, with all its inadequacies, into a new company whose employees cooperate, show loyalty, and appreciate quality.

There are four methods used to bring about a transformation process. The first, put forth by Deal and Kennedy (1982, 1984) and Kilman, Covin, (1988), is "shared cooperation," where the emphasis is on changing the behavioral or cultural infrastructure by removing real and symbolic barriers of power and authority. Cooperation among all levels of employees is valued, and the traditional notion of managers giving orders and subordinates following is dramatically changed. The assumption is that the lower-level employees know their work better than anyone else in the organization and they are in the best position to suggest better use of machines and labor.

The second method, proposed by Kanter (1983), is the "parallel system," where a modeling technique is used to bring about the transformation. An alternative structure is created alongside the traditional structure. The alternative structure possesses the qualities and characteristics deemed desirable by management. This structure interacts with the traditional structure and as a result, the old structure incorporates qualities of the new structure and becomes more open to change.

The third method of transformation, often called the "motivational method," is found frequently in the writings of Peters and Waterman (1982) and Peters and Austin (1985). Their focus is on identifying and explaining the cultures of what they consider to be "well-run companies." "Excellence," as they put it, is obtained through the creation of a strong commitment from employees, as well as visionary leadership (as opposed to traditional management) and a "passion" for excellence. As with other transformational methods, this one assumes that the traditional authority structures that promote obedience, control and conformity lead to lowered job satisfaction, alienation, and apathy among all levels of workers. They seek to alter the organization's culture and create leadership qualities that promote esprit. Peters and Austin (1985) maintain that management connotes control and controlling is demeaning to employees. On the other hand, leadership connotes unleashed energy and has the potential to increase trust and respect for the dignity and creative potential of all employees. It assumes, as Drucker has long maintained, that employees are self-motivated and strive to find meaning and fulfillment. It is the manager's job to function as a leader who is able to create a culture that will maintain this motivational level and not destroy it. This is generally accomplished by creating a culture in which employees believe that they are shareholders in the corporation, and as such, they are assessed on their efforts to create satisfaction among consumers and purchasers of their goods and services.

The final transformational method, often called "top-initiated change," is put forth by Deming and refined by Crosby (1984). Here the consultant works to alter the values, attitudes, and ways in which top-level managers think and operate. These consultants identify "change drivers" among the organization's elite. Their approach is to improve the quality of the work, and it is based on an assumption that employee commitment and trust can be obtained only through the desire for high quality. It is the job of management to communicate the values and ideals that will optimize quality of output. These authors have developed a 14-step plan for transformation, which is broken down into four phases: conviction building, commitment, implementation, and celebration. In the first phase, senior management instills its conviction for quality, which is filtered down through the organization. The second phase is anchoring the commitment throughout the organization. The third phase, implementation, is actually putting quality-control apparatus into place, and identifying and removing the obstacles to quality. In the final phase, celebration, the employees are appreciated and rewarded for their efforts. Transformation consultants expect that the energy that evolves from the celebration will be infectious and will stimulate repetition of the process. This approach is a prescriptive process in which key members of the organization use their authority and learn the necessary tactics to promote and support the achievement of quality.

In general, these transformational methods attempt to deemphasize authority by placing operational decision-making and responsibility for quality in the hands of work groups or teams of employees throughout the organization.

Based on Japanese success, and perhaps reacting to it, transformation consultants are in fact operationalizing many of the efforts put forth 20 to 30 years ago by NTL trainers and many organizational development consultants.

Summary of Characteristics

Definition of Consultation

Transformation consultation completely transforms the organization into a cooperative endeavor that emphasizes quality.

Focus

Beginning with top management, the transformation consultant aims to alter the value system in the entire organization.

Assumptions Underlying the Effort

The traditional management-oriented organization promotes alienation and destroys morale. This must be changed if the organization is to compete successfully in the global economy.

Roles

The transformation consultant hopes to educate top- and middle-level managers and assist them in adopting new values and methods of operation. The client's role is to learn as students, to place the new methods into operation, and to report back to consultants.

Objectives

The transformation consultation aims to eventually bring about a total organizational transformation that stresses cooperation and quality.

Entry

The transformation consultant enters the organization through the top.

Key Intervention Techniques

The transformation consultation process uses lectures and meetings with top-level employees in groups and individually.

In the next chapter, a new method is proposed, psychoanalytic consultation. Chapter 7 lays the groundwork for a discussion of the work of psychoanalytic consulting in the chapters that follow.

Psychoanalytic Consultation

It is impossible to escape the impression that people commonly
use false standards of measurement—that they seek power,
success and wealth for themselves and admire them in others,
and that they underestimate what is of true value in life. And
yet, in making any general judgement of this sort, we are in
danger of forgetting how variegated the human world and its
mental life are.

—SIGMUND FREUD (1930/1961, p. 62)

P sychoanalytic theory alone can-
not provide a conceptual framework for understanding organizational issues. Even when psychoanalytic theory is used as a psychology of
the individual, its clinical application requires "clinical technique" as a
method to apply it. Similarly, when psychoanalytic theory is applied to
the organization, a technique is required.[1] Without a technique, conducting an analysis is fortuitous, antidotal, and encumbered with
speculative symbols and metaphors. To apply psychoanalytic theory
effectively requires a framework that explains both the general work
of the organization and the issues facing employees that are common
to all organizations.

Among an array of organizational theories and methods of consultation, the one that lends itself to the application of psychoanalytic

---

[1]This is not to suggest, as Ellul (1964) does, that in our attempts to be predictable and
exact, technique must prevail over the human being, or that technique must reduce the
human to a "technical animal" or "the king of slaves of technique." In the attempt to
understand the person at work, we must caution against the double constraints offered
by the use of technique. First if one assumes that "organizational man" is encumbered
by the constraints of the technical framework of the organization and its demands for
"objectivity," the researcher must avoid increasing these constraints by the techniques
used in trying to understand organizational man.

theory is "social systems theory." Historically, social systems theory has ties with psychoanalytic theory, and a review of a number of writers supports the idea that these two theories are compatible.

Social systems theory has its basis in the analogies between the organization as a system and its correlates found in all living systems. As a living system, the organization is open to interaction with its environment. This interaction occurs in three areas: taking in resources from the environment, converting these inputs, and exporting these resources as finished products or waste products. Of significant influence among systems theorists has been von Bertalanffy (1950), who identified formal entities found in all living systems. Comparing the organization to other living systems has a distinct advantage in that it provides a theoretical model in which to understand the operations of the system. Consider what Boulding (1953) suggests when he describes the commonalities between organisms and organizations:

> Both . . . can be described in terms which are suggestive of the accountant's concepts of the balance sheet and the income account. In describing an organization or an organism as it exists at a moment of time, we make a listing, or perhaps a map, of the parts. Such a listing may be called a "position statement," if one may borrow a phrase from the accountants and use it in a somewhat wider sense. A chemical formula of a compound, a map in anatomy or in geography, the balance sheet of a firm, the organizational chart of an organization, even the credal statement of a church, are all examples of position statements at various levels of abstraction. They all represent the analysis of a whole into parts which are not further analyzed and which for the purposes of the problem in hand are regarded as homogenous. These parts I shall call "components." Thus the atoms H and O are components of the chemical formula H_2O; the organs, veins, arteries, etc. of an anatomical chart or the provinces, cities, railroads, etc. of a map are components of the body or that of a region; the assets and liabilities are components of the balance sheet of a firm; the organizational categories and lines of communication and authority are components of an organization chart; and the various articles are components of a credal statement. (p. xviii)

Boulding goes on to say that all living matter, including organizations, has unstable components. Decay, trauma, conflict, and entropy are components that must be managed to deter deterioration of the system. This is the work of management and the rationale for the design of a structure. This way of seeing the organization has been embraced by a number of organizational theorists including Rice and his associates at the Tavistock Centre, in London, England (Rice 1963,

1969; Miller & Rice, 1967/1973). Over the years, the systems view has included the sociotechnical model (Emery & Trist, 1960), the open systems model (Katz & Kahn, 1966), the contingency model (Lawrence & Lorsch, 1970), and the general systems model (Miller, 1965). These models present a view of the organization that is a part of a larger system or environment, as a system that is open and continually engaged in transactions with its external environment through the exchange of resources in the form of material, money, people, and information. These models view the organization as a system containing a set of units that maintain relationships with each other (Miller, 1965). The state of each unit is partially dependent on the state of the other units (Alderfer, 1972).

According to Alderfer (1972), relationships that are established within a system provide for integration, coherence, and stability, thereby strengthening the system's security. The relationships that are established across the system's boundaries facilitate the system's interaction with its environment and thereby provide an opportunity for the system to send out its exports (waste products) and to bring in nourishment and stimulation. Miller and Rice (1967/1973) propose a basically simple conceptualization of the organization which forms the foundation of systems theory. According to Miller and Rice (1967), any organization may be seen as an open system as long as it engages in an exchange of material and resources with its environment. Imported materials are transformed by means of a conversion process. Some of the imported products are consumed for internal maintenance, and the remainder are exported as either waste or finished products back into the environment.

Outputs are converted into additional resources which enter into the organization. Over time a continuous process develops where materials, information, and finished products are transformed internally by the organization, and are then transported into the environment where they are again transformed into useful inputs. Survival of the organization depends upon the capacity of the organization to manage the flow of outputs into the environment and transformation of these outputs into useful inputs.

These input–conversion–output processes are the primary work of the organization. Indeed, they are necessary for survival. This view of the organization's structure and function provides a unique opportunity for the consultant to assess the important relationships between these three primary activities. (A more complex model of the organization from a systems perspective is given in Figure 7.1.) It is this understanding, then, that enables the consultant to help the organization to engage in these basic processes more effectively and, in effect,

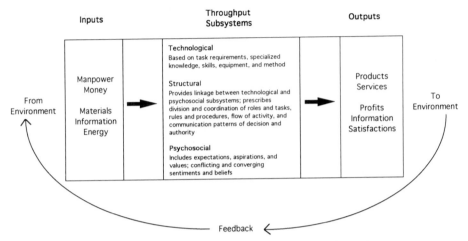

Inputs	Throughput Subsystems	Outputs

Technological
Based on task requirements, specialized knowledge, skills, equipment, and method

Structural
Provides linkage between technological and psychosocial subsystems; prescribes division and coordination of roles and tasks, rules and procedures, flow of activity, and communication patterns of decision and authority

Psychosocial
Includes expectations, aspirations, and values; conflicting and converging sentiments and beliefs

From Environment

Manpower
Money

Materials
Information
Energy

Products
Services

Profits
Information
Satisfactions

To Environment

Feedback

FIGURE 7.1. The organization as an open system. In the throughput system illustrated above, three subsystems (Technological, Structural, and Psychosocial) are defined.

to ensure its own survival. All organizations and organisms survive as a function of their ability to manage their boundaries, and according to Cox and Walderson (1949), this applies to "bacteria, mice, and men, and social organizations, like labor unions, churches and states . . ." (p. xviiii).

As the organization engages in the work of boundary management, it must perform tasks. These tasks, which require efficient and effective performance, are vital to the survival of the organization. At the same time, they function on a vulnerable psychological base, which at various points in time constrain performance. Identifying these tasks and analyzing the issues that may contribute to their dysfunctioning are necessary if the organization is to function optimally over time.

FOUNDATIONS OF PSYCHOANALYTIC CONSULTING

The conceptual foundations for understanding the organization from a psychoanalytic perspective come from the works of Bion (1948/1962), Lewin (1947), Jaques (1951), Menzies (1960), Miller and Rice (1967), Sofer (1961), and others affiliated with the Tavistock Centre. Their collective view holds that the personal needs of an employee, as well as the motivation to fulfill these needs, are a constant. However, it is the organization and its very structure that may frustrate these needs. The course of study, therefore, becomes an analysis of the methods, defenses, and cultures that evolve over time as these employees seek gratification of their conscious and unconscious needs. Psychoanalysis maintains that these needs are so compelling that employees may subordinate the task of the organization to obtain gratification. Management often mistakenly responds by increasing control and using incentives and threats to get the employee to "keep working" and to "follow orders," and by doing so, management avoids the essential function of management: to design and manage a culture and structure to avoid frustration of these needs.

In psychoanalytic consulting, as in other methods of consultation, the consultant enters the client's system for the purpose of enhancing stable patterns of behavior. These patterns of behavior are products of a balance of forces that both oppose and support the system, and a consultation is required when the forces opposing system functioning are greater than the forces supporting it. The consultant's aim is to reduce those forces that keep the organization from functioning effectively. Because the consultant enters the organization intent on reducing opposing forces that are contributing to dysfunction, he/she conceives of his/her job as not adding to the resources of the organization but strengthening its positive recuperative capacities and eliminating factors that prevent functioning by reducing capacities (Jaques, 1971). In addition, the psychoanalytic consultant as an astute observer is concerned with what is missing. Konrad Lorenz once remarked that "the most difficult and often most important observations are those that detect that an object is missing, that an action fails to occur, that an anticipated phenomenon is absent" (McDougall, 1980, p. 216). The consultant observes not only what may be missing but also what does not fit, or is out of sequence or synch. This may be an inappropriate affect, a missing role or some aspect of the organization's structure that is missing, a cultural event that is inappropriate or missing, an employee who is absent or terminated, and so on.

In Chapter 9, an incident is described that provides information that seems inconsequential but sheds light on the nature of the dysfunction being examined. It occurred during a meeting with the consultees, who appeared disinterested and gazed out of a window into a parking lot with an empty space reserved for the departing CEO. An analysis of this simple incident turned ambiguity into clarity. Often when faced with confusion, a consultant feels inept and frustrated because he cannot find the missing pieces of information. These feelings are generally a function of two unconscious motivations: (1) the consultant cannot see things clearly because he is defending against some frightening affects associated with the missing information, and (2) the organization wishes to keep the consultant in the dark for the same reasons. These feelings may also be an attempt to keep the consultant at a distance, to control the endeavor, and to avoid submission to the intervention that may eventually bring about change, improvement, and health. It is a natural human impulse to shut down, to deny, repress, dilute, and avoid basic psychoanalytic discoveries (Orgel, 1990). The fears associated with psychoanalytic inquiry are basic and real, and they are a function of the nature of psychoanalytic work, to discover the origins of unconscious conflict.

As Freud (1912–1913/1953, 1937–1939/1964) explained, one leaves behind events (of a sexual and aggressive nature) which are forgotten and defended against as one moves ahead, and in doing so one creates "phenomena similar to symptoms in their structure and purpose" (1937–1939/1968, p. 80). Psychoanalytic intervention, if successful, will move the consultee to a dangerous place in time, back to the origins of the symptoms, to the source of the anxiety. This movement is then fraught with anxiety and defenses and resistance associated with dread. Consequently the consultant is experienced as a sadistic object bent on pushing the consultee headlong into this terrifying experience. It is illogical that one should want to return to the scene of the "crime" and reexperience all the discomforts and pain one worked so hard and long to make disappear. The psychoanalytic consultant can engage in this work, and the apparent hatred associated with the resistance to change, only if he believes that change is possible if the source is reunderstood and that the compulsion to repeat can be altered by undertaking this journey. Faced with this almost impossible task and the anxieties associated with the resistance to truth, the consultant will have a number of reactions and will unconsciously seek to dilute the process. In doing so he/she will join those consultants engaged in the work of instruction who suggest to consultees ways "to do things differently," thereby avoiding the work of psychoanalytic consulting, which is "knowing things differently."

The foundations of psychoanalytic consulting are contained within its theoretical integration of an organization's structure, its groups or departments, and its members into a holistic system. These variables—structure, groups, and individuals—are continuously interacting to make decisions, perform tasks, and import and export resources (material, energy, and information). The efficiency and effectiveness of an organization are influenced by the conscious and unconscious motivations or wishes that underlie the capacity to engage in the work involved in these three variables.

For example, a relationship exists between an organizational structure and a psychic structure (see Chapter 4). The consultant assesses how the organizational structure contributes to or detracts from psychic gratification. Involvement in formal and informal groups also presents opportunities for phychic gratification as well as conflict, and deprivation. Finally, the consultant assesses the employees' attachment to activities of a task, its role requirements, and the opportunities for psychic gratification found in the work.

Membership and the capacity to work in a group or department may be influenced by both group-level needs and individual personality characteristics. These variables are understood through an integration of personality dynamics and group dynamics. Ashbach and Schermer (1987) call them the third paradigm in the study of organizations. This area of study is the focus of psychoanalytic consulting, and it borrows heavily from the work of Lewin (1947), Chein (1946), Bion (1961), Freud (1912–1913/1953, 1921/1955), Winnicott (1965), and Foulkes (1948, 1964). Stated simply, these theorists suggest that the mental processes of the individual that are behaviorally observed are significantly altered when one observes that same person interacting within a group or institution. Behavior observed in a group or institution appears outside the person, that is in the "field" or "social system," and these behaviors are governed by the laws and norms of the larger group.

Of major concern in applying psychoanalytic theory to organizations are environmental influences that impinge upon the mind and promote human thought and action. While most psychoanalytic consultants maintain that the unconscious lies at the base of human decisions and the capacity to work, others maintain that it is the environment that influences unconscious life, which in turn precipitates an interaction. Just how much the unconscious life influences a person's actions and how much the environment influences these same actions is given considerable debate in psychoanalytic circles. Bowers (1984) suggests that there are two types of influences— influences that will always go unnoticed, and remain beyond our conscious awareness, and influences that are unappreciated but still have an influence, but because they are unappreciated they go unnoticed. The psychoanalyst pays close attention to the latter types of influence. The work and the consequential interpretation become of value only after that which was unappreciated becomes valued. Bowers (1984) maintains that these uncomprehended influences affect unconscious life, and if the consultant is able to bring them to the consultee's awareness, they will have a profound effect on the system. Thus the work of the consultant is conceptually to illuminate the influence the person has on the "system" and the impact the "system" has on the person. Consequently, the system and the person are not considered separate entities.

Ashbach and Schermer (1987) suggest a similar process to the work of the consultant when they discuss the difference between an individual in clinical practice and the same individual in an organization. When the individual in clinical practice is observed, the boundary around that person is closed. As a result, one sees regression to primitive forms of imagery which are experienced as internal and a function of the person's history. When the observer sees the individual in an organization, this boundary is opened and one sees the external manifestation of the person's behavior which now becomes a product of group interaction, group fantasy, structure, and myth. For example, every system has a boundary that separates it from the immediate environment without closing it off completely. A number of subsystems are contained within the organization; for example, technology may form one subsystem, the classification of employees may comprise another, and a division may form yet another.

The same individual employee may be part of any one or all of the various subsystems at the same time. Just as a person in society moves through many systems during the course of the day, the member of an organization does the same. The effectiveness of the system in completing its task is a function of (1) how effectively the relationships necessary to manage or regulate the flow material are, (2) how the energy and information between systems flow and operate, (3) and how the person moves through the various subsystems. However, as the employee moves through these various systems and crosses multiple boundaries, they all influence him/her. These influences have the cumulative effect of altering his conscious and unconscious motivations and work-related capacities.

ASSESSING THE PRESENTING PROBLEM

Typically a consultant focuses on the presenting problem and aims to correct that problem; rarely will he/she entertain the possibility that the presenting problem is a distortion. Psychoanalytic consulting maintains the position that the presenting problem may at best be a symptom and often is an issue that serves to protect the real problem.

For example, a consultant is called into an organization to correct dysfunctions within a subsystem or department. This department is viewed by the executive constellation (consultee) as problematic. The consultant who focuses on the presenting problem will attempt to alter or change this deviant department and bring it into the fold. This is accomplished when the larger system no longer views the deviant subsystem as bothersome or unproductive. However, consulting to the presenting problem presents a twofold problem:

1. An organization often calls in the consultant after other departments complain. Rarely does a deviant department itself call for assistance. When the consultant sees the deviant department as the object to be changed, the deviant subsystem responds to the consultant as an agent of the complaining subsystem, that is, as an enemy.
2. The consultant, by focusing exclusively on bringing the deviant department into the fold, runs the risk of losing sight of the functional nature of the deviancy. The consultant makes a mistake when he consults to the symptom and asks the wrong question, such as, "Why is this subsystem dysfunctional?" On the other hand, the psychoanalytic consultant asks, "Why does the larger system view this subsystem as dysfunctional?" This question allows the psychoanalytic consultant to focus on the functional nature of the symptom. Failure to ask this question increases the risk of engaging in a consultation that ends in "blaming the victim" and neglects total organizational functioning.

The following is an example of how a consultant would go about consulting with a dysfunctional subsystem. The consultant consults to a poorly functioning division of a major conglomerate. This division is blamed by the top management of the conglomerate for causing significant problems throughout the company. An overeager and perhaps naive consultant, on hearing the stated problem, would approach the dysfunctional division and attempt to correct its problem(s) without investigating an important aspect, the functional nature of the dysfunctional division. On the other hand, the psychoanalytic consultant would investigate the function that the problem division performs throughout the entire system, or more specifically, how the dysfunctional system actually contributes to the overall health of the company.

As often happens with living systems, especially human systems, an ill component can serve a number of functions, and one of its functions can be to hold or maintain the health of the larger system. Psychologists report this in the social functions of scapegoating. Psychoanalysts report this in the function of projection, and certain biologists report this in the function of aberrant organisms and their role in ecological survival. Therefore, merely to go ahead and correct a dysfunctional division could have the negative consequences of spreading dysfunctions throughout the entire organization. Here, we see the utility of the concept of positive recuperative capacities of the organization. A question the psychoanalytic consultant must formulate is, Why can't this conglomerate care for or cure this dysfunctional division itself? Second, why is the conglomerate content to blame rather than understand that it may in fact be a contributor to this dysfunctional division? Until the consultant discovers why a particular problem exists and the secondary gains involved in holding on to a problem, the consultant cannot be certain whether the intervention will help the organization gain the necessary insight to heal or to take care of its own dysfunctions in the future.

If it can be assumed that unhealthy systems rarely call for a consultant, it can also be assumed that the healthier an organization is, the more likely it is to seek assistance. Most often, healthier systems more readily discuss their problems and seek changes. This may very well be true for the entire field of consultancy. Unprofitable and troubled organizations find a consultant to be a luxury, and in their attempts to economize, they often shut the door to the possibility of help. An exception can be made for organizations near bankruptcy, that is, symbolically on their deathbed. In desperation, they are generally forced to recognize the need for help.

Thus, consultants are most likely to be called into organizations that lie at the extremes of a continuum of health: either optimistically healthy or near death. This situation is unfortunate because the bulk of the organizations that make up the middle of the continuum need to struggle to maintain their competitive edge, and in most cases they are the ones that can benefit the most from a consultative effort.

UNDERPINNINGS OF PSYCHOANALYTIC CONSULTING

As recognized earlier, in the application of psychoanalytic theory to consultation, boundary management assumes a special position, and analysis of boundary-related issues in the consultant–consultee relationship is a major theoretical thrust.

Psychoanalytic consulting maintains that an external boundary forms around all organizations and subsystems within the organization. This boundary separates the system from its environment and the subsystems from each other. A vital aspect of systems consulting is an assessment of by whom and how the boundaries are managed.

This view is applied to the consultant–consultee relationship, where the consultant conducts an analysis of the dynamics and issues that evolve during the establishment of the boundaries around this relationship. The psychoanalytic consultant believes that an analysis of this relationship will provide important insight into the areas of authority in the organization and how it is delegated; subsystem dependency and autonomy; and clarity of task definition, how the organization views the multiple tasks, and how the organization manages its boundaries. Finally, analysis provides important clues concerning the nature of the request for a consultation, not only about the issues that precipitated the request but also about the organization's resistance toward intervention and change.

The consultant views himself as a system, a system merging with another system (the consultee's system), and so on. Therefore the success of any given consultation depends on the transactions across the boundaries of these systems. It is assumed that the fluidity and the dynamics underlying these transactions will change during the course of the consultation. Therefore, it is vital that the consultant understand the stages or phases through which the consultation typically moves. Three general stages have been identified: beginning the consultation, the intervention stage, and the termination stage.

Beginning the Consultation

There are three major activities in which the consultant engages during this stage. The first focuses on the nature of the contract between consultant and organization; the second is the consultant's capacity to view and understand his/her entry into the organization as a microcosm of the organization's capacity to manage its boundaries; and the third is the consultant's capacity to conduct an analysis of the dynamics and unconscious forces at play in the consultant–consultee relationship.

The Contract

Because a well-thought-through and mutually agreed-upon contract provides the structure for the work, the consultant engages in the work of this stage with an obsessional zeal for clarity and caution. The work of this stage sets the groundwork for all later work, and the consultant spends as much time as necessary to gain the necessary clarity. Difficulties in clarifying the contract are important indicators of the degree of ambivalence the organization or the consultee may have about the consultation.

For the consultant, the contract is a highly personal object. Some consultants view it as a structural guide and a legal document that spells out the nature of the problem, the meeting times and place, points of review and evaluation, expected outcomes, and fees. Other consultants who have not taken the advice of those who have had experiences with uncooperative staff, have endured foiled interventions and have ended up terminated and without payment for services. Some consultants proceed cavalierly and begin to operate on a handshake. Sometimes these consultants maintain that there is an advantage to having a loose contract; they are not constrained by a document and can suggest and make necessary changes as the consultation proceeds. These consultants say that drafting a tight contract in the beginning is like deciding to operate without examining the patient.

Although the psychoanalytic consultant believes that clarity at the beginning is vital, he/she tries to keep the options open. This may be accomplished by drafting more than one contract. The systems consultant will draft a contract called an "exploratory" or "diagnostic" contract, which is terminated at a given point in time when the consultant and consultee agree to draw up a "set" or "intervention" contract. In the diagnostic contract, the consultant has the freedom to assess the nature of the problem, the target of the intervention, intervention techniques, length of time, and other necessary inclusions. But most important, this period gives the consultant an opportunity to assess the nature of his/her relationship with the consultee and the depth of the resistance to a consultation. It is here that the consultant begins to receive an education about the firm, and the consultee begins to gain a sense of what the consultation is all about.

Not only is the contract an articulation of a mutual set of expectations, it is also an agreed-upon set of specifications that have the potential for forming a viable evaluation system. If the contract contains agreed-upon outcomes and details specific areas where improvements in organizational functioning are expected, both client and consultant can access their work together. According to Lippitt (1959), the consultative process is not just a matter of the consultant's competency and/or creativity; the process is a collaborative effort in which both parties are attempting, in their own way, to achieve the same identified goal.

Entry as a Microcosm

The consultant begins the entry process with a major assumption: that the entry into the consultee's system represents a microcosm of the consultee's abilities to manage the entry of resources from the environment into the system. The consultee's ability to understand and attend to critical issues is indicative of boundary management. It is therefore assumed that poor boundary management in this area will become apparent in the entry process.

During the entry process, the consultant has the rare opportunity to view the client at work. The consultant observes the nature of authority invested at the boundary as well as the manner in which the system transacts business with its environment. For example, the degree of formalization of the contract is generally viewed as a representation of how the organization formalizes its structure at the boundary, and further, how it formalizes its relations with other systems in its environment.

At entry, the consultant–consultee relationship begins. This relationship has external and internal boundaries, with their respective psychological and physical characteristics. The external boundary comprises a spatial aspect that is concerned with the meeting place and physical surroundings and a temporal aspect that includes time and length of the consultative sessions. The internal boundary contains psychological aspects that may include material, information and emotional conditions, and the expectations that both parties bring to the sessions.

The Consultant–Consultee Relationship

The consultant–consultee relationship is viewed in two ways: as a microcosm of the dynamics that exist in the organization (i.e., what goes on in the organization will be replicated in this relationship), and (2) as a process where the consultant occupies the role of a helper. The dynamics of this relationship are often difficult to assess. For example, the consultant must be able to ferret out information from the array of defenses the consultee utilizes when communicating. The degree of intensity of these defenses is a function of the degree of anxiety the consultee experiences in this relationship and also of his/her experience within the organization (in his/her role, relations with others, and the culture of the organization). The dynamics of this relationship are a reflection or a mirror of the organization's dysfunctions. The second aspect of the relationship is a function of the role of being a consultant and the impact this role has on the consultee and the organization in general. An effective psychoanalytic consultation requires that the consultee internalize aspects of the consultant through the process of identification, where positive facets of the consultant's functioning become part of the consultee's experience of self. According to Pine (1985), these identifications may occur through tone of voice, form of humor, an attitude of calm under conditions of anxiety, the habit of questioning assumptions, toleration of ambiguity, style of expression, and focus of interest. In addition, the authority of the consultant is significant to the identification process. The information given to the consultee from an "awesome" authority figure will most likely be taken in. This information includes interpretative data, insight into dynamics, modes of functioning, and options for choice. Finally, the consultant has the potential to confirm the inner experience of the consultee if he/she is able to create an environment of safety, to respond to the consultee in a supportive and empathic manner, and in some cases merely to listen to the thoughts and experiences of the consultee. Then, through this identification process, the consultee's recuperative capacities will be increased by adding to his/her self-esteem and confidence.

The consultant–consultee relationship stands or falls in relation to the exchanges across the internal boundary. The internal boundary is an artifact of the division of labor that exists between the two parties, and it is influenced by an array of resistances and expectations. The task of managing this internal boundary is to understand the expectations brought to the sessions, reduce the resistances, and clarify the overall work. The ultimate aim is to create a climate of openness, trust, and clarity. To attain this state is indeed problematic, and failure to do so often lies at the base of consultation failure.

Viewed from this perspective, one can conclude that consultations fail because of the inability of the consultant to understand the reaction his/her presence is having on the consultee and the organization. This is perhaps most clearly understood from the perspective of transference.

Resistance to a consultation evolves from powerful emotions, some conscious and some held from awareness by defenses. In all consultations, the consultant triggers transference reactions in the consultee that evoke conscious reactions that are motivated by unconscious wishes and fantasies. These wishes, fantasies, and their derivatives produce anxiety, guilt, and rage, which bring forth defenses.

Consider the following vignette: A consultee says that he cannot work with the vice president because he is too aggressive and selfish, and the consultee wants the consultant to meet with the vice president and change him in some manner. The consultant asks himself the following question: How does this consultee see me? From an unconscious perspective, the consultee is viewing the consultant as the idealized parental figure who will save him from the aggressive man. Perhaps this is a derivative from an unresolved oedipal issue or some derivative of an intense sibling rivalry.

All consultations trigger transference reactions. These reactions begin very early in relations with parents and sometime siblings, and later they are transferred to institutions such as school, church, organizations, and other people. Transference reactions are ubiquitous and can be either positive or negative, depending on whether the earlier experiences that are being replicated were conflicting and frightening or loving and supportive. Failure to understand these reactions will increase the potential for a failure.

Because of the power of transference reactions in the consultant–consultee relationship, the consultant must be able to recognize that many times the consultee is reacting to the consultant not as a "real" figure but as a representational object. Of course, this works both ways, and the consultant must be aware that he/she may be unconsciously using the consultee to gratify some wishes. It can be assumed that the direction in which the consultation moves and the success of the work is a function of these transferences and the consultant's failure to recognize them.

The consultant is generally invited into an organization with limited information and considerable ambiguity. The consultant reduces this ambiguity or tolerates it by maintaining clarity of the internal boundaries, that is, clarity of authority, division of labor and task performance, and responsibility. A collaborative analysis of these characteristics is essentially the basis of the consultation.

At the beginning of the consultation, the consultee is expected to produce a high degree of verbal communication and the consultant is expected to suggest and direct responses. The collaborative nature of the consultation implies that to reach an optimal work climate, the relationship must change. The relatively contained role of the consultee must expand to include characteristics that the consultant initially exhibits; that is, the consultee must be able to provide, on his/her own, interpretations and suggestions, and present direct responses to experiences that were initially ambiguous.

Another important aspect of consultant–consultee relations is the ability of the consultant to assess the capacities of the consultee to function effectively. This requires a personality assessment that focuses primarily on the ego functioning of the consultee. If the consultee is demonstrating an inability to manage boundaries, the consultant must be able to determine whether this is a personality dysfunction or a system dysfunction. The consultant assumes a relationship between the system and the personality. The consultant leans toward the position that the system has considerable influence on the personality. In addition, the consultant strives to create an appropriate balance between the organization's forces and personality forces. Effective management is only possible when this balance is reached. However, in some cases this balance may never be reached because of severe organizational dysfunctions or a personality disorder in the consultee. Working with a consultee who is experiencing a personality disorder or a "life crisis" is exceedingly problematic and not recommended.

The consultant assumes that being in the role of consultee precipitates stress. It is the intensity of this stress that determines the utility of defenses and the degree of harmony the consultative relationship will contain. In the initial assessment of the consultee's ability to manage boundaries, the consultant assumes that effective management cannot occur if the consultee is aloof and unable to join in the emotional life of the organization. It is also assumed that dysfunctional ego capacities will limit the consultee's ability to join in the work of both the organization and the consultation. The inability to engage in these tasks will manifest itself in the consultee's inability to negotiate boundaries between him/herself and the organization.

If the consultee demonstrates difficulties in managing the boundaries around the consultant–consultee relationship, it is assumed that the consultee will also have difficulties managing his/her own ego boundaries as well as boundaries around groups or departments in his/her organization. This position draws its theoretical support from Rice's (1969) concept or definition of the mature person:

> The concept of the self . . . (the ego) . . . mediates the relationships between the internal world of good and bad objects and the external world of reality, and thus takes, in relation to the personality, a leadership role. The mature ego is one that can differentiate between what is real in the outside world and what is projected onto it from the inside;

what should be accepted, what should be rejected and what should be incorporated into experience. In short, the mature ego is one that can define the boundary between what is inside and what is outside, and can control the transactions between the one and the other. (p. 13)

Difficulties in coming to terms with the role and the task within the organization will occur if the consultee is so immersed in the emotional life of the organization that he/she defends a system that is clearly dysfunctional. It will also occur if the consultee cannot become involved in recommending and carrying out change, or if he/she is unable to locate boundaries or acquire adequate boundary definitions for the organization and its subunits. According to Miller and Rice (1967), confusion concerning boundaries will lead to organizational as well as individual "breakdown," and inefficiency and failure will follow.

Often in a particularly regressed organization, the consultee internalizes the dysfunctions that abound and, in the process, becomes deeply troubled. Under such stressful conditions, the consultee may press the consultant to help in such a way that the consultation begins to resemble psychotherapy. According to Miller (1973), this is a mistake. The task of the consultant is not to consult to the personal defense mechanisms or interpersonal issues the consultee may present. The consultant should not be interested in changing individual behavior but rather in assisting clients in developing an understanding of their roles and relationships in the organization, and of managing themselves within these roles and relationships. According to Miller (1973), Rice believes that clients have the responsibility and resources (ego strength) to work through for themselves the personal consequences of role issues within the consultative relationship, and it is not the consultant's job to undertake a personal therapeutic stance.

The Intervention Stage

If the initial phase is successful and adequate diagnostic work has been accomplished, the intervention phase will function smoothly. Of course, this is an ideal; rarely are interventions fully accepted by organizations. Often organizations display no resistance until this phase is reached. This is why the initial phase is important. The consultant does not want to reach the intervention stage, "the stage of performance," to find out that he/she did not do an adequate job and resistance is apparent. If resistance does appear at this stage, it is often impossible to reduce. It generally means that the consultant has missed something in the diagnosis, and he/she must go back to the beginning. Often this is too late.

Often resistance toward an intervention will come from sources not identified in the diagnostic stage. Merely obtaining clarity and commitment for an intervention from employees in authority positions is not enough. Employees can form pockets of resistance based on real or imagined fantasies about the consequences of an intervention. These concerns are often exaggerations and may contain paranoid ideation associated with loss. Under these conditions the consultant, the consultee, or their ideas for change become the object of fear. It is important that the consultant differentiate between the object of the employees' paranoid ideation and the nature of their fears. Employees may project fear onto a consultant while at the same time accepting the intervention, and vice versa. In addition, employees may demonstrate the acceptance of a consultant or group of consultants while quietly sabotaging the intervention.

During the intervention phase the consultant assesses his/her feelings about the endeavor. If the consultant's feelings about the consultation change, he/she must understand what has brought this about. It may be that at this stage the work of leaving the organization begins. Far worse is the consultant who feels that the consultation is not going well but refuses to admit that the intervention is problematic. Under this condition the consultant may defend against his/her anxiety through denial and may engage in a forced intervention. This consultant will view employees who resist as a problem that must be dealt with, and the consultant may alter the intervention to harm these employees.

Once the target of intervention is identified, a strategy for bringing about the desired change is formulated. Here the consultant and the consultee may work in collaboration, or the consultee may work alone. If the consultant has made a clear and adequate diagnosis, he/she may not need to be a part of the intervention process. This is consistent with the idea of increasing the recuperative tendencies of the organization. The idea is to work with the consultee in such a manner that he/she is able to bring about the desired change. To this end, the nature of the relationship between the consultant and the consultee is, in effect, redefined at this important stage. The consultant may withdraw, ending the consultation. The consultant may partially withdraw, allowing the consultee to conduct the intervention but to meet occasionally with the consultant. Or the consultant can become actively engaged in the intervention. This choice evolves from discussions with the consultee about the best strategy for precipitating change. Once decided, an intervention contract is drawn up. If the consultation continues the contract will include a description of strategy, meeting times and places, fee, duration, expected outcomes, and evaluation/documentation.

The Termination Stage

The psychoanalytic consultant thinks of termination as an important part of the consultation process. The work of termination is an area where unresolved issues concerning the consultative effort are discussed. Another important part of the termination phase is to reduce dependency. It is assumed that if the consultant has made a significant impact and has been successful in intervening in the organization, the consultee will have become increasingly dependent on the consultant. The consultant attempts to reduce the dependency by assisting the consultee in taking over the consultative effort after the consultant's departure. The consultant convinces the consultee that the work does not end with the termination of the contract. From a theoretical perspective, one will be able to discern whether the consultant has been successful in increasing the organization's capacities and recuperative tendencies if the organization can function well without the consultant.

Termination occurs once the time set in the intervention contract expires. The psychoanalytic consultant holds firmly to this contract. If the work stated in the contract is not completed, or the outcomes achieved, the consultant and consultee may draft a new contract or add an addendum to the old contract. Casual extensions or violations of any conditions of the contract are not tolerated. If the consultant cannot complete the expected or agreed-upon work within the contractual time boundaries, it is generally assumed that it is the result of organizational resistance to the consultative effort. It is generally assumed that discussion of the resistance at the same time a new contract is formulated will prove more successful than merely extending the time in an effort to overcome the resistance. The work of redoing the contract will include the important authority figures in the organization, who may not tolerate resistance because of the resulting increase in time, energy, and, most important, money. In most cases, if the consultant cannot complete the work within the agreed-on time period, he/she will not be able to complete it even with an extension.

No consultative effort can be considered a success if the system returns to its "old ways" or degenerates after the consultant leaves.

Following Lewin's (1947) suggestion, an important aspect of the consultative effort is "freezing" the change that occurs once the organization is "opened." An important sign to look for, which indicates that the consultation is going well and that a nonproblematic termination is near, is the consultee's desire to convey what he/she has learned. This includes some basics of systems theory to others both inside and outside the boundaries of the consultative effort.

Consultants are often left with two burning questions after a consultative effort is completed. One has to do with whether success, if achieved, will be long term or whether the organization will quickly return to its "old ways" after the consultant's departure; the other has to do with a sense of failure. Both of these questions are explored here under the rubric of evaluation.

EVALUATION

The most serious deficiency within the field of management consultancy is the failure of a consultative effort to be adequately assessed against standards of efficiency and effectiveness. The field has operated on the ludicrous assumption that success is a function of popularity and growth. This is clearly not the case. Experienced consultants can identify successful consultants who do poor work and excellent consultants who starve. Additionally, examples exist of consultative efforts that were described by consultants as disasters but which at a later point proved to have been successful. The reverse of this is perhaps more common.

The reason for the reluctance to evaluate consultations is perhaps the same reason that consultants do not freely discuss their failures: Consulting firms and change agents know it is "bad" for business to discuss problems, mediocre interventions, and failures. It is clear that practitioners are not interested in having their consultative efforts evaluated. According to Mirvis and Berg (1977), consultants, in their zeal to propagate their successes, leave the public with an inflated, but distorted perspective of their ability to bring about change. It seems that organizational consultants are trapped in what may be a self-defeating cycle, in which a backlog of assured successes has spawned demands for future ones.

For practitioners who think of their work with a marketing mentality, success is determined by how well they sell a commodity, and rarely by testimony from satisfied customers or independent evaluations. An unfortunate aspect of the lack of evaluation is that there is very little research information available. Those who want to learn about consulting or who are thinking about becoming a consultant receive little information about what works and what does not. However, the major losers are the consultants themselves. The entire field suffers because it paves the way for charlatans equipped with slick rhetoric, who offer a confusing array of theories, models, techniques, and formulas to baffled clients.

The lack of a unified evaluative instrument and structure is understandable. Organizational change is perhaps the most difficult of human endeavors. What type of intervention actually caused change and the assessment of change over time are exceedingly difficult to evaluate. Consider the statement by Marcus (1978), "[A]ll interventions have consequences, and one of the things we should keep in the forefront of our consciousness is that the most important consequences of any intervention almost always turn out to be the consequences that were not intended" (p. 66).

Perhaps the clearest and most informative method of evaluation is an assessment of the relations between the consultant and the consultee. Assessing the relationship gives the consultant important information about how the consultation went and the probability of success. Using some of the guidelines for evaluating the process proposed by Swartz (1975) and Lippitt (1959), consider the following points when assessing the consultant–consultee relationship:

1. Did the consultant form a sound interpersonal relationship with the client?
2. Did the consultant pay attention to the nature of the dependency relationship that might evolve in the client? (It is considered bad consulting practice to promote client dependency. Conversely, the ideal outcome is to assist the organization in realizing its own potential and maximizing its capabilities.)
3. Did the consultant focus on and think clearly about the problem?
4. Did the consultant respect the client?
5. Did the consultant appropriately achieve influence in the organization? (Some consultants "put on a show" and dramatize their plans and outcomes.)
6. Did the consultant communicate clearly to client that the skills the consultant possessed related to the client's needs or the problem at hand? (Sometimes consultations fail because the consultant tried to force-fit a limited range of techniques to a particular problem. This occurs generally because the consul-

tant lacks the skills and experience to draw on an abundance of intervention styles and methods. Perhaps the worst consultation occurs when the consultant refuses to admit that he/she cannot be of assistance.)

7. Did the consultee fully understand the nature of the consultant's role and contribution? (Some consultants are clearly nondirective, while others are exceedingly directive. The role a consultant assumes is often a function of his/her intellectual foundations as well as individual personality.) All consultants vary about how they view the problem as well as how they intervene. The style or manner in which a consultant intervenes must be communicated clearly so that the client does not have a set of expectations that cannot be realized. Consultations have been known to fail because the consultant and the consultee had different ideas about how the results of a diagnosis were to be communicated. The consultee who expects the consultant to make a major address in front of the board of directors will be in for quite a shock if the consultant expects to give him a written report.

8. Did the consultant express a willingness to have his/her services evaluated? Most reputable consultants will have a clause in their contracts stating that their work will be evaluated at a specified point in time. The consultee should have an opportunity to evaluate the consultant's work not only during the consultation, but even months after the consultant's departure.

LACK OF STANDARDS FOR EVALUATION

Overall, if a consultation is to be deemed effective, the consultant must work toward enhancing the client's system and drawing on the system's recuperative tendencies. If this evaluative indicator seems vague, it is because standards of evaluation in consultative practice are lacking. A major question facing those who wish to establish such standards is as follows: Is it possible to establish standards when there is so much uncertainty concerning what constitutes change and what factors within a given effort bring about change?

With so many competing consulting styles and ways of bringing about change, hopes for a consistent, standardized valuative process are bleak. The best we can do at this point is to examine those methods and styles of intervention that are most commonly used in management consulting.

A critical question that may shed some light on these difficulties in evaluation can be borrowed from the health profession: Did the client get well? Of course, this is not easy to define; the health profession has struggled with this issue for over 100 years. In fact, the health profession has been preoccupied for generations with issues of what is *un*healthy. A lack of health is relatively easy to define. Similarly, we find that organizational literature is filled with writings about "sick" organizations. There are many answers to what constitutes an unhealthy organization. What follows are some common characteristics of an unhealthy organization: unprofitability; interpersonal conflict; high turnover; low morale; internal conflict; high absenteeism; no growth; poor labor–management relations; and work sabotage.

On the other hand, what constitutes a healthy organization is more complex. For example, if one asks a consultant who has just worked toward lowering the turnover rate whether the organization is healthy, he/she would most likely find it difficult to answer the question because evaluating the health of an organization requires a far greater understanding of the organization's complexities. Another problem that makes finding this answer difficult is that all organizations suffer dysfunctions from time to time. Over time, every organization will move in a manner of degree along a healthy to unhealthy continuum.

Realistically, the answer to the question is not to ask the question at all, for by doing so, one is seeking a simplistic answer to a complex question and increasing the risk of being reductionistic. Perhaps a better way to ask the question, if one asks it at all, is, once again, to take a page from the health profession's book: Does the organization have recuperative powers; that is, does the organization have the power to correct the tendencies that will move it toward a dysfunctional state from time to time? Asking this question gives the consultant a chance to assess the organization's recuperative powers, and by so doing, increases the probability that the intervention will enhance these powers.

Consultations fail for many reasons. Following are the most common:

1. Management hires consultants as outsiders to do work that they are clearly capable of doing but are fearful of.
2. Consultants are hired to supplement in-house staff and then end up doing the work while the in-house staff sit back.

3. Consultants do not obtain a clear understanding of the problem and their effort goes toward the resolution of the wrong problem.
4. Consultants attempt to correct a problem or deficiency that is beyond their expertise, time constraints, or interest.
5. Management uses consultants to try to affix blame or to do management's dirty work, and the consultant cooperates unknowingly.
6. Management hires a consultant to support an already-made decision.
7. Management is content with the thought that the problems will be solved simply because the consultant has arrived.
8. The consultant underestimates the degree to which resistance to change exists in the organization.

Additionally, consultants fail either because they are too subjective or because they use too much objectivity. Consultants might also fail because they are overextended and cannot devote adequate time and attention to an organization. But perhaps the overriding reason why consultants fail is that they did not formulate a proper and thorough contract with the client.

If the contract contains agreed-upon outcomes and details specific areas where improvements in organizational functioning are expected, both the client and the consultant can assess their work together. According to Lippitt (1959), the consultative process is not just a matter of the consultant's competency and/or creativity; the process is a collaborative effort, where both parties are attempting, in their own way, to achieve the same identified goal.

GUIDELINES USED IN PSYCHOANALYTIC CONSULTING

Diagnosing the source of stress is often difficult and requires a considerable amount of patience and skill. The reason why identifying the source of problems is difficult, is that organizations cover the source with layer upon layer of resistance and changes in structure. For example, when stress occurs in the organization, a period of rapid change in the organization generally occurs. The members of the organization use this "we need to do something period" to increase their own opportunities for gratification by suggesting and implementing structural change that they consciously and unconsciously find beneficial.

When problems occur in organizations, it is generally viewed by the organization's members as a time to become opportunistic and "feather their beds." Another way of looking at this is to think of the secondary gains members derive from problems. For example, a member of the organization dies, all of the employees feel a sense of sadness and loss, but the departure of this important person in the organization unfreezes the structure of the organization and increases opportunities for members to increase their social and economic status.

Most often, the organization has gone through numerous attempts at correcting a stressful source before the consultant arrives on the scene. Sometimes an attempt to reduce stress gives rise to much more pronounced types of stress, similar to an ill person's arrival at the hospital after having attempted to doctor him/herself, only to exacerbate the original problem. Sometimes attempts to correct a dysfunction create structural changes in the organization that have benefited some employees so much that they do not want the initial stress reduced. So stress in the organization can be viewed by the consultant with an old phrase in mind, "problems go deep."

Often a consultant is called into the organization long after the stressful or traumatic incident has occurred. Usually the organization has already failed repeatedly to resolve the problem, and in its attempts has created a number of other problems. The "presenting problem" may be far removed from the initial problem. This requires the consultant to engage in skillful detective work to come up with an etiological analysis. Why is this important? The psychoanalytic consultant assumes that change is exceedingly problematic without a thorough analysis because analysis is what allows the consultant to identify real and potential resistance. The consultant looks for problems in one of six areas. It is assumed that the source of all organizational difficulties can be traced back to one of these areas.

Rice and his associates at the Tavistock Centre, as well as numerous others, have identified formal entities of a system. It is these following entities that not only function as the guideposts for psychoanalytic consulting but provide a framework within which psychoanalytic theory can be applied. They are:

1. *Boundary maintenance and regulation* (Aldrich, 1971; Baker, 1969; Beer & Huse, 1972; Chin, 1961; Dolgoff, 1972; Emery & Trist, 1960; Katz & Kahn, 1966; Klein & Gould, 1973; Newton, 1974; Rice, 1969; Rice & Miller, 1967; Sofer, 1961)
2. *Task analysis* (Dolgoff, 1972; Emery & Trist, 1960; Howenstein, 1975; Rice, 1963; Sofer, 1961)

3. *Authority and leadership* (Aldrich, 1971; Dolgoff, 1972; Howenstein, 1975; Newton, 1974; Zalesnik & Kets de Vries, 1984)
4. *Role definition* (Aldrich, 1971; Dolgoff, 1972; Katz & Kahn,
   1966; Kahn, Wolfe, Quinn, & Snock, 1964; Bensman & Lil-
   lienfeld, 1979)
5. *Interorganizational relations* (Aldrich, 1971; Baker, 1969; Chin,
   1961; Emery & Trist, 1965)
6. *Subsystem dependency and autonomy* (Argyris, 1964; Baker, 1969;
   Bennis, 1962; Dolgoff, 1972; Emery & Trist, 1960; Kahn et
   al., 1964; Rice, 1963; Schein, 1969; Sofer, 1961)

A key educative concept used in systems consulting is "insight,"
specifically, insight into the psychodynamics or covert processes
found in organizations. The systems consultant gains insight by
following the following basic concepts of systems theory: First, the
organization is a living system and ought to be viewed according to
the principles and laws that apply to all living systems. Second, as a
living system, the organization is open to interaction with its environment and engages in three major activities: taking inputs from the
environment, converting these inputs, and then maintaining an output system. Third, what differentiates the organization from other
nonhuman living systems is the assumption that unconscious motivation plays a significant role in the day-to-day functioning of its members and influences the entire system.

The psychoanalyst uses systems theory to apply psychoanalytic
theory. Psychoanalytic theory is applied within these six basic areas of
the organization. According to systems theory, these six characteristics are structural realities of all organizations. Systems theory suggests that in order for an organization to function efficiently and
effectively to increase its adaptive and recuperative abilities, it must be
able to clearly understand the dynamics within these areas (Czander,
1985). If stress exists in any one of these six areas, the three major
activities of input, conversion, and output will break down and systems dysfunction will begin. For example, it is often helpful to look at
the organization as one would view a natural ecological system. Just as
an oil spill can upset the ecology of a river bed, an inappropriate input
will upset the ecology of the organization. Or, just as an important
conversion subsystem like the liver can cause the deterioration of
one's body, so can a vital subsystem breakdown in the organization
lead to total system stress. The chief mechanisms for survival of the
organization are to be found within the six suggested areas.

The consultant follows a series of deliberate and consistent steps
while proceeding through the entire consultative effort in an attempt

to isolate and analyze the organization's dysfunction. These steps follow a set of guidelines to provide a conceptual framework for isolation and analysis of dysfunctions. They are firmly embedded in theoretical works often referred to as systems theory, general systems theory, open systems theory, or organization–environment theory.

In the following six chapters each of these guidelines will be examined.

CHAPTER 8

Boundary Maintenance and Regulation

A stone's throw out on either hand
From that well-ordered road we tread
And all the world is wild and strange:
Chruel and ghoul and Djinn and sprite
Shall bear us company to-night,
For we have reached the Oldest Land
Wherein the Powers of Darkness range.
—RUDYARD KIPLING,
Dusk to the Dawn (1925, p. 131)

As a living system, the organization is subject to the universal laws of nature. Miller (1965) contends that there are principles and hypotheses that describe living systems in general, regardless of the nature of the systems or its components. The central principle that applies to all living systems is that they must interact with their environment in order to survive. The work of interacting with the environment is twofold: to procure inputs to keep the system fed and functioning, and to locate space and consumption of the system's outputs and waste products. The process of taking in is the work of surviving, and this requires continuous interaction with other systems. All of these interactions are boundary interactions.

An assessment of the human being as a living system provides an excellent example of the nature of boundary management. The human system needs resources from its environment in order to survive. The internal subsystems break down these raw materials by consuming them for energy and converting them into finished products. The human system relies on harmonious, consistent, and productive interaction with its environment to ensure consistency and quality of inputs over time, and when this fails the system fails. Consequently, the major function of boundary management is to maintain continuous interaction with the environment. This work is exceedingly complex and difficult. Consider what Gerard (1968) suggests:

> The individual, qua biological organism, constitutes a nicely integrated hierarchy of molecules, cells, organs, and organ systems. Looking into the space enclosed by the boundaries of the skin, one can rightly assert that a person is complete and unique, a whole. But facing outward persons are constantly, sometimes pleasantly and sometimes painfully, reminded of their existence as a part, as an elementary unit in one or several social hierarchies. (p. 52)

The same principle applies to the organization. It is a distinctly unique system that functions as a single and seemingly self-enclosed unit, but as a whole it exists within the larger community of organizations and in society as a small unit. Like the individual, and all living systems, the organization must seek to attain harmony with its environment if it is to get on with the work of survival in the world.

THE FUNCTIONS OF THE BOUNDARY

The boundary of the organization has many functions, its chief one being to delineate where the boundary differentiates what is inside the system from what is outside. The boundary functions as a point of entry for all of the system's inputs, members, materials, information, and so on. It is also at the boundary that the organization meets its environment, including those constituents and significant others who formulate impressions and views of what occurs within the organization's conversion process. The boundary is often the only point where nonmembers can witness what goes on inside and obtain information about the organization's ideology, culture, and member preference. The basic operational function of the boundary is to protect the technological core of the organization. The technological core is where the conversion work occurs, where inputs are converted into outputs. Boundary management ideally serves to protect the integrity of its core; to give the core the resources necessary to do its work so that it can maintain high standards of efficiency and effectiveness.

Consider what happens when faulty boundary management occurs: the technological core may be presented with inferior material, poorly trained personnel, inadequate equipment, or disruptions. A more relevant example is a professor who is trying to teach a class when outside the window a maintenance employee is blowing leaves with a machine that makes sounds equivalent to those of an outboard motor. This is a boundary violation. It is the professor's job to protect the boundary around his small system, the classroom. Because of the violation, the professor may have to stop the class and attend to the boundary. In other words, the violation takes him away from his primary task, and the work within the technological core is violated. The maintenance subsystem has as its primary task to protect the work within the technological core, the classroom; however, both the professor and the maintenance person end up violating the work. This is a function of a set of dynamics within the organization and the maintenance department where personnel feel free to engage in their work without consideration of the core. This violation would be interpreted as an expression of hostility toward the technological core, and it may be an expression of rage toward the administration. Any effort by a support subsystem to violate the integrity of the technological core is an expression of acting out organizational conflicts. Consider what would occur if the boundary manager, the professor, were to move outside the boundaries of his/her system and attempt to stop the noise. It might be as simple as telling the maintenance employee to stop his work. But suppose the maintenance employee does not; suppose the maintenance employee says, "It's my job." Then the professor has to search for this employee's superior. Suppose the head of maintenance says "no" to the professor's request.

As one can see, this simple violation has the potential to escalate into a major event. All boundary violations have this potential. This is why many boundary managers are reluctant to engage in the vital work of protection of the boundaries. And, this is why violations of the boundary are considered expressions of organizational conflicts. Typically, boundary managers who unconsciously experience violations as an expression of organizational conflicts will withdraw into apathy. They fear the consequences of entering the fray.

It is the task of management to work to support the efforts within the core; however, in contemporary organizations, the opposite is often witnessed. This means that the efficiency and effectiveness of the organization will be limited, especially within its technological core.

BOUNDARY PERMEABILITY

The boundary varies considerably with respect to its degree of openness versus closeness to its environment, that is, what gets in and what does not and the ease with which a resource enters. Consider two restaurants, McDonald's and Lutèce (a fancy French restaurant). The primary task of a restaurant is to keep the seats occupied. However, at one the seats must be turned over with speed and at the other with slowness. The nature of time in seats is a function of boundary management.

At McDonald's, people spend a short period in seats; therefore the boundary has a high degree of permeability; it is easy to enter. The task of the boundary manager is to keep a constant flow of people with minimal delay, reducing time in seats. This is accomplished by having few seats so that people are pressured to leave, by making the seats uncomfortable, and by placing them close together. In the 1970s, Bickford's and the Automat, two highly visible New York restaurants, went out of business because the elderly would sit for hours, therefore reducing turnover. McDonald's solved this problem by making its restaurants children oriented. The organization was well aware that the elderly do not like to spend an afternoon with noisy children around. In addition, taking children to a restaurant generally means that the adults will eat quickly and run.

At Lutèce, the boundary permeability is low and is marked by requirements such as reservations, dress, a visible manager (the maitre d') at the boundary, and a preentry waiting room. These boundaries are carefully controlled; the boundary manager is expected to know the entrants and will match up entrants with waiters in an attempt to maintain system harmony.

Schwartz (1981) developed a view of boundary management that applies the queuing and waiting process to customer satisfaction. He suggests that the degree of expectations of satisfaction the entrant has is a function of the degree of permeability at the boundary. The queuing and waiting process is significantly correlated to the degree of satisfaction one expects to obtain once one is inside the organization. Consider the following example: In a strange town one gets ill, is alone in a hotel, and picks up the telephone book to call a physician. The physician answers the phone and says, "Come on over." The ill person hops in a cab and goes to the office, enters an empty waiting room, and is greeted by the physician. What is the ill person to assume? That the physician is a quack, that he has no customers, etc.? The immediate response is one of fear. The ease with which entry was gained brought lowered expectations of the type or quality of service expected inside. If the physician had made the ill person wait, it is likely that the ill person's expectations of satisfaction would have increased.

The boundary is managed purposefully with the intent of creating satisfaction. In addition to the subtleties of the queuing and waiting process, how one is treated as one enters a system will impinge upon expectations of satisfaction. Consider the following: A patron enters Lutece and the maitre d' treats the patron with disrespect. The patron is told to wait, and as the patron is waiting others appear to go ahead of him. After a long time, he is finally given a table near the kitchen door, and after another long wait a disinterested waiter is signaled. The waiter arrives and says, "I'm sorry let me get someone for you." Time passes and another waiter finally arrives and asks for the patron's order. The patron tells the waiter that he has not been given a menu. The waiter quickly returns with a menu and stands over the patron, pressuring him to decide quickly on his expensive meal. These experiences at the boundary will influence the patron's expectations of the meal, and under these conditions the meal is ruined before it arrives and the patron leaves, vowing never to return.

During the workday, an employee crosses many boundaries— meetings, departments, lunches, other organizations, and so on—and the experiences inside these systems will be a function of each experience crossing the boundary. Even if the employee does not enter or cross the boundary, how he/she is treated will create a sense of what goes on inside, or what the organization is all about.

A small manufacturing firm in a rural town had a history of treating job applicants with disrespect. A rather cruel personnel officer made each applicant wait for half a day for a brief interview, fill out numerous forms, and take a lengthy test. The interviewer then asked highly personal questions. After the interview, if the company was not interested in the applicant or had no openings, the interviewer would not contact the person and would toss out his folder. The company began to find that it had a reputation in the community of being a terrible place to work, and despite the CEO's attempts to treat his employees fairly, he could not overcome the negative reputation. The action at the boundary, the way in which potential entrants were treated, was responsible for the rumors that the company was insensitive and a bad place to work. These applicants, "filled" with the bad experience at the boundary, spread the rumors and made the reputation.

When a person enters the organization for the first time he/she is filled with symbolic representations communicated to him by the organization. It's not only the encounter with a receptionist but the physical layout, the paintings on the wall, and the general ambiance that generate a perception of the organization. While what is communicated by the organization at the boundary can rarely be articulated by the entrant, it does create a feeling state, a feeling about what goes on inside.

The most graphic example of this feeling state is why people choose one bank over another. The most significant factor is proximity; however, a close second, and first when banks are close to each other, is the feeling a potential depositor gets when he/she enters. The feelings are related to questions concerning safety, competence of the staff, the ability of the staff to work for the depositors, the attractiveness of the other depositors, and other factors (e.g., seats for the elderly, speed of service for the young, and special lines signifying status). The boundary is exceedingly important to the life of an organization. Who the organization decides to place at the boundary is a symbolic representation of the value the organization gives to the entrants. Also, how these employees manage the boundary—its queuing and waiting process, its degree of permeability, and its general sensitivity to potential entrants—will influence expectations. The way in which an organization manages these boundaries is a reflection of the manner in which the executive constellation manages its boundaries both within and outside the organization, including how they go about the business of bringing in resources as well as how they keep out noxious stimuli.

THE PSYCHOLOGY OF BOUNDARY MANAGEMENT

Given the turbulent nature of the contemporary business environment, the CEO is required to spend increasing amounts of time at the boundaries. The CEO is frequently called on to represent the organization in myriad relationships with federal, state, and local government regulatory agencies, financial institutions, national union representatives, consumer groups, sales and marketing organizations, and so on. For example, it has been estimated that the heads of Japanese firms spend 80% of their work time at the boundary of the organization negotiating relationships between their organization and the various groups and institutions in the environment.

There are two reasons why a CEO would choose to stay inside an organization and not attend to boundary management: the first has to do with the nature of the organization and the culture that is established over time; the second has to do with the personality of the CEO in the organization. This raises questions concerning the capacity to engage in the work of boundary management: Why is it that in one type of organization, a manager is capable, and in another, the work is neglected? Is this capacity to engage in the work a function of the organization's culture, of the personality of the manager, or of a combination of both?

It was Rice (1969) who suggested that the function of boundary management is similar for all living systems. He suggests that what the ego stands for in terms of understanding individual boundary management, the CEO stands for in the organization. The CEO and the ego perform similar functions; their primary functions are to mediate relationships between the internal world of the system and its external environment. The psychoanalytic consultant, relying on experience in assessing ego functioning, is able to expand or apply ego functions to CEO functions and to further elaborate the principles underlying boundary management. For example, Peterfreund, (in Rogers [1980]), sees the concept of ego or ego functions as "built-in (structural) strategies for self regulation available for the control of behavior of an open system, such as the self-preservative tendency of living organisms to maintain a steady-state homeostasis of functions" (p. 665). To extrapolate this view of the ego to the functioning or capacities of the organization, one can now see the CEO as serving similar functions for the organization. The CEO sits at the boundary of the organization, between the organization's internal world and its external environment. The boundary is the membrane and protector of what is internal, and the task of the CEO, in a manner similar to the ego, is to maintain internal harmony and order. Failure to do so will precipitate internal stress and disharmony, and it will make it difficult for the organization to adapt to its environment in an efficient and effective manner.

The CEO, like the ego, has a limited amount of energy, and if the CEO's energy is devoted to controlling the organization's internal complexities, he/she will be unable to engage in the efforts necessary to adapt the organization to its external environment. To put this another way, if the ego's energy is devoted to controlling the organization's internal complexities, it will be depleted and unable to make the necessary effort to exercise efficient and effective boundary management. For example, a weakened ego will allow inaccurate or inappropriate information into the system; it will engage in unrewarding or destructive relationships with important other systems in the environment and will allow harmful resources to enter the system. If the system is a person and has a weakened ego, the person's capacity to function optimally will be significantly reduced through faulty boundary management. This person may allow the following to enter his/her system: alcohol, nonnutritional food, cigarettes, or damaging, stressful relationships. Similarly, a weakened CEO will allow into the organization inappropriate resources, or will fail to bring into the system resources necessary for survival. When this occurs, the consequences are internal subsystem stress, subsystem decomposition, and eventual system death.

This conceptualization also holds true on the output side of the system. Just as the ego differentiates objects in the real world and what is projected onto it from within the system, the CEO must be able to manage what leaves the organization and enters into its environment. In short, a mature ego or a well-functioning CEO can define the boundary between what is inside and outside and control the nature of the transactions between them. When this executive function is damaged, the boundary cannot be managed properly and the system is threatened.

Boundary activities can be conceptualized as having concrete duties and responsibilities, while the ability to carry out these duties has psychological underpinnings. The work of psychoanalytic consulting is not to assess the nature of the duties to be performed but to diagnose why the duties are not performed, or why the boundary is not managed responsibly. Although there may be a structural deficit in the employee's cognitive understanding of the duties of the role of the CEO, the answer is most likely to be found in an understanding of the dynamics and genetic considerations of the organization's pathology.

The CEO, like the ego, has capacities, which here are called skills. The ego contains conscious and unconscious mental processes. The ego releases and binds affective energy and influences the process and content of information flowing into and out of the human system. Anna Freud (1966) places the ego at the seat of observation.

> The function of the ego is to adapt the human system to its environment and provide gratification for unconscious impulses, i.e., to maintain a sense of adaptative peace between the internal and external world. When peace is obtained, the ego can fulfill the duties of correctly perceiving external reality and improving, as well as the systems positions in the world. (p. 51)

The consultant looks for those things in the individual consultee and within the larger organization that interfere with these skills. Essentially, the consultant wants to know if the CEO is able to master his/her environment relative to the resources available. This is accomplished by assessing the CEO's objective performance, subjective sense of competency, expectation of success, and degree of concordance between actual performance and his/her experience. A performance analysis of the CEO assesses two of the CEO's primary tasks: (1) to ensure that the boundaries of the system are maintained and regulated and (2) to ensure that the "conversion" work is effectively and efficiently carried out. Maintaining the boundaries is the "gut" work of managing. It entails working in strange and alien environments. Making deals, trying to obtain resources for his system, and ensuring his/her system's survival will bring the CEO into hostile, competitive, and depriving environments and expose him/her to failure and degradations. For these reasons, the CEO often avoids this work. He/she prefers to stay "at home" inside the organization where it is safe and where narcissistic injury is least likely to occur. Inside the organization the CEO can use his/her authority as a protective cover against these real and imagined injuries.

When the CEO does venture outside the organization and experiences failure and humiliation, he/she will use the organization to sooth narcissistic vulnerabilities. The CEO responds to fears of going into the environment by meddling in the internal life of the organization. He/she may begin by restructuring the organization or establishing new internal rules and regulations. The CEO's actions have a dual purpose. In addition to avoiding the boundary management work, the CEO can obtain idealized responses from subordinates. If the CEO is unable to obtain idealized responses, he/she may react by becoming overinvolved with rules and regulations and may actively seek and punish violators.

When the boundaries are well maintained and regulated, the internal subsystems (the conversion system) will function well and require minimal leadership. If management develops a primary structure, the remainder of their efforts should occur at the boundary where the staff, money, materials, machines, intelligence, and other resources that facilitate work are imported or enter. If the employees receive all they need in order to get on with the job, they will engage in their work without difficulty. Difficulty arises when the employees do not get the primary resources necessary to do their job, and often the result is that the CEO has to spend an inordinate amount of time "putting out brush fires" or handling internal problems.

Faulty boundary management invariably leads to internal problems within the organization. For example, would we have had race riots in the 1960s if the leadership of our country had listened to Thomas Jefferson and others who believed that the practice of slavery was a poor policy and would come back to haunt us? Would we have a drug problem if we could successfully prohibit large quantities of heroin and cocaine from coming into the United States? The point is, what occurs internally within the organization, or for that matter within any subsystem, can be traced back to the management of boundaries. Decisions or the lack of decisions made at the boundary will affect the internal life of any system. Therefore, the psychoanalytic consultant who is asked to consult about any type of internal dysfunction begins the investigation by assessing problems at the boundary.

CONSULTING TO THE BOUNDARIES

Some consultants (e.g., Ferguson, 1968) suggest that the primary focus of any consultation should be on the organization's boundaries and those who manage them. This includes not only the boundaries surrounding the system but also those surrounding the subsystems that make up the organization. Ferguson (1968) believes that relationships among and between subsystems make for either collaboration and health or imbalance, stress, and dysfunction. Furthermore, he says that it is along the interface between systems and subsystems, (i.e., between its parts) that the system is either welded and linked or stressed and broken.

Every boundary between every system offers opportunities for either collaboration or conflict. It is the managers of these interfaces who hold the key to organizational success, and it is these people who generally benefit most from a boundary focused consultation.

The consultant assesses four types of boundary management within the organization and its respective subsystems:

1. Regulation of the task system boundary (the system's input, conversion, and export systems and their relationships);
2. Regulation of the sentient[1] group boundary (this includes role and division of labor);
3. Regulation of the organization's boundaries; and
4. Regulation of the relationships between task, sentient, and organizational boundaries.

No assessment of the boundary activities of any organization is complete without an assessment of the entry subsystems where those things needed for internal conversion work are imported and where

---

[1]This refers to the emotional life of the members of a system. It is assumed that emotions and feelings will influence how group members perceive and respond to their work activities and the activities of other groups and organizations with which they interact.

noxious factors that may damage the system are rejected. The consultant assesses three points of entry into the organization: (1) of people, whether members or nonmembers; (2) of materials and resources; and (3) of the consultant into the organization.

Entry of People

Entry is a fundamental aspect for the individual as well as for organizational life. For the individual, the task of "getting in" is often an overriding and lifelong effort. Seeking admission to school, professional societies, neighborhoods, clubs, social networks, and jobs requires considerable preparation and, in some cases, many years of education, training, and socialization. For the individual and the organization, the act of getting a job means, in effect, achieving entry into the world of work. Thus we find that the personnel office serves a crucial function not only for the organization but also for the individual. For the organization, this office, or subsystem, is a major element in the relationship of the organization to its environment. The personnel office determines the character and composition of applicancy population. In service organizations, the entry office determines the composition of the client population. In this case, if the office is functioning inefficiently, the organization may well be faced with a variety of problems stemming from the improper regulation of clients, such as an overabundance of clients, incompetent recruitment of staff, or entry of ill-suited clients.

Entry of Material and Resources

It often follows that personnel responsible for the procurement of resources, material, and intelligence have little knowledge of the overall operation of the organization and function with limited authority. This subsystem requires continual intersystem communication with the operational subsystems within the organization. The subsystem also must engage in continual exchange with those systems in the environment that provide the necessary ingredients to keep the organization functioning. In addition, this subsystem is required to assess the quality and cost of materials gathered in the environment and to predict the future of supply availability and cost over time.

For example, if one assesses the importance of the purchasing subsystem of a peach cannery, one finds that this subsystem has a direct effect on the survival of the organization. This subsystem must be able to purchase high-quality peaches at the lowest cost, and, additionally, it must be able to predict crop production and develop a method to assess the future of the market. This unit must also assess the market in terms of competition, especially if crop reduction occurs. And finally, this unit must be able to work harmoniously with the sales or marketing subsystems and offer intelligence concerning the control of consumption via advertising and pricing. A major advertising campaign begun at the time of a severe crop shortage could spell both short- and long-term disaster for the company.

The entry subsystem has the potential to promote either harmony or dysfunction among the production subsystems found in the conversion system. In addition to bringing high-quality material into the system for the conversion process, the subsystem must regulate the flow of material into the conversion system. The authority existing in this subsystem is of special importance. If the entry subsystem does not have the authority to control the flow of material or information into the production subsystems, it will operate merely as a viaduct, continually sending into the system whatever comes its way. In the entry subsystem and production subsystem relationship, each has the potential to undermine the other. The entry subsystem can withhold vital material or send inappropriate material or information into the other subsystems of the organization. Predictably, the production subsystem will continually blame the entry subsystem. Both subsystems must have harmonious relationships with the experimental or research subsystems where material changes can be adequately assessed before they are allowed to enter the production units. A common problem in production companies occurs when contracts are procured and the company has neither the technology nor the expertise to complete them satisfactorily. This leads to cost overruns, which jeopardize the reputation of the company and in some instances lead to bankruptcy.

Nonprofit human services organizations invariably fold because of an inability to bring into the organization adequate funding. This occurs for a number of reasons: ignorance of the grant-writing process; inadequate fund raising; the blind belief that as long as the staff keep doing their good and important work an angel will appear in the form of a wealthy donor or, at the last moment, the politicians will realize they cannot in good conscience eliminate this "valuable" program. In the meantime, during this moment of crisis, which occurs with frightening frequency, the work of the organization comes to a standstill as the organization's resources are put to the test of gathering funds. Calamities of this sort are often the result of the CEO's devoting too little time or energy to the planning and development of an adequate entry subsystem until it is too late.

Entry of the Consultant

The first task of the consultant is to assess the entry subsystems. The consultant tries to answer the following questions:

1. What is the nature of authority in this subsystem when compared to the overall hierarchical structure?
2. How is the manager of the entry subsystem perceived by the management constellation of the organization?
3. Does the CEO show an active interest in the entry subsystems?
4. Is the delegation of authority given to those who are considered competent by others in the organization?
5. Who is placed at the boundary of the organization and why?

Second, the consultant works toward specifying the major tasks of the entry subsystems. He/she assesses how the entry system is receiving and performing its work with the clients, staff, material, and information that enter the organization. The consultant investigates the relationships between the entry subsystem and the production (technological core) and maintenance subsystems. Finally, the consultant assesses the quantity and quality of effort that goes into developing and maintaining those necessary relationships between the organization and its environment. In other words, the consultant carefully assesses the relations with those subsystems that are responsible for fulfilling vital needs and ensuring the organization's survival.

The most productive method of gaining this valuable information about the entry subsystem is for the consultant to assess his/her own experience on entering the organization.

It should be clear by now that the boundary has significant social and psychological characteristics which are projected onto the consultant as he enters. These characteristics contribute to the development of a psychoanalytic understanding of this process. Attitudes and values can be assessed through an analysis of the symbolic effort management gives to the work of boundary management, and how the organization collectively responds to the consultant as an entering object. The response to the consultant contains conscious and unconscious motivations. For example, some executives see the organization as symbolically protected by a wall, insulating itself from the dangerous environment. This attitude is a reflection of both individual and group concerns about external dangers, which are a reflection of unconscious experiences with a dangerous world. This attitude is interpreted by the consultant as he assesses his/her own experience as an entering object. For example, if the employees respond to the consultant as a fearful object, the consultant can begin to generalize from this experience and make assumptions about the prevailing attitude.

These perceptions of the environment may be a function of irrational fears or they may have a firm base in reality. The psychoanalytic consultant is most concerned with irrational fears and responses to the environment. For example, irrational fears may precipitate an array of defenses against interaction with a strange and new situation. The basis for these fears is rarely lodged exclusively in either the personality of the CEO or the organization's culture, but to varying degrees in both. Irrational fears are considered generalized representations of earlier experiences. These fears must be assessed if the consultation is to continue.

Irrational fears of the environment, or what lies beyond the boundaries of the organization, are indicated by the affects and anxiety the CEO feels when he/she enters the environment. These affects and resulting anxiety are a function of unconscious derivatives stimulated by relationships that have occurred in the past. Going into the environment will precipitate the trauma or reawaken a dormant trauma.

In this case the CEO shrinks from any experience that increases anxiety. The organization suffers because the CEO cannot attend to the work of boundary management. Consider the following: a chief executive began to curtail his business traveling. He told the consultant that he and his wife were having marital problems, that he feared she was having an affair, and that he considered it vital to stop travel to save his marriage. After further inquiry the consultant discovered that these fears were associated with an encounter one evening while the executive was out of town and staying in a hotel.

The executive met a man at a bar. After an enjoyable conversation, the man invited the executive to join him for dinner. The executive had a wonderful time. However, he drank excessively, which resulted in his disclosing information of a highly personal nature to this complete stranger. He had never done this before. He went to bed late and found himself overwhelmed with anxiety and an inability to sleep. The executive could not get the thought out of his head that the man was a homosexual and that he might be attracted to the man and thus he was a homosexual. He was in a full-blown homosexual panic. The executive was supposed to meet with the man for breakfast the following morning, but he quickly left and in the process canceled all his business meetings. On the plane home he developed the fantasy that his wife was being unfaithful. Over the course of the next several months, the executive found multiple excuses to avoid travel. In the meantime, the company suffered.

Kramer (1977) and Rohrlich (1980), in their exploration of the homosexual dynamics stimulated by the submissive requirements of organizations, suggest that unconscious homosexual wishes are often at the base of what Rohrlich (1980) refers to as "hypermasculinity." This is where the male defends against these wishes by being "abrasive, driven, competitive, arbitrary, impolite, and excessively aggressive." For this executive, going into the environment meant that his repressed and threatening feelings of being weak, passive, and vulnerable would emerge and be observed by all. So he opted to stay "at home" where he could be idealized and feel a sense of power and control.

In another organization, a company also suffered because the CEO was incapable of engaging in the necessary boundary work. The board of directors, in its search for a new CEO, selected a vice president who had been with the company for many years. He was an excellent vice president, the employees were fond of him, and everyone applauded the choice. He was an excellent number two person. He worked well managing the internal life of the organization; enjoyed this work and was good at it. However, he did not like to travel and disdained hotels, restaurant food, conferences, and parties. He was happy in his office, in familiar surroundings, with people he knew. The CEO position required that he travel, enter unfamiliar environments, meet with new people, and act polished and gregarious. Needless to say, the boundary work of this organization did not get done. The organization suffered.

The question for analysis is, Why was this person chosen? The board of directors knew this man well. This choice can be explained in light of the dynamics within the board and the organization. In its choice, the board denied the relevance of boundary management. The decision represented the culture of the organization, which demonstrated a distinct preference for insulating itself from the environment. In a collusive manner, the board represented the wishes of the staff. The board chose a person who was incapable of doing the work. The board perceived that the organization's environment was too unpredictable, chaotic, and dangerous, and this fear was symbolically represented throughout the organization and most likely embedded in its culture. Consequently, the board chose a person who was unconsciously viewed as a symbolic representation of the organization. However, in this case the employee chosen was a symbolic representation of a dysfunctional culture. Additional issues may have influenced the decision, relating to guilt, loyalty, a response to the previous CEO, or an unconscious desire to destroy the company.

When consulting to a situation like the one described or any boundary issue, the consultant must seek answers to the following questions: What is feared from the environment? What are the internal conflicts that make it difficult to engage in environmental interaction? What are the fears associated with leaving the organization and entering the outside environment?

To reiterate, one can obtain an increased understanding of the unconscious meaning associated with boundary management if one assesses how the work of boundary management is manifested. One does this by assuming that the boundary is established to protect the system. All stimuli that enter the system are considered impingements. Over time, the organization and the CEO come to view these impingements with joy and acceptance or fear and rejection. This is often a function of the organization's history, past conflicts (internal and external), and compromise formations (methods historically used to reduce conflict).

The consultant assumes that as a new object entering the system, he/she will be treated in a fashion similar to other objects that have entered the system. The consultant looks for behaviors among those employees at the boundary that are replications. He attempts to answer the question, Am I being treated in a fashion similar to the manner in which other objects entering the organization are treated? Furthermore, the consultant investigates the motivations that boundary-spanning employees have for treating new objects the way they do. For example, is the consultant treated with respect, fear, devaluation, hope, grandiosity, and so on, and what does this mean in the context of organizational dynamics and for the future of the consultative effort?

This information is ferreted out in the early phases of the consultation. Particular attention is devoted to the manner in which initial negotiations are conducted. The consultant must clarify the following issues: (1) the nature of the initial request for consultation; (2) the authority inherent in the request vis-à-vis the organization; and (3) task expectations. Clarity is important because there are usually many covert reasons for requesting the consultation. Careful examination of the reasons for the request can reveal various resistances to change and to the consultative process in general. By conducting this assessment, the consultant essentially arrives at a picture of the entry process as a microcosm of how the entry subsystem operates in general.

CASE HISTORY: A CONSULTATION TO A COLLEGE

After hearing the consultant lecture, the dean of students of a small residential New England college called and requested his assistance. The dean said that the school had a student drinking problem which was getting out of hand. The drinking had precipitated "rowdy" behavior on the weekends, and the school needed to make some sense of why the sudden increase in problem behavior had occurred and to develop methods of solving the problem.

The consultant felt that he could be of help only if the dean and the college president would agree to assess the problem in terms of the entire college. The consultant went on to explain that he could only assess the problem from the perspective of an organizational consultation, which would include an organizational diagnosis beginning with the college president. To assess the problem as existing exclusively within the student population would be too limited and might end up in "blaming the victim." The dean agreed and a meeting was set up with the college president. The fee was satisfactorily negotiated and they agreed to a 2-hour meeting in which they would discuss the scope of the problem and a structure to be followed in conducting the consultation.

The consultant arrived at the college president's office and was immediately ushered in by the president's secretary. Coffee was ordered and the consultant asked the president if it was possible that they not be disturbed. The president agreed and informed his secretary. The dean was absent. The president said that the dean had other issues to attend to and that his function had been only to locate a "good" consultant. When discussing the college's problems, the president demonstrated little concern about the alcohol consumption on campus and only peripherally recognized the problem. He proceeded to discuss enrollment issues, the entry of women into the college, and the deteriorating quality of its students compared with students in the past. He explained that the traditions of the college had been forgotten, and that competition with other colleges, even those with a poor reputation, had recently increased. He was worried that his college might be losing in the competition for students.

The consultant conveyed his uncertainty as to why he was needed or how he could be of help. After a period of silence, the consultant said that he could see a number of areas that needed exploration but that the president would have to be a bit clearer about his expectations of the consultant. The president replied that a consultation was in order, but he could not seem to articulate why, and he indicated some embarrassment. The consultant, sensing an eagerness for assistance but difficulties in talking about the college's problems to a complete stranger, suggested a meeting with some of the president's administrative staff. The president immediately suggested three administrators—the dean of students, the academic dean, and the dean of admissions—as well as the chair of the history department.

The consultant asked the president if he was aware of the fee arrangement made with the dean. They then agreed that there would be two fees: a low fee for the exploratory work and a higher fee for the diagnostic, formulation, and intervention work. The consultant said that he wished to meet with the suggested staff group for 2 hours, and then with the president once again.

Analysis of the Initial Meeting

It was clear that while the consultant was assessing the nature of the problem and the receptiveness to a consultation, the president was conducting an interview assessing the consultant's ability and his suitability to work in the institution. The college is an institution of academic excellence, with a long history and tradition. The president's inquiries were to help him assess the consultant's ability to understand and support that tradition. The president was also concerned about trust, and he wanted to allay his fears that the consultant would use information gained from the consultation to damage the institution. The initial question facing the consultant concerned the nature of the president's fears. Were these fears appropriate to the situation? If not, could they be generalized to fear of other objects entering the organization (e.g., freshmen)? If this were the case, the consultant could focus on boundary issues. This important question would be answered later in the consultation.

The tradition of the college would give the consultant important clues to the existing culture and the possibility of conflicts between the old traditions and the new values established by the current student population. At the initial consultation, the dean of students had maintained that the conflict centered around student alcohol consumption. The president had not legitimized the alcohol problems, but had clearly recognized other issues, such as the conflicts between the old traditions and the behavior of the new students and conflicts between the "old guard" and new employees.

The president seemed to be a dominant force in the college, both on the interpersonal level and in his role as president. This was demonstrated by his self-presentation to the consultant and by the fact that he was able to delegate work responsibility. He agreed to delegate the responsibility for the consultation to other staff members. This delegative effort was especially important considering the material to be discussed and its threatening nature to the perception of the president's competency.

The initial interview with the president led to the formulation of a structure to accommodate the consultative work. It seemed vital to the consultation, and to its ultimate effectiveness, that the structure for the consultative process come from the president. The president would assign all consultees with whom the consultant would work and the consultant would report to the president. This structure permitted the president maximum access to the information that would come out of the consultation and also solidified the work bond between the primary consultee (the president) and the consultant.

Initially the consultant focused on establishing a structure for work. However, the consultant suspected that the desire of the president to control the consultative process did not necessarily mean that he was ready and willing to fully cooperate. It may very well have been that the president's desire for control was a resistance.

In order for the consultee to join in a viable work relationship with the consultant, a motivational level must be maintained. This motivation is a function of the consultee's feelings of involvement and responsibility for the problem under consideration. If the consultee's involvement in the problem precipitates anxiety, the consultee may be unable to work and will resort to behaviors or perceptions of the problem that are defensive in nature. Often in discussions about the nature of the problem with the consultee, the consultant will be able to assess the nature of the consultee's resistance. The consultant must be aware that merely being invited in by a consultee is not sufficient for a successful outcome. The key for the consultant is to maintain an awareness of shifting motivational levels and to discuss them openly with the consultee. In essence, ancillary to the work of the consulting are paying careful attention to the emotional state of the consultee and working in such a way that anxiety and resistance do not undermine the consultation.

Some major questions remained at the end of the initial stage (entry stage) of the consultation. Why did the dean, who actually made the initial contact, transfer the consultant to the president? Why didn't the dean collaborate with the president? And finally, what was the real difference between the dean's perception of the problem and the president's? While the dean quickly focused on a single issue, the president was more comfortable with the larger factors that were negatively influencing the system.

An additional word about the president is helpful: He was able to communicate to the consultant, as the consultant crossed the boundary (entered the system), the importance of the institution and the respect given to the learning process. He communicated to the consultant what the institution was really like inside. The consultant developed the idea that if everyone who entered the college had an opportunity to spend an hour with this person, who so completely loved the institution, the college might be perceived differently. This observation, coupled with the president's initial fears of the consultant, would have implications for a diagnosis and intervention. For now, it seemed that the president's withdrawal from boundary activities was based on his fear of new students and new administrators. They were seen as aggressive, insubordinate, and volatile.

Second Meeting with Senior Administrators

The following week, the consultant met with the three administrators and the head of the history department in the college boardroom. The dean of students introduced the consultant, and the consultant quickly set the time boundary by announcing, "We will spend 2 hours together." The consultant did this to establish his authority in the room. The three administrators hurriedly began to move into what seemed to be prepared statements about the degree of drinking on campus and their personal views of the causes. They presented charts, graphics, demographic data, and even figures on alcohol-related crimes and problems in the surrounding town. They monopolized the first hour of the meeting, with each administrator having an opportunity to present information. Entangled in the presentation was a complaining tone about how the quality of life at the college had deteriorated. Collectively they expressed hopelessness about the dilemmas they faced, at the same time drawing up a long list of the causes of the problem. The list included changes in student character, backgrounds, attitudes, and parental supervision, or lack of it; the failure of the larger educational system; the lowering of the drinking age in the state, and the resulting increase in alcohol consumption; the increase in drug abuse in the larger society; and the difficulties the liberal-arts-educated person faces in today's society.

After listening to the administrators, the consultant said, "How can we possibly solve such a complex problem?" They laughed, and one of the administrators said, "Did you say *we?* It's *your* problem."

The consultant observed three characteristics of the administrators that suggested that working with them would be difficult: (1) their rigidity and formality; (2) their desire to shift the blame for the problem to a multitude of external factors; and (3) their wish to give the entire package to the consultant. After a few moments, the consultant said to the administrators, "After hearing your presentations, I quite frankly do not know what to do, or where to begin."

Feeling anxiety, the consultant called on the history professor with the hope of saving himself. The professor happily jumped in. He quickly aligned himself with the consultant by saying that he had been at the college for almost 35 years and during this time had "seen everything" and "heard it all." He said that he agreed with the consultant's initial reaction, and that they could either waste time in speculation or develop a framework for understanding the problem better. The consultant agreed and said that he thought he could provide a structure for examination, but before doing so, he would find it helpful to hear about the history of the college. One of the administrators startled the consultant by stating that he had never heard the history. The other two administrators both scurried off to get coffee and returned, prepared and eager to listen.

The history professor began a brilliant description of the history of the college, highlighting its high and low points with a sense of meaning and empathy.

At the end of the meeting, the consultant said that he certainly had a lot to think about[2] and that he would like to meet with them once again but first he wanted to talk to the president. The consultant then asked them if they felt that others from the college could be helpful and should be included. They said yes, and the consultant quickly suggested that they might want to go ahead and discuss with the president the inclusion of additional staff. The consultant was also aware that he was suggesting that the senior administrators meet with the president. He was also encouraging a continuous discussion of the issues at hand. It is important that the consultant either directly or indirectly suggest to the staff that they work on the problem when he is not present. This is one way to avoid dependency on the consultant, as well as to minimize the belief that only a consultant can solve organization's problems.

The evening before meeting with the president, the consultant developed an initial formulation.

[2]Due to the exploratory nature of this meeting, and the early stage of the consultation, the consultant took notes. With practice, it is possible to write notes and participate in a meeting of this type.

Formulation

Clues to the stresses that occur internally in a system can be assessed with greater clarity if one is able to examine the changes or jolts that occurred at the boundary of the system over time. The boundary system of the college had altered significantly over a 4-year period prior to the consultation: in 1975, women students admitted for the first time; in 1977, admissions requirements were lowered; and in 1975–1979, freshman-orientation programs were gradually phased out.

Entry of Women

In 1975, the first major change in the boundary regulatory system occurred since World War II. The entry of women into a 180-year-old men's college brought with it major strains on the resources of the system. Women entered without adequate housing arrangements. No dormitory space was available so space was allocated in local rooming houses and in one defunct fraternity house. There were few female faculty members, administrators, and counselors, and a rush to hire women staff members brought in outsiders with little or no knowledge of the existing internal system or its traditions and values. Prejudices were acted out by male staff in the form of neglecting newly hired women; the institution thus offered little in the way of socialization as these women crossed the boundary. The college-board scores and high school grade averages of the women students were higher than those of their male counterparts, but after the first year the women's grade-point ratio was almost identical to the men's.

The all-male "club atmosphere" at the college suffered a trauma. While some all-male subsystems opened their doors to women, most actively developed covert arrangements to eliminate women students. In the past, the thrust of the social life for male students had taken the form of a linkage with four all-female colleges in the region. These linkages became strained as structured nonacademic events (dances, conferences, etc.) between the schools were phased out to reflect the fact that the college now had women on campus. The phasing out of these structured events increased a sense of isolation among students on the campus and fostered an entrepreneurial social life for the students.

Creating a social life outside the formal authority structure of the college left the students alone without authority, parental supervision, or structure. Being left to their own devices, away from parental authority and in a relatively new environment, produced considerable anxiety. From a psychoanalytic perspective, the previous organizational structure provided an externalized superego control system to defend against libidinal drives. The new structure proved to lack the authority of the (parental) structure to repress sexual aims, which led to regression. Initially, "naughty" behavior was intended to upset the administration. However, this behavior soon turned to anger. Both sexes experienced resentment and complaints proliferated. The major complaint was that the administration no longer cared.

Lowering Admissions Criteria

In 1977, another jolt was received at the boundary. While lowering the admission requirements actually brought no significant change to the intellectual life of the college, or to the quality of work and grade-point averages among the students, an image was created that the college was "slipping." Another fact that contributed to this view was that graduates were finding it increasingly difficult to gain admission to the better graduate schools. This was no reflection on the quality of the school. It was, in fact, the result of the proliferation of college graduates throughout the country seeking admission at the same time, and thus increasing competition. However, these two factors reinforced the impression that the college was losing its tradition of academic excellence. This view was expressed by alumni, who became increasingly discontented with the course the college was following. The college staff, being pragmatic, feared that alumni discontent would be reflected in donations, a vital resource to the college.

Phasing Out the Freshman-Orientation Program

The third jolt to the boundary occurred during the 1975–1979 period. While this change was of little interest to faculty and administrators, it was the most significant change in the boundary regulatory system. The college began phasing out its rather intensive freshman-orientation program. The phaseout reduced the program from what was once an intensive one-week socialization process during which entrants had the opportunity to meet with the president, senior administrators, and key professors and counselors. Alumni were invited to talk and the history, traditions, and values of the school were firmly entrenched in the mind of every entering freshman. The phasing out of this program resulted in severing the connectedness that new students could feel to the history of the institution. It also facilitated a failure to provide the entrants with a role that was tied to tradition and values. The absence of role accommodation gave new freshmen a sense of alienation from the institution. The students' need for a psychological connection shifted from the institutional boundary to small informal groups of peers. Now the students had to find their own way in the college and develop their own culture. This culture was radically different from the old culture of the larger system. The sense of alienation from the larger institution created stresses among the student population, and it brought out stress-relieving activities, such as drinking. The "rowdiness" could now be interpreted as an expression of hostility or anger toward an institution that was perceived as uncaring.

Another factor that needed to be included in the consultant's formulation was the apparent rigidity and anxiety demonstrated by the three senior administrators assigned to meet with him. Their lack of knowledge about the traditions of the college suggested that they might be in a position similar to that of the student population. Additionally, they appeared to be under considerable pressure to return the college to its original state of existence, where old values and traditions were internalized by the institution's members, a state they knew little about. How could the students be expected to internalize the values of the institution and feel comfort in what was supposed to be a serene academic climate when the institution's three senior administrators demonstrated little knowledge of what the institution's values were?

The consultant was comfortable with this formulation and the next step was to develop a structure where consultee receptiveness was high and an atmosphere for change was possible.

Second Meeting with the President

When the consultant arrived, he was promptly invited into the president's office. The president announced that all calls would be held and then stated that he had invited the senior administrators and the history professor to the meeting. When the consultant asked why the president did this, considering that he (the consultant) had not discussed the nature of the meeting, the president replied, "My staff all said they felt the consultation was necessary and were highly impressed with the consultant." He went on to say, "We want to get on with the consultation and their presence may speed things up a bit." The first thought that passed through the consultant's mind was that the president was undermining the consultant's wish for a structure. Then the rationale for the president's decision became clear. The consultant had in effect suggested that the three senior administrators meet with the president and it seemed possible that the president did not want to have such intimate contact with them. If this were the case, some additional work was required to assess the dynamics between the president and his staff.

The administrators arrived without the professor. The consultant did most of the talking and presented his diagnosis, leaving out any references to the apparently strained relationship between the president and his administrators. At the conclusion of the discussion, the consultant firmly recommended to the president that he meet with a group of six faculty members whose opinions the president respected, and who were aware of both the traditions of the college and some of the present problems. The consultant also recommended that he and the president meet for six, 2-hour meetings. The president thought for a few moments and then said, "What about these guys," referring to the administrators. The consultant said as gently as possible that he thought they were too close to the problem at hand. The consultant said that he would need to talk with them later and that bringing them in at a later point would be more beneficial. The president agreed. Later, the consultant and president quickly reached an agreement on the fee and the president agreed to have a contract drawn up. The consultant gave the president an outline of what he wanted in the contract and the meeting ended.

Leaving the administrators out seemed to be a logical choice. When making decisions of this type, concerning whom to include and whom to exclude, a major criterion is the degree to which the consultee is altruistically involved. The professor wanted their college to "get well," but the administrators seemed to have a greater investment in preserving their jobs and status or, perhaps even more suspect, using the problem to increase their status. Under conditions where employees see the consultation as a vehicle to improve their condition in the organization, the consultation will suffer. With this in mind, the consultant chose to keep these administrators out of the consultation.

Diagnosis

The critical issue at this point was the development of a structure that would provide a receptive environment and would increase the likelihood that the president would act on the recommendations. This was especially important because the consultant felt that the greatest resistance to change would come from the president. To successfully complete this consultation, the creation of an atmosphere of trust was vital. The professors, a group of trusted colleagues, would help the president overcome what had been a confusing climate of administration. It seemed that the only group capable of influencing the president was the professors.

Meeting with the Professors

The meeting with the professors went remarkably well. An atmosphere was established for engaging in an analysis of the history of the college, and assessing the major shifts in the college's boundaries. The consultant's original formulations were viewed as accurate and were accepted with enthusiasm. New information that turned up reinforced the initial interpretations. During the meetings, the consultant found it helpful to assign the professors two papers to read; at one point he also gave a half-hour lecture. Although this may seem like an attempt to place the professors in a student role and convince them of the consultant's position, it was not the case. The professors were genuinely interested in how their organization functioned and greatly appreciated the theoretical underpinnings of the consultant's recommendations.

Discussions focusing on the executive constellation of the college proved especially enlightening. The following picture unfolded: When the college began experiencing some recruitment difficulties, the trustees moved to bring in more business/management-orientated administrators. The dean of students and the academic dean returned to teaching. The men who were hired to replace them were young, had limited or no teaching experience, and were professionally trained in school or business administration. By acting to increase the managerial expertise of the executive constellation, a gap was created between the newly hired administrators and the faculty.

As the problems at the college progressively worsened, senior faculty close to the president and important alumni began to view the administrators as inept, and the gap increased. These meetings with the consultant were the first time faculty explored issues openly instead of griping and complaining to or about the administration. The faculty concluded that the president had been adrift in recent years, aloof from the students. Also, they were not at all impressed with the new administrative team surrounding him. They saw the president as a scholar, as a person who enjoyed the company of scholars. He led the college by using the tradition of the office of the president, and he had previously enjoyed participating in activities with students, which was a critical part of the school history. He was now isolated and conflicted. He was the only link between the past and the present administration, and he was also a buffer between the faculty and a group of trustees who seemed bent on moving the college toward a corporate form of school management.

It appeared that the president's withdrawal from boundary activities and his isolation evolved from the demeaning actions of the board of directors. When they intervened and chose the president's administrators, the president felt inept. The new administrators were loyal to the board and assumed values toward the college that were the board's and not the president's. The president's wish to see himself as an academic leader, and not a CEO, were in contradiction to the board's view of the president's role.

The faculty cautiously accepted the view that the president ought to assume a CEO–business management role. They maintained that academic leadership ought to value the technology of teaching and the learning process.

With this in mind, the consultant and faculty committee worked toward integrating contemporary management practice with ideals associated with academic leadership.

At the final meeting, the consultant presented the unanimously approved recommendations of the faculty committee to the president:

1. Institute a new freshman-orientation program. Place the program under the management of a senior faculty member and increase alumni input, especially from the board of directors.
2. Develop meetings and events to integrate the new administrative staff into the institution. Organize events to formalize social activities for the students and reduce the informal activities on campus.
3. Create a presidential committee containing the new administrators. Have the committee meet regularly with the faculty senate to give the faculty an opportunity to communicate their thoughts about their roles, as well as about the traditions of the institution.
4. Institute a professor of institutional history, who would give lectures about the history of the college periodically.
5. Set up a committee headed by a chief librarian to record an institutional history.
6. Set up a committee that would meet weekly to plan the activities of the Office of the President, with the purpose of integrating the president into the life of the institution.
7. Return admission criteria to their pre-1977 conditions.

All of the topics were discussed at length, with particular emphasis given to the last recommendation. The president's response was, "Suppose it doesn't work?" The consultant responded, "I believe that these boundary activities will communicate an accurate picture of the college to entering students, but more important, they will bring students into the fold and reduce alienation. The thrust of any president's job is to maintain standards for entry, to sell the college and increase the size of the applicant pool. If successful, he will increase the quality and quantity of resources entering from the environment." The president smiled approvingly, and it was clear that the criteria enabling a new structure to develop were established.

The consultant met with the president a week later. The president praised the consultant and said he was beginning to observe changes already. The initial request for the consultation to reduce alcohol consumption was not directly answered, but everyone involved felt that there was a good likelihood that things in that sphere would change for the better.

Of particular concern to the consultant was to restore a sense of cohesion among the president, administration, faculty, and entering students. "Cohesion" in the sense that they all knew the nature of their respective tasks and that these tasks would be integrated into a conscious effort to work on a superordinate goal. This was eventually accomplished by returning the institution to a level of operation where esprit increased. Without a unifying sense of esprit, the college would have remained fragmented.

Conclusion

Put simply, this organization had lost a grandiose view of itself. It no longer viewed itself as being capable of accomplishing its primary task and succeeding in the world. Often, jolts or disruptions at the boundary precipitate internal changes. The major problem associated with internal changes is that they estrange the institution from its past. In this case, the "newcomers" did not know the subtle culture of the organization and were not aware of the delicate psychological glue that bound employees together. Therefore, they were seen as "bullies," indelicate marauders who were only out for themselves.

Another view suggests that disruptions at the boundary are experienced by those who have labored in the organization for a long time as narcissistic injuries. These injuries trigger feelings of depression, rage, and fragmentation, and often these feelings are projected onto the newcomers. The typical response of all involved is to search for objects to blame, so that the wish to restore an inner sense of cohesion can be maintained. Splitting often results from such injuries (see Chapter 2). In this organization, it resulted in a structural splitting which was nothing more than the creation of a "we versus they" type of climate.

When the organization recaptures its "glory days," it promotes a compensatory grandiose experience and the employees tend to over-assess the institution, its management and technical staff, and the work it accomplishes. This is sometimes necessary. In a psychological sense, it is a good thing. The organization can only come out of the depths of despair or depression when it is able to see itself as a viable self-object. This means that organizational dysfunction can be seen as a stimulating, involved experience. When this occurs, all employees can obtain "fuel" from the grandiosity associated with the institution's accomplishments. This promotes a greater degree of cohesion within the employee's self system and promotes internal cohesion in the entire organization.

According to Kohut (1977), all institutions must be able to function as a "mirror" for their employees. This means that the organization in a general sense must be able to communicate to employees that they are good and capable of having idealized wishes fulfilled. The absence of "mirroring" perpetuates the experience of worthlessness, causing employees to feel empty and fragmented. This is the psychic equivalent of faulty parenting. When the employees understood the organization's history, they felt connected to the past. Now they are capable of experiencing the organization and its leadership as having empathic and nurturing capacities. According to Ashbach and Schermer (1987), this is especially important for organizations engaged in promoting growth and development in a client population. Of particular concern in a consultation to a service organization is the impact staff issues have on the clients, in this case, students. Considering the vulnerability of the students (in the crisis of late adolescence), it is vital that the organization have the capacity to offer to entering students an "empathic net." This is especially relevant to first-year students who generally enter college in a late adolescent crisis.[3] Thus the entry

---

[3]There are many views of what occurs during late adolescence. Some see it as a phase of consolidation of character formation, the concretization of a compromise formation (see Brenner, 1982), the development of stable object constancy, the stabilization of psychic mental apparatus, the resolution of early trauma, the recapitulation of unresolved infancy conflicts, and a compromise solution with defined sexual identity.

process must be considered a process that is vital to the well-being of the student.

When the organization is not perceived or experienced as empathic and nurturing, the splitting phenomenon increases and various groups, in this case faculty, administrators, and students, view each other in blameful ways. Although splitting may help to restore a sense of self/group cohesion, the initial feeling of being intact is short-lived and the regressive mode required for splitting to occur will return, scapegoating and projection will increase, and conflict will escalate.

If the consultation had not occurred, the defenses of splitting, projection, and scapegoating would have continued, causing irrevocable harm to the organization.

CHAPTER 9

Task Analysis

The central question is whether the organized life in its present and potential forms, offers man the opportunity to establish a sense of commitment and dignity in his life; whether, in effect, the sacrifices he makes extend or limit the freedoms he values most.

—C. B. KAUFMANN (1967, p.17)

The organization is designed to perform tasks, and each task requires a technological or operating system and a system of functions to control, coordinate, and service its technology. These systems are delineated by boundaries. Therefore, consulting to any task system requires identifying both the task and the boundaries of the task system (the place where the task is performed). Dysfunctions within any given task system, which make it impossible to perform the task optimally, are a function of the ambiguity found in these boundaries. Trying to locate and define the boundaries around a task is difficult and complex. This difficulty is exemplified by Kuhn's (1974) definition of a boundary:

[T]he boundaries of a system are logically defined by listing all the components of the system; any elements not listed are construed as falling outside the system. For some systems, or real models of them, a boundary line or surface may be so located that all elements of a specific sort within it are components and all outside are not. All elements within it can then be construed to be "listed" by the boundary. Whether elements not in the system should be ignored or be listed as part of the environment depends on whether they are relevant. . . . (p. 64)

The challenge for the consultant is to ascertain the boundaries around the task, that is, what is to be included and what is to be

233

excluded. This requires much more of an analysis of specific work activities to be performed within a given period than a "scientific" manager or efficiency expert would make. The psychoanalytic consultant sees much more as lying within the boundaries of a task system. The activities go beyond the specific and include all the interdependencies and interactions with other subsystems necessary to get the task accomplished, as well as the psychosocial climate necessary to engage in the work with enthusiasm and mental clarity (sentient effort).

In an early publication, Rice (1952) introduced the concept of the "primary task," as a means of discriminating between the different tasks operating within the organization. He defined the primary task as that one thing the organization had created to perform. This performance would then justify the organization's existence.

In a later publication, Rice (1963) recognized the problems associated with treating the organization as if it had a single goal or task, and he suggested that organizations ought to be studied as systems with multiple goals, all operating simultaneously and ideally in supportive relationships with each other. He cited teaching hospitals and prisons as examples of organizations that perform multiple tasks simultaneously. He then suggested that these multiple tasks could be understood as existing in some hierarchical form, and developed the notion of the heirarchy of tasks. He redefined the primary task as that which the organization must perform if it is to survive. In addition, this primary task is followed by a number of other tasks that can be ranked in order of importance. Rice believed that these tasks are not static and will change over time. For example, at a certain point in time, a task ranked as number two could become number one, and the number one task could become number ten, and so on.

Rice conceptualizes the organization as two major subsystems: (1) the operating subsystem, which performs the work of the primary task of the organization, and (2) the managing subsystem, which is external to the operating subsystem but has the responsibility of managing and regulating the boundaries of the organization. The operating subsystem has also been referred to as the technological core of the organization, where the actual conversion work takes place. In other words, it is here that the inputs are converted into outputs. Two dimensions are intrinsic to the technological core and help in understanding its task(s): time and territory (Miller, 1973). The dimensions of technology, time, and territory function to differentiate tasks among the various subsystems within the organization. This means that the function of every subsystem is not only to attain a given task but to relate these tasks to other subsystems in some type of timely and coordinated manner. This work of coordination is left to the managing subsystem, who is responsible for managing technology, time, and territory in terms of the activities related to internal tasks within the system and their relationships to other systems and how these other systems support and constrain the task(s).

It is the task of management to arrange these tasks in hierarchical form, create these hierarchies to accommodate the requirements of the organization and its environment, and finally, to understand the constraining versus supportive nature of these tasks, avoiding the possibility that secondary or tertiary tasks may constrain the work on the primary task.

FACTORS THAT CONSTRAIN WORK ON THE TASK

The psychoanalytic consultant is concerned with factors that constrain or make work on the task(s) difficult. Isolating these factors is extremely difficult because constraining factors are rarely obvious. As a matter of fact, they generally evolve over a long period and are usually embedded in the culture of the organization. Obtaining a clear picture of possible motivations for allowing tasks to constrain each other is difficult for many reasons, compounded by the fact that an analysis of task(s) or any task system will take the consultant directly into an analysis of the culture or the psychosocial climate of the organization.

Task constraint is generally apparent when subsystems define their primary task(s) or their work in ways that are different from those of other subsystems, or their work is at odds with the task(s) of these other systems. The consultant begins the investigation by asking the question: Why does one subsystem constrain the task of another subsystem?

To clarify the constraining nature of tasks consider the following example: At an urban teaching hospital, three tasks must be performed in order for the system to survive: health care, teaching, and research. The following incident demonstrates how teaching a secondary task can constrain the primary task. The dental school, in its desire to teach the depth to which students should drill into teeth before a nerve is hit (the teaching task), had its students give placebos instead of novocaine to indigent clinic patients and then drill. The young students quickly learned how close to the exterior of the tooth the nerve is when their patients jumped in excruciating pain. The students not only learned their lesson about drilling but also gained experience in dealing with distraught patients. Word of this practice reached the black and Hispanic communities and caused an uproar, and nearly cost the clinic its license. The efforts of the dental school to engage in the task of educating had constrained the task of providing health care. In the literature, and especially in case analysis, many accounts can be given of an organization and its management who wholeheartedly engaged in efforts for one task and in doing so actually constrained or abandoned the required efforts for another task. This is most apparent in organizations in which tension exists over issues of quality versus quantity.

Often the organization's environment will actually constrain the organization's ability to work on its tasks. This is always a function of poor boundary management. It is the work of the consultant to isolate that which constrains the task, and when an organization is engaged in multiple tasks, the consultant must examine the difficulties associated with the organization's capacity to plan and avoid constraints. Consider the following example: A fish restaurant in the urban Northeast is experiencing a harsh winter, the Northeast ports are closed, and the market has no fish. The manager, who has not planned for this occasion, cannot call other markets to obtain fish. Consequently, the chef must make do with frozen fish, which will cause stress in the kitchen subsystem and among the waiters and will disappoint customers. Contrast this restaurant to another: The manager of the second restaurant calls up a market in the gulf, where he is on a first-name basis with the owner, and has an ample shipment of fish delivered by air express. This system survives a potentially stressful period. None of the subsystems experience stress, but more important, the employees, aware of the manager's efforts, demonstrate a greater sense of esprit as they perform their tasks. Under these winter conditions, the primary task becomes one of procuring fish in distant markets. Under plentiful conditions, this task would be lower down on the task performance hierarchy, and most managers would pass the task off as insignificant. However, the manager who considers all the tasks in a hierarchy and plans contingencies for each task is a manager who understands and devotes efforts to the supportive requirements of each task and thus will ultimately avoid conflict and stress. A key question often faced in the analysis of tasks is, Why is one manager capable of managing the equivalent of the fish market scenario while another suffers from a type of task myopia and tends to a task that is completely irrelevant to the survival of the organization?

Conceptualizing the hierarchical nature of tasks allows the manager an opportunity to create a matrix on which the task(s) of the organization can be plotted against the three dimensions of time, territory, and technology. For example, if one views time, territory, and technology as resources and plots this against the hierarchy of tasks the organization must perform at a given point, one can begin to develop a schemata for the allocation of the necessary resources. A manager who has the capacity to develop this schemata will survive under conditions that require major boundary management efforts.

TASK AND SENTIENT SYSTEM MANAGEMENT

At the base of task constraint is the inability of a subsystem to be part of the overall coordinated effort of the organization. This inability is generally a function of internal dysfunctions. Internal subsystem dysfunctions can be viewed from a number of perspectives, but perhaps the clearest descriptive explanation can be found in the sociotechnical systems model presented by Emery and Trist (1965). Simply, they propose that conflict occurs when the sociological and technical aspects of a system are not coordinated. All subsystems have two functions: a task function and a sentient function. When these functions are not merged, the system increases its propensity to constrain the efforts of other subsystems; that is, the system will be out of synch with the work of the organization.

To explore this view further, the task and sentient functions must be defined. The task function is the equivalent of the technology of the subsystem. It is defined as the work assigned to the subsystem. The task function not only includes the work of the subsystem but the instruments used to produce the subsystem's outputs and the knowledge used to engage in the conversion work.

The sentient function is where social and emotional bonds develop among employees. Ideally, an organization's sentient life is a powerful force in contributing to and maintaining job satisfaction, which further contribute to the establishment of an increased capacity to sense and respond to environmental issues. It is the quality of these bonds that infectiously moves across the boundaries of other systems and ultimately affects the perceptions outsiders have of the nature of the work inside the system. An organization's sentient life will affect both the quality and the quantity of new and potential entrants. The quality of the sentient life within each subsystem is primarily responsible for the motivation to work and the quality of the product. Under conditions of successful sentient functioning, the work itself is secondary. Miller and Rice (1967), Mintzberg (1988), Herzberg (1966), and Maslow (1954) confirm this by suggesting that whether an employee experiences satisfaction or deprivation is a function of the quality of the interpersonal and group relations within that employee's subsystem.

Thus, the efficiency and effectiveness of any subsystem are determined by the degree to which the task boundaries and sentient boundaries coincide. Satisfaction and subsystem productivity are at their highest when the emotional content of the work is fused as opposed to separated. How an employee feels about his/her work is a function of the employee's feelings about his/her coworkers. If the employee perceives his/her fellow workers as friendly, supportive, and interesting, the organization will be similarly perceived and the work will be experienced as gratifying. Even the most routine of jobs will be experienced as gratifying under these conditions. On the other hand, employees who feel emotionally unconnected at work, or in conflict with others at work, will experience the job as dismal and emotionally draining.

PSYCHOANALYSIS OF THE SENTIENT SYSTEM

The psychodynamic explanation of the sentient experience may help to illuminate the general psychoanalytic theory of work. The sentient experience is essentially a play experience, especially when play is considered an engagement in some type of task. When one says, "I am lost in play," one is saying that he/she is lost in the task. Very few people consider work as something to get "lost in." It is generally play in which one gets lost. The process of "getting lost" is similar to the child's being happily engaged in play, talking to him/herself and unaware of his/her surroundings but with an underlying awareness that mother is nearby. "Getting lost" means losing one's sense of the boundaries of time, territory, and technology. This experience may occur when the person is at work and suddenly realizes that it is late and he has been engaged for a long time, although it did not seem long, or the person is engaged in work and suddenly realizes that he has forgotten where he is, as if he has entered into another state of consciousness. Sometimes after being engaged in work, the person reflects and realizes that he has worked with extraordinary effort and has accomplished difficult or perhaps tedious or creative tasks with ease. Some report that it felt like they were "on fire," "alive with inspiration," "filled with creative passion," "I could accomplish anything."

The experience can be described as an enactment of an omnipotent fantasy, but closer to the mark would be to consider it a dissociative experience in that through engagement, the employee separates from his/her personality thoughts and emotions. In doing so, the employee compartmentalizes the work activity from other parts of his/her life. This differs from a dissociative disorder because of its temporal nature. It is as if the employee is suspended for a while and then can return to the self system and utilize its integrative capacities. If the employee did not have the capacity to utilize the integrative capacities of the self system, he/she would experience depersonalization and possibly lose contact with reality.

The ability to lose oneself in the task can be in isolation or in a group activity. At work, most task-related activities take place in groups. In these groups, it is not only the nature of the task that produces sentient gratifications but also the social bonds that are formed with coworkers. In many instances gratifications associated with the actual task system are secondary and it is the emotional bonds with fellow workers (bonding in a social group) that are primary.

This position contradicts the classical psychoanalytic view of work, which suggests that it is the work itself and the symbolic value of the tools of one's labor that provide gratifications. The reason for this somewhat limited view is that classical theory has focused almost exclusively on autonomous, entrepreneurial, creative endeavors, where work is not confined to the office or within social groups.

In the office, because of its highly social and interactive nature, the employee will not be psychically connected to his/her work in the same manner as, perhaps, a craftsman or a writer. In the bureaucracy, the office and the group, the social activities associated with work take on profound importance and present a very different psychodynamic explanation. This may also explain why employees who work in bureaucratic organizations appear to value status, competition, and advancement to a much higher degree than does the craftsman or professional entrepreneur. Status, competition, and perhaps greed may be tied more to the dynamics of the social group and the competitive culture that is created by the group than they are to individual motivations.

The social group is defined as the organization, the department, or the various informal groupings with which the employee will interact. The employee's capacity to work and perform a task is a function of his psychic connection to these social groups. The psychoanalytic explanation of this psychic connection can be understood as a transference type of relationship. The following section explores how the employee's capacity to perform a given task is a function of his/her transference connection to the institution, a primary group, and his/her superior and peers.

FORMING A TRANSFERENCE RELATIONSHIP:
THE PSYCHOANALYSIS OF COMMITMENT

Similar to Romzek's (1989) view, organizational commitment is generally considered by organizational scholars to be a "sense of attachment to a work organization." Attachment is typically defined as "investing in" or having an "affective emotional component" with one's place of work. The nature of an employee's commitment is a description of the quality of the transactions between the employee and others at work. To be committed enables the employee to reach beyond him/herself to another. To be committed also carries with it an increased sense of intimacy. This is not the type of intimacy found in love relations, but the type that can bring about a "meeting of selves that share in a mutuality or some trusted reciprocity . . ." (Ingram, 1986). Commitment can also be explained as a positive transference reaction where the employee displaces his/her feelings and attitudes, which are applicable, in an historical sense, to some significant person, onto another person in the present. These objects from the past that influence the present can be parents, siblings, and teachers, but also inanimate objects such as buildings. They can be either positive or negative depending on the types of feelings the person is displacing. Transference has been given the most attention in the field of psychoanalytic treatment, and the general consensus is that an analytic cure cannot take place unless the transferences that arise during the treatment are analyzed. In treatment, the analyst becomes the target of appropriate and inappropriate affects which are repetitions of earlier experiences, and these affects, communicated in the context of the patient's feelings about the analyst, will bring about the cure.

Although the psychoanalytic literature abounds with research on transference in the clinical sphere, little attention is paid to transference as it occurs in an organizational sense. Greenson (1967), following Freud, explored the pervasiveness of transference and implied that transference reactions could be applied to institutions. He suggests that while transference reactions are essentially unconscious, some aspects may be conscious. For example, a person may be aware that he/she is reacting strangely or with excessive anxiety to a particular situation, although that person may be unaware of the meaning or the motivations for his/her strange reaction. Also, a person may be intellectually aware of the source of his/her reaction to a particular environment, but the important emotional basis that motivates the reaction may be beyond awareness.

Assuming that positive sentient attachments or negative responses to organizations or subsystems within organizations may be the result of a projection of displacement earlier experiences, wishes, and affects, the following explores the psychic basis of the repetition of early experiences that are played out in transferences to organizations, and how these transference reactions are precipitated by the organization.

Organizational Transference

Organizational transference is generally understood as a phenomenon where the organization over time becomes a haven or refuge for the employee, who comes to feel a sense of security and a maternal sort of protection (Reider, 1953). The concept of organizational transference is not merely understood as the displacement[1] of an employee's inner objects onto a blank screen as it would be in the analysand–analyst relationship. It is far more interactive and induced. The organization is capable of promoting transferences through its hierarchical arrangements, authority structure, and role requirements; it can be suggested that organizations may actually wish to elicit transference reactions of a certain type ultimately to create commitment and loyalty. However, this does not invalidate the significance of the employee's earlier experiences and the notion that transference reactions are repetitions of these experiences.

Because of the highly interactive nature of the organization, the scope of a transference reaction is widened. For example, transference reactions are derived not only from other employees but also from the organization's culture and such inanimate objects as computers, office space, furniture, and architecture.

Even Freud (1912/1958) suggests widening the scope of transference. He says that transference can be viewed from two perspectives: as a repetition of infantile wishes and as a function of social interactions. Freud claims that transference permeates all perceptions and communicative processes and it can be understood beyond the dyadic processes of psychoanalytic treatment. He goes on to say that transference will have implications for institutional settings.

Durkin (1964), in agreement with Freud, suggests that in groups and organizations transferences collide, meet, and fuse. She says that in organizations, transferences are generated by the organization's structure, which provides communicative channels (status differen-

---

[1] The classical view of transference is the displacement of emotions belonging to some unconscious ideation to a representation of that same object in the external world. For example, this view would see hostility initially directed unconsciously toward the same-sexed parent in childhood as being displaced onto a superior at work (Stolorow & Lachmann, 1985–1986).

tial, proximity, and roles). Also, as stated earlier, they evolve out of the organization's culture, history, rituals, customs, and norms as well as out of the organization's demands for performance, duty, and task requirements. For the individual employee, transference reactions can be thought of as responses to external objects that are colored by mental structures that were organized in the past and have continued to be functionally effective and have remained available for periodic mobilization. Viewed from this perspective, transference reactions may be considered organizing activities (Stolorow & Lachmann, 1985–1986). As such, transferences may serve a number of functions: (1) they can "fulfill cherished wishes and urgent desires, (2) provide moral restraint and self-punishment, (3) aid adaptation to difficult realities, (4) maintain or restore precarious, disintegration-prone self and object imagoes, and (5) defensively ward off configurations of experience which are felt to be conflictual or dangerous" (Stolorow & Lachmann, 1985–1986, p. 23). To fully understand just how the organization promotes transference reactions, it is helpful to understand that the organization and its constituent players are capable of promoting regression in their employees. The employee's response to organizationally promoted regressions is to rely on transference reactions to help stop the regressive slide.

Organizational Regression

Research on organizational regression begins with the efforts of Lebon (1985), Freud (1955/1920), McDougall (1973), Tiger (1989), Menzies (1960), Turque (1975), Durkin (1964), and others who have analyzed the effects of being in large unstructured groups and have added to a theory of collective behavior. In organizations, structure is established to reduce the regression one generally experiences in large, unstructured groups. The purpose of structure, the assignment of roles and a division of labor (tasks), is to protect the employee from the regressive pull associated with structurelessness (see Chapters 9 and 11). However, while the function of structure is to reduce regression, organizations have the capacity actually to promote or increase regression.

It is generally assumed that the key to understanding the etiology of regression[2] and its precipitated transference responses is to see it as

[2]Regression as it is used here is a move away from higher levels of mental organization to a more archaic organization. It is not used in the sense most often used in the psychoanalytic literature, as a return to some earlier period of childhood or a reenactment of some childhood trauma. Regression is not used here as a reflection of a return in the temporal sense.

the damming up of outlets for affects. At work, an employee is particularly vulnerable to regressions. For example, Halpern and Halpern (1983) suggest that job settings are breeding grounds for regressions for two reasons: the need to deny and repress emotions at work and the fact that at work, an employee assumes a role that also dictates which behaviors to engage in and which to refrain from engaging in. Other factors that contribute to regression are the overt and covert requirements for becoming a member of a small group and the absolute pressures to create a friendly, supportive, cohesive work group (sentient group) despite the competitive, hierarchical, and sometimes hostile nature of the work environment. The desire to become a member of this sentient group and to obtain the almost therapeutic benefits provided motivates employees to repress the fears and anxieties associated with issues related to entry and sustaining membership.

Groups continuously utilize projection[3] to maintain an inner state of cohesion by projecting bad, hateful, aggressive feelings onto its own members as well as onto objects outside the group. Projection is used to stop or halt the regressive pull when the group is faced with some real or imaginary anxiety-producing event(s). However, when projection fails to stop this regressive pull and internal cohesiveness is not obtained, regression once again starts up. The group will fragment and members will unconsciously project paranoid affects onto each other in an attempt to reduce the now intensified regressive pull. This will increase anxiety by threatening to destroy the sentient life of the group. The group is now in a state of helplessness and vulnerability. Under these conditions, the immediate environment is perceived as uncertain, unpredictable, and uncontrollable, and the group experiences the environment as containing exaggerated dangers. Feeling helpless, the group will turn to the leader for assistance and members will disregard their active tasks and roles (Appelbaum, 1963; Kaplan, 1967). The leader will successfully reduce the regressive pull when he becomes an object of the collective group's transferences where the terrifying wishes and paranoid dread are relinquished, resulting in aim inhibition (Saravay, 1978). Saravay goes on to say that the regressive pull is reversed when:

[3]The concept of projection used here is referred to as simple projection, where the person unconsciously attributes to another object a characteristic that is his/her own. These attributes are generally anxiety-producing affects such as hatred, envy, greed, or other feelings that are experienced as intolerable. Another way of viewing this defense is to consider it a process whereby an internal threat is made into an external threat. This is most apparent in groups where collective or collusive projections become a powerful force in fostering cohesion. According to Jaques (1951), this is one of the most powerful elements binding individuals together.

> Identifications with the leader are . . . formed, internalizing object repre-
> sentations of him, producing sublimations of the associated instinctual
> wishes . . . earlier infantile conflicts, regressively mobilized in the group,
> are resolved with the addition of newer and healthier identifications to
> the original conflict resolution, providing greater ego and superego
> strength. (p. 502)

Regression is thwarted when the employees' externalized ego ideals are attached to the leader, who then serves as an object around whom object representations are reprojected. According to Freud (1921/1955), the leader serves as a common object for the group because he is a substitute for the ego and superego functions that were lost or given up as a result of "group induced regression" (Redl, 1942; Semrad, Kanter, Shapiro, & Assenian, 1963; and Saravay, 1978). Kohut (1985) takes a similar position and adds that identification along with idealization of the group or a leader will protect the group from its own feelings of inadequacy, powerlessness, and fear. He says that identification and idealization "protect the individual member of the group against certain states of narcissistic disequilibrium which are experienced as envy, jealousy, and rage" (p. 438). Consequently, if leadership can protect the employee, it can also produce narcissistic disequilibrium.

REGRESSION AND THE FAILURE OF LEADERSHIP

When identifications with the leader are not available or apparent, the once idealized leader will be perceived as an impingement. The employees' defenses will become vulnerable, a regressive pull will become apparent, and the employees will become increasingly dissociated.[4] Their behavior takes a form similar to conversion hysteria.

[4]All groups maintain the potential to a regressive pull toward dissociation. The fact that organizations may promote transference reactions is itself a regressive phenomenon (Reider, 1957). The regressive pull toward dissociation is most apparent in organizations in which the group is "robbed" of its defenses. The definition used here is of a disorder where gross psychological distortion results and a specific breakdown in perceptual and/or sensory/motor behavior results. In organizations, this dissociative type of disorder can be quite compartmentalized, that is, the employee can function well at home and appear to be a good spouse and parent, but at work the same employee regresses and functions in a dissociated manner, often acting out in ways ranging from inappropriate behavior to outright delusional behavior. For example, employees report feeling shocked when they meet a fellow employee on the street with his/her spouse and children because at work the same employee appears regressed, that is, childlike, enraged, prank pulling, or sadistic. The question they struggle with is, How can this person be one and the same?

Halpern and Halpern (1983) describe the onset of this type of reaction with a quote from Joseph Heller's novel *Something Happened*:

> In the office in which I work, there are five people of whom I am afraid. Each of these five people is afraid of four people (including overlaps), for a total of twenty, and each of these twenty people is afraid of six people, making a total of one hundred and twenty people who are feared by at least one person . . . I . . . find it impossible to know exactly what is going on behind the closed doors of all the offices on all the floors occupied by all the people in this and all the other companies in the whole world who might say or do something, intentionally or circumstantially, that could being me to ruin . . . I have the feeling that someone nearby is soon going to find out something about me that will mean the end, although I can't imagine what that something is. (1974, p. 13)

These types of paranoid responses are typically a function of a collective projection of the employees in a company or an office. Ouchi (1981) sees this as a "behind closed doors" phenomenon where the closed door is a "fire alarm signal to an employee that his job is in danger." Consequently, the employee becomes obsessed with a search for signs or signals that confirm his/her belief that something terrible will soon happen, and finds evidence all around. In this instance, the leader is not viewed as loving, benevolent, and empathic but as harsh and destructive.

Leaders can consciously and unconsciously contribute to a regression to this type of paranoid state when they find themselves in frustrating conditions in which they feel powerless and frightened. A significant contributor to frustrations occurs when the leader (CEO) is attempting to transform the organization and increase its competitiveness. Under these conditions, the CEO may unconsciously structure a regressive pull among his/her employees in the hope of obtaining some magical solution to the problem. In effect, the CEO actually contributes to the creation of what Kets de Vries (1980) refers to as a *folie à deux*, which is described as a type of "shared fantasy."

According to Blum (1988), the *folie à deux* fantasy can be understood as a group's "adaptation and identification vis a vis the stronger individual's fantasy or delusion . . ." (p. 330). It is a type of symbiotic attachment to the leader who is perceived as an object ranging from "caretaker" to a "god." The basis of the attachment to the leader is a function of the shared fantasy that contains both aspects of reality as well as earlier wishes for parental attachment, affection, and approval (Bergmann, 1982). Kets de Vries (1980) suggests that these types of unconscious demands and wishes for a magical solution occur in "a world in which absolute good is fighting absolute evil, that there is a lack of compromise and, consequently, unrealistic goal setting, which only heightens the participants sense of frustration." (p. 197).

Consider the following example where a CEO unconsciously contributes to regression by the creation of a paranoid state among his employees: During a banking convention, the CEO of a large urban bank meets a training consultant who has a reputation for being charismatic and a guru among motivational consultants. The CEO, under considerable stress due to his company's recent failures, spends an afternoon with the consultant and is convinced to spend a week free of charge at the consultant's "Retreat for Executives."

During the retreat, the CEO participates in group therapy, massage therapy, sensitivity training, and a number of public and private motivational talks with the guru. He is impressed and leaves feeling his life has changed. Returning to work he feels rejuvenation: He feels his mind is clear and he is no longer worried. His interactions with employees take on a new dimension and he now wants to get to know them on a more intimate level (he wants to know what they feel and he now expects them to be open). Feeling disappointed when they do not respond, and sensing that the problem is as the guru suggests, that they are closed off and detached from "themselves," he calls in the guru and his trainers to bring "new life" into his company. A memo is sent to all vice presidents and senior managers instructing them to attend weekly training seminars. One employee reports the following:

> In the group the trainer had these cards and she read off instructions to each member of the group. Each member had to discuss some very highly personal thing about himself, something that occurred in his childhood. I was told to talk about my mother and father and what they did for me at Christmas when I was 10. It was a time when my father was drinking heavily and they were going through a divorce. It was a particularly painful period of my life. I remember saying to myself, "Oh what luck, I can't talk about this." I struggled through it and when I was finished the trainer said I would begin next week and would continue to discuss my feeling about my parents' breakup. We all had to tell about early traumas and painful experiences. If we didn't have one, the trainers would get impatient and push for a story. Hal, who everyone knows is uptight, got red in the face when his turn came and he got up and walked out. Everybody was real nervous. After the meeting we met and discussed how angry we were; what's the purpose? What the hell are they up to? Why are they trying to humiliate us? [Anonymous interview by author]

Between the first and second meeting, the employees decided that they would have to join together to protect themselves from the trainers. The employees showed great disdain for the trainers and this guru, who was perceived as a mind controller who had gotten hold of the boss and "brainwashed him." They openly questioned the professional training of the trainers and spread the word that they were "New Age" charlatans. They also gave support to members who were injured by the initial experience and they decided that at the next meeting they would make up stories.

In this vignette, the CEO unconsciously uses the training program to serve two functions: (1) His identification with the guru allows him to avoid the responsibility of worrying about the nature of his task, which is to keep the company profitable and to avoid the calamity of layoffs and termination of staff. Through his identification he can deny the real work and instead focus on that which makes him "feel good" in an irresponsible manner. (2) By imposing the training program upon the staff, the CEO uses it to displace his paranoid feelings onto them. The staff now contains the paranoid feelings, and they in turn see the trainers and the guru as the villains. In projecting their hate onto the trainers and guru, the staff can now see the CEO as a "poor victim," which is unconsciously what the CEO wishes. He no longer will experience the hostility the employees initially projected into him; these affects are now projected or displaced onto the trainers and the guru.

Over the course of 3 weeks, the employees projected their paranoid fears into the trainers, and the trainers began to feel frightened about their work and the employees. The program trainers projected their paranoid fears onto the guru, who promptly called on the CEO and "dumped" the paranoid feelings back onto him. Thus the cycle was completed and the feelings that began with the CEO returned.

The unconscious motivation, underlying the conscious wish to promote cooperation and intimacy among the staff, had the aim of increasing the CEO's advantage by fostering dysfunction (apathy, conflict, and competition). Brocker (1984) confirms this when he says that "the search for remedies and the uncritical application of various encounter group methods have created a phoney atmosphere of pseudo-instant intimacy [These actions arise out of] . . .'a desperate need for unreflected action' " (p. 385).

In structuring this event, the CEO's painful and self-punitive attitude toward his own sense of inadequacy was relieved by the guru, and these affects were projected into his subordinates. The subordinates are now in a frightening and anxiety-producing situation, and the CEO is briefly freed from the torment of failure. However, this does not last long; the subordinates rebel and break the cycle.

A critical question is, What happens when these paranoid feelings are not recycled and get located in a group, a department, or a single employee? Regression is precipitated and the employee(s), over time, experiences increased disassociation. Under conditions of extreme psychic stress, regression is fostered by the failure of the internal defensive structure. The failure of the defensive structure to reduce anxiety brings forth the wish for an externalized defense in the form of an increased demand for social control and the wish for an idealized leader. The wish is gratified when a type of concordant transference is established where the subordinate identifies with the superior's experiences and then feels that he/she and the leader are very much alike, the extreme being a symbiotic attachment where fantasies are shared.[5]

According to Blum (1988), Freud discovered shared fantasies about the same time he discovered the oedipal complex, and he placed the oedipal complex in the realm of his thoughts about shared fantasies (Masson, 1950/1985). Later on, Freud (1923/1961) reported shared fantasies in the context of the child's capacity to share his parent(s)' fantasies. Of all the motivations for shared fantasies, the most probable is that they provide for adaptation to stressful environmental conditions. An extreme example of this is the "sick-building syndrome."

SICK-BUILDING SYNDROME

The sick-building syndrome is often referred to as a situation in which employees collectively or individually experience a mysterious illness. The employees experience a physical response to something in the building (a fume, water, air, dust, food, etc.). This illness generally strikes suddenly, and scores of employees can fall ill, experiencing stomachaches, dizziness, vomiting, fever, headaches, rashes, coughing, and in some cases paralysis. The illness subsides after a few days and rarely is a definitive chemical or environmental cause isolated. This reaction is called hysterical contagion. Kerckhoff and Bach (1968) define hysterical contagion as

[5]The concept of the shared fantasy is also similar to the "altruistic surrender" (Wangh, 1962), "chronic losers" (A. Freud, 1967), "focal symbiosis" (Greenacre, 1959), "symbiotic attachment" (Anthony, 1970), "personal myth" (Kris, 1956), "ghost sickness" (Gutmann, 1965), "hysterical contagion" (Kerckhoff & Bach, 1968), "primal fantasies" (Freud, 1916–1917/1964), and "secret sharing" Blum, (1988).

one in which a set of experiences or behaviors which are heavily laded with emotions of fear of a mysterious force are disseminated through a collectivity. The type of behavior that forms the manifest content of the case may vary widely from one example to the next, but are indicative of fear, and all are inexplicable in terms of the usual standards of mechanical, chemical or physiological causality. (p. 25)

Other authors also discuss the mysterious nature of some type of force that impinges upon the group and brings about a physical reaction. Sometimes this is referred to as mass hysteria (Faigel, 1968; Polk, 1974; Stahl & Lebedum, 1974; Jacobs, 1965; Kirkpatrick, 1975; Wheeler, 1966; Smelser, 1962; Medalia & Larsen, 1958). It can also be referred to as epidemic hysteria (Knight, Friedman, & Suliante, 1965; Friedman, 1967).

These extreme reactions generally occur in two types of work situations: The first is, for example, a manufacturing plant where work is experienced as repetitious, monotonous, and physically or psychologically constraining. The physical and psychological constraints associated with a repetitive task such as toll collecting or parts assembly can trigger a reaction, but can also occur in physically confining situations such as small windowless offices or basement cubicals. These types of situations increase the psychological susceptibility for the use of projections and regression. The second work situation where this type of regression is most likely to occur is one in which the task is exceedingly stressful. The employees may be terrified of death, layoffs, or some form of psychological or physical injury. In both situations, the sick-building syndrome is an attempt to self-regulate, or a self-righting method, and a defensive reaction to the regressive pull the employees collectively feel when the structure in their work environment, or that which was provided by the organization, is perceived as failing.

Typically employees combat the regressive pull associated with the task by collectively projecting paranoid fears and anxieties. It is the intensity of these paranoid projections that brings about the irreversible regressive pull to group dissociation. In Meissner's (1984) study of cult phenomena, he suggests that deep-seated feelings of paranoia, or a "paranoid ethos," underlie the more extreme cult behaviors or collective madness. He goes on to define primary elements of the irreversible paranoid process:

(1) the core introjects around which the subject's inner world is structured; these introjects represent critical internalizations of significant object relations in the . . . [person's] . . . developmental history and provide the basis for the organization and integration of the self-system;

(2) projections that derive from the core introjects and contribute to the progressive modification and differentiation of object-representations and their correlative object-relations; and finally, (3) the paranoid construction (the group and its behavior) by which the meaningful and sustaining patterns of environmental reference are cognitively organized to provide a congruent context for the support of specific projections. The integration of these projections within the framework provided by the paranoid construction gives rise to the subjects projective system. (p. 103)

The paranoid delusion is sustained through the creation of a paranoid construction. The construction has two purposes: (1) to provide relief from the anxiety associated with the paranoid delusion, and (2) to reinforce the construction through some form of activity or behavior. The key to understanding the intensity of these projections and their apparent psychotic manifestations is provided by Waelder (1951), who offers a hypothesis as to why simple projection is subject to correction by experience and why paranoid projection is not. In simple paranoid projection, aggression alone is projected, and this can be corrected over time or can function as a catharsis. However, when it is irreversible, the aggressive wish is fused with love for the object and the hidden wish that the object will be "all giving." According to Reider (1957), Waedler (1951) says that "it is the forcible, disguised, return of the person, love for whom is denied and perhaps, projected" (p. 170).

This phenomenon is apparent in situations in which a once idealized leader is destroyed. The aggressive wishes are produced by a failure to maintain the idealized imago and are fused with the now more repressed wishes of love toward the object. The once loved leader is now hated because during the group's struggles with ambivalent representations of the leader as ideal and nurturing, they also experienced him as persecuting and frustrating (see the discussion of the schizoid position in Chapter 2). Events easily push the group's regression toward the negative pole of this ambivalence. The regression then continues because the leader can no longer provide the illusion of trust and security. In this instance, the leftover positive attribute, the affects associated with love and idealized wishes, is repressed and becomes fused with these newer aggressive wishes. The regression begins when the group, as all groups do, tests the leader and the members discover that because of the leader's ineptness or environmental factors, the leader is incapable of being trusted. This then confirms affects associated with the persecutor position. Consequently, it is not the projection of aggressive, hostile impulses that leads to the regressive pull, but the love for the object that is attached to the aim of the projections. This hate for the object is split off and is repressed and denied and then turned inward against the self (group). This creates within the group an experience of the members as dirty, unloved, unworthy, unproductive, and bad.

These types of projections (paranoid), as all projections, are based on internally intolerable ideas or affects, but within this context they differ in that they will undergo a transformation before they actually become projections. Therefore, of key interest in understanding these regressions are two phenomena: (1) the paranoid projections that form the basis for the most extreme type of regression are most likely layered and the original projections are altered over time, and (2) the intensity of the regression is a function of the degree to which the organization actually promotes or detracts from the creation of defense utilization through a positive transference or a psychological sense of community.

Another way to understand these phenomena is to assess the nature of resistance that occurs when the organization is attempting to bring about change. Change is usually upsetting and promotes anxiety because the employees are not trusting and are uncertain of the new situation. In most cases, change can occur with minimal anxiety when the organization provides something resembling a transitional object to the employees during this stressful period.

In Chapters 2 and 4, the role of the transitional object in stopping regressive pulls was investigated. It was suggested that with change, the employee will seek, as he/she had done in childhood, a representation of mother to hang onto so that the employee can master the anxiety he/she experiences. In groups, the regressive pull ceases when it can locate this object. However, if the object is not found, regression will continue. It is in this area that the organization will contribute to either stopping or promoting regression.

An example of the conditions that foster group dissociation and the failure of the organization to stop the regressive pull (absence of a transitional object) occurred at a large urban teaching hospital when employees on a surgical ward were suddenly stricken with a mysterious illness. The employees experienced vomiting, dizziness, and fever. The surgical rooms were shut down while teams of investigators from state, city, and federal bureaus conducted tests and investigated everything from the air ducts to cleaning fluids. Nothing was found and the problem disappeared in a few weeks.

The analysis begins with the assumption that leadership robbed the surgical team of their defenses. Two prior events caused feelings of powerlessness in the surgical team: (1) The administration and union were engaged in a conflict because budget promises made earlier were retracted, leading to a perception of the leadership as apathetic and failing; and (2) performing surgery on chronically ill patients was no longer considered a life-saving task but more in the interest of the financial well-being of the hospital. These factors contributed to a regressive pull. However, a major contributor was the task of surgery.

Hospitial employees unconsciously fear they will kill or be killed by their patients or patients' families and friends. Fantasies associated with death are advanced through the belief that the hospital is filled with disease. The fear of death is pervasive, and it is the function of leadership to protect employees from these real and fantasized fears.

The paramount fear associated with hospital work is the fear of AIDS. A patient to be operated on by the surgical team had AIDS. To perform this operation the team had to wear equipment of heavy cloth that covered them from head to foot. Each team member's head was encased in a heavy hood with a plastic opening for vision. One employee commented: "The outfit makes us feel like spacemen." This comment is often used as a metaphor; like being "spaced out," it is an unconscious representation of someone who is experiencing temporary disassociation or is not connected to reality. Moreover, the outfits altered the communication patterns in the operating room. Defenses are maintained by communication patterns, the most common defenses being small talk, joking, or gossip. These patterns stopped. In addition, the masks made it impossible to maintain eye contact. Unconsciously the masks stimulated earlier fears associated with masked monsters (consider the response by small children to someone in a mask). Finally, a major defense against anxiety associated with surgery is the conscious wish to save patients, to do good. This wish conflicts with the unconscious wish associated with aggression that is played out in the activity of cutting and entering into the body. In this case unconscious ideation was fueled by the fear that the patient might kill the team. The patient unconsciously was viewed as a symbolic representation of evil. This made unconscious wishes more conscious, thereby increasing the team members' anxiety. As a surgeon prepared to cut, two nurses fell to the floor, two physicians immediately left the room feeling ill, and a third nurse began to vomit. The staff blamed the air.

By blaming the bulding, the team evoked effective counteractivity among the hospital's leadership. The empathic responses from leadership allowed the team to reconstruct defenses and forestall fears associated with death and destruction. The administration was once again the "good parent." In all cases of the "sick-building syndrome" a similar pattern exists. What was once a homey, safe environment becomes unsafe, unpredictable, and murderous. In these cases the rage experienced toward such elements as leadership, the task, and the patient is displaced onto the building.

FORESTALLING REGRESSION

It is generally the experience of a psychological sense of community that holds the greatest potential for self-system integration, group cohesion, and the creation of positive transference attachments to fellow employees and the institution in general. On the other hand, an administration can foster fragmentation of the self system by not providing a sense of community and fostering alienation, or, as the case above suggests, by not providing a transitional object in a situation of flux where anxiety is increased. When these failings occur, the employee feels he is not in a caretaking, empathic environment.[6]

One view of the task of the sentient system is that it is responsible for the creation of a work climate in which the task and the relationships among fellow employees can offer to the employee a kind of "spiritual" involvement. That is, the employee views his/her involvement in the organization, inter alia, as a derivative of his/her real or fantasized family romance. This would be creation of a transference in a positive sense and would serve as a defense against regressive pulls.

When a positive transference is attained, the employee is capable of increased awareness of his/her environment. It is as if the employee has a heightened consciousness of the surrounding stimuli and his/her sentient needs are gratified through a mental and physical attachment to the organization. At work, satisfaction and subsystem productivity are at their highest when employees can autonomously locate and regulate their boundaries and internal activities with minimal intrusion or dependency on the larger system. When this occurs, the boundaries of both task and sentient systems are merged and it is as if the employee can focus without distraction in a manner in which his/her thought processes are fully devoted to the work and distraction is no longer an issue.

DEFENSIVE NATURE OF THE SENTIENT SYSTEM

When consulting to the task system in the organization, the employee's connection to the task, and for that matter to the organization, is of crucial importance. Merely to identify the task and its boundaries is not enough. In order for employees to work effectively

---

[6]On the other hand, the quality of the organization's psychosocial environment may be of little consequence because the organizational environment will attract personality types that find the climate appealing. The key here is matching the personality of the recruits with the psychosocial environment and then accommodating that environment to suit the collective personality of the organization, and the subsystems within it.

and efficiently on a given task, a support system is necessary. It is assumed that an employee's connection to the task in the form of a positive transference will produce an effective sentient life, and this sentient life will be an important mediator of stresses associated with the task. Consequently, it is the culture of the organization that is the underpinning for either support or destruction of the sentient life that supports the task.

The culture of the organization, referred to here as its psychosocial climate, is an ambiguous concept. It is largely concerned with the employee's feeling state. An easy way to think of culture is to imagine how one feels when one enters an organization for the first time, whether it is a bar, restaurant, bank, or corporation. Entering the organization for the first time evokes feelings ranging from trust to suspicion and fear, from warmth to coldness, from friendliness to rudeness, from clarity to confusion, from comfort to anxiety, and so on. The perception one obtains is a function of both the physical presence projected by the organization and that which is projected by the people employed.

It is not being suggested that all one needs to do to create an effective and efficient work climate is to make it happy and friendly. There certainly are nice places to work that are not productive organizations, and vice versa. What is being suggested is that the consultant, when consulting to task systems, focus on mergence of the task and sentient system boundaries. This requires an analysis of how the task system impacts the sentient system, and how the culture of the organization impacts the sentient system. The term *impact* means that the consultant is concerned with the process by which anxiety and stress contribute to reducing the clarity necessary to engage in the work. To obtain this clarity and attachment to the task system requires an assessment of the psychodynamics associated with attachment to the organization. An attachment to an organization (a positive transference) begins early on during the employee's entry. An examination of the entry process and the employee's entry into a formal and informal group at work will offer vital clues toward isolating forces that undermine commitment and avoidance of the task.

INTRAPSYCHIC ATTACHMENT TO THE ORGANIZATION: BECOMING A MEMBER

Intrapsychically, personality consolidation is characterized by a solidification of a compromise formation, the development of stable object relations, and the attainment of a stable intrapsychic mental apparatus. Entry into the organization for most employees precipitates the equivalent of an intrapsychic crisis. This crisis stems from the completely unfamiliar environment, which stimulates intrapsychically a recapitulation of unresolved conflicts. Of primary significance are conflicts related to early separation–individuation issues, that is, separation from parents, entry to school, and other strange and anxiety-producing environments the employee remembers from early childhood.

If the employee carries into the organization intense and unresolved separation–individuation issues, his/her personality will remain unconsolidated. This type of employee is exceedingly vulnerable to regression during entry. Regression is used here as a symptomatic indication of ego disturbances, and it is marked by hostility and depression characterized by a withdrawal of libidinal cathexis of the self, resulting in anxiety spurred on by demonstrative disinterest in work or the organization as well as an increase in feelings of grandiosity or hypochondriacal concerns. Under these conditions, the employee experiences illness and takes frequent sick days. The ability to develop an emotional connection to the organization reduces these regressive pulls. This occurs if the employee is able to form a positive transference and is able to transfer libidinal attachments to the organization and to its employees. The critical question that emerges here is, How is a positive transference established?

The employee brings into the organization experiences of self-doubts, heightened self-consciousness, oversensitivity to criticism, rejection, and defeat. The already fragmented self system is strengthened by the resurrection of the idealized self system which contains fantasies of being successful, powerful, and brilliant. The idealized self-image is often vulnerable at entry and easily tarnished. If the employee is able to receive or experience gratifications associated with the idealized self, the employee is able to develop a positive transference with the organization, commitment is heightened, and loyalty has the potential of being formed. Very early, as the employee enters the organization, the employee will attempt to capture experiences consistent with the wished-for self-image and to avoid experiences of the unacceptable self. This is where membership in a group becomes vital, for if the employee is able to gain membership, he/she will be able to use it to shore up the vulnerable, unacceptable self, especially in situations where he/she experiences narcissistic injury. Reider (1953) confirms this when he says that transference "is a way of regaining a lost omnipotence by participating in a great organization" (p. 62).

If the employee does not have adequate ego strength or strength of self to tolerate narcissistic injury, he/she will rely on the group to protect the idealized self. The group does this by encouraging the employee to project bad objects outward. The group will support the employee by saying, "Yes, that boss is a real bitch," or by encouraging the employee to seek revenge: "Let us tell you how you can get him back, so he will let up." Thus, the group works with the employee to defuse the injury and reduce the content of the affects associated with the unacceptable self by creating an empathic net. This is the equivalent of creating a psychological sense of community, a psychic phenomenon similar to a positive transference.

A positive transference is established when members encourage others to join and identify with the organization, and when members construct a "we are alike, and all in the same boat" experience, which lessens narcissistic concerns and consequently reduces vulnerability to narcissistic injury. According to Kohut (1971), this identification process helps the person defend against the reactivation of archaic narcissistic (grandiose) affects that originally stem from the experience of being powerless, impotent, and unimportant in the world. When a member of an organization is on the fringe and not a member in a social group, he/she will have little or no identity and, according to Kernberg (1975), will experience a psychic void that can lead to excessive and futile use of defenses such as projection. He goes on to suggest that defenses do not work because boundary differentiation is absent.

Membership in the social group promotes a positive transference by providing a source of narcissistic gratification that fills the narcissistic wish for power. If the group and the organization cannot provide an empathic net, the employee can only receive imagined gratifications (narcissistic supplies) by engaging in self-serving, unempathic, aggressive, and competitive behaviors. In his review of French psychoanalysts writing about group phenomena, in particular Kernberg (1971) in his review of Anziew, suggests that under conditions of group and organizational regression, "the relationship of the individual to the group as an entity acquires characteristics of fusion of their individual instinctual needs with a fantastic conception of the group as a primitive ego ideal equated to an all-gratifying primary object" (p. 14). Later on, in his review of the work of Chasseguet-Smirgel, Kernberg (1971) states that the group selects not a paternal/superego type of leadership, but a pseudopaternal, "merchant of illusions" "which confirms the narcissistic aspirations of fusion of the individual with the group as a primitive ego ideal. . . . Basically, the identification with each of the other members of the . . . group permits them to experience a primitive narcissistic gratification of greatness and power" (p. 15). This illusion is so powerful that whatever interferes with this illusion will be destroyed by the group.

Masterson (1981), in contradiction to many analytic theorists, claims that the need for a psychological sense of community begins in adolescence[7] where the adolescent and peers join together to begin and complete the process of integrating sexuality into their self-image, and to begin the process of emancipation from parents. This community arranged by adolescents not only provides the support necessary to help them through this difficult period, but also helps them with other traumatic events in their life such as divorce, death of a parent or sibling, poverty, crime, and so on.

In an organization, the informal social group serves the same purpose: to help employees through the difficult period of entry and the narcissistic injuries experienced on the job. Tolpin (1971) suggests that the psychological sense of community (the social group) is exceedingly powerful, and it prevents a loss of cohesiveness, disintegration, and rage within the employee.

CONSULTING TO THE TASK OF A HOSPITAL UNIT

The hospital represents an optimal laboratory for analyzing the relationships between the sentient system, the multiple tasks that are required to be performed, and the psychosocial climate. The hospital, as with many service-oriented businesses, represents a "climate" to the client. In the case of the hospital, that climate is expected to facilitate healing. The climate is expected to be merged with the technology or task to optimally heal the patient, and a stay in the hospital is viewed as being in an environment conducive to getting well. This is seen when patients are asked to define the characteristics of a hospital they prefer, and psychologists explore factors that contribute to a "healing climate." The results of numerous studies of hospital climate suggest that while technological advances are important, it is the psychosocial climate of the hospital that receives the most attention as a curative factor.

Climate can be best expressed by both patients and staff in terms of a semantic-differential continuum. For example, the hospital can be described in terms ranging from caring to bureaucratic, warm to cold, respectful to disrespectful, and so on. Patients who live in the hospital observe this climate, and it has a significant impact on their

---

[7]Most psychoanalysts point to the onset of the capacity to develop or acquire a psychological sense of community at about the age of 5, when the child enters school.

well-being. The staff also experience the climate, and it influences how they go about working on their respective tasks, namely, tending to their patients. Consequently, patients experience the nature of the psychosocial climate from their perceptions of the hands-on caretakers, namely, the nurses.

The following case is a consultation to a hospital subsystem, and an example of how the tasks within this subsystem become problematic when the culture of the larger hospital system fails to provide necessary support and contributes to subsystem dysfunction.

CASE ANALYSIS

The consultant received a call from the director of nursing to consult to the staff of an intensive care unit (ICU) of a small suburban hospital. The director explained that the unit was experiencing an absenteeism rate that was five times greater than the rate in the hospital in general. Morale was low, and the nurses were reported to be in constant conflict about the scheduling of work shifts and duties. In addition, the director said that the nurses were not responsive to physician orders and a viable, harmonious working staff unit was nonexistent. The head of the ICU was spending increasing amounts of time away from her staff, isolated, often closing her door and remaining inside her office for long hours.

The consultant contracted to engage in six 90-minute meetings with the director of nursing, and to assist her in diagnosing the situation and planning an intervention. In his meetings with the director, the consultant sought answers to two questions: (1) how does the psychosocial climate of the larger hospital system contribute to the problems within the ICU, and (2) what was the nature of the task(s) within the ICU that required support from the larger system?

Psychosocial Climate of the Hospital

Of all the factors that influence the work within a hospital, the dual system of authority has the greatest influence. Administrative authority, the nonphysician managerial authority, begins with the board of trustees and moves down the hierarchy to lower-echelon hospital employees. The second line of authority is professional authority, those within the technological core. This form of authority has its base outside the hospital, in professional associations where values and norms of professional conduct are learned and reinforced. Health care organizations are unique in that they lack systemic organization. The subsystems often function as a collection of privately run mini-organizations with loose financial and professional ties. This makes coordination exceedingly problematic because loyalty is to the subsystem and not to those within the higher managerial levels of the organization.

Following the general view of the dysfunctions inherent in the dual authority system, the consultant sought the answer to the following question: Did either of the authority structures lend support to the ICU? The administrative or managerial authority system was primarily concerned with issues of efficiency and cost control. The administration viewed the ICU as an efficient operation, which brought a considerable amount of money into the hospital. The equipment and space utilization were efficient and the hospital administration supported the efforts of the unit and held it in high esteem. The staff of the unit, the nurses, felt especially loyal to the hospital administration, and in particular to the CEO. They depended on his support and attention, and he demonstrated considerable appreciation for their efforts, often singling the nurses out as a special group.

On the other hand, the professional staff, those employed and loyal to the professional authority structure, were viewed by the ICU nurses as unsupportive. The chiefs of the professional staff were viewed by the ICU staff as apathetic to both the ICU staff's work and their apparent difficulties. The director of nursing was singled out as among these unempathic administrators. She was an elderly woman near retirement. She seemed more concerned about the older and more traditional units of the hospital, such as pediatrics, obstetrics, and surgery. Similarly, the chief of medical care, an elderly physician, had a history of greater investment in time and resources to units other than the ICU. The director of nursing quoted him as saying, "The ICU is a place where we wire up the old people and hopeless cases to collect some high-priced, medical care dollars before they die." This information was communicated by the director in a manner that demonstrated her agreement with his observation.

These two organizational leaders, the chief of medical care and the director of nursing, the consultee, can be described as "from the old school." The new technologies housed in the ICU were alien to them, and their resistance to the new technology was interpreted by the ICU staff as an indication of apathy. This type of resistance and the emotional consequences are frequent occurrences in high-technology organizations that experience rapid technological change. Resistance or the slightest hint of discouragement or disinterest will be interpreted by the staff as a form of abandonment. These feelings are generally heightened by the increased anxiety associated with mastery of the new technology, which falls on the shoulders of the staff. However, in the case of the ICU nurses, the experience of anxiety was heightened by another factor, which was more generic to the task of their unit.

Task of the ICU

The values held by the chief of medical care, the director of nursing, and the larger hospital system, and their attitude toward the ICU, were a function of the work of the unit. The ICU cared for the severely ill and dying. Some 75% of the patients that were in the unit during the year were terminally ill. The physicians viewed the unit as a place where they could "dump" the patients they had failed to cure, the hopeless cases. The ICU came to be known as the "dumping ground" for those patients the larger system wished to avoid. These patients were the ones most likely to elicit feelings of despair among the staff. The theme of "out of sight, out of mind" was most apparent, and the ICU was utilized by the staff of the larger system as a social defense. By placing anxiety-producing patients in this unit, and then by keeping away from the unit, the staff could avoid the anxiety. Once the terminally ill were sent to the ICU, the staff from the larger system experienced relief. They did not have to experience death or engage in the work associated with removal of a body from their unit.

The ICU staff felt isolated from the larger hospital system, and consequently they experienced the larger system as devaluating their work. The hopelessness associated with the task was compounded by the abandonment, both psychically and psychologically, by the larger system. The director of nursing exemplified this in the following comment: "We did find a good spot for them [ICU], near the parking lot on the south wing, kinda out of sight." This issue of abandonment was reinforced by another issue that was looming, an issue raised offhandedly by the director at one of the meetings. She said, "Oh, they're also probably upset because their dear is leaving soon." She was speaking of the hospital administrator, the CEO.

The CEO was near retirement and was absent from his office with increasing frequency. The CEO took on symbolic significance for the staff of the ICU. He had been seen by the staff as an inspirational leader who gave them a strong sense of security, and in doing so, he protected the ICU staff from feeling alienated and devalued. This impact was evident at a meeting the consultant requested with the ICU staff, which was arranged by the director of nursing. The purpose of the meeting was to meet the staff and discuss how things could be improved in the unit. The meeting took place in a small conference room that overlooked a parking lot. The consultant observed a depressed-looking staff drift in at various intervals: No one was on time. At about 10 minutes after the meeting was to begin, when all the nurses had finally arrived, one nurse looked out the window and commented, "He's not here again, he's out more than he's in." At this point the director of nursing began to speak.

DIRECTOR: The schedule needs to be looked at.

NURSE (1): *(Interrupting her)* Why do we always need to fill in empty spaces? Why can't they [meaning the administration] find someone from one of the other units, or a student or something—I've had it.

NURSE (2): You know it's not our fault. You need to fill the empty spaces soon or everything is going to go to pot. We're overworked and we can't continue at this pace.

NURSE (3): I'm getting sick myself. It's too much.

DIRECTOR: You work a couple of extra shifts and then complain. You have everything you need. Why when I was on the floor. . .

NURSE (2): For Christ sake . . . *(Buzzer goes off and three nurses get up and run out)*

CONSULTANT: I think we had better stop for today. I am glad to have met with you and I would like to meet with you again sometime. Thank you! *(Everyone leaves, and the director is visibly angry)*

The psychological significance of the CEO was evident at this meeting. The ICU staff, when faced with feeling abandoned by the larger system and their immediate supervisor, and working with a patient population that precipitated primitive anxieties, required empathic support, but as the metaphor "empty" implied, their only source of support was, indeed, empty. The experience of emptiness is underscored by Menzies (1960), who suggests its utility in coping with work-related anxiety. She says:

> In developing a structure, culture, and mode of functioning, a social organization is influenced by a number of interacting factors, crucial among which are its primary task, including such environmental relationships and pressures as that task involves; the technologies available for performing the task; and the needs of the members of the organization for social and psychological satisfaction, and above all, for support in the problem of dealing with anxiety. . . . (p. 100)

The problem of anxiety among the ICU staff became clearer through an analysis of the task within the unit.

The nature of the work within the ICU was particularly anxiety producing. Patients near death and dying, as well as the presence of the patients' friends and relatives in the unit who were overwrought with grief, guilt, and rage, presented the staff with deeply felt depressive burdens. Being so close to the experience of death and dying resurrected in the staff feelings of being deserted and lost. It is as if the staff, through identification with the patients, felt that they too would die if they were not attended to and supported. The CEO symbolically represented life to the staff. His retirement was experienced as another death. However, his death assumed profound proportions, because with his death, the last object utilized by the staff to defend against and ward off depression would be lost. In the past, the staff had been able to ward off depression through the process of denial of affects and by taking refuge in the physical action associated with the performance of duties on the unit, and with the knowledge that the CEO appreciated and valued them. The significant issue for the ICU staff was concentrated around identification with the CEO. By identifying with the CEO, the staff could effectively work on its tasks without a regressive pull. This was accomplished by internalizing the power and strength of the CEO. They could perform their tasks because they had the CEO's strength inside them. Schafer (1968) supports this conceptualization by suggesting:

> Internalization is the fantasy of taking objects into the body, and this is the incorporation of fantasies about others. We are not referring to internalization or imitation, or copying . . . but internalization of the external object molded in such a way so that it conforms to the persons inner objects. Before internalization can occur a leader must be idealized, that is, the subordinate must see the leader as exceptional in comparison to himself. (p. 32)

This type of internalization brings followers together. It is the combination of the idealization and then internalization of the CEO which forms the bonds among employees in the ICU. The staff's identification with each other and the idea that they are indeed a group sustains the idealization of the CEO.

The ability of the group of nurses to form a bond and be protected from the anxieties associated with the task is a function of (1) the idealization of a leader, in this case the CEO, (2) an internalization of some utilitarian aspect of the leader to serve as a defense, and (3) a partial identification of the followers with each other.

The lack of support exhibited by the staff from the larger system became increasingly apparent as the CEO moved closer to symbolic death, retirement. Without adequate identifications and internalization with a pseudoparent, the ICU could not defend against either the projections from the larger system or the anxieties associated with the task. For the ICU to maintain the necessary defensive structure, two characteristics would need to remain. First, the unit needed a strong sense of unity or internal bonding, and second, the staff needed to utilize the defenses associated with professionalism in the relations with patients and families. Of these characteristics, bonding within a group has the greatest degree of relevance. For example, nurses are expected to abstain from certain types of behaviors in their relations with patients. When abstinence fails for a nurse, as it often does, it is the staff who are expected to respond to this failure, first, by empathically seeing that the failure is a response to some stress, and second, by helping to ameliorate the stress. It is the staff whom the nurse experiences as a social group that helps establish and restore defenses that are necessary if the nurse is to avoid becoming "too involved" or emotionally attached to work or patients. However, in order for the ICU staff to become this powerful protective and "therapeutic" group, the larger system must support their work. When it does not, the defensive structure breaks down and the staff members experience abandonment. This reduces the support structure the nurses need to defend against the powerful anxieties triggered by the activities associated with their task.

Failure of the Defensive Structure

The defensive structure failed because the leadership of the hospital and the staff of the larger system failed to lend support to the ICU. A critical issue for the consultant concerned the nature of the intervention that would bring about the establishment of the necessary structure and relationships to support the task of the ICU. To begin to develop the intervention, it was necessary to assess how the hospital in general conceived of itself as a supportive system.

In many organizations, support is rare, or it is given to the subsystem that needs it the least. Often the units that receive the most support are those that have a glorious history, have graduated a CEO, or have added to the prestige of the organization in general. Also, the organizational system fails to offer support to a particular subsystem because those within the larger system unconsciously wish to keep that subsystem stressful or unproductive. This often is the equivalent of scapegoating the subsystem; that is, rendering the subsystem dysfunctional. Blaming the subsystem for all the organizations problems follows. This is equivalent to blaming the victim (Czander, 1983).

In the hospital, support was given to those units that added prestige to the larger system. Pediatrics, surgery, and obstetrics added power and prestige to the male-dominated group of physicians. In addition, these were units where staff could talk and brag about success. The "real work" of the hospital, saving lives and giving birth, occurred in these units. All the ICU could do was to ease the pain associated with death, and not many wanted to discuss it. Thus the values and attitudes in the larger system led the ICU nurses to the emotional experience of worthlessness and depression, which, added to the emotionality connected to the work, brought about a general decomposition. The larger system projected onto the ICU affects associated with fear of death and fragmentation. The larger system was critical of the work of the ICU; devaluation was a method of reducing these affects. It was as if the larger staff could be relieved of these burdens and the affects associated with death if the ICU carried them.

The thrust of the intervention was to develop a system of support for the ICU. But before this intervention could begin, one last question needed to be answered: Why had the larger system failed to recognize this on its own, rather than needing a consultant to make the suggestion? Until this question is answered, the consultant cannot be certain of the nature of the resistance to the intervention.

The reason the larger system failed centered around the hospital administrator. The staff in the larger system had an attachment to their leader that, surprisingly, was just as strong as the ICU staff's. He was retiring after 40 years of building a good, quality hospital and he was revered by all. His departure would be experienced as a great loss for the institution and for many of the employees personally. This brings the analysis to a psychodynamic understanding of the lack of support for the ICU. The staff in the larger system were losing a highly valued leader. In a symbolic sense he was dying. There was no one to take his place and the staff unconsciously felt abandoned and feared that with his death all around them would also die, the hospital would die. The symbolic function of the ICU now becomes clear: It was the place that people went to die. Unconsciously, the larger staff saw the ICU as both responsible for and the cause of their leader's death. They projected onto the ICU, their rage toward the leader for abandoning them and they wanted to see the ICU die. The unconscious fantasy was that if the ICU would disappear, all would be correct and the leader would not have to die.

Intervention

Because of the vulnerability of the ICU staff, the intervention began as soon as possible. Failure to begin the process of changing the situation would have resulted in resignations and termination. However, the consultant was also aware of the need for caution because of the apparent resistance that would come from the staff of the larger system. The staff of the larger system would resist change or undermine the change process because they had found the role the ICU played in their work life to be most functional. If the intervention were successful and the situation were to change, it would be the staff in the larger system who would have the most to lose or give up. For example, the staff of the larger system could no longer project their anxieties onto the ICU.

With this in mind, the following steps were taken:

1. The head of the ICU and the CEO would have two hourlong meetings with the consultant to discuss issues within the unit and his departure.
2. The CEO would meet biweekly with the ICU staff for the next 6 months until his retirement.
3. A search committee would be formed with representatives from the staff (including the ICU head) on the committee. This committee would report directly to the board of trustees about the process of selecting a new CEO.
4. A guest speaker would present a series of lectures to the larger system in grand rounds on the subject of death and dying.

The guest speaker had the greatest impact on changing the values and attitudes toward the ICU that were held by the larger system. The staff began to respond to the ICU staff with a greater sense of empathy. The lectures raised the consciousness of the staff and the ICU staff began to feel a sense of appreciation. Soon after, physicians and nurses began to visit the ICU.

The internal structure of the ICU was altered, an increased sense of bonding among the nurses occurred, and esprit returned. This came about because the task and sentient systems received support from the larger system.

CHAPTER 10

Authority

"Social Class" refers to the universal tendency of men who
are similarly situated socially and economically to develop
common ideas and engage in collective actions. "Bureaucracy"
refers to the universal tendency of men who are employed
in hierarchical organizations to obey directives and to identify
their own interests and ideas with the organization and
with all those persons in it who share identification. These
are rival tendencies of action.

   —REINHART BENDIX (1956, p. xx)

Ideologies of management are attempts by leaders of
enterprises to justify the privilege of voluntary action
and association for themselves, while imposing upon all
subordinates the duty of obedience and the obligation to
serve their employers to the best of their ability.

   —REINHART BENDIX (1956, p. xxi)

One thing is clear. After studying the family and making the
father its pivotal point, psychoanalysis had more to say about
authority and the leader than anything else.

   —SERGE MOSCOVICI (1985, p. 241)

Authority assumes a special
place in psychoanalytic consulting because of its profound influence
on the relationships that are both formally and informally established
and maintained in the organization. Authority is the only legitimate
instrument for the promotion and maintenance of obedience and
conformity in the organization. The nature of authority influences
the type of structure the organization adopts, the relationships among
workers, and the manner in which the work of the organization is
accomplished.

Within the field of organizational theory, authority is a poorly understood concept. Authority and power are not differentiated, and many writers on organizational behavior automatically assume that authority and power are one and the same. This presents a confusing picture and often leads both writers and students to assume that power is a commodity to be used, that they have power or they can get it in some fashion. An example of this is articulated by Morgan (1988), who sees power as being the equivalent of a resource:

> All organizations depend for their continued existence on the adequate flow of resources, such as money, materials, technology, personnel and support from customers, suppliers and the community at large. An ability to exercise control over any of these resources can thus provide an important source of power within an organization. (p. 161)

To conclude, as Morgan has, that the source of power lies within resources, is similar to making the assumption that because one is bigger and stronger than all others, one's size and strength are a source of power. Morgan concludes that the source of power can be located in an object or source. However, this conclusion denies the interactive nature of power and dismisses its psychological components. Also, assuming as Morgan and others have that when an employee has power, its source has been located, is to muddle or dismiss the idea of authority, or worse, to imply that power and authority are synonymous.

Authority is defined as a right given as a result of rank or office occupancy. It is a right to issue commands and to punish violations. While the person occupying a position of authority may have power, psychologically it must be differentiated from authority. Power is a perceptual phenomenon; that is, one attributes power to another. Power only exists within the eyes of another, within the perceiver, and a person's perceptions are a function of the personality of the perceiver, the perceptual field, and the attributes of the perceived. Additionally, power can only exist when the observer attributes power to another. This is based on a set of characteristics that the observer believes to be associated with power. A person occupying a position of authority can be perceived by subordinates as having little power and vice versa. If power is a perceptual phenomenon, then in psychological terms the person projects power onto another as a function of meaningful attributes.

The projection of power onto another may be based on a number of characteristics such as money, family, education, knowledge, and appearance, as well as status and areas of discretion contained within a given role. Therefore, authority, that which is given to a role occupant, will merely influence the observer, thus creating the perception of power. Although authority is only contained in a role, the role itself can command power, but it will only do so if it is projected by another. A person who occupies a particular role may be perceived as having power because of the nature of the role.

An important question for the analysis of leader–follower relations is the nature of the psychological mechanisms involved when one attributes power to a role. This type of power, that is, power attributed to a person because he/she occupies a role, results when the characteristics of the role influence the perceivers' fantasies of the power contained within the role. The observer may not know the role occupant; however, he/she may attribute power to its occupant from a distance. In this instance, the power that is attributed to this person in the role has very little to do with the role occupant. When one responds, he/she is responding to the role and not to the person at all. When the observer moves closer to the role occupant and is capable of getting beyond the trappings of the role, power takes on a different function. It moves away from fantasy and has the potential of moving closer to reality.

POWER FROM AN ORGANIZATIONAL PERSPECTIVE

The most common definition of power considers it to be connected to the ability of one person to influence another; however, this is not true in all cases, because this definition fails to take into consideration the perceptual field, the context within which the perceiver observes or attributes power. For instance, a superior might influence a subordinate without the subordinate's knowledge, or vice versa.

Let us consider two employees, P and O. We might speak of P's power over O, but in reality this power is invested in O and not in P. This confusion is clarified when one thinks of power in terms of control (i.e., P's control over the behavior of O). Power becomes an issue not over the actions, rules, or regulations that evolve under these conditions but over the state of affairs that rules, actions, or demands will influence and formalize in one's perceptual field (Chein, 1947).

It is true that in hierarchically structured organizations a person occupying a position of authority does, in fact, control significant aspects of the life and fate of others, and thereby possesses great influence over the activities of these others. But it is not the person who occupies the position that exerts the influence. It is the organization and the roles that facilitate the perception of power. In this instance, *P* may have the power to fire *O* for various reasons, but *O* has power: the power to resist. Perhaps resist as Bartleby did in Melville's *Bartleby the Scrivener,* or by undermining *P*'s authority by not working correctly or by slowing down the work by intentionally or unintentionally distorting commands, or by engaging in direct confrontation.

We all can agree that a CEO is only perceived as having power if the subordinate accepts these conditions, and although it is believed that in hierarchical systems, with structured inequities, some have more power than others because of their right to reward and punish, however, this often is not the case. Subordinates may not have the same rights as their superiors, but when it comes to power, both subordinates and superiors have equal access.

The issue of power is exceedingly complex, and it is reasonable to assume that merely having more legal rights (authority) than another does not imply that a similar power arrangement exists. To see power as a function of perception requires the conclusion that a psychology underlies all of these relationships. This is also true for authority relationships, which are formed and are forever influenced by the person's first relationship with authority, mother. To understand the psychology of these relationships (i.e., the belief that motivations for conflict within the organization are a function of conflict within authority relationships) presents to the student of organizations an opportunity to ferret out the motivations that underlie most organizational dysfunctions.

PSYCHODYNAMICS OF AUTHORITY RELATIONS

Authority has a profound effect on the psychic life of subordinates. This is especially apparent in vertically structured bureaucratic organizations where subordinates are removed from their corporate superiors by layers of personnel, formal rules, and regulations. From a distance, the role of authority will produce what psychoanalysts call transference reactions in the subordinate. When the subordinate is unable to move close to the person occupying a role, that is, cannot see the occupant as a real person, the subordinate will demonstrate a greater tendency to project or transfer onto the superior (the role and its occupant) feelings, fantasies, and wishes that are often experiences of earlier relationships with authority in the subordinate's life.

Consider the following example: A young student falls in love with her professor. The professor responds to this love as if it were real. To do this is to commit a grave mistake. This love has very little to do with reality. It is based exclusively on the student's fantasies which are influenced by the role the professor occupies. The role contains authority and other characteristics that appeal to the student and produce feelings of love. However, this love is not love for the occupant of the role (the person), but love that evolves from projections resulting from the role itself. Also, it evolves from the characteristics of both roles, the teacher and the student.

Being in the role of a student precipitates wishes and fantasies associated with passivity, subordination, and being nurtured and loved. When this is coupled with the characteristics associated with the role of the professor (parental, nurturing, dominant, admired, etc.), one can see how the role interactions might facilitate unconscious and conscious transferences which contain elaborate fantasies and wishes. Additionally, once this interaction is placed into the context of the university, where closeness increases libidinal urges, and where idealization abounds under the guise of romantic truths, one can consider how the system itself promotes such transference reactions. The question the professor may ask is: If I were not in this role, would this young student still love me? Probably not.

In consulting to authority, the psychoanalyst stresses the interactive nature of the relationships that are a necessary part of the utilization of authority. The consultant assumes that these relations have powerful fantasy components. Understanding the dynamics associated with fantasies of authority underlies the work of reducing organizational conflict. Superiors must always be aware of the reactions to authority from followers (Wolff, 1950). Relationships of dominance and subordination are highly complex interactions of reciprocity, and conflicts can be apparent even when followers appear purely passive in the relationship. On the other hand, even an unconditional ruler rules by some degree of mutual contract. The consultant assumes that all superior–subordinate contracts are psychological in nature and are supported by intrapsychic projections and projective identifications.

We have established that authority contains strong elements of unconscious ideation. In the example of the young student in love, the love contains unconscious projections based on role characteristics. Often those who occupy roles of authority perpetuate false idealizations among subordinates to compensate for the lack of power they experience within the role they occupy. Frequently organizational leaders will respond to a consultant's question concerning their relationship with their subordinates by saying, "They love me." This has the same spurious connection to reality as a leader's saying, "They hate me," although in this case, this observation would be prohibitive and taken as a sure sign that the leader is defective in some manner. However, as in the case of the professor, to personalize these observations, or to believe they are true, means that one is at the mercy of them. The leader, by attributing power to his/her subordinates—the power to love or to hate—is at their mercy. However, the overriding concern when a leader personalizes his/her subordinates' responses is that it leaves the leader with little room to conduct a careful analysis of the nature of his/her relationship. The leader's perceptions of reality become just as colored as his/her subordinates.

The profound importance of authority relations can be exemplified by assessing the similarity between work and play. Many psychoanalysts suggest that what play is to children, work is to the adult, and that the psychic components of play will actively find their way into adulthood within work activities. If one investigates play activities of children, authority relations are most apparent. In play, the child expresses psychic concerns associated with oedipal struggles and works toward a resolution of the very same affects that are carried over into adult life. However, at work, authority objects are not the creation of one's fantasy, one cannot mold and shape them into psychically gratifying situations as a child can do in play. Yet the employee carries manifestations of early play activities into work arrangements, especially into authority relations.

Consider the play of children where one child plays the parent, teacher, or policeman. One observes in play the psychic representations of authority as one child expresses his/her wish to be dominant as opposed to passive, harsh as opposed to loving, and obedient as opposed to rebellious. Also in play one observes the manifestations of internalized sex-role stereotyping. Yet at work, when these early manifestations cannot be realized, defenses are called forth, especially denial, projection, and displacement. At work, one rarely has opportunities to shape authority relations. At work, the authority relationship must be accepted. This creates a number of dilemmas. Each dilemma contains conflict and can result in work inhibitions.

WORK INHIBITIONS AND AUTHORITY

Success or failure at work has very little to do with reality and is a function of the subordinate's fantasized relationship with authority. The power of the role of authority and its impact on subordinates requires observational sensitivity on the part of the consultant when consulting to authority relations. Consider the following: An authority figure may turn his shoulder in front of an employee. This may be perceived by the subordinate as a slight, as an impingement upon his self-worth and status in the organization. In other words, it may be perceived as a narcissistic injury, which may have a profound effect on the subordinate's work life.

The fantasy of being loved, valued, and admired at work, which is contained within the wished-for self-image, is exceedingly vulnerable in authority relations. Consequently, while the superior sees turning his/her shoulder as insignificant, the employee occupying the role of subordinate experiences it as a narcissistic mortification. Narcissistic injuries result from the inability to gratify preoedipal and oedipal wishes. Preoedipal injuries will create panic, excessive clinging to the object in the form of obedience, or schizoid withdrawal. Oedipal injuries result in the experience of shame, inferiority, and worthlessness, which is most likely to cause aggression and conflict of an interactive nature. Gouldner (1954) suggests that in authority relationships, conflict increases as those in subordinate positions attempt to evade or rebel against perceived control and dominance, and those in authority roles react to their subordinates' behavior in a parental manner by increasing their control and dominance by establishing new rules and regulations. This process continues and escalates over time, eventually ending in a psychic stalemate where oedipal conflicts are repressed through the creation of an organizational structure that resembles a machine bureaucracy.[1]

In order to maintain an authority structure, member compliance is required. The members of the organization are expected to lend credibility to this structure by following orders and respecting the hierarchy. An organization cannot be coordinated internally unless it effectively induces its members to follow an established set of conditions where stability of authority is maintained through the establishment of regulatory boundaries.

Regulatory boundaries are established by defining and clearly maintaining standards for performance, rules and regulations, requirements for participation, and closeness of supervision. However, increases in these areas (i.e., excessive control) will increase the potential for conflict and the motivation to deviate. As mentioned earlier, conflict is inherent in all authority structures, and conflict is perpetuated by the subordinates' desire to increase their degree of freedom from controls.

A critical issue for the psychoanalytic consultant is the analysis of the conflict that results when those who occupy positions of authority attempt to influence and direct their subordinates. These conflicts are

---

[1]Mintzberg (1988), writing about types of organizational structures, suggests that the machine bureaucracy is the most dominating and controlling of all structures.

common in all organizations and they arise wherever dominance and control are apparent. It is generally assumed that all psychic conflicts are the result of developmental arrest, often referred to as unresolved developmental disorders. These developmental disorders form the intrapsychic structural foundations of the adult personality. The two areas of developmental concern that seem to contain a special relationship in adult life with authority are the anal stage and the oedipal stage. Of these two, the oedipal stage is most problematic, because at this stage external social repression is concomitant with the internal repression of impulses (Horkheimer, 1949).

The source of the oedipal complex was explored by Freud (1920/1955), as he applied the myth of Oedipus to his explanation of infantile sexuality and psychosexual development. Freud placed this complex at the center of his theory of neurosis: "It . . . is the nuclei complex of the neurosis, and constitutes the essential part of their content. Every new arrival on this planet is faced by the task of mastery of the Oedipus Complex; anyone who fails to do so falls victim to neurosis" (p. 28). Additionally, Freud maintained that the oedipal complex could help explain the relations of man to his leader and perhaps to civilization.

For Freud, the critical component of this complex is rivalry with the same-sex parent. The same-sex parent is seen as the ultimate authority who is both feared and hated. When the little boy experiences love for the mother—for the girl love for the father—this love, in its primitive form, comes under severe societal taboos and dread of the retaliatory powers of the same-sex parent. To psychically survive this phase requires a defensive reaction where the child must alter sexual impulses into socially acceptable behaviors. Thus, the critical step in this developmental phase is to successfully negotiate a satisfactory relationship with both parents. When this occurs, the child can successfully move into the latency period, where sexual drives are put on hold.

According to most developmental theorists, including Erikson (1950), the latency stage of development is crucial because it is the period in which the young person begins to develop values and attitudes toward work and achievement (Neff, 1977). Considering the importance of success in prior developmental stages, and the fact that at the beginning of the latency stage the child is still resolving oedipal issues, one can see the impact that the successful resolution of oedipal issues will have on the latency period. If the child does not resolve the oedipal issues, the child will carry conflicts with authority into the latency stage. This will severely limit the child's ability to sublimate and engage in the relationships required for work.

If the child is unable to sublimate libidinal drives, and is conflicted with authority as a result of unresolved oedipal issues, the child will not be able to reap the benefits of the latency period. Successful resolution of the oedipal period is only accomplished through parental love and understanding combined with tolerable degrees of frustration and prohibition. These will enable the child to develop both a strong autonomous ego and a benign superego.

During the oedipal period the child learns to control his/her impulses when fear of an external authority (the same-sex parent) is internalized. This internalization of authority never gives as much to the child as it takes, and the child's attitude toward authority and to its psychological agency, the superego, assumes an irrational aspect. For example, according to classical theory the child achieves social adjustment only by taking pleasure in obedience and subordination. Overindulgence, severe frustration, or deprivation by either parent during childhood will increase the likelihood of induced regressive oedipal or preoedipal fantasies in adulthood. The adult, when faced with a frustrating relationship with an authority (an oedipal type of situation), will psychically split the ego into one part that is rebellious and aggressive and another part that is dependent and submissive. Either part can be projected onto the leader or superior. If the submissive, dependent part is projected, the leader is seen as loving and gratifying. If the rebellious, aggressive part is projected the leader is seen as controlling and mean. To keep this part from being destructive, it may be projected onto someone other than the leader, some real or imagined enemy (generally an enemy of the beloved superior), or the aggression can be turned against self.

According to Kets de Vries (1978), employees who have conflicts with authority continuously engage in what he refers to as a rebellious position, and they perceive work as a duty, as something of a demand imposed by authority figures. Consequently, work turns into a symbolic struggle for obedience and control. The struggle becomes one for freedom against oppression associated with authority (the parent, who is seen as a constraining fearful object). This type of conflict is the result of the employees' failure to identify with authority figures (the parent[s]) early in life; that is, they are not able to invest their aggression against authority into their superego; consequently, they are not able to internalize authority. Instead they use the superego to defend against a replication of early struggles of an oedipal nature (Grunberger, 1966). They do this through projection, where they create an excessively idealized object in their superior.

Projections of this type help employees avoid resurrection of early oedipal struggles. The avoidance is complete through projection of magical power onto the authority figure. This may sound similar to the defenses used by young males who invest magical power in an object, but it is different. In the case of the young male, an identification takes place and the defense is used as protection against an external threat. In the case of the employee, no identification takes place. The object serves to protect the employee from internal dangers, his/her own aggression. The projection of magical power onto the authority role, making the authority into a powerful figure, is created to protect the subordinate from these conflictual oedipal issues. According to Grunberger (1966), in this case the wish is to make the authority a protector against the self, to keep the subordinate from the adult world. In the process the authority becomes the "bearer of the megalomaniacal narcissistic projections of his followers; he is their rallying point as well as the purveyor of an ideological content that feeds their defensive impulses against the Oedipus . . ." (p. 296).

Underlying this wish for a powerful leader, and the passive desire to be an obedient son or daughter, is a powerful aggressive motivation. This aggression is often repressed and can remain repressed if the authority keeps the promise and gratifies the unconscious wish. This repressed aggression against authority is subject to rapid and wild shifts in feelings. It is tenuous, and if the authority demonstrates the slightest fault, aggression erupts. These shifts are often observed in situations where a leader who was once perceived as a saint is suddenly perceived as a frustrator and evil.

Hatred and aggression left unresolved, as a carryover from earlier oedipal conflicts, reduce the probability of attaining libidinal gratification from work-related activities and may contribute to or distort the motivations connected with occupational choice and career success. The employee who is continuously engaged in a struggle with authority figures, a struggle filled with rivalry, envy, jealously, or suspicion, is unable to derive pleasure from work. When overwhelmed with conflicts the employee cannot obtain love. Hate resulting from early oedipal conflicts makes the idea of love in a reparative sense unattainable. This is evident when an employee reports frustration and deprivation at the hands of his/her superior. The employee cannot delay his/her need for gratification and is quick to become frustrated and to experience a withdrawal of libido. For this employee, authority is, as it always was, depriving and frustrating. The superior has little chance of filling the void. Everything around the employee is empty, including work.

Frustration of the wish to be gratified may also take the form of narcissistic demands. Employees constantly look for signs and symbols from authorities to support their wishes for love and admiration. When gratification is not forthcoming, early unacceptable self-containing feelings of inferiority and worthlessness come to the fore. Under these conditions, employees respond by withdrawing from the burdens of responsibility and decision making. In doing so, they avoid the fears associated with oedipal struggles. Complete reliance on authority (i.e., obedience) is also considered an avoidance of oedipal conflicts. Here the subordinate seeks the regressed comforts associated with the dependent, infantile preoedipal state as a way to avoid the aggression and hatred associated with oedipal struggles.

Often the organization promotes this type of regression. This occurs when the executive constellation unconsciously fear oedipal struggles and respond to them with increased control and demands that subordinates adhere to rules and regulations. The superior takes on a harsh parental attitude. Over time, the subordinate, in response to organizational pressures, moves away from oedipal struggles through regression to a preoedipal stage. Now the subordinate responds to authority with dependency as opposed to aggression. Oedipal conflicts are most anxiety producing for superiors, who often respond by terminating or symbolically castrating the troublesome employee. Superiors feel greatest comfort with compliant, dependent employees, and if they cannot promote an environment in which preoedipal regressions prevail, they will selectively recruit employees with preoedipal pathology.

Of all the relationships in an organization, it is authority relationships that make the most powerful contribution to psychic stress. It is well documented that the superior's age, sex, race, and other more subtle characteristics will greatly influence the intensity of the subordinates' reaction. The simple statement of a male subordinate, "I can't work for a woman boss," is the consequence of powerful conflicts, some conscious (some that can be articulated), but many that are unconscious ideational stereotypic projections of affects associated with oedipal and preoedipal wishes.

INTERACTIVE NATURE OF AUTHORITY RELATIONS

All authority relations are psychically based on the projection of fantasies. Even those relations that give the appearance of a being satisfying have the potential of becoming problematic because they are based on fantasy life and have little to do with reality.

Given the vulnerable nature of authority positions, role occupants wish for and actively pursue projections of adulation from their subordinates. Seeking adulation helps to reduce the anxiety associated with the demands of the position, such as responsibility and gratification of subordinates' wishes. Although superiors actively encourage projections,•projection can be especially damaging. Consider the superior who encourages the projection of unconscious fantasies onto him/her and who attempts to gratify these projected fantasies to obtain adulation. The superior's intent evolves from his/her need to be admired and loved. However, most superiors fail to recognize how complex and vulnerable an admired type of relationship is. This is most evident when an authority feels bewilderment because a subordinate who once admired and loved the authority figure suddenly turns and now hates and admonishes the authority. The confusion exists because the person in the authority position believes that it is actually he/she who is being loved. If superiors understood that what is projected has little to do with them and is a function of their role and the unconscious wishes of their employees, these superiors would not experience this shift with confusion, or worse as a personal affront. The psychoanalytic consultant seeks to reduce these damaging projections by working with the superior to increase his/her knowledge of the power of projections and role of authority, and of the dangers associated with his/her wish to be admired and loved. The consultant seeks to create relationships between superior and subordinate based more on reality and less on fantasy.

The psychodynamics associated with authority will influence and permeate many aspects of organizational functioning. For example, psychodynamics influence a subordinate's ability to perceive or comprehend communications, especially those from a superior. Dynamics also influence decision making, and whether a given system is compatible with a subordinate's personal interests or goals within the organization, and the degree to which a subordinate is capable of compliance. The allocation and the structural arrangement of authority have a decisive influence over the kinds of adjustments people are capable of making in the organization, and ultimately over the practical results and effectiveness of the organization (Crozier, 1964). In spite of its importance, in most cases, authority operates ineffectively. In most organizations, violations of authority are accepted as matter of course, with implications that are rarely considered. This is especially problematic when employees experience authority as ambiguous.

THE PROBLEM OF AUTHORITY AND AMBIGUITY

Consider an organization in which no one knows who is in charge, who is responsible for the results of a specific project, or the scope of responsibility and discretion. It is reasonable to assume that lack of clarity is one of the most prevalent reasons for organizational conflict and failure. The lack of clarity concerning the nature of the organizations's authority structure creates two responses: (1) a considerable amount of anxiety among subordinates and (2) increased projections.

The lack of clarity concerning the nature of authority is most apparent when an employee is asked to lead a work group or committee. Both superiors and subordinates experience anxiety and do not work well when ambiguity exists. The most common areas of confusion are in defining time boundaries, defining membership requirements, the nature of the task to be completed, access to resources, and the scope of the leader's authority. Still, committees are ubiquitous, and they are often a wasteful and ineffective means for decision making because of a lack of clarity.

The lack of clarity is most dangerous for an organization when it occurs at the organization's boundary. Consider an organization that sends out a subordinate (e.g., a vice president or an assistant) to negotiate contracts or to develop associations with other organizations. The nature of authority given this organizational representative must be absolutely clear if the best interests of the organization are to be served. For example, a large textile company involved in union negotiations at one of its mills found that a vice president had given concessions to the union that the organization described as extraordinary. The problem resulted from the organization's failure to define the nature of the vice president's authority during the negotiations. The vice president, uncertain of his authority, was pressured into making bad agreements by sophisticated union chiefs, who were highly skilled in the art of negotiation. If the organization had stated clearly what the vice president could or could not do, the apparent giveaway would not have occurred.

Formal authority requires clarity if the work of the organization is to proceed with minimal difficulty. Promoting clarity of the authority structure has the potential of freeing subordinates from extraneous issues found in informal power arrangements. From an organizational perspective, authority, when it is defined and clearly understood, provides a structure for objective problem analysis and decision making. When subordinates have unclear expectations and responsibilities, the political and informal social system will prevail to harness the competition and maneuvering that will most likely emerge under conditions of ambiguity.

TYPES OF AUTHORITY RELATIONS

The psychoanalytic consultant attempts to assess the subordinates' perception of authority along a number of dimensions that form the subordinates' conception of the executive role constellation. Hodgson (1965) suggests three types of authority constellations that can be found in the organization. The first type is a single, highly controlling, and assertive superordinate constellation. Here the subordinate hopes that "freedom from personal anxieties will be found in perfect subservience to omniscient superior" and the subordinate is left with the choice of rebellion or conforming to these pressures for control and conformity. The second type of constellation is built around the conception of a maternal-nurturant superior. Once again, there is ambivalence in this relationship between superior and subordinate, but the dynamic issues are different. The superior may obtain a certain amount of gratification through the process of giving and receiving affection. However, the superior lives in fear that the subordinate is insatiable and that unrealistic needs may replace more realistic needs. The superior is left feeling that he will be faced with the impossible task of keeping all the subordinates happy and well-fed. The souring of this constellation occurs when the superior views the subordinates as demanding, whining children, or "cookie monsters,"[2] who are never satisfied. The superior no longer finds it gratifying to give nurturance and he feels "burned out." Two other aspects of this constellation are discovered when sibling-type rivalries occur among the subordinates as they struggle to seek nurturance from the executive constellation. Additionally, the superior often finds considerable aggression and destructive behavior from subordinates when he tries to pursue his own goals and gratify himself, rather than satisfying the subordinates. The third constellation is characterized by the friendly, egalitarian superior. This constellation often evolves as an avoidance of understanding or working through of the primitive dynamics that occur in the other two constellations. While this mode of functioning is often more permissive and open, in actuality it creates an artificial form of friendliness and democracy that is fraught with suspicion and serves to cover over fears of reprisal from the boss. The superior communicates that he/she wants to be "a friend," "one of the guys," and fully pursues a democratic ideal, but covertly, the superior strikes fear and dependency in the hearts of his/her subordinates.

The psychoanalytic consultant maintains that these three types of superior–subordinate relations are formed and held together by reciprocal exchange of intrapsychic projections, introjection, projective identifications, identifications, and displacement. In these relationships, as in any relationship, survival depends on the gratification

---

[2]This refers to the character on the children's television show *Sesame Street,* who continually seeks and devours cookies by using cunning as he schemes to outsmart others.

of dependency needs and wishes. Even in a pathological relationship, the gratification of infantile wishes ensures psychic survival.

PSYCHOPATHOLOGY OF AUTHORITY RELATIONS

The organization is an interactive environment where needs meet head on, sometimes resulting in mutual gratification but often in frustration. Under the best of conditions the members of the organization work together to clarify their abilities to offer gratification to each other so that they can use each other positively; that is, they utilize their strengths and weaknesses in ways that are consistent with social reality. Ideally, this is what organizations are all about—creating structures designed to use the talents of members to accomplish tasks in ways that are respectful of and concerned about the preservation of one another's sense of self-worth and dignity.

However, in rigid hierarchical structures where authority is protected at the expense of creativity, innovation, and spontaneity, these relationships go awry; they become pathological and ultimately destructive to those involved. Instead of creating an optimal cooperative system, the system becomes competitive and dogmatic, where status is protected at the expense of others. When consulting to relationships of this nature, the psychoanalytic consultant attempts to understand what has contributed to the dysfunction. Contributors to authority dysfunction are located in two major areas: in the structure of the system and its motivation for control and dominance, and in the psychodynamics of an interpersonal and intrapsychic nature. If the motivations or dynamics are not uncovered, these potentially destructive relationships will be repeated time and again, increasing harm to the organization and to its employees.

Among an array of damaging relationships, the most problematic is a superior's use of his/her position to psychologically play on the emotional vulnerabilities of a subordinate in order for the superior to increase his/her own psychological gratification. In effect, this is the equivalent of a commonly used phrase—taking advantage of one's subordinate. Those who have an authority role are in a position to take advantage of others, namely, their subordinates. This is made possible by the vulnerability one unconsciously experiences when in a subordinate position.

Authority, as it exists in organizations, is alienating to one's unconscious wishes. If one considers the structural arrangement one typically has had in the past, as a child with parents, teachers, elders, and so on, it has always been apparent that identifiable characteristics such as age and size have been powerful concepts used to differentiate oneself from authority. But entry into the organization as an adult is a unique situation in which authority comes to the fore as the only identifiable distinguishing physical and psychological characteristic separating superior and subordinate. To the adult subordinate, authority is experienced as alienating primarily because those identifiable characteristics that were functional in the past are no longer functional. Authority relationships in adulthood are without mother, father, or teacher. The people who occupy authority positions do not even resemble those older, traditional authority figures. However, this is not to say that transferences cannot occur. It is the general structure of the organization, its vertical or horizontal nature, that promotes various types of transference reactions, that is, where employees react to authority as they had reacted to authority in their past.

When transference reactions abound, the subordinate has little choice but to use the defenses and characterological responses that worked in the past. Typically, the subordinate experiences dissonance precipitated by the large gap between the characteristics of the new authority relationship and that which the subordinate brings with him. Consequently, the relationship becomes strained, distant, and artificial, and the arrangement closely resembles play activities in which one child is the boss and the other the nonboss. They are adults playing a children's game. They are adults of similar age, background, intelligence, and perhaps experience, at play.

The experience of authority under the best conditions still leaves subordinates with anxiety as they tire of the game or seek a change or reversal of roles. When this occurs, the person in authority responds by engaging in an evaluation, the purpose of which is to shore up the inequitable relationship and put the "uppity" subordinate back into his/her place.

From a somewhat different perspective, authority relationships are understood as being capable of producing powerful debilitating emotions because of the expectations a subordinate may have. The subordinate may be fixed into a transference reaction to his/her superior. Transference reactions are ubiquitous. Subordinates react, repeating actions and having similar reactions, as if the superior were a mother, father, sibling, or some other significant figure. From these reactions, a set of expectations evolves, not from the real situation but from projections. These projections determine the degree and the nature of the reactions. Consider employees who react to their superior with the expectation that he/she is an idealized parent. Psychologically the search for an ideal and powerful authority figure is similar to the quest for a duplication of the ideal benevolent parent, or the wish to continue the sadomasochistic struggle in the family. Consider employees who react to their superior as a sibling. Inherent in this reaction are remnants of intense sibling rivalry. These subordinates react to their superior as a rival and manifest many of the affects contained in their relationship with their sibling from the past.

Employees unconsciously wish to replicate the nucleus of love, protection, hate, and rivalry that was present or wished for in earlier relationships. Typically employees seek ideal relationships in which love, status, and protection are possible. They are motivated by fantasies associated with a wish, a wish to obtain that which was not obtained in their earlier relationships. However, this wish for an ideal relationship is never found, and the subordinate responds to the apparent disappointment by manifesting one of two types of reactions to the psychological state associated with being a subordinate: (1) a splitting phenomenon where the subordinate protests the lack of gratification through the manifestation of unconscious rage which is acted out within or against the organization and the superior (the sadistic trend); or (2) a defense against this rage where the subordinate quietly suffers and assumes a position of obedience and compliance, as one who fears the wrath of authority and the loss of love (the masochistic trend). Under these conditions, the subordinate responds by withdrawing from the burdens of responsibility and decision making and in doing so avoids the fears associated with the oedipal struggles.

The following case is an example of how earlier conflicts become repeated at work. We will examine how an authority relationship can precipitate a transference reaction at work, and how a series of organizational events can rupture the delicate nature of this relationship and influence the tragic act of suicide.

CASE ANALYSIS

The following is an analysis of a consultation to an organization whose 42-year-old chief engineer had recently committed suicide. As part of the consultative work, the consultant investigated the work context within which the suicide took place. This analysis is of the events that preceded the tragedy and the psychodynamics that may have influenced it. The analysis focuses on the relationship between two individuals in the context of the organization, the chief engineer (who committed suicide) and the CEO. The analysis focuses on the nature of their relationship, how their respective roles and types of psychopathology contributed to their problematic relationship and culminated in a series of events that eventually influenced the suicide. The case analysis was begun after the suicide. The CEO called the consultant and the following conversation took place:

CEO: A wonderful employee and friend has just killed himself. He was our chief engineer in this company I own . . . and I feel the consequences are great . . . well they're going to be . . . yeah . . . real . . . bad, crazy, I'm worried.

CONSULTANT: What are you worried about?

CEO: I don't know . . . just worried . . . they . . . we all need help with this issue . . . we have to understand it . . . this has been a real shock. I don't know . . . I feel responsible in some way. Do you feel you could come in . . . talk to some of the men . . . me, to . . . give them a chance to talk about it? It would help.

Two critical issues are examined: the CEO's construction of a relationship with the engineer and the CEO's decision to delegate his responsibilities to the engineer. The chief engineer committed suicide 3 days prior to the CEO's departure for a 3-week stay in the hospital for minor surgery during which the CEO had appointed the chief engineer to act as his replacement.

The case has been altered significantly to protect the privacy of the parties involved. The material is drawn from a consultative effort and later on a case presentation at the Department of Psychiatry and the Institute for Social and Political Studies at Yale University.

Before we examine the relations between the CEO and the chief engineer (Mr. O), we will examine the background each brings to the relationship.

The Chief Engineer

Mr. O was the only child of a depressed, alcoholic mother and a physically absent father. His father was a sailor who was absent from home for long periods. When his father was home, he rarely talked to Mr. O as a child and did not participate in hobbies or sports with his son. When Mr. O was a teenager, his father left home permanently. Mr. O was not aware of this fact until 3 years had passed and his mother announced that his father wasn't coming back. Mr. O's mother did not work and they lived in a small apartment. As a teenager Mr. O obtained an academic scholarship to a local college and lived at home. He went away to graduate school and was away when he learned of his mother's death. He did not return home for the funeral and ordered his aunt to dispose of all of his and his family's belongings.

Mr. O thought of obtaining a doctoral degree and pursuing a teaching career, but he met his future wife shortly after his mother's death. After a courtship of 6 months Mr. O married and left college for work, with a master's degree. Mrs. O described her husband as a lonely and depressed man who found great pleasure in his workshop, repairing and creating electronic gadgets. She called him a "tinkerer." She described herself as being able to care for him as his "mother and therapist." Sex was infrequent, and she reported that she did not mind the quiet house. Raising the children was her joy. After the birth of their third son, sexual contact between husband and wife ceased. She claimed that they never discussed it. She described Mr. O as a good father to his sons and reported that he became interested in them when they reached the age of 8 years, when he brought them into his workshop activities.

Mr. O's coworkers described him as a "strange" person who was "aloof." They said he would frequently go to lunch at noon and would remain at a local bowling alley watching people bowl for hours on end. They also said that once or twice a year he would disappear from work and home. His wife would call and the company would be buzzing with speculation as to where he was. Some jokingly referred to him as "having a secret life" or being "an eccentric millionaire." Many of his coworkers disliked him and they collectively agreed that he was a troubled man. They saw his relationship with the CEO as similar to a father–son relationship, but they expressed dismay that the CEO did not take a stand, either to help him (although some believed that it was not the CEO's job) or to terminate him.

The CEO considered Mr. O a valuable employee. He had saved the company thousands of dollars in man-hours and material costs through many of his inventions and suggestions. Some of his inventions had been patented and were bringing money into the company. Over the years, he averaged two to three inventions or significant suggestions per year. Thus, the CEO felt that as long as such wonderful ideas flowed, the company would tolerate his eccentricities. One employee stated, "He's been driving us crazy for the past 7 years, he had better be inventive."

Mr. O's frequent absences and wandering often brought admonishments from the CEO, but the CEO admitted that it was difficult to be punitive and that he would often end confrontations with a comment such as, "If I didn't love you so much, I'd fire you. Do me a favor, shape up and stop punishing me, now get out of here and leave me alone."

The CEO was well aware of Mr. O's dependency on him. He stated, "If I fired him I knew he would be finished. No one else would hire him, even though he was brilliant; he is too much trouble. . . . I had a softness for him, and I was committed to keeping him on the payroll. . . . I truly felt he was worth the trouble, even though many here felt differently."

Mrs. O said her husband idealized the CEO. "He was like a father figure." Even though she had never met the CEO, she gathered from Mr. O's reports and her brief telephone conversations with the CEO, that he was a kind, benevolent man.

Only the employees saw their relationship (CEO/Mr. O) as strange. Their comments: "It was a weird relationship." "The boss felt he was a shrink sometimes, you know, he wanted to get in your head, he [Mr.O] liked that." One employee reported that once, when he was angry, the CEO ended the conversation by telling Mr. O, "You're a bad boy, but we still love you." He said Mr. O looked pleased.

While aware of her husband's past job difficulties [he had had many jobs] Mrs. O believed Mr. O had found a "home" at his present job, and she knew nothing of the recent stress he was experiencing at work.

Mr. O apparently spoke very little to his wife or to his fellow employees, but he would speak to the CEO about three or four times a day. Some speculated that when the CEO was out, Mr. O looked distraught and would often leave work.

The Chief Executive Officer

The CEO was a tall, strikingly handsome man, meticulously dressed, who had a new, expensive sports car parked in front of his office window. He appeared better suited for Wall Street or Madison Avenue than for the small, dirty manufacturing plant he owned. "What is he doing here?" was answered by closer examination.

The CEO characterized himself as a democratic leader. He claimed to have always rejected the idea of tyrannical leadership found in larger corporations. He was proud of the fact that he had created a pleasant, cooperative work environment for his staff of 120 (employed on double shifts in good times), mostly unskilled workers. He described the organization proudly as his creation, and the story of his reason for running this type of company contained numerous boasts of his benevolence.

He had founded the plant after obtaining a small contract to produce railroad parts. Over the years he had obtained more contracts and the plant grew. The CEO thoroughly enjoyed his creation and felt joy about the fact that he cared for so many people and their families. He proudly reported taking on high-risk employees, visiting them in the hospital, and even attending employee family events. He truly felt he was "doing good."

However, the CEO reported that about 6 months before Mr. O's suicide, he began to experience the feeling that things were not going as well as he had led himself to believe. The CEO reported the following: "The employees have become too dependent on me."

This realization, coupled with the fact that he needed to enter the hospital for a minor operation, led the CEO to take action that had major repercussions for the organization and its employees. He issued a memo announcing that Mr. O would be in charge of the company in his absence, a period of about 8 weeks.

By appointing Mr. O, an acknowledged incompetent leader and troubled person, the CEO passed over the vice president, the second in command and widely viewed as capable. When asked about this, the CEO responded, "I felt it would be good for [Mr. O], to put him in something that required responsibility, plus I would be close by. They could get to me. It was not as if I was going off to China."

This case exemplifies the underlying motives associated with all appointments, promotions, or transfers. In these instances Levinson (1984) suggests that guilt is often a motivating factor. This case points to the more unconscious, destructive wishes at play. Destructive wishes are associated with the wish to hurt or destroy an employee or the company. An appointment or promotion can be unconsciously motivated by the wish for revenge that evolves out of past experiences. In this appointment, as with many appointments, an inadequate employee is given the position so that the former office holder can maintain his/her esteem in the organization. In cases where one leaves an organization, the forbidden wish is that the organization will suffer in the departing person's absence, develop a fond appreciation of his/her efforts, or long for his/her return.

The actions of the CEO horrified his staff. The staff reacted by vacillating between feeling punished by the CEO for being too dependent on him and feeling outrage at the appointment of someone they viewed as incompetent. Placing Mr. O in a CEO position brought about an opposite reaction than what the CEO had consciously hoped for. He said that the "staff's dependency on him increased instead of decreasing." It now seemed evident that the CEO wished for and needed the dependency relations with his staff and Mr. O. This need can be understood in the context of the consultant's diagnosis of the CEO. The CEO's decision and his personality suggest a narcissistic personality type.

At first, the narcissistic personality generally appears to be mild and gentle. He believes himself to be a benevolent leader but reports his actual benevolence vaguely. A closer examination of the narcissistic leader uncovers resentment, anger, and rage simmering behind an attractive veneer. This type of leader uses subtle rage and derives great pleasure and gratification from damaging others. Shortly after an interaction with the narcissistic type, one feels annoyance and anger, as if one has been deceived or depleted of something.

According to Kernberg (1980), among different types of pathological character traits found in leaders, narcissism is perhaps the most troubling of all. This is especially true in small organizations, such as the one described here, where the leader's potential to both generate and promote psychopathology among the staff is greatest. These leaders demonstrate a considerable amount of insensitivity and a lack of awareness of the pathological human relations they foster around themselves which pervades through the entire organization. The narcissistic leader is debilitative because of the lack of mutual identifications in his interactions with others, especially subordinates. In this leader, identification is a one-way street: There is no give and take. Consequently, subordinates feel both deprivation and seduction. That is, the feeling of emptiness in the relationship is also marked by the expectation that fulfillment will be forthcoming if the subordinates continue to admire. They frequently use grandiose defenses to protect themselves from dangers. Additionally, Kernberg (1980) says that the narcissistic leader will "be surrounded by people similar to himself, people suffering from serious behavior disorders."

This is how the CEO maintained control. He claimed that his organization was democratic but he established a kind of fascism by surrounding himself with employees similar to Mr. O: employees who would be dependent and compliant and would not threaten him.

Employees are used by the narcissistic type of leader to regulate his/her widely shifting sense of self-esteem. If the leader feels down and depressed, he/she will use the employees to get up and feel elated. If the leader feels elated, he/she will use the employees to stabilize the affect. Very little that goes on in the organization is accomplished with altruistic motives; much is done with the leader's self-esteem and wishes for grandiosity in mind. The effects of this type of leadership are troublesome. Kernberg (1980) confirms this when he says, "[W]hen the organization is small, the negative effects of this type of leader can be overwhelming. Everyone is hampered by the leader's insatiable appetite for power and admiration and by his extreme psychological fluctuations" (p. 424). Kernberg emphasizes an oral nature, and it appears that this is precisely the seduction of the narcissistic type. Narcissistic types are never able to "take in" or introject that which is projected by their subordinates. They demonstrate little in the way of merging as they continuously struggle with self-object differentiation. It is as if that which is projected is attached to nothing, yet the narcissist demands that the subordinates keep on trying.

In contrast to Kernberg, Bursten (1978) suggests that in the analysis of the narcissistic personality type, the following question needs to be answered: "Why do these people have such a high interest in themselves?" Bursten claims that they cannot take themselves for granted; they constantly need to confirm themselves. It seems that having such a high investment in themselves leaves little left over in the way of being able to invest in others. The quantity of compassion and empathy that is available is only for themselves. The narcissists' inability to gratify both assertion needs and dependency needs, and to identify with or introject with the projections of others (their staff), is a function of their rejection of the adult world and their regressive narcissistic retreat into themselves. Unfortunately, in an organization, this type of leader promotes relationships with his staff that lead to extreme forms of passivity and depression.

In his interactions with Mr. O, the CEO had established a relationship that satisfied his own narcissistic needs for admiration and control. The unfortunate consequence of this relationship was that the CEO was insensitive to the impact of this relationship on Mr. O. In this case, the CEO was not only demanding power over others; he was also creating a situation where he would return from the hospital and have to correct the problems certain to arise. The CEO, by promoting this type of situation, was unconsciously expressing his wish to maintain the dependency and admiration of his staff, as well as expressing his fear and vulnerability by ensuring that he would not be replaced by someone else.

Mr. O was being thrust into a position of authority over a staff who perceived him as incompetent. To complicate the situation, the staff felt personally betrayed by the CEO's departure and even more so by his appointment of Mr. O. This precipitated feelings of anger that eventually would have been displaced onto Mr. O when he moved into the CEO's position. The CEO, the father figure, had rejected Mr. O and left him in charge of an angry group. It is clear that the appointment of Mr. O enhanced the CEO's wish to feel invulnerable, just as the appointment of a more appropriate employee, the vice president, would have been threatening to him.

Mr. O's intrapsychic attachment was strongly encouraged by the CEO. He found that this relationship offered the potential for meeting his own needs for love and admiration. Thus, the CEO not only permitted Mr. O's regressive behaviors but even rewarded them. This is characteristic of a narcissistic leader. He encourages permissiveness among staff members as long as it promotes submissiveness and increases his ability to control others and gain admiration.

The creation of a submissive–dependent environment in the organization was psychically comforting for Mr. O, and he responded to the CEO's personality by projecting unconscious dependency needs onto him. The CEO accepted and encouraged these wishes because he found them gratifying.

The staff responded to the CEO's personality by withdrawing into passivity. However, over time the staff became increasingly angry. The CEO feared this and responded by placing Mr. O in his position. This defused the murderous wishes from the staff and displaced them onto Mr. O. The CEO further reacted to the employees' rage by assuming the sick role, thus removing himself from responsibility and their rage. By placing Mr. O in his position, the CEO ensured his return to his former position as the admired, benevolent leader over a dependent, guilt-ridden staff. In the process, he successfully neutralized the rage toward him; his fantasy was that he would enter the hospital as a tragic figure and would receive sympathy along with admiration. The revolution from his staff would be aborted and Mr. O would become the surrogate victim. Mr. O was set up by the CEO in much the same way that Mr. O's father had set him up years before when he died, abandoning Mr. O and leaving him in the care of an orally devouring mother. In this case, mother was the staff.

However, Mr. O would not cooperate. Replacing the CEO, coping with an enraged staff, and experiencing the loss of a father figure who had promised so much in the way of gratifying dependency wishes was an untenable situation for Mr. O. Three days before the CEO's departure, Mr. O committed suicide.

A Theory of Suicide

In this case, the psychoanalytic consultant views the suicide as precipitated by environmental impingements or trauma. Most studies of suicide have focused on trauma as the loss of a significant loved one, physical disability, aging, and other factors involving the person's interaction with his/her immediate environment. Few studies have investigated suicide attributed to work. Brodsky (1977) suggests that the following work conditions contribute to suicide: sudden change in working conditions, conflict of loyalties, poor person–role fit, impossible work demands, the ending of a love affair at work, persistent and cumulative interpersonal conflict at work, and sudden dismissal. An analysis of this case suggests that five of the seven contributors suggested by Brodsky existed at the time of Mr. O's death.

Over time, Mr. O became increasingly dependent on the CEO. Unknown to the CEO, Mr. O was creating a world in which he was seeking a relationship with his own father, who was deceased. This idealized relationship was promoted by unconscious fantasies. The CEO's own desires and psychological needs assumed an overwhelming place in the conduct of Mr. O's own life. The relational network between the CEO and Mr. O was twofold: (1) dependency was established by demonstrating irresponsible behavior that gave Mr. O a uniqueness and special stature in the company, and (2) testing authority through disobedience assured Mr. O that he was still loved. It was precisely these conditions that formed the basis for the psychodynamics that precipitated the tragic act.

Over time, Mr. O settled into a depressed state that became socialized through his involvement in complex projects that took a long time and were completed in isolation from others. The choice of the engineering profession gave Mr. O the opportunity to work alone and limited his interactions with people. But his work in the company, and his association with the CEO in particular, began to have an impact Mr. O and made his use of isolation as a schizoid defense less functional. Specifically, the affects associated with his longing for love and contact and the disappointments experienced in his paternal relations began to emerge. Depression and rage increased as his defenses weakened as a result of increased contact with the CEO. As this relationship increased in intensity and Mr. O's search for an ideal figure had come close to being complete, his schizoid isolation defense lost its power. Mr. O began to enter into a full-blown oedipal struggle with the CEO. However, his oedipal struggle repeated a masochistic quest for duplication of parental authority as well as a continuation of his sadomasochistic struggle with his father.

As with most oedipal struggles, Mr. O could not release or direct his aggression because this would jeopardize the wish that love and nurturance would someday be forthcoming. When oedipal aggression was aroused by Mr. O's relations with the CEO, it was turned inward against the self as opposed to outward against the CEO (the object of frustration). The turning of aggression against the self is a repetition of an earlier pattern. It is a repeat of Mr. O's relationship with a punitive, withdrawn father and an indulgent mother who encouraged rebellion against the father. When mother encouraged aggression against the father, it placed Mr. O in a compromised position. If he carried forth her wish, the father would retaliate. If he did not carry out her wish, mother would withdraw her love. Therefore, he introjected her aggressive wishes toward the father and turned them against the self. The introjection of aggression against the self was defended against by schizoid isolation. However, the events of the CEO's departure and the appointment of Mr. O to replace the CEO intensified the aggression and weakened the ego defense.

For Mr. O, work was a meaningless activity. At times he was able to demonstrate creativity and productivity; however, these activities lacked purpose and goal-oriented motivation. Work was merely a method to gratify powerful dependency wishes and neutralize aggressive affects. Work failed Mr. O as a defense; it did not move him out of the self-defeating vulnerable position. This was because for Mr. O, work was nothing more than a sublimation of affects for the purpose of being valuable only to others, and not to himself (Khan, 1960).

Another way of looking at this suggests that Mr. O's creative efforts were accomplishments only to maintain his wish for a bond with the CEO. However, as stated before, the CEO was a withholding, narcissistic figure, capable only of using Mr. O. Consequently, Mr. O had no choice but to maintain a torturous tie to the CEO, a replication of Mr. O's tie to his father. The meager gratifications Mr. O was able to obtain from the CEO were dramatized, and this enabled him to continue to use the relationship to fuel the wish for a symbiotic attachment. As stated before, Mr. O dealt with anxiety stemming from aggressive wishes by schizoid withdrawal. If he could withdraw from people, he could not hurt them. Occupational choice, hobby, place of employment, and behavioral activities served as defenses against his anxiety.

On being informed that he would be replacing the CEO, Mr. O regressed to a point where the functional nature of his schizoid defenses, and their organizing principles which had held the aggression in check, no longer worked. Now Mr. O's aggressive wishes directed at the abandoning father, which had been displaced onto the CEO, were fully experienced. In the past, the nature of the CEO's narcissistic character unconsciously colluded in fostering Mr. O's defense against these wishes by offering some gratifications of Mr. O's unconscious symbiotic wishes. The gratification of these symbiotic fantasies tenuously held the aggression in check. Put another way, the relationship functioned as a container for the dangerous aggressive wishes and provided avenues for self-punishment.

In effect, this relationship was a replication of Mr. O's wish to be close to and distant from early representations of his father. In his relationship with the CEO, Mr. O was able to move back and forth freely from closeness to distance. This movement back and forth allowed Mr. O to neutralize or regulate the powerful affects. Being both close and distant when psychologically needed provided for weak but functionally stable internalized object elations. In this way the CEO could function as an object for refueling. When he was refueled he could distant himself and assume a hostile posture from which he could project aggression outwardly.

However, the illness of his boss and the anxiety associated with the wish to kill the father brought about two psychic reactions. First, Mr. O could no longer distance himself from the aggressive wishes of patricide. He was to replace his father, the object he unconsciously wished to kill. Second, by being pushed into the CEO's role, his father's position, utilization of the defense of schizoid withdrawal became impossible. Mr. O was left with the affects of being an oedipal winner, namely, guilt and fear. The fear was associated with mother (the staff). The staff would consume and destroy Mr. O for killing the father and assuming his position. If one considers that suicide is the turning of aggression against the self, one obtains some insight into the mechanism involved here: Aggression against the paternal object can be taken in against the self through a splitting process. In this instance, Mr. O psychically splits the self into the murderer and the murdered. When he kills himself he is killing part of the self responsible for his rage, his father. This occurs, as suggested above, when Mr. O occupies the father's position, the CEO's chair. The CEO facilitates the splitting by placing Mr. O in this intolerable position and abandoning him just as his father did.

The staff represented mother, who Mr. O experienced as cold, uncaring, and demanding. Mr. O also feared mother's oral rage, the fear of being consumed by her. The staff, also abandoned by the CEO, would displace their oral rage onto Mr. O. Of critical importance is why Mr. O failed to use the schizoid defense as he had done in the past. Why didn't he flee from the situation?

Mr. O was imprisoned by his relationship to the CEO. Mr. O unconsciously believed he would reach nirvana through this relationship and the fantasies attached. He could not give it up. By maintaining the CEO in the position of an idol, Mr. O was freed from the harsh, punitive superego. Grunberger (1971) confirms this when he says that the "idol is not the super ego, on the contrary, the idol is proof of the nonexistence of the agency" (p. 296). Thus the idol, the CEO, becomes the superego and in the process hope is renewed that the superego may become something other than harsh; it will be loving and benign. However, when the idol is gone, externalized controls and hope also vanish. The dark rageful affects return. When they do, they are turned against the self.

Mr. O could not flee, visit the bowling alley, tinker in his basement, or vanish for a few days. He could not feel free from the rageful affects; they followed him.

CHAPTER 11

The Taking of a Role

Not only the possession of skills but the creation or
maintenance of overall mood and affect are intrinsic parts
of successful role performance.
—JOSEPH BENSMAN AND ROBERT LILIENFELD (1979, p. 13)

In the past decade, we have witnessed an important change in the way people value work. The value of success in one's career has had an enormous impact on work life and aspirations. The "work ethic" now has a sense of urgency about it. The career, or more closely the career path, must be maintained at all costs, and to deviate from this linear road to success in one's career means failure. This is true for both men and now women, who gaze in amusement at vignettes and stories of people who "packed it in," opted to stay home with the kids, or decided to reject careerism for a job. Work for most people involves being in a role, either as an autonomously employed professional or within a large or small corporation. For some, self-realization can be attained by being the best at what one does in one's work, which is the equivalent of being the best within a given role.

To study work and to consult to problems associated with work inevitably bring one to the threshold of the relationship between the employee and the role he/she occupies.

Various conceptualizations of role and its relationship to work have been proposed. Of primary importance is the power a role has over the employee. For example, learning, perception, and motivation are influenced by the role an employee occupies. Role influences the required level of motivation and behaviors that are expected to be displayed or to be abstained from. Also, role and its attributes contrib-

294

ute not only to employee satisfaction but to the employee's emotional well-being.

Role is defined as a mode of adaptation to authority, structure, culture, duties, and responsibilities. It defines behavior (actual, implied, or potential) subsumed under a formalized title which is recognized and more or less valued by others. From an organizational perspective, the intention of role is to promote stable patterns of behavior by creating a structure that offers a climate of consistency and reliability. From this perspective, roles are considered the substance that holds the structure of the organization together in a coherent form and permits the tasks of units, as well as the larger organization, to be carried out. Roles define the expected behaviors of the organization's members. By defining roles, employees have defined for themselves the relationships they are expected to maintain with others, subordinates and superiors, as well as with other units, departments, and systems both within and outside the organization.

Sociologists have devoted significant attention to the processes involved in role acquisition. This is often referred to as the "taking of a role." Furthermore, they give "role" a central place in the theory of organizations, often referring to the organization as a system of roles. In conceptualizing the nature of roles, sociologists are concerned with how roles are defined by organizations and how the individual is socialized into a role. However, the sociological view of role and role acquisition, while providing important insight, fails to explain the process of role taking as a function of the relationship between personality and the characteristics of a given role. In addition, within this discipline there is little agreement regarding the meaning of role and its utility in explaining conflict or dysfunctional behavior.

Psychoanalytic theorists do not fare much better than sociologists do in explaining the processes and meanings of role acquisition. Whereas psychoanalytic theory exhibits a greater capacity to explain dysfunctional behavior, it pays less attention to the processes involved in taking a role, or the influence role has on personality and psychic structure. While literature on the psychodynamics of occupational choice has increased in recent years, there is no mention of occupation as having anything to do with role. The literature on occupational choice instead focuses on the performance of work-related activities as related primarily to metapsychological theory. Additionally, the psychoanalytic literature focuses on a limited area of work—the autonomously functioning professionals who engage in creative efforts (e.g., artist and writer). With a few exceptions, the employee working in a large bureaucratic organization is virtually left out of psychoanalytic analysis.

THE SOCIAL MEANINGS OF ROLE

Role is related to two sociological concepts that may be analytically distinct but often are empirically overlapping in their meaning. The first concept related to role is status. The second is the meaning of the label associated with the role.

In its most general sense, "status" is a conception of social reality, specifically to parameters and categories or titles that confer status and are considered meaningful in the context of the organization's culture. The function of role is to define or delineate status differentials and how the occupant of one role relates to the occupant of another. Bensman and Lilienfeld (1979) claim that the status attributed to a role will make its occupancy sought after, and despite the negative characteristics associated with high-status roles, one is rarely reluctant to accept such roles. They claim that high-status roles "validate our personal sense of self-esteem and gain us personal recognition from others, even when we know that much of that esteem is based not on our personal qualities but on our public position" (p. 23).

In play and games, the child learns about the significance of roles, especially status differentiation. It is quite remarkable to see young children argue over who shall occupy the high-status role. The loser is invariably the one who must grudgingly accept the lower-status role. Often the child will call off the play rather than accept such a demeaning status. The power of role playing in the psychological development of children and its contribution to occupational choice have received meager attention.

Beginning with Mead (1934), the development of self was considered a function of the child's taking on or identifying with the attributes of a particularly relevant role. Strean (1968) suggests that by taking the role of a significant other, the child learns to identify with the other and learns to regard him/herself from an external point of view. It is as if the child learns to mirror himself as he observes himself functioning within a given role. Garvey (1984) and Garvey and Berndt (1977) suggest that in childhood, through imagination and play, the child will experiment with many roles, and over time the child will select and identify with a role that is consistent with his/her self-role. The interactive and imaginal aspects of role, where the child makes imaginal identifications through play, facilitates the development of a sense of being in the world. Consider the following example: In play, the child assumes the role of teacher, parent, or some type of authority figure, and the other child assumes the role of a small, powerless child, someone similar to him/herself. Both children are afforded the opportunity to clarify their feelings and attitudes toward their role occupied in the present (a role consistent with their views of self and their views of how others see them) and the role they may occupy in the future.

ROLE AND LABELING THEORY

Another conceptualization (second meaning) of the meaning applied to role refers simply to the socially meaningful labels that can be attached to the role (e.g., boss, chief, janitor, and accountant). A label is socially meaningful when it alters the expectations others hold for the behaviors of an individual (the role occupant) and consequently the options available to them. From this perspective, a role defines an employee's place in the world, functions as a container for the employee's inner experience, and lends stability and reliability to an ambiguous environment. Another meaning attributed to role is that it specifies a component of stratification in the organization. In this sense, various positions are hierarchically ranked as they are differentially evaluated and rewarded.

From a psychoanalytic perspective, the concept of role is the subject of considerable controversy and speculation. Some theorists suggest that over time, the role an employee occupies will alter that employee's personality (Sampson, 1971; Kohn & Schooler, 1983). Zalesnik and Kets de Vries (1984) suggest that the decision to enter into a role "is part and parcel of character/structure . . . [and the employee's] habitual modes of responding to internal and external stimuli" (p. 309). Those few psychoanalytic writers who have explored this topic are concerned with how the role influences the employee, how the role serves an adaptive and defensive purpose, and how a given role may contribute to conflicts and dysfunctional behaviors. From this perspective, it can be concluded that the motivation to enter into a specific occupation may be rethought as a motivation to enter into a specific role, a role defined by the occupation.

OCCUPATIONAL CHOICE

The classical psychoanalytic view suggests that one chooses an occupation because of the defensive functions it serves. Psychoanalytic theorists claim that the activities within a given occupational role serve as a vehicle for gratification of instinctual impulses or their derivatives. These activities and behaviors expected to be displayed or refrained from are defined by the role. It is the role itself that allows for utilization of the defenses of projection, sublimation, reaction–formation, and repression, which allows for the transformation of instinctual impulses into aim-inhibited derivatives. Psychoanalytic theorists see role performance as a constraining phenomenon and the more "public" the role, the more the occupant must refrain from displaying the less public aspects of self. Bensman and Lilienfeld (1979) describe the constraining nature of role occupancy in terms of the required behaviors of any given role and the demands for mastery of role performance. They see these demands as going beyond the training necessary to have adequate skills to function in a given role:

> Mastery of the means to give off the desired effect may entail . . . endless performance practice. At the level of mood, role performance involves training the body, the muscles, the voice, the emotions, to be available to the will of the performer at the moment of performance. (p. 13)

Herein lies the function of acquiring a role and performing. The defensive utility of being in a role is found not only in the skills necessary for performance, but in the "mood" required of the role. The use of body and the requirements of displayed emotion suggest that being in a role will assist the employee in renouncing instinctual affects and their derivatives for purposes of "public" display. Consequently, the choice of an occupation, and a given role, is essentially the unconscious and conscious desire to use the role to cathect or discharge affects associated with aggressive and sexual drives.

The ego psychology position places the ego and its capacities at the center of occupational choice. For example, Santostefano (1977) lists the following ego capacities, each serving as a primary influencer of occupational choice: the capacity to act upon an object, the capacity to delay gratification, the capacity to identify with or internalize the standards of parents and other ego ideals, and, finally, the congruency or fit between opportunity in the environment and the capacity of the ego to delay and construct means–ends alternatives. Santostefano (1977) sees occupational choice as the result of fixations in certain characterological modes of behaviors: reaction mode, action mode, and passive mode. These modes can be physical (body oriented) or intellectual (mind oriented), and they are constructed from a wish to gratify the dominant or core fantasy. Therefore, these characterological modes are operational methods used to gratify the wishes contained in fantasies about occupational success and they form the basis for the selection of occupations as means–ends opportunities.

In agreement, Brenner (1982) suggests that occupational choice is a function of an elaborate conscious and unconscious attempt to gratify a childhood wish. For example, he says that if this childhood wish is a wish to see the primal scene, the person may choose an occupation where observation is the major activity, (e.g., filming or investigative research). For Brenner (1982), occupational choice is determined by a compromise formation, namely, a combination of drive derivatives, anxiety, depressive affects, and superego controls (fears), that is met head on by external circumstances that will influence and inhibit actual choice of the role. While Brenner sees choice as a means–ends method to gratify the wish, he also maintains that it may be a defense against feelings of helplessness, rage, or forbidden impulses.

Watkins (1986), in a manner similar to Brenner, suggests that it is the symbolic meanings the role occupant attaches to a role and the behaviors within a role that will influence choice. She says:

> With symbolization in mind, however, the child never just practices a role, but uses the role as well to express himself and to create an alternative world. Thus, one is not a policeman for the mere practice function of exploring "policeman" as a role, but because issues of power, protection, and vulnerability are afoot for one. To look at it in this way is similar to dream interpretation, where one must ask, "Why out of all the possible day residues, is this particular detail around which a dream has grown?" The child does not ask himself how to express a sense of some naughtiness; he becomes and acts the part of a dirty, slippery, hungry little pig. Instead of saying one is needy, one acts the part of a crying, hungry, whining infant. (p. 65)

Consequently, the role serves a symbolic function. It offers the child, and later the adult, opportunities to gratify unconscious wishes. These wishes serve to reduce some early conflict or trauma, and also reduce the anxiety associated with these early repressed wishes. Watkins (1986) presents an excellent example of how the role serves this symbolic function. She says that the little boy creates a lion image as a way "to spare the boy the anxiety of dealing directly with the father image" (p. 64). In the lion image, the boy adopts the role and characteristics of a lion to avoid the anxiety associated with castration. In this role he becomes bigger and more dangerous than his father. Later on, in adulthood he still holds on to the image and behaviors associated with the lion image, and at work he scares his partners and he is preoccupied with demanding from others his idea of the respect the lion should command in his terrain. At work, he symbolically roars as he once did as a child, and he scares his fellow workers. In this instance the lion is an expression of his characterological style, which is capable of gratifying the wish in symbolic form through his occupational role. He uses his role to structure his work environment to expand and justify the unconscious meaning associated with the role and defend against the repressed fear of castration.

Concerning the relationship between these conflicts, wishes, and resulting anxieties and one's role (environment), Brenner (1982) says that "the environment sets the stage by furnishing material that is seized upon and utilized by each of the components of conflict that give rise to the compromise formation in psychic life" (p. 225). It is the environment that offers options, that is, an array of roles, and among these available roles, one is seized. If the characteristics of the role can be utilized by the components of the compromise formation, then the role will serve an integral psychic function.

This mode of utilizing a role to serve components of psychic conflict is apparent in the analysis of a middle-aged woman who decided to pursue a career in law. Psychodynamically she experienced herself as a lost child, and in her past, she had demonstrated a profound need to protect lost animals which she identified with. Her initial career choice was in veterinary medicine, but she gave this up because she could not gratify the aggressive wishes. She continued to locate a stray or lost animal and impulsively embrace it and then search to locate its owner. In this way, she could experience the grandiose wish to save a lost object and be saved herself (a counter-dependent wish). Underlying this wish was a fear of her aggressive impulses (which could not be gratified in the veterinary occupation), and the activity of saving lost animals was a defense against the anxiety associated with the wish to kill them. An analysis of these affects leads to an exploration of her wish to enter law.

The choice of being a lawyer allowed her to internalize into her psychic structure a system of external laws (superego control) to serve as defenses against aggressive wishes and create a clear separation between unacceptable and acceptable wishes. She chose to enter environmental law, and here she has the opportunity to gratify the demands of a psychic compromise: She can continue to protect animals from people (parents) who abandon and kill. Also, she can now aggressively pursue people (parents) who pollute and bring into the environment toxins that kill harmless animals. Her occupational choice permits a compromise of her intrapsychic conflict centered around aggressive wishes. In her practice she can cathect or discharge her aggressive wishes directly against authorities who function symbolically as her parents: the ones who abandoned her and permitted psychic toxins into her "environment."

THE DEFENSIVE FUNCTION OF ROLE

The work of Neff (1977), Kramer (1977), Hendrick (1943), Holmes (1965), Lantos (1943), Jahoda (1983), and Oberndorf (1951) suggests that occupational choice serves a binding function. Following Freud's (1930/1961) statement that work binds the employee closer to reality, these authors suggest that occupation, if properly chosen, will bind psychic conflict by imposing reality on one's activities.

One can conclude that classical psychoanalysts and ego psychologists see occupational choice as serving a defensive function. However, they are unclear about the specific mechanisms involved in the process of choosing an occupation. For example, they fail to define the nature of the binding function of the person's choice of a occupation. Is it the activities of the work itself, the status the occupation provides, or the interpersonal relations required by the work? One can conclude that in an occupation, the role provided by the occupation and the organizational definition of the activities to be performed will provide status and discretion. One can also conclude that the role and the characteristics of the role will serve as a link between the person's intrapsychic life and external reality. One also can assume that the role provides a defensive function and at the same time allows for certain types of gratifications.

Perhaps a key to understanding the binding function of role can be understood from the perspective of time, namely, delay. The role and its requirements give assurance to the employee that through behavior and effort, gratifications will be available. Consequently, the gratification of a wish can be delayed if the role gives to the ego assurances, in fantasy and reality, that gratifications will be forthcoming. For example, a characteristic of those with a narcissistic personality is a relentless desire to achieve and prevent interference with the fulfillment of a wish.

Consider the following: A female employee, who was a firstborn child, experienced herself as never being able to "get enough" from her mother. Mother had given what little she had to offer to the employee's younger siblings, and this employee had to work especially hard to obtain anything from mother. In adulthood she occupied the role of a teacher. This role unconsciously became a way to obtain gratification from mother. This gratification was obtained from students who idealized her and gave her love and attention. This wish to "get enough" from mother was consciously expressed by being a "good" and "loved" teacher and is associated with the unconscious expression of a wish for blissful union with, and an idealization of, mother. The achievement, that which this person aspires to, is found in the role this employee aspires to. The role then encapsulates her wish for blissful union and idealization. The key issue that would determine success or failure then is her ability to tolerate delay, to have patience, and to trust, as she attempts to attain the idealized role.

Now we can see how employees can feel depressed even though they have achieved an aspired-to role. They discover that their unconscious wish is not gratified in this role, and all their efforts to achieve have been for naught.

It is the role that defines the behaviors an employee will display or refrain from displaying. The role also defines the mode of adaptation to the authority, structure, culture, and responsibilities within the organization. If the chief function of the role is to provide stable patterns of behavior, it follows that this can be accomplished only if the role serves a binding function and can ameliorate psychic conflict and not contribute to it. The binding function of a role is tested out and either accomplished or rejected during the process of entering into a role. This is often referred to as the socialization process.

ENTRY INTO A ROLE

Entry into a role is a complex psychological process. Identification is at the core of this process. One way to understand this process is that the activity of joining, where the entrant "takes on" the requirements of a role, involves a renunciation. The employee is required to renounce behaviors typically displayed outside the organization. The employee must accept "abstinence" as a role requirement. The employee can conform to the requirements of the role if the role can serve a binding function, that is, serve as a defense against the anxieties associated with drive derivatives, infantile wishes, and early trauma.

An important way for the employee to defend against the stress associated with entry into a role at work is to develop or support the professional ego. The professional ego, sometimes referred to as the work ego, contains fantasies associated with the idealized self-image (for an expanded discussion, see Chapter 3). The wishes contained in this self-image and the nature of the characteristics of the actual role at work are assessed by the professional work ego. Initially, the decision to enter a role at work is motivated by the fantasy of the idealized self-image. Contained within this image is the idea of what the employee wishes the role to be. Stress upon entry is reduced when this self-image is consistent with the employee's view of what the role will provide. In other words, the employee will ask the question: Is this role consistent with the fantasy of "what I want to be"? If activities within the role allow the employee to gratify the wishes contained in the fantasy, the employee will accept the requirements of the role, including abstinence. On the other hand, stress will result when the employee experiences an incongruity between his/her fantasies and the actual duties of the role and the nature of the interactions with significant others on the job. This is why the first few days on the job are important.

Stress resulting from incongruities can be ameliorated during the entry process in several ways.

1. The employee must be adequately socialized into the role and the organization. Adequate time and preparation must be given so that the employee has ample opportunity to introject the organization's history, myths, and significant events into his/her professional ego.
2. The employee must be able to experience closeness with those who occupy positions of authority. He/she must be able to obtain a sense that the authority figures are benign and supportive.
3. The employee must be accepted into or join into the informal social groupings in the organization.
4. The employee must be able to gratify his/her motivation for mastery. This is accomplished by giving the employee opportunities to perform tasks in a manner that not only instills a sense of competence but contributes to increased self-esteem.

Frustration is the primary source of stress one experiences when joining an organization and entering a role. Frustration results from the employee's experience of deprivation; the employee is deprived of the freedoms or the resources to seek or obtain gratification of needs and wishes in a fashion that he/she is accustomed to. The employee must give up old habits and possibly habitual ways of obtaining gratification. The employee gets out of this stressful quandary in two ways: (1) by joining the organization's informal social system which provides gratification; and (2) through the process of identification, where the employee identifies with the authority figure (supervisor) and incorporates aspects of this object into the self. Here authority is incorporated into the ego ideal and this allows the super-ego to neutralize aggression associated with the frustrations associated with the role requirements.

THE FIT BETWEEN PERSONALITY AND ROLE

Joining the organization is completed and the employee becomes a member in the psychological sense when he/she internalizes parts of the role he occupies and the role or aspects of the role become part of his/her professional identity. Also, the employee responds to attributes or activities of the role as if they were his/her own. For example, if the organization is criticized, the employee feels criticized. It is as if, over time, the employee responds to the role phenomenologically from the experience of depersonalization to one of personalization.

When an employee is properly socialized into a role and has a sense of clarity concerning role expectations, duties, and responsibilities, the probability of psychologically joining and maintaining a "best fit" between the personality and the role is increased. However, many employees experience stress on the job because the work activities within a given role impinge upon their characterological structure and precipitate excessive anxiety.

Recently the Michigan Supreme Court granted worker's compensation to a General Motors employee because of the incompatibility between the employee's personality and the activities of his role. He was a parts inspector on the assembly line and he suffered mental strain because the workers kept installing defective parts on the assembled autos. In court he was diagnosed as an "obsessive–compulsive perfectionist" (Ivancevich & Matteson, 1987). The personality of this worker demanded order, correctness, and cleanliness. On the job, he experienced dread. Working with messiness and defective parts had a direct bearing on his mental health. According to Ivancevich and Matteson (1987), the courts have dramatically moved away from the position that workplace stress is the result of "gradual wear and tear" and is not a compensable personal injury under law. Now the courts have indicated that the employer can be legally liable for an employee's mental illness.

In this case, as in all cases where an employee is viewed as demonstrating schizoid characteristics, depressive affect, or obsessive characteristics that are out of step with the organization's culture, the employee was perceived as a troublemaker. It is a mistake simply to see this employee as being psychologically dysfunctional, or at odds with the organization and its members. To do so is to blame the victim. Such employees are at odds with the role they occupy, and this role does not "fit" their personality. If the GM quality-control inspector were able to manifest and gratify his obsessional zeal, he might have been a content employee, and furthermore, the organization as a whole might have benefited.

The fit between the person and the role may be considered a function of the degree to which the characteristics of the role are integrated into the personality of the occupant, especially his/her ego ideal. The overriding concern for the person going through the process of joining an organization is to establish this fit. It may occur over a short period of time or it may never occur at all. The way one feels about one's work and duties is a function of the ability to move from the domain of an assumed role, that which the organization gives us, to the domain of familiarity (Blos, 1974). When a fit does occur, it is through the incorporation of the characteristics of the role into the member's professional ego. According to Waelder (1936), when this fit occurs, multiple function is gradually achieved with the newly required behaviors of the role and this role will shape particular modes of gratification, defense, expression of conscience, and adaptation. A new self evolves—the self as worker.

OTHER CONTRIBUTORS TO ROLE STRESS

When a fit does not occur between personality and role characteristics, the employee is psychologically unable to join the organization and remains on the periphery. If the employee is unable to utilize defenses, stress will increase over time. This is referred to as role stress. Role stress contributes to conflict between the role occupant and the organization, especially its authority. The role occupant may experience such negative psychological and physiological responses as depression, aggressive outbursts, peptic ulcers, coronary disease, and alcoholism or have such mild reactions as tardiness, absenteeism, low morale, or excessive disagreements.

Isolating factors that contribute to role stress is an exceedingly complex endeavor because of the variance in the fit between personality and role characteristics. Some employees may demonstrate good productivity and work relationships and be considered good workers and yet be under a considerable amount of stress. This is evidenced by the secret alcoholic or the lonely, depressed individual who is perceived on the job as a jovial, friendly person. Additionally, some employees thrive on stressful conditions, seeking occupations that would be considered by many to be too stressful, while other employees avoid stressful conditions, because they experience long working hours, deadlines and conflict as emotionally exhausting. Stress has become more common on the job because of the increased job complexity brought about by rapid technological change and increased economic pressures placed on individuals (Gordon, 1987).

Also, a number of organizational theorists have suggested that organizational factors create role stress with a high degree of consistency (Raslin, 1983). They maintain that role is a factor in harnessing aggression. Aggression is required to complete tasks and to seek accomplishments and challenges. The role, if clear and well bounded, will provide avenues for the release of aggressive and libidinal drives.

If role behaviors are to be performed with satisfaction, they must be ego syntonic. If not, the "results will yield superficial performance or substantial resistance or even emotional breakdown" (Grey, 1988, p. 485). Bensman and Lilienfeld (1979), in agreement, suggest that occupational roles that allow for the presentation of "oneself," or allow persons to be "themselves," will lead to greater degrees of satisfaction. These are roles that offer a wide variety of behaviors and allow the role occupants to integrate attributes of the role into their personality, where they do not feel constricted. Bensman and Lilienfeld (1979) conclude that when a role is congruent with the personality, it will "allow individuals to be more honest and truthful with one another, to express the full range of their emotional attitudes" (p. 16).

The process of internalization, where the employee incorporates aspects of the role in varying degrees over time, will alter the psychic structure. The employee will adapt his self system to the role requirements, and through this process use the role to create a link between his/her self system and external reality. Additionally, the person will incorporate the role and its characteristics into the psyche and the role will serve as an attachment function similar to a transitional object. In this sense the person will adapt to the role and at the same time take it in, identify with it, and obtain a sense of well-being in the world. On the other hand, there are those who suggest that over time, the role occupant will alter the characteristics of a role to suit his personality. This is particularly evident in a study of the role of psychotherapist by Sherman (1972). Sherman explores the particular style of performing the tasks associated with "curing" their patients and concludes that the style adopted by psychotherapists is a function of their personality.

In assessing this controversy, it seems apparent that whether the person changes a role or stays within a role is a function of the following factors: the intensity and stress associated with the role, the degree of autonomy the role offers its occupant, the duration for which the employee occupies the role, the age of the role occupant, and most significantly, the fit between the occupant's inner experience and the characteristics, gratifications, and social meaning provided by the role. On the other hand, if the role is too constraining or not constraining enough, the person may displace his feelings onto another object, withdraw into a schizoid position, or stretch the boundaries of the role (act out). Acting out is common in the organization when employees cannot contain their anxiety and engage in overt displays of inappropriate behaviors. In addition, stress can also result from a lack of resources (e.g., time, material, staff, or money) needed to meet the requirements of the role and a lack of socialization or proper preparation of the occupant for a given role, which also contributes to ambiguity. Finally, stress results from a concept referred to as "multiple role occupancy," where a member simply occupies too many roles and the demands of each role overlap. This is a common occurrence in the case of the single parent who is working and attending school in the evening. This person occupies an organizational role as well as the roles of parent and student. From time to time the demands of one role are so great that the person will be required to reduce the effort required to fill the other role, causing a vicious cycle that culminates in "burnout."

Kets de Vries (1984) has identified three categories of factors that contribute to role stress: occupational level, career stage, and the stage of adult development the employee is in. In addition, major events in the employee's life outside of work may contribute to stress on the job. Death of a loved one, marriage, divorce, birth of a child, sexual difficulties, fear of being fired, and so on, will all culminate in job stress. Gordon (1987) suggests that interpersonal factors and leadership or supervisory character style, as well as factors related to group cohesion and participation, will contribute to role stress. Recent studies say that professional women experience role stress as a result of discrimination, stereotyping, conflicting demands of family and work, and feelings of isolation (Nelson & Quick, 1985; Cooper & Davidson, 1982).

It is often said that humans are "creatures of habit." This thought applies to the concept of role stress and is particularly apparent when one must change one's role. Over time, a role occupant often finds that the role becomes increasingly more comfortable. This is especially apparent where the employee's professional ego is strongly identified with the role and the employee finds that the activities, status, and social meaning of the role are exceedingly gratifying. When a role is altered, the role occupant experiences discomfort and stress.

Contemporary organizations are frequently involved in reorganizations, and rarely does the executive constellation consider the negative effects of frequent role alterations. Often the occupant of a role responds to this change initially by resisting. The change is often experienced as an impingement or violation because it alters the predictability and consistency that the employee values and finds psychologically comforting. When a role occupant is moved into a new role, he/she usually experiences a sense of loss and will suffer mild to severe forms of depression. Stress and the effects of anxiety and depression are considered less apparent when a member moves on to what is considered a "better" position; however, even here the new role occupant will experience a sense of loss.

In a study of the movement of blue-collar employees into white-collar positions, it was found that half of the newly promoted employees requested their old job back. It seemed that the shift from labor to management precipitated considerable stress. Not only did the employees have to change roles at work, but the change also impacted on their relations with family, friends, children, and community.

The following case history is a consultation to a role occupant who became a victim of role change. Ironically, the change was brought about by the occupant herself. The consultant was actually brought in to look at issues other than role dysfunction. This is not uncommon, for it is rare for an organization to have the insight to recognize role stress. Often organizations seek consultations because of behavioral aberrations, but they rarely see these aberrations as responses to role stress.

CASE ANALYSIS OF A CONSULTATION

The request for this consultation was made to the School of Public Health at a major urban university. The request was transferred to the director of education and consultation at the same university and then was passed on to this consultant.

The request was to consult to a small community-based public health clinic for women, which was located in the same city. The consultation was to the CEO of the clinic (the consultee), who was experiencing a depressive episode that might have resulted in a clinical depression if there had not been an intervention. The director of education and consultation arranged for the CEO to contact the consultant by telephone:

CEO: I'm Ms. _____ Dr. _____ suggested that I give you a call. Do you know about the problems at the clinic?

CONSULTANT: A little.

CEO: Well, I'm having a hard time of it, with the new organization and all. A lot of problems in general. I don't know if I need a consultant or a shrink *(laugh)*. Like I'm feeling bad these days, I'm really personalizing this. I know it's the job, and not me. My friends say if I can straighten out things at work I'll be OK. I guess that's why we, well, I'm told you're good at this stuff.

CONSULTANT: What would you like to do?

CEO: I guess we should meet.

CONSULTANT: I think that would be good. We can meet in my office or if you'd like, at your office. What do you think?

CEO: I don't know, uh . . .

CONSULTANT: How about meeting at your office?

CEO: OK, when?

CONSULTANT: How about——? We can meet for 90 minutes. My fee is $__/hour.

CEO: That's fine. Do you know where I'm located?

CONSULTANT: No.

(CEO gives directions)

Before we continue with the actual consultation, it will be helpful to view a critical factor that is apparent when consulting to a rather small entrepreneurial organization, namely, its developmental history. The consultant was informed by those who were familiar with the organization that it had recently experienced a major developmental leap. This information stimulated the consultant's desire to know more about the history of the clinic before he actually entered into the work.

The women's health clinic was established 5 years earlier by a group of women determined to increase the level of medical and preventive services to a population of lower- to lower-middle-class women within an urban community that can best be described as being in transition. The clinic was staffed by women who were all volunteers. They occupied a small storefront in a blighted industrial section of the city. All the equipment had been donated and the technical services were performed by three volunteer nurses and a female medical doctor, who volunteered her time for 2 to 3 hours per week. Little direct patient care was given, and the clinic functioned during this period as a referral service. Ninety percent of the referrals were made to the large university-based hospital located approximately 5 miles from the clinic.

Description of the Problem

When consulting to role definition, it is important to assess the nature of change that has occurred in the role. This can be accomplished by assessing the developmental growth of the organization. It is assumed that as the organization passes through developmental stages, the definitions of the roles within the organization change. It is these kinds of changes that precipitate role stress. This organization had passed through two phases during the previous 5 years. What follows is an outline of these phases, which were isolated as a result of three 1-hour conversations with the director of the clinic.

Phase One

One of the first characteristics of phase one was the minimal entry requirement for staff (i.e., fluid membership). All volunteers came from the community; some were long-term community residents and others had come to the community because of an appointment to the university. Still others had come in a student capacity and had stayed on. There was also an undifferentiated division of labor; everyone was permitted to do everyone else's work. Specialized duties were nonexistent. The clinic had a strong ideological commitment to women and their health, and a belief in equality was an equally strong commitment. For example, anyone on the staff could take a pap smear or lead an obesity group.

The staff rewards were high, and there were consistently high levels of energy. The clinic was open Monday through Friday from 9:00 A.M. to 6:00 P.M. on Thursday, with extended hours until 10:00 P.M. The staff rewards were also found in a high degree of social contact as well as in the strong commitment to ideals. In spite of the lack of a division of labor, a high degree of autonomy existed. Staff members were permitted to go off and work on their own, supervision was nonexistent, and duties were delegated collectively in group meetings attended by the clinic's total membership. It was at these meetings that all decisions were made.

The leadership was charismatic and described as informal. The person who began the clinic (the consultee) was a unifying and organizing force. She was a woman in her mid-30s who had a master's degree in public health as well as being a registered nurse. She was recently divorced from a medical doctor and lived in the community with her three children, supporting herself on alimony and personal funds. Among the core group of eight women, three were on welfare and the remaining four had part-time employment elsewhere. Four of the women had shared living arrangements. In addition to providing a social network, the clinic also provided a very valuable financial support system. Even though leadership was not formalized, it was quite clear that the leadership of the clinic was lodged in the CEO. She made most of the day-to-day decisions and provided counseling and, at times, loaned money to clients and staff.

The nature of these arrangements appeared to foster dependency relationships that gave a sense of power to the CEO rarely achieved in formal organizations. It was precisely this power arrangement between the consultee and the staff that precipitated the request for a consultation. The consultee had realized that as the organization began to formalize, she experienced a sense of panic at "losing control of the organization." The factors that stimulated this fear will become apparent as we move to the second phase of organizational growth.

Phase Two

The determining factor that moved the clinic to phase two was the need for a license. This required that the clinic move toward formalizing relationships with the university-based hospital. The consultee had decided that to ease the formalization of relations, arrangements could be made to provide learning opportunities for interns from the schools of public health and nursing. Graduate students entered the organization. In addition, the clinic applied for funds from a federally sponsored work program. All of the eight core staff members had received federally funded salaries. In addition, volunteers entered. All at once, there was an extraordinary amount of crowding within the small storefront clinic.

The influx of new staff created demands for supervision. The consultee, having negotiated these contracts, was the only staff member qualified to conduct the supervision. At this point, there was a total of 15 full-time staff and 25 part-time staff, serving a population of 50 clients per week. Clients received special attention and were examined extensively for even the most minor complaint. If hospital treatment was required, the client was often driven to the hospital, another special service.

The supervision of the large number of students was inadequate. However, demands by the students to be supervised were minimal, and the students were gratified by an involvement in the strong ideological atmosphere of the organization and its high esprit. It became quite apparent now that the consultee was in fact the CEO. She had to sign forms for students, VISTA volunteers, and CETA employees, of which she was one herself. And the new staff frequently referred to her as the boss. This formalization brought relief to the staff and concerns about any damage to the ideological belief in equality was not apparent at this point. In addition, a group of students began meeting with the CEO to discuss the possibility of writing a grant application. One of the application stipulations was that there be a board of directors.

The grant application was approved and the clinic became a fully licensed medical clinic with a newly renovated building. With this tremendous growth came a rapid increase in the demand for written procedures, increased complexity of operations, formalization of referral linkages, inclusion of specialists, and most important, formalization of the role of CEO. The organization was now moving into its third phase of growth.

The Consultative Work

The organization had begun to settle into the third phase when the consultant entered.

The consultant met the CEO in her new office. The CEO had a secretary and in the offices next to her were a bookkeeper, medical director, business manager, and records office. The friends and associates who had been with her since the clinic's inception had either left the organization or were phased into specialized, meaningless paid positions. The limited skills of the old staff became less valued as the technology of the clinic increased, and staff members with greater technical training were hired.

The CEO appeared unhappy and depressed. She invited the consultant into her office, which appeared cold and impersonal. She sighed deeply and began to describe the organization and her problems in a dull, dispassionate manner. Only when she spoke of the "old organization" did she light up with joy. While describing the "new organization," she was indifferent. She appeared to be lonely and uncomfortable in her new role and surroundings. After about a half hour, she announced that she had forgotten that she had a board meeting she would have to attend. She invited the consultant to attend and he agreed. She spoke very little at the meeting. Under some circumstances this might be considered a sign of good management, but in this case it was not.

In discussions with the director of education and consultation, who had suggested the consultation and was familiar with the CEO, the CEO had been described as vibrant and challenging, eager to provoke, and always stimulating. This was confirmed in discussions with colleagues prior to the consultation. At the board meeting, however, she demonstrated none of these characteristics.

The board was composed of people successful in their respective professions and capable of offering financial, political, professional, and technical assistance. At one point during the board meeting, the CEO looked aghast at a board member, a physician, who suggested that they close the original storefront, where the operation had begun. He commented that it was not an efficient part of the operation and had become a "hangout for local people." The CEO, in anxious rage, spoke up and began to present a counterargument, but she suddenly fell silent and excused herself.

Two weeks after the board meeting, the consultant appeared for the second meeting with the CEO and was told she had been at home for the past week. The consultant immediately called her and suggested that they meet at her home.

The consultant arrived at the CEO's home and found her in a night dress and looking distraught. Over coffee, she spoke of her desire to resign, her recent divorce, insomnia, and drinking. The consultant raised the issue of the "old" organization and the "new" organization. The CEO described herself as missing the old place, old friends, and good times. She described the new organization as stressful, particularly commenting on the loneliness of her position, the demands for administrative detail, and the lack of "real" human interaction. She came to the conclusion that above all, she needed a position in which she could interact with people and meet the "real" human needs of people. She was asked how the "new" role could be made more appealing and they focused on the types of structural changes she could make that would accommodate her needs.

Intervention

A structural design was developed to ease some of the role stress. A community advisory board was created to meet weekly for the purpose of discussing both community need and the organization's responsiveness to the community. The CEO appointed some of her "old" staff to this board. This intervention was a mistake. The community board did little to reduce the symptom of depression. The CEO still felt emotionally exhausted.

At the third consultative meeting, the CEO spoke at length of her unhappiness. She was asked about the community board meeting and she spoke about how many people felt that the clinic was not able to offer services to a large enough catchment (geographical) area. The CEO spoke about the needs within the surrounding communities. She said that the clinic now had a catchment area to be served that was determined by the state. She went on to say that the area the clinic was to serve had excluded one of the poorest sections of the city, and that this oversight was a tragedy.

The consultant suggested that they examine the type of organization the CEO would be most happy with and the activities she found most rewarding. She spoke about the "old" organization. It appeared that it was the activity of creating an organization, as well as the entrepreneurial aspects of managing it, that was most appealing.

The consultant suggested that the CEO ought to do what she does best—that is, create an organization and develop a service, such as a new clinic. This prospect intimidated her and she said, "How can I leave my baby?" The truth of the matter was that "her baby" had grown up. It was now time to raise a new baby. The metaphor was well received by the CEO and it seemed clear that her ambivalent attachment to the clinic was no longer in her best interest.

The CEO offered her resignation and suggested to the board that the CEO's role should be filled by someone more adept and comfortable managing a well-structured, formal clinic.

Some of the "old" staff joined the CEO in the new endeavor and with a small amount of funds, they began the operation of a storefront clinic, similar to the way the "old" clinic had begun. They opened the new clinic in the poor section of the city that was not served by the "old" clinic because of the catchmenting demanded by the state funding agency. Esprit was high and everyone felt that the CEO had made the correct decision.

Analysis

The success of this consultation is found in the help given the consultee in seeking a role in which she would be more comfortable. Often, roles change over time, and employees who are experiencing distress are unaware that the basis of their distress may be a function of conflict between their personality and the changes in the role they occupy.

Congruency between one's personality and a given role is often something employees take for granted and rarely analyze. Often, one does not realize that a fit has not materialized until the time of termination, burnout, or demotion. Then, it is often too late to assess the situation accurately because the employee's self-esteem is already severely damaged and the employee is unable to see alternatives clearly.

When consulting to a changing organization, the psychoanalytic consultant investigates how the roles employees occupy may have shifted in such a way that the defensive characteristics of a role that once enhanced health may be restored. The key to this intervention was the consultee's statement, "I was once happy." From this point, the investigation led to an analysis of what had changed.

For this consultee, functioning as the CEO of the old organization provided ample opportunities for the narcissistic gratification that contributed to a cohesive self-system. The old organization was at an elementary stage of development, and the lack of bureaucratic characteristics enhanced the CEO's sense of power and gratified her wish to be idealized. This organization, with a dependent staff, strong ideological commitment, low degree of specialization, and almost flat structure created for the CEO a utopian psychological environment. Later on, trying to experience the same degree of gratifications in an organization with a much higher degree of bureaucraticness made it difficult for the CEO to function.

We can assume that the CEO's wish for grandiosity represented an attempt to capture the self-object relations that may have been unavailable in childhood, and like an unempathic parent, this new organization failed her. In her present role the CEO was challenged and criticized and she experienced this as a narcissistic blow to her already vulnerable self. Her depressive response was a function of her inability to use her role of CEO to maintain the illusion of her grandiose self. Although she still maintained the title of CEO, she did not experience this work as important; in fact, it was without value to her. The work was devalued because it contained none of the important gratifications associated with her wish to be idealized. Within and outside the organization, she became increasingly depressed, feeling alone and unloved. Inside the changed organization, she regressed to the paranoid position and experienced the board of directors as insensitive bureaucrats who deprived her of her much needed gratification.

When the CEO left the clinic to begin a new one, which would be at a primitive stage of development, she was once again in a role that allowed her to receive gratification. She could be in caring, intimate relations with employees who admired her. These unconscious wishes or motivations are often characteristic of the "entrepreneurial personality," who requires a close knit, loosely structured organization that will offer to the person who occupies the role opportunities for gratification of omnipotent grandiose fantasies.

A final note addresses the behavioral requirements of the roles the CEO occupied. The behaviors associated with the old role allowed her to repress her dependency wishes. In this role, which required frenzied activities, constant interaction, and execution, she could utilize a manic defense. This defense is common when unconscious feelings associated with dependency are aroused. In the new role, the required behaviors demanded more obsessional and detailed responses in a formalized and structured manner. The hierarchical nature of the new organization and the rigidity of the role failed to allow her to use a manic defense against these feelings.

Conclusion

This consultation is an example of the interaction between the role demands of the organization and the specifics of a member's personality. The intervention helped the CEO make a change before her emotional decomposition forced changes in the role she presently occupied. In making this change, she was able to avoid the experience of failure. The CEO was able to leave her organization with feelings of goodwill and satisfaction. In most instances this does not occur. As with this CEO, most employees would experience conflict and would unconsciously project their internal dissonance onto the organization, which would eventually culminate in termination or an angry resignation.

This type of consultation is most helpful to those employees who are experiencing role stress by focusing on problems with the person's present role and what types of roles the person found fulfilling in the past. The thrust of the consultation was helping the consultee discover a role that was suitable, by assessing the nature of the gratifications the role offered as a function of the consultee's personality. Once this diagnosis was made and the nature of the role analyzed, the CEO was able to be helped to realize that her problem did not have to be personalized and her difficulties did not have to become a personal failure. She could obtain gratification if she was adequately helped to discover a role that was suitable. Stated simply, this type of consultation succeeds when the consultee chooses the work she enjoys most and does best.

It is evident that the consultee was also experiencing other factors in her life that contributed to her depression. For example, a good clinician would have considered her recent divorce a significant contributor. However, while other contributors to her condition should not be discounted, the consultant must maintain clarity of boundaries to be able to work effectively. The thrust of the consultation was to organizational issues. If this consultation had not succeeded, it might have been evident that these other factors could not be avoided, but to explore issues such as divorce would have moved the consultation out of the realm of its intended purpose. If this had occurred, the consultant would have recommended clinical treatment and would have made a referral.

CHAPTER 12

Interorganizational Relations

The lust for power is not rooted in strength but in weakness.
—ERICH FROMM (1941, p. 32)

Contemporary organizations are required to engage in exchanges among other organizations at a rate that far exceeds any in the past two decades. Increasingly, interorganizational events now permeate all aspects of organizational life. Contemporary organizations are expected to engage in relations with their vendors and suppliers with increased intimacy and continuity. In addition, organizations face real or potential mergers, acquisitions, and joint ventures on a scale never before witnessed. Internally, organizations are expected to engage in continuous exchanges among subsystems. Current textbooks and literature proclaim that in order to compete in the international marketplace, management must develop a particular type of structure with their vendors. Metaphors used to describe these relationships are called "just in time," "participatory," or "fluid." Management theorists tell us that for the organization to survive, cooperation and teamwork are vital. In most cases this means that organizational systems, internal subsystems, or departments must be capable of working with each other within a culture that promotes harmony and continuity.

In spite of demands that organizations engage in interorganizational relations[1] little is known about the nature of these events. In organizational textbooks, the focus is on the methods, procedures, or structures that management uses in interorganizational relations,

[1] Interorganizational relations include interactions between one or more organizations, departments, units, divisions, groups, and so forth.

317

and a theory of these events does not exist. In the area of applied psychoanalysis, the efforts to contribute to an understanding of these events are paltry.

Understanding interorganizational relations is important for three reasons. First, it is through the interaction of various groups and subsystems that the goals and objectives of the organization are accomplished. Second, management coordinates the flow of work, communications, and people across the boundaries of departments and subsystems. If one subsystem breaks down, the remaining subsystems are affected, often negatively. Third, understanding the intergroup process provides a foundation for studying the larger system and the nature of the relationships the larger system or organization engages in with other systems in its environment.

Interorganizational relations are defined by Levine and White (1961) as any voluntary activity between two organizations (systems) that has consequences, actual and anticipated, for the realization of the organizations' respective goals and objectives. From a systems perspective, the system being studied is the "focal system" (Evan, 1966). Interactions between systems are studied from two perspectives: (1) the "input–organizational–set"—those systems that send inputs into the focal system; and (2) the "output–organizational–set"—those systems that receive the focal system's outputs. This simple conceptualization can be applied to an organization interacting with its environment as well as to subsystems within an organization that are interacting with other subsystems. The linkages necessary for optimal systems functioning are the subject of study from the following perspectives: the types and nature of transactions, the nature of cooperation and conflict in these transactions, the functional nature of these conflicts, and finally, the conscious and unconscious motivations for these events.

THE TYPES OF AND NATURE OF TRANSACTIONS

In organizations, the activities of one unit are dependent on the activities of another. Effectiveness is included among transactions that cross boundary regions separating these units. For a transaction to affect or impact a unit, the boundary must be managed in a manner that contributes to, and does not detract from, effectiveness. Consequently, management of the boundary region assumes special importance. In psychoanalytic consulting the transactions of intergroup relations are a direct result of how the unit controls and coordinates the boundary region.

Exchange theory is particularly helpful in this type of analysis of boundary transaction management. The consultant assesses the elements that are exchanged in transactions, such as giving or receiving labor, services, technical help, etc., or sending or receiving resources other than labor. In addition, the consultant assesses the overt and covert motivations and interests leaders may have for engaging in transactions. It is important to understand the unconscious motivations for engaging in transactions. If they are not understood, it is almost certain that at some point during the transactions spurious motivations will surface and negatively will hinder the event. Consider the following example of an interorganizational event where covert motivations destroyed the collaboration.

A large, urban East Coast hospital purchased a multi-million-dollar software program from a West Coast company. Markus (1984) described what can happen when a company seeks to use the technical services of a computer vendor: "[T]he vendor may wish to make a profit from a quick sale with little follow-up service, whereas the system using the organization may desire to obtain cheaply the expensive talent required to install and maintain and train the people who will use it" (p. 122). The hospital could not use the software and it remained inoperable for almost a year. The hospital could not get the vendor to "properly install the program." The vendor claimed that the 3-hour time differential made communication impossible. The truth of the matter was that each organization had conflicting objectives; the vendor wanted to make the sale and had little desire to spend time on the East Coast. The hospital wanted the vendor to install and train the employees to use the program properly. The failure to realize and communicate these covert wishes created conflict later on; consequently, the relationship failed.

In the exchange theory approach, the consultant examines factors that may lead to a dysfunctional relationship. The most common are organizational affiliation, function, authority, prestige, proximity, and personal characteristics. Also examined are the actual elements involved in the exchange and the direction of that exchange—its unilateral and reciprocal nature and the degree of dependency the focal organization has on the source of supplies in the exchange. Most important are the covert motivations for the exchange. These motivations will always influence expectations.

Exchanges between organizations or within subsystems in organizations are influenced by the following:

1. Accessibility of elements and information involved in the exchange;

2. Objectives of the organization and the subsystems involved in the exchange;

3. The degree to which the systems involved have knowledge of each other's functions and their relative degree of importance to one another; and

4. Unconscious expectations of each other, namely, matters that are not discussed or agreed on.

THE NATURE OF CONFLICT AND COOPERATION IN TRANSACTIONS

In interorganizational relationships, conflict in inevitable, and in many cases conflict is expected and considered functional. With this in mind, the consultant must enter into an interorganizational event with an open mind, withholding any activity that is intended to reduce the conflict until he/she carefully assesses the source of the conflict as well as its impact on the systems involved.

The consultant can assume that conflict is related to the following:

1. *Goal incompatibility.* Goal incompatibility is the result of competing views and the lack of agreement of the larger systems' goals and objectives.

2. *Differing decision-making philosophies.* Often systems will develop their own styles and methods for reaching decisions. Two organizations may eventually reach the same decisions, but differing styles can cause the appearance of differences when in fact there may not be any.

3. *Differences in status and prestige.* Authority and power may affect interorganizational performance and precipitate conflict. For example, in hospitals, intergroup conflict often emerges among various professional groups located on a continuum from high in power and prestige to low in power and prestige. This is most apparent in the relationships between the nursing and physician staff. Additionally, the manner in which an organization structures itself may generate conflict. The issues of centralization versus decentralization, horizontal versus vertical, configuration, and division of labor will all influence the sociotechnical climate of the organization. However, the stability of the organization's structure is the most common reason for conflict. Whenever an organization reorganizes, relocates, or adds or detracts from its structure,

the power and politics within the organization escalate. Employees respond to the change by maneuvering to improve their position in the organization. The psychoanalytic consultant maintains that a critical motivation for creating a centralized, vertical, or controlled structure is to promote dependency. Management operates on the assumption that by establishing dependency, they can avoid conflict. However, they often create conflict. If management responds to potential conflict by repressing it, they will increase the intensity of the conflict over time.

4. *Interorganizational competition.* Conflict is most apt to occur when both systems are engaged in competition for scarce resources.

5. *Unconscious motivations.* Unconscious motivations evolve internally and are present when the interorganizational event is viewed as a means to reduce internal conflict.

THE FUNCTIONAL NATURE OF CONFLICT

The psychoanalytic consultant is aware that conflict may have both functional and dysfunctional consequences. For example, conflict generally precedes change in organizations, and sometimes it is necessary if change is to occur. In addition, conflict may increase the cohesion or bonding among members in a group or an organization. It is often pointed out in psychological studies of groups that when one group is engaged in conflict with another, there is a heightened tendency for each group, independent of the other, to reach quick agreement on its goals and tasks. Also, during an interorganizational event, employees tend to interact with greater frequency, and personal attractiveness increases. Additionally, there is a greater agreement on rules, regulations, and procedures. Under these conditions, employees are less conflicted about authority and in many cases desire strong, definitive leadership.

Finally, during an interorganizational event the entire system may engage in the event with the belief that the "other" organization is the "enemy." When this belief is apparent, the event becomes structured in such a way that the process unconsciously perpetuates the belief. Organizations frequently seek to engage in or perpetuate conflict with an external system to defend against some threatening internal conflict or struggle that is completely separate from the event. Consider the metaphor "going off to war." This is a way of avoiding internal conflicts, a way of smoothing them over while the employees mobilize for battle. The motivation for creating this type of culture is found in the research on "scapegoating," that is, using an external object to project hateful or aggressive impulses to relieve internal stresses. When this type of conflict exists and assumes a functional purpose for the organization, the chances of successfully intervening and reducing conflict will most likely be aborted by the employees. They resist reducing conflict during the event because of the function the conflict serves. Under these conditions, the consultant initially can reduce interorganizational conflict only by reducing the internal stresses.

AN OPEN SYSTEMS VIEW OF INTERORGANIZATIONAL RELATIONS

The psychoanalytic consultant focuses on the nature of the authority established within the boundary of the interorganizational relation. For example, in all interorganizational relations, a transactional task zone is created for the purpose of accomplishing the work of the respective systems.

Representatives of the respective systems become negotiators and consequently become members of the transactional task system. The negotiators require authority from their base organization to act on the base organization's behalf in the transactional system.

When the transactional system is established, a new boundary is created. According to Miller and Rice (1967/1973), the transactional system contains four new boundary dimensions (see Figure 12.1).

1. Between Organization A and Representative a;
2. Between Representative a and Organization B;
3. Within Organization B with the addition of Representative a; and
4. Within Organization A with the addition of Representative b.

The interactions become increasingly problematic when more than one organization is involved in the intergroup events (see Figure 12.2).

When consulting to an interorganizational event, the intergroup relations are assessed from the perspective of the nature and quality of authority given to each representative. The representative is expected to function as a negotiator, and what he/she may or may not do in the transactional task system is important if the organization is to be

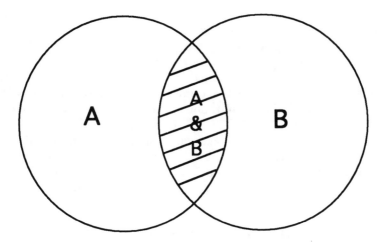

FIGURE 12.1. Two organizations creating a transactional task zone.

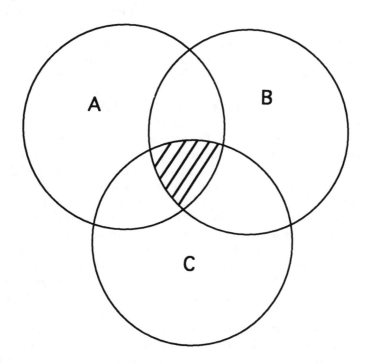

FIGURE 12.2. Three organizations creating a transactional task zone.

properly represented. Conflicts over contracts, information, values, communication, and resource exchange are often a function of a lack of clear authority given to the representative.

The dynamics that underlie interorganizational conflicts are played out in the transactional zone area. The representative, whether he/she is the CEO or a unit head, becomes a receptacle for the projections of the organization's feelings and fantasies about the other organization. The choice of a particular representative, how he/she is prepared by his home organization, and the information the representative is given as he/she leaves to enter the transactional zone will have a significant impact on the negotiations. For this reason, a psychoanalytic understanding of the event is required.

THE PSYCHOANALYSIS OF THE INTERORGANIZATIONAL EVENT

According to von Bertalanffy (1950), all living systems have boundaries and all living systems are defined by their singular boundary. For the organization's members, the delineation of a boundary provides security. Ashbach and Schermer (1987) confirm this when they say that the boundary is experienced as the "holding arms" of mother. When a boundary is ruptured, the organization's container is "unable to hold." Consequently, the employees no longer feel safe; they feel anxiety and dread. It is analogous to the weakening of a dike during a fearful storm. The "container," all that held the employees and provided security and predictability, is now perceived as fragmented. Old rules, regulations, roles, and structures are experienced as fractured. The anxiety employees experience produces a number of regressive responses. One reaction may be the unconscious wish for the omnipotent leader who will bring security, control, and comfort. Another may be the projection of annihilation fears outward against an enemy, which is often followed by the construction of a belief in the organization as all powerful and better than all else.

The belief that a fantasized enemy can be defeated will bring order and stability to the organization. Consider the following: A leader announces to employees, "We are going to merge." The immediate response is regressive, which triggers an array of adaptive and defensive responses, all in an attempt to establish a state of emotional equilibrium by delineating new boundaries. Typically, in response to a potential merger, the organization will seek to tighten its own boundaries by dramatizing rules, ceremonies, and procedures in an effort to differentiate itself from the prospective merging system.

The boundaries are tightened by decreasing the organization's boundary permeability. This action is motivated by the wish to protect the organization from persecutors, the "other" group.

When the intergroup event is experienced as a rupture of the boundary, reactions fluctuate wildly and rapidly, usually ranging from omnipotent fantasies to vulnerability and dread. The chief motivations for the intensity of anxiety and a particular reaction are existing organizational issues. For example, if employees are already feeling insecure and anxious, the intergroup event further increases anxiety and regression. Another factor contained in the organization also contributes to the type of reaction employees have. If the intergroup event is an unconscious attempt to reduce or mask some organizational conflicts. the event itself will have extraordinary potential to either increase or decrease anxiety. For example, consider the CEO who enters into an interorganizational event with the conscious purpose of merging with another organization. However, his/her unconscious motivation is to act out some omnipotent fantasies. The historic understanding of the CEO's behavior, his/her successes and failures, and the employees' understanding of his/her motivations will influence their reaction. If the employees experience the CEO's wish to engage in the event as being a gain for the CEO and a loss for the employees, conflict will result. Generally, an intergroup event proves positive for those employees immediately close to the event. They will generally experience their job with a heightened sense of importance, and they will inflate their importance to the organization. Now one can see that perhaps one motivation for an intergroup event is to mask feelings of powerlessness and vulnerability. Generally, omnipotent responses are attempts to ward off anxieties associated with the experience of being vulnerable and intruded upon by outsiders. It is helpful to view the outsider, the other organization, with suspicion and fear. Leaders can often remain in power as long as they are able to contain the members' anxiety by demonstrating in reality and fantasy that their organization is all-powerful. Former President George Bush's "Operation Desert Storm" is an example of this phenomenon.

THE MOTIVATION FOR AN INTERGROUP EVENT AND ITS RELATION TO LEADERSHIP

A critical function of leadership is the capacity to establish routes and routines for carrying out relations between groups and organizations. Inherent in these relations with other groups is real and potential conflict over territory, resources, control, and status. Most of what occurs in organizations, and that which is often taken for granted, is often the result of long-standing disputes, conflicts, bargains, coalitions, and agreements between different groups (Homans, 1950). How much a group gets in these strugges is a function of the capacity of the leader, for it is the leader who enters the fray and returns a winner or a loser.

Groups whose members meet to negotiate may have a defined task, but they also have other tasks such as the need to reconcile divergent idologies, statuses, or cultures. This is most apparent in contemporary organizations, with their heterogeneous employee populations. All intergroup events are attempts at merging, bringing together these heterogeneous groupings. The merging may be temporary (i.e., formed to resolve some crisis or perform some service), or it may be longer lasting (as in company–vendor relationships), or it may be permanent (as in two companies that "blend together"). The wish to merge is often considered to be rational and a function of reality-oriented issues such as provision of service, proximity, common inputs, tasks, or outputs. However, from a psychoanalytic perspective the motivations often have a powerful unconscious basis. As stated above, the main motivation for a merging is a function of the omnipotent striving of the organization's leader. Underlying the wish to enter into a merger is the leader's wish to be perceived as an "omnipotent self-object who serves as a representative mythological figure" (Ashbach & Schermer, 1987, p. 197). A critical question for analysis of an intergroup event is, Why is the leader motivated by this wish to seen by his/her subordinates as a mythological figure? Another question is, Why would the leader wish to leave his/her "home" and venture into strange and unfamiliar and perhaps dangerous territory to obtain this status? From a psychoanalytic perspective, the intergroup event is unconsciously motivated by a reparative wish. The leader believes that he/she has caused some grievous harm to his/her subordinates and the leader seeks reparation by bringing them a great gift. The gift will "make up" for the conscious and unconscious feelings that the leader created a "mess." This wish is triggered by the leader's feeling of vulnerability, which is often precipitated by some real or imagined trauma that the organization has experienced in the marketplace, or that the leader has experienced. The leader then sets out to save the organization and its employees and restore his/her position.

At the start of an interorganizational event, when the employees become aware of the leader's plans, their feelings of vulnerability increase. The leader's absence from the organization heightens this experience of vulnerability, which usually results in increased dependence on the leader. This dependence is dramatized when employees search for news of what has occurred in the transactional zone.

The leader's absence presents a paradox, because while the leader wishes to save the organization, the leader discovers that his/her actions actually increase anxiety "back home." If the leader carries into this event the wish to save his/her employees, to make reparations for ills, and to resolve unconscious guilt for the havoc he/she has created, the leader might make serious negotiating mistakes. These negotiations will not be based on any sense of reality, but they become a "game," designed unconsciously to win back or solidify a status that the leader perceives as crumbling. The leader's capacity to negotiate in the transactional zone is further confounded by his/her employees' dependency needs. Fearful that they will lose their leader, employees will unconsciously create "situations" that require the leader's attention. The function of these "situations" is to get the leader to "stay home."

During the interorganizational event the leader unconsciously sees him/herself as having attained the omnipotent position, as powerful protector of the organization's boundaries. This fantasy is spurred on by the fragmentation that is left behind in the organization, as the leader leaves "home" and enters into this ambiguous spatial territory to negotiate. Winnicott (1965) refers to this space as "potential space" and calls it a region for play and sublimation where the leader is able to "act out" omnipotent fantasies. Consequently, the interorganizational event unconsciously becomes an attempt for the leader to repair the damage to his own organization, and increase his own scope of power through realizing his omnipotent fantasies by increasing his domain or territory.[2] However, the flaw in this wish is contained in the instability the leader leaves behind, as he/she ventures out, and the dangers the leader may experience in foreign territory. The employees feel abandoned. This feeling is motivated by the unconscious fear of being swallowed or annihilated by the other organization. Under these conditions the employees are left with the experience of depletion and fragmentation, and they regress to the paranoid–schizoid position where they engage in the work of protecting themselves from real and fantasized impingements.

---

[2]Of course, there are leaders who take a different route with mergers. They see the intergroup event as an opportunity to "get more" for themselves, such as a "golden parachute." This type of greed is a defense against the guilt associated with their destructive acts. By aggressively taking money, they project their destructive wishes onto the organization, experience themselves as victims of the now perceived hateful company, and receive the money as a reparative act. The more money they receive, the less guilt they experience.

Why does this occur? According to Astrachan and Flynn (1976), in order to perform work employees invariably wish to see themselves as being members of a "happy family"; this self-image may take the form of a work-related view of themselves as "we physicians" or "we engineers," or it may be formed on the basis of common territory as "us on the third floor" or "we in the north building."

In intergroup relations, this sense of community is threatened. The employees fear that the organization's purpose, history, traditions, values, and very culture will be destroyed. Additionally, the employees feel that they will be "stripped of [their] usual professional or organizational role and [their] usual habits of behavior in work groups" (Astrachan & Flynn, 1976, p. 62). Consequently, disciplined groups such as professionals and highly technical staff may experience themselves as suddenly deskilled, as the old and honored ways of behaving and achieving status are restructured. A paranoid position takes the form of believing that management has constructed some grand and manipulative scheme with the purpose of offering more to the "new group," who are now seen as siblings. The leaders are no longer trusted and are viewed as persecutory objects. Under these conditions the leader is allowed to return to the organization only if he/she fulfills the fantasies of its members and "slays the dragon," that is, the leader returns triumphantly. If the leader is not victorious, he/she can only return to the throne by creating fear and intimidating his/her members. Another response to the anxiety associated with this event is to revolt. In this case the revolt is a restorative activity in that it allows the employees to move out of the dependent, passive position and the anxiety associated with waiting for "news" from the transactional zone.

The function of revolt or crisis in an organization about to engage in an interorganizational event is motivated by the wish to bring the leader back "home," to quell the storm, and to get the leader out of the dangerous transactional zone and end the negotiations. When this occurs the leader responds by resolving the difficulties in order to receive adulation from his/her staff. In the process the leader often responds to the negotiations by sending a subordinate into the transactional zone. Given the anxiety in both the leader and employees whenever an interorganizational event is about to occur, one can see how a leader might unconsciously use his/her employees to escape the transactional zone. Here the leader may actually precipitate the crisis knowing that the employees will demand that he/she remain in the organization. The leader then avoids the transactional zone with a sound excuse, thereby saving face, and sends out an expendable subordinate to negotiate in the zone. When this occurs, the subordinate is invariably scapegoated. The following example bears this out.

A university-based medical health center had a history of conflict with the surrounding black and Hispanic communities. The center staff experienced the surrounding communities as a threat and maintained rigid boundaries separating the center from the communities. For example, the front entrance of the center was located away from the community and faced the perceived friendly, white academic community. When the center received a multi-million-dollar grant to treat alcoholism, the center's CEO and staff feared that indigenous community leaders would demand the bulk of the funds to establish treatment programs in their community under their control. The center staff reacted to this fear with feelings of omnipotence. They began to demonstrate a heightened sense of professionalism and expertness. They suddenly discovered drug treatment experts in their midst. They started giving lectures to each other on alcohol addiction, invited experts to speak, and started collaborating on papers.

The grant instructions stipulated that the center had to create liaisons with its communities. This meant that the center had to establish a relationship with agencies in the black and Hispanic communities. The staff feared these liaisons and responded to the demands by becoming increasingly involved in internal conflicts at the center. Their conflicts centered around treatment ideologies, drug treatment versus the talking cure, and direct treatment as opposed to ancillary services and rehabilitation. Some even suggested the Alcoholics Anonymous treatment approach, which intensified the conflict. At the same time, the staff constructed an illusion that the CEO would make these problems go away. Instead, the CEO exacerbated the internal problems.

The CEO feared meeting with the community. The grant instructions were quite clear; he would have to enter into negotiations with dangerous groups. The possibility that he would fail in these negotiations was strong. The CEO, feeling vulnerable, avoided direct contact with community leaders by canceling meetings and then becoming ill. His fear was that the community agencies would demand a significant part of the grant award and considerable involvement in the decision-making process.

The CEO was caught in the middle between a staff who wished for victory and a community who wished to castrate him. He wanted to hold on to the idealized fantasies the staff projected onto him and to avoid situations that might damage these fantasies. These projected fantasies gave him strength and instilled in him a sense of power where little existed. To avoid the experience of castration and vulnerability, the CEO stimulated the internal conflicts in his organization. He set up a large staff meeting to address their issues. On the day of the staff meeting he discovered that he had set up a meeting with community leaders at the same time. The CEO was quietly pleased; now he could avoid the community groups. He announced to two community leaders that he would not attend their meeting because of urgent issues at the center, and he would send a senior psychiatric resident as his representative. The resident he chose was inexperienced in community relations and he was white and middle class. In the negotiations he was met by a hostile and angry community group. Under pressure and experiencing considerable anxiety and fear, the senior psychiatric resident gave away a significant portion of the funds and allowed the community leaders considerable participation in the decision-making process concerning the allocation of the funds. The following day, the director had no choice but to agree to the commitment. The center staff and university administration were very upset.

In this case the chosen representative, the young resident, was scapegoated. He was set up by the CEO in an attempt to gratify the demands of the community leaders and maintain the projected fantasies of his staff. The community leaders were still viewed as "evil" and this view was now intensified because of the belief that the community leaders had taken advantage of the "lamb." The CEO maintained his fantasied position, and he reduced the guilt associated with sending the resident out by giving him a major promotion. On the other hand, the community leaders were quite pleased. It was the first time they had obtained a significant portion of a federal grant that had been obtained by the university. The CEO had dramatically improved in the eyes of the community; he now had achieved the ultimate, becoming an idealized figure by both groups—staff and community.

In the following example, we explore the dynamics that exist when an intergroup event is internal to an organization (i.e., between subsystems). This type of event provides an opportunity to examine more clearly the dynamics of intersubsystem or interdepartmental relations, and how these dynamics are influenced by the CEO and the organization's culture.

CASE ANALYSIS

This consultation was to a small metallurgical plant, which was a division of a large multinational corporation. The division had been established during World War II to produce weapon accessories under Department of Defense contracts. Production peaked during the Vietnam conflict, when the plant had three shifts in operation. The employees, most of them World War II veterans, made a significant amount of money during this period by working long and hard hours. After the conflict, production began to slip consistently. The plant equipment was not replaced and this severely reduced the quality of the parts produced. In addition, the plant could not produce the high-quality accessories required for contemporary sophisticated weaponry. The plant had trouble procuring adequate contracts, and the existing contracts were often not completed on time because of poor quality control.

Corporate management decided to make significant changes in the plant management.

Management Changes

The average age of the management team members, as well as the line staff, was over 50 years old. Approximately half of the staff were ex-union employees who had worked their way up the plant ladder. A number of other management employees were transfers from other divisions of the corporation. The plant culture was represented by an image of toughness and marked by a high degree of interaction between union employees and management. There were very few official trappings to be found in the complex of management offices, and in some cases, management-level employees had no office and simply spent their workday on the plant floor. The plant cafeteria was an area where staff and union gathered each day. Here they worked out production problems and the labor and management issues that occurred infrequently. A high commitment to the corporation existed and there was a willingness to work long, hard hours.

Among the management staff, the education level was low and most had received management training on the job or through corporation-sponsored workshops. Both labor and management had close contact outside the plant. They lived in the same communities and sent their children to the same schools. Weddings, baptisms, funerals, and other gatherings were attended by both management and labor. Union grievances were rare, and when they occurred, they were quickly settled. Often these meetings took place in a joking atmosphere where trade-offs were made that were often based on the long-term work histories of the employees. Both union and management shared the same locker room and also washed up together after work. Dress and amount of grease and dirt often made it impossible to differentiate management from labor by appearance.

A traumatic change occured when the plant director, who had held the position for almost 20 years, was forcibly retired. The assistant director, who had worked his way up the ladder from the position of laborer, was demoted. Two other management employees, who were also ex-union, were demoted to supervisory positions over a very small segment of the plant.

Corporate management appointed a new plant director. He was a 35-year-old who had recently received a combination MBA and MS in engineering from a prestigious Ivy League school. He brought with him a PhD in metallurgy who was in his early 30s, as well an associate director also in his early 30s. The associate director was a younger brother of the local politician. Together, the new management constellation had no years of plant-management experience. Once on board, the new director hired two additional managers. Both of these young men were previously employed as metallurgical technicians and attended evening college; they also had no experience in plant management. A total of five new staff members entered to form a new management team. The result was disastrous, conflicts permeated the plant, two distinct groups emerged, and the struggle lowered morale and eventually precipitated sabotage.

Request for a Consultation

The consultant was called in by the new director after the director had been on the job for 6 months. The director chose the consultant based on a recommendation from one of the newly hired management/technicians who had been involved in a previous consultation at another plant.

The director's complaint was stated very simply: "poor communications amongst the management staff . . . training in communications and possibly human relations were needed."

The consultant met with the director. They discussed the director's entry into the organization and how he was received by his new staff. After a lengthy discussion, the consultant began to focus on the employees who were with the organization prior to the director's arrival. The consultant requested that the director set up three meetings: one with the old management staff, another with the new employees, and a third with both groups and the director.

The consultant met with the old management staff in the cafeteria 2 hours before lunch. This was done to give a message to the remainder of the plant employees that a consultation was taking place and that the old management staff was involved. To conduct this meeting behind closed doors would have added to the fears already in the plant that something negative was once again happening to the old management team.

In spite of the lack of privacy, the managers spoke openly about the problems, and they isolated a number of conflicts they were having with the new group of management employees. They outlined the following issues:

1. A new emphasis on formal meetings, where management only talks to itself;
2. New management's inability to deal with union grievances, and their lack of experience in general;
3. Poor planning;
4. Lack of quality-control mechanisms;
5. A growing gap between management and union; and
6. The feeling that they were no longer involved in the work of the plant and no longer needed.

Of the feelings and thoughts expressed, the most salient was that they were no longer needed. This, at least initially, seemed to form the basis for the apparent lack of communication and collaboration that were desperately needed by the new director.

Immediately after the consultant's meeting with the old management staff, he telephoned the director and asked to set up a meeting with the consultant and the newly hired management staff. The goal of this meeting was the same as that of the first: for the consultant to acquire a list of the problems as the group viewed them. A comparison of the two lists would indicate the closeness or degree of disperity between the two groups. The consultant hoped that the list of items would provide the basis for a common meeting ground, or what Sherif (1966) would call a superordinate goal, where both groups could actively work together to accomplish something that was mutually rewarding.

At the meeting with the new management team, it was collectively stated that the plant was viewed by corporate management as "on its deathbed." The management team could not discern whether corporate management had given them their positions because top management didn't care (i.e., had given up on the plant) or because they really wanted and expected the new team to turn the plant around. The new management team was clear on one issue: If they did not turn the plant around soon, the company would close it.

The management team isolated several reasons for the present condition of the plant and some of the major obstacles in reviving the plant:

1. Poor quality of equipment;
2. Failure to institute effective quality-control mechanisms and efficiency;
3. A history of a lack of strong leadership;
4. An old management staff who were too old and close to retirement and no longer interested in working to bring new life into the plant;
5. Resentment felt by the old staff, both management and union, for the new management team;
6. The crisis orientation of the plant: old management desired to work together with high esprit on crisis and this mentality left no time for planning; and
7. Sales and contract acquisition staff who were unimaginative and unable to procure new or challenging contracts for the plant.

After this meeting the consultant departed the plant and spent a week formulating a diagnosis.

Diagnosis

Two distinct groups existed in the plant. Each group became the victim of the other's projective fantasies. These fantasies were complicated by the fact that the plant was not doing well. As a matter of fact, closing the plant, death, seemed a real possibility.

Considering the dynamics of each group, it was apparent that each sought to project onto the other the fantasy that it was responsible for the pending death. In doing so, each group could avoid its own responsibility in the matter. The conflicts did nothing but confirm the projected fantasies.

In reality, the conflicts meant that a collaborative work environment was unobtainable. The new management group and the old management group were not contributing to the overall goals of the organization. In fact, their conflicts were constraining both their individual and their collective efforts. At a time when the plant desperately needed strong and creative leadership, none existed. Of all the dynamics that were being played out because of the conflict, the most disturbing, and perhaps the most dangerous to the organization, was each group's response to the conflict. The greater the conflict, the more each group tended to protect itself from the other; the greater the energy spent on protecting, the less energy was available to engage in the work necessary for organizational survival.

The consultant concluded that the conflict between the groups served a function: It promoted internal cohesion. Over the months, each group was rapidly becoming an entity unto itself, as it worked to strengthen or fortify its respective boundaries. Feeling threatened, each group spent increasing amounts of time attempting to maintain its own system of beliefs and values and ways of operating for the purpose of survival, status, and prestige, often at the expense of the other group. Because the plant had ceased to function as a collaborative enterprise, the conflicts significantly reduced the plant's ability to overcome the strong pull the organization was collectively experiencing: to give up and allow the plant to close. Let's look more closely at the two groups.

The Old Management Group

The old group was experiencing frustrations on many levels. The appointment of the younger, and clearly "outsider" management group was symbolically interpreted as a statement from top management to the old management team that they had failed. The experience of failure was unacceptable, and to avoid this experience the group projected failure and incompetence onto the new group. Unconsciously, their efforts were directed toward undermining the new team to make certain they failed, even if it meant plant closure. The leadership of the corporation had set this type of response in motion by taking power away from the old team and communicating to all that the old team was not capable of pulling the plant out of its desperate state, and implying that the new group would.

Given the threatening nature of the new management team and the condition of the plant, the old management team tightened its boundaries and regressed to a persecutory position. The collective fantasies projected onto the new group increased bonding among the old group members. In addition, the old group intensified its relations with the union employees and actively sought the union's support in the fight with the new group. As long as the old group could project fantasies onto the new group and tighten the boundaries, the fear and vulnerability could be reduced.

The New Management Group

The new group had a clearly articulated view of its task, which was to make certain that survival was ensured. This view was personally internalized because the success of a major taks such as this, given to a young manager, was considered the chance of a lifetime. If the new management group succeeded, major promotions would certainly follow.

The new management group members experienced feelings of omnipotence. They fantasized that they could turn the plant around. The fear of failure was displaced onto the old management team, enabling the new team to successfully avoid the experience of vulnerability associated with potential failure and narcissistic injury.

The new management group reacted to the experience of potential failure by projecting the paranoid fear that the old management group was out to ensure their failure. They had expected the new director, "their boss," to engage in the necessary battle with the old group, and had fantasized that the new director would destroy the old group and save the organization from the "pain of death."

The alignment that the old management group had developed with the union employees was seen by the new team as another indication of their attempt to destroy. The new group's response to the conflicts was similar to the old group's response to the conflicts. The new group also intensified their relationships among themselves. They began to spend increasing amounts of time together, both during and after work hours. The new members formed a golf foursome, which competed in the company golf tournament. The cafeteria, an arena where the dynamics of the plant were acted out, as well as a place where the plant's conflicts were resolved, ceased to serve this function. The new group members were excluded from the lunchroom conversations. After a number of attempts to join, the new members began to eat lunch at a local restaurant.

The New Director

The new director was an exceedingly personable, relaxed, and empathic individual. He was married to an artist, and in contrast to his work in a military–industrial plant, he lived a somewhat bohemian/intellectual life-style. He was bright, articulate, and physically attractive. His young mannerisms, blond hair, blue eyes, and relaxed intellectual orientation presented a sharp contrast to the poorly educated, ethnic, and burly members of the old management crew.

The new director brought with him a management team who idealized him and responded to the new director as a benevolent father figure who wanted to protect them. The narcissistic preoccupation of the new director demanded an "audience" response from the new team, that they experience him as an idealized parent. Given the terrifying aspects in the plant, this was an important anxiety-reducing function for the new team. Additionally, for the new director it served a "mirroring" function by helping him defend against the fear associated with his own inadequacies as a leader.

The response of the old management team to the new director was one of confusion. They said such things as: "We cannot figure him out; he is a nice guy and friendly, but strange." In an offhanded comment, one of the old management members described the new director as a "hippie in a suit and tie."

The ambivalence expressed by the old management team was the only optimistic note in the consultative effort. It meant that they were still unconsciously hold off their judgment of the new director. Although there was a wish to see the new director as a "bad" object, the splitting experience was weak and had the potential of being integrated into a more healthy perception.

Intervention

The consultant isolated many factors that had led to the intergroup conflict. The major question was: What could be done to reduce the conflict and promote a collaborative environment? The consultant thought about a number of possible interventions but was uncertain as to which would be most effective. The major reason for his uncertainty was his impression that the new management crew were "in over their heads." They were intensely frightened and suspicious of the old plant employees, almost as if they were in a foreign land for the first time. An intervention that would expose their naivete and lack of managerial confidence in the old staff could prove disastrous. An intervention that acknowledged that the new management team needed support—even mentoring—from the old staff would be the ideal. The concept of a mentoring relationship between some of the old management staff and the new director's staff was met with disapproval by the new director. He appeared threatened by the suggestion of the old and experienced staff teaching the younger members, and he stated that he had "a better plan." The director wished to take the lead in reducing the conflict himself and he felt that he alone could "win over" the old management staff.

The Party

The new director suggested that he could reduce the conflict with a get-acquainted party at his home. The consultant agreed, on the condition that he be invited. The consultant did not attempt to convince the director of the potential for failure because he was not at all certain of the impact. At the very least, the consultant thought the party would present an opportunity to observe interactions and gather data about who was most willing to associate with whom.

The director's wish for a party and his expectations had a magical quality to them. The party, its place away from the organization, was unconsciously perceived by the new director as an arena in which he could mix external reality (the two groups coming together) and fantasy (that all of the conflicts and problems would dissipate). The party was an attempt to structure a group feast, but it was devoid of a celebration, a victory, or an achievement. It was clearly too late, in that the dynamics were already established, simply to view the party as a "get together" or as an opportunity to meet. The party needed some symbolic function. It had to be perceived as an occasion on which members from both groups could join together; otherwise it would fail and perhaps exacerbate the problem.

The results of the party were disastrous. It was attended by the new management staff and a number of the director's friends and his wife's friends. The old management team did not attend. Written invitations had been sent out with an RSVP, and even though only one of the members responded negatively, the others did not show up.

On the Monday after the party, the consultant met with the new director. The director was depressed and asked for help in understanding what had gone wrong. Experiencing a narcissistic blow from the old management team created a sense of desperation. He now pleaded for help and was ready to try anything to resolve the conflict. He openly spoke of his vulnerabilities and fears of a ruined career if things did not work out. The importance of the old team to the director's survival was now solidified. Both the director and the consultant realized that if the director was going to survive, it was he, himself, who had to be integrated into the old team and into the organization. He now experienced himself on the periphery, alone and incapable of functioning as a leader.

It was clear that as long as the new director and his team remained on the periphery of the organization, the conflicts could not be resolved. The consultant decided that the openness of the old staff and the open personality of the new director lent itself to a T-group type of intervention, where everyone involved would be given an opportunity to share their concerns and their feelings about the plant, corporate management, and each other. The new director's management staff presented a problem because of their timidity and acknowledge discomfort with the old management team. The consultant wanted to avoid a situation in which the director would become integrated into the organization at the expense of the new management team, who could become scapegoats and consequently alienated. In spite of his apprehension, the new director told the consultant that the new management team would do fine.

The consultant asked the director to arrange a meeting of the entire management team in the cafeteria after work hours one week following the party. While the new management team arrived promptly, the old management team drifted in over a 20-minute period. The consultant remained silent during the first 30 minutes and allowed the discussion to evolve. The director spoke at length about some work-related issues, and the group seemed content to avoid the emotionally powerful issues.

The consultant finally spoke and said that the purpose of the meeting as he saw it was to discuss some particularly difficult issues and the group seemed to be having difficulty raising these issues. After a moment of silence, the director spoke: "I'm having a lot of difficulty working here. I know this because I have a great deal of difficulty coming to work each morning. It's as if I'd rather be somewhere else." This brought a smile and nods of agreement from the employees. With a sense of relief, the members began to speak freely. The discussion was open and focused on the central issues. The old management team aired their sentiments about the plant, the new director, and corporate management. The old team was particularly shocked when the director announced that the plant had been very close to being closed by corporate management and might have been if he had not quickly initiated changes in production and quality control. But he had felt stymied by the old management team, who seemed content to allow the plant to die. The old management team was pleased that the director seemed to need them.

After some silence, the consultant intervened by asking: "What happened to the director's party?" This precipitated an in-depth, almost therapeutic discussion of their difficulties in getting to know each other. Also, the theme of pushing aside the old management team was thoroughly explored. The new management team expressed their feelings concerning their need for assistance and support from the old management team.

The consultant steered the group in the direction of the specific needs of each member of the director's new team, and asked the old management how they could help. It turned out that the old management team felt they had an awesome task, for they had to work not only to save the plant but also to mentor a team of young management employees. The best they could hope for was a sense of satisfaction that their efforts, if successful, would save the plant and turn the reins over to a new group pending their retirements. The new management team said that they would be appreciative of such an effort, and that this form of graciousness was a necessary part of learning the work and advancing their careers.

The thrust of conflict resolution centered around the identification of a superordinate goal, a collective effort to save the plant. The director responded to the old managers' commitment with a commitment of his own to them as a group. He said, somewhat surprisingly, that he was requesting corporate management to bring back the recently retired director as a consultant to the new director, for he too needed mentoring. The old management team felt valued and pleased at the outcome of the meeting. Each new manager was paired with an old manager who was to serve as a kind of protector and mentor. Each pair would be required to meet each day for an hour to discuss issues, and they all agreed that as a group they should meet weekly after hours.

The plant operated very well for the next 3 years, although quality control and meeting contract deadlines remained a problem. Corporate management had allocated some monies to improve production equipment. A major contract had been negotiated that was expected to be the production job that would save the plant, but an inability to meet quality and cost standards moved corporate management to the decision to close the plant. All members had made a herculean effort, and even though they were exceedingly disappointed at the closing, they felt a great deal of satisfaction that they had collectively given their all in spite of overwhelming odds.

The critical questions are: What has been resolved and how can the dynamics be understood?

In all instances in which group or intergroup conflict is resolved and collaboration and a sense of community evolve, the groups have resolved oedipal-related conflicts. Their revolt against the leader (authority) allowed the old team to work through conflictual issues. The guilt associated with their rejection and hurt of the leader established a conscience and brought about increased development of superego functioning. Additionally, the old group, who had experienced themselves as old, near retirement, and narcissistically depleted, now experienced rejuvenation. They were then capable of assuming a paternal, mentoring stance vis-à-vis the new management team. The leader (authority) was not perceived as castrating and the old group believed they could function competently. The new team functioned as the favorite sons of the restored old team. The leader was now seen as benevolent and as a figure capable of being idealized by both groups. The powerful dependency wishes could be given up. When the director publicly demonstrated his hurt feelings and vulnerabilities, he reduced both the oedipal conflicts and the splitting processes that had depleted the effectiveness of both the old and the new management teams.

CHAPTER 13

Dependent and Autonomous Structures

[O]ur cultural emphasis on technology, competition, individualism, temporariness, and mobility has resulted in a population that has frequently experienced the terror of loneliness and seldom the satisfaction of engagement.
—JERRY HARVEY (1988, p. 25)

When analyzing an organization, it is necessary to assess its internal subsystems for the purpose of differentiating their boundaries. When boundaries between subsystems are clearly differentiated, the nature of the transactions that cross them can be observed. Differentiating boundaries will provide information concerning the continuity or discontinuity of intersystem regulation and maintenance. The primary purpose for developing subsystems is to differentiate. This will increase the ability of the organization to work effectively and efficiently.

As organizations increase in size and complexity, their subsystems multiply and the transactions between these subsystems become increasingly active. In an era of increased specialization, organizations require specialized subsystems to perform the many complex, exceptional, and sophisticated tasks. These tasks not only include highly specialized boundary tasks in the form of legal work, personnel, and marketing, but also internal tasks where union–company and professional association negotiators are needed to work with the organization's management through contractually affiliated subsystems (e.g., insurance providers and government regulators) that are permanently established at the boundary. Additionally, with increased specialization, the interdependency among subsystems dramatically increases, significantly altering motivations for autonomous functioning.

Attempting to identify the boundaries around a system will provide information that attests to the organization's capacity to differentiate. This is important for four reasons.

1. From a biological perspective an organism cannot grow or reproduce itself unless it is capable of differentiation.
2. From a sociological perspective, all groups utilize role, statuses, etc., to promote differentiation, and division of labor is not possible without differentiation.
3. From a learning theory perspective, whenever an organism must make two or more different responses to two or more different stimuli, its ability to make reasonable responses is a function of its ability to differentiate, and perceptually, the various aspects of an array will only become distinguishable through differentiation.
4. From a personality developmental perspective, differentiation occupies a significant place. Differentiation is defined as the ability to separate the object from the external world. Poor capacity in this area leads to faulty perceptions and communications, vital attributes in organizational effectiveness.

To fully understand dependency and autonomy requires an understanding of developmental psychology and how the human moves from dependency to autonomy. Differentiation as an ego capacity occupies a significant place in developmental theory. For example, when considering issues of dependency and autonomy, the lack of differentiation capacity within individuals, groups, and systems leads to dysfunctions. It is the ability to separate the self from others and the external world in general that leads to optimal functioning. It allows one to see objective reality with clarity. This is stressed by Mahler, Pine, and Bergman (1975) in their infant research. Mahler suggests that differentiation occurs when the infant develops an ability to see mother as separate. She considers this an important developmental phase where the infant develops his/her capacities associated with mental organization, namely, the capacity to cognitively know the meaning of place, time, and the affects of others. In addition, this phase is marked by the infant's capacity to seek autonomy, which begins as the infant begins the process of movement away from the primary caretaker (mother). This is the onset of the long, arduous road to autonomy.

When applied to work, differentiation is defined as the capacity of an employee to cognitively isolate the boundaries within the organization, which include the boundaries around the system, the boundaries between respective subsystems, and the boundaries separating work activities and work-related relationships.

The concept of autonomy is relevant to the understanding of the employee's relationship to work, because it refers to the capacity of the employee to function independently. Closely related to this concept is delegation of authority—an important aspect of organizational leadership. Delegation means offering the employee an opportunity to function autonomously; that is, without the closeness of supervision and the debilitating and intrusive effects of a watchful authority. However, one just does not delegate authority: The effectiveness of delegation is a function of the employee's ability to function autonomously.

From a developmental perspective, one can only function autonomously if one has been able to separate and function without the need for attachment to a superior. Attachment is necessary when the employee fears that if he/she differentiates, he/she will experience anxiety and fear for his/her safety. It as if the employee says, "If I do this on my own I will be in danger. If I fail, then I will be blamed. If I stay attached and avoid separation, then I can be protected: I will be safe." Unfortunately, this is a common occurrence in contemporary organizations. While organizations seek to promote autonomy and delegate authority, they often create situations in which they use delegation to induce fear in employees. The realities of the modern workplace are not conducive to separateness or individuated responses for two reasons. The first has to do with the difficulty management may have with "giving up" control; the second has to do with the subordinates' fears associated with autonomous functioning. The first issue was discussed in Chapter 10, where the psychodynamics associated with authority are explored; the second aspect is explored here.

To varying degrees, employees experience anxiety when they are forced to function autonomously. They unconsciously wish for and seek situations in which they can avoid the affects associated with autonomy, such as depression and anxiety. After all, employees seek to join bureaucratic corporations rather than strike out on their own because the company provides shelter from these basic anxieties. In reviewing Fromm's writings related to the neurotic fears associated with autonomy, Greenberg and Mitchell (1983) suggest the following:

> [T]he fact of separateness is acknowledged and accepted, and the relations with others proceed on the basis of intimate yet differentiated involvements. The other possibility entails denial of the reality of one's separateness and of individual responsibility for fashioning one's life. A wide variety of regressive, neurotic orientations may be relied upon, and

Fromm argues that differences among them are less salient than the similarity of their essential function: they all provide illusions and fantasies that enable the . . . [employee] . . . to avoid the actuality of his separateness and support the pretense that he continues to reside in the earliest state of blissful security. (p. 108)

According to Fromm (1941), one is not motivated by pleasure as classical analysts suggest, but instead by desire for safety. In seeking this state, the employee denies autonomy, separateness, and his/her own vulnerability. The consequence is a regressive pull where the ability to differentiate is deadened and the employee becomes susceptible to illusory symbiotic unity (Pine, 1985) and a belief in "magical substances, powerful saviors, [and] strategies for self-protection" (Greenberg & Mitchell, 1983). It follows, then, that the employee seeks the safety of the bureaucratic organization and hides within the confines of an organizational structure that promises predictability and security.

In the bureaucracy, an employee can avoid anxiety associated with individual action and autonomous functioning by escaping from the freedoms associated with these activities (Fromm, 1941). This employee "escapes" into an illusion, into what Ashbach and Schermer (1987) refer to as the psychic equivalent of the experience of the "holding arms" of mother, a state of abject dependency. The question is, If the employee is unconsciously seeking this state of blissful symbiotic attachment as an alternative to the anxiety associated with autonomy, how does this employee function in the corporate world? This employee functions in the corporate world by splitting, where wishes associated with autonomy and individualism are denied and the employee operates within a created social image. This split is abundantly examined in the psychoanalytic and social psychological literature. This employee is referred to by Winnicott (1965) as having a "false self"[1]; Lifton (1968) refers to the employee as the "protean man"; Reisman et al. (1950) call him/her the "other-directed person"; and Whyte (1956) refers to him/her as the "organizational man."

These views collectively suggest that the employee behaves as

---

[1]Of particular relevance is the concept of the false self. According to Winnicott (1965), this self system is a response to early threats and impingements to the nascent self system. The false self is created to cover for what the person is "really" feeling or needing. According to Zaleznik (1970), organizations over time develop ways of communicating what resembles the false self. These are organizations that cannot permit full expression of feelings and rely on distorted views of themselves and reality to protect the "real self." It is apparent in this type of organization that any threat to the false self would be destroyed, and one way of controlling the possibility of threat is to create a dependent environment.

others would have him/her behave. His/her internal responses are consciously and unconsciously denied. The result is a deadening of spontaneity; risk taking is avoided and the employee's experience of "being in the world" is recorded through the accumulation of material possessions and status. In actuality, this form of splitting increases unconscious motivations for dependency, because in giving up the internal wish for autonomy, the employee also gives up ego capacities such as creativity, spontaneity, and perhaps most important the ability to enact aspects of his/her fantasy life as it relates to work-related wishes. This not only reduces imagination but also the ability to differentiate. Stimuli are responded to in a "false self" manner where the employee's innermost feelings and fantasies are contained and repressed because they are felt to be fearful and threatening. Primary process ideation is psychically considered off limits, as being impulsive, and the employee is ruled and controlled by secondary process thought. The employee responds to new and challenging experiences with a heightened sense of anxiety and fear which precipitates a greater need for safety and security, promoting a vicious cycle.

When the employee is in a situation in which autonomous functioning is required, as in delegation, he/she feels insecure and vulnerable. These feelings are projected onto the superior, which in turn creates a vicious cycle whereby the superior responds by adopting an authoritarian leadership style, a style that is unconsciously welcomed by the subordinate.[2]

The employee retreats from autonomy, and in doing so communicates to the superior, "I cannot do it. I am fearful and I am convinced that the world is a dangerous place." This is a reflection of the powerlessness the employee experiences and this experience is projected onto his/her superiors. The superior may react to these projections in one of two ways: He/she may recognize the employee's powerlessness as an opportunity to structure a parent–child relationship, or he/she may identify with the projection and experience himself as powerless. According to Kanter (1977), when this occurs superiors will become increasingly "rules-minded in response to the limited options for power in their situation, turning to 'the rules' as a power tool," or they are "provoke[d] [into] . . . a cautious, low-risk, play-it-safe attitude" (p. 256). Kanter (1983) goes on to say:

[2]This is a defense process similar to projective identification, where unacceptable feelings are projected onto another, eliciting a response to the unwanted affects. In this instance, both subordinate and superior respond to the affects associated with powerlessness. However, the response from the superior to the experience of powerless is very different from that of the subordinate. The superior responds in a controlling, paternalistic manner and demonstrates the behaviors the subordinate unconsciously wishes for.

[T]he organization's concern with regulations reduces administrator's spheres of autonomy, limits their influence and decision-making power. The very provision of graded careers stressing seniority, in which incremental advances are relatively small and all must wait their turn, fosters dependency. . . . It removes incentives for assertion and reduces people to a common denominator—one in which they did not participate in defining. . . . Another organizational cycle is set in motion. As each manager protects his or her own domain, the sense of helplessness and power of other administrators in intersecting units increases. They, in turn, may respond by redoubling their domination over their territory and their workers. (p. 256)

Kanter claims that these responses emanate from the superiors' feelings of powerlessness; however, she is unclear about how these feelings arise. It is maintained that the superiors' feelings of powerlessness come from two sources: from their own internal fear of autonomy, and from their subordinates' projections. If these responses from the superiors are to the feelings of powerlessness that are projected onto them by their subordinates, the responses are exactly what the subordinates wish for, a climate of certainty, protection, and control.

In an environment of powerlessness, superiors respond by increasing their control and domination, and subordinates respond by seeking positions of dependency and protection.[3] Thus, Horney's (1937) contention that people will respond to the affects of helplessness and inferiority by becoming dominant and controlling may only apply under certain conditions. That is, in addition to personality factors, the role one occupies and the environmental conditions of the organization influence employee response. Role and environmental options influence choice of response in the following manner: Some employees may choose to become bossy or authoritarian; however, for others the options may be dependency and acquiescence. Dependency and acquiescence are the most frequent responses described in the literature on infant and child development. These

[3]The current trend in organizational theory is away from the control/authoritarian model of the workplace where top management controlled all aspects of its internal functioning. The traditional rationale for the control model, based on Taylorism, was founded on the belief that management (a certain class of people) alone had the expertise. This view has shifted and the motivation for control is now seen as the desire for power rather than the use of expertise. The current view suggests that expertise is located at the bottom of the organization's structure, suggesting that those who labor, have, in addition to muscle and psychic skills, brains as well. It is still uncertain if this "empowerment" approach will be a short-lived fad or will take on the same lasting qualities as did Taylorism and the school of scientific management.

are predictable responses when one is in a position or environment where one is, in actuality, powerless and dependent, such as in a hierarchical bureaucracy where powerlessness can be the only response for one so little and powerless to begin with. Perhaps this is why in children's play, children tend to identify with the aggressor and adopt exaggerated punitive roles (e.g., teacher–student or parent–child).

It is not suggested that an organization will only increase control and domination because its subordinates unconsciously wish it. There are a number of other motivations for increased control. For example, from an organizational perspective, increased control is often a response to the anxiety associated with interacting with a turbulent and uncertain environment from sudden downturns in the market and decreased profitability, to the departure of a CEO, to rumors of a hostile takeover. The crucial point is that the wish to seek to control in the work-place environment is a response to insecurity, fears, and the wish to be safe. Anxiety associated with these fears can be reduced by taking measures to confront the reality; however, the typical response is to retreat from reality and increase efforts to create the "illusion" of safety.

CLARIFYING SUBSYSTEM BOUNDARIES

According to Ashbach and Schermer (1987):

> The group boundary is equated in the unconscious with the ego boundary and with omnipotence. Social boundaries are given the implication of control of the environment and of guarantees for the self, creating a potential space of possession in which one feels secure and victorious. The dissolution of a group boundary is experienced as a loss, a failure, a death. Boundaries have primitive, narcissistic emotional significance. (p. 117)

The issue that has been explored is how an organization contributes to or detracts from autonomous functioning. It is suggested that the mere delegation of authority will not influence autonomous functioning, and may in fact reduce it. Then, just what does contribute to autonomous functioning? It is argued that clarity of boundaries is directly related to the degree of autonomy that an employee and an organization experience. Slater (1966) confirms this position by suggesting that "boundary awareness" is central to autonomous functioning, and that boundarylessness will lead to system fragmentation and a lack of differentiation concerning what is inside and what is outside the system. In addition, a lack of boundary awareness increases anxiety and, along with fragmentation, results in faulty ego adaptation and increased dependency. Once again, this creates a vicious cycle.

When the system fragments, anxiety increases because of confused boundary maintenance, and discontinuity between subsystems will result in a greater degree of effort to bring about internal regulation and control. Typically, discontinuity between subsystems is necessary because it defines boundaries and establishes a control region. However, when discontinuity between subsystems is established for the purpose of creating the illusion of safety, it results in the establishment of a barrier between subsystems. This barrier ultimately decreases cooperation and intersystem transactions. Discontinuity should not be confused with the concept of differentiation. Discontinuity suggests that the subsystems are segmented in such a way that integration and cooperation are hindered. In addition, it is also a cognitive segmentation where the organization does not "move" in collective agreement as to what constitutes its culture. This perpetuates differences in attitudes and values and creates differing and possibly competing and constraining subsystem cultures.

Lawrence and Lorsch (1970) suggest that when segmentation exists, it makes the task of management "to integrate the organization into a harmoniously functioning whole, close to impossible" (p. 188). This view is underscored by March and Simon (1958), who maintain that under these conditions, each subsystem has the tendency to pursue its own goals, often at the expense of other goals within the organization. However, the greatest impact of segmentation is experienced within the individual employee who, while experiencing segmentation as an attempt to provide security, creates a situation in which the experience of security can only be obtained within the employee's primary social grouping or department. This results in a "we versus they" situation. Obtaining security under this psychological arrangement makes an emotional connection to work problematic because the employee must continuously devote time, effort, and psychic energy to maintaining a of the belief in the weakness of others and maintaining constant vigilance, lest the boundaries of the subsystem become violated.

Returning to their view of the function of the boundary, Ashbach and Schermer (1987) and Slater (1966) claim that the establishment and maintenance of the boundary strengthens ego boundaries. However, for an employee to accomplish this requires the psychic attainment of two types of illusions: (1) the experience of omnipotence of the group and the impervious nature of its boundaries, and (2) the idealization of the leader. Unfortunately, these illusions promote dependency and reduce autonomous functioning. Under these conditions, the ego's capacity to engage in the work of the organization is significantly diminished because of the employee's preoccupation with these illusions and idealizations. This state of affairs can only be altered if management takes the responsibility of managing the boundaries away from the employees and assumes the responsibility themselves. If management fails to do this, they allow the boundaries to become confused or ambiguous and they promote regression to a dependent position, where the work capacities of the employees are reduced because they must now engage in boundary work. When employees must work to create boundaries, they accomplish this task within their informal social group, and when this occurs they begin to seek gratifications not from work-related activities but through informal group activities. The reason work does not get done is that employees are invested in the illusion of safety that results from deficient boundary management.

The illusion for safety occurs within informal groups. These groups collectively create ego ideals. These ideals contain real or fantasized characterizations of the group and leadership. The group investment is in the belief that these idealized objects will protect the members from the fearful, external world. Corporate management is invariably included in this cabal of fearful objects. For example, when management responds to the employees' inability to engage in the task, management is viewed by employees as critical and judgmental. Management's criticisms are denied as the employees attempt to hold on to the experience that they are good and competent. If the organization is encumbered by low morale, low productivity, and poor quality, it is "management's fault"; the bad objects are projected onto management, thus preserving the ideal associated with the group or department.

AUTONOMY AND ITS IMPACT ON TASK AND SENTIENT SYSTEMS

In an analysis of dependency and autonomy issues the informal social system occupies a special place. The informal social system is defined as a grouping of employees who are aligned around sentient values. These groups are not sanctioned by the organization, although the organization may be aware of their presence and may actually support their events and activities. Membership in an informal group may be centered around work tasks or some specialized duties, but most often alignment is formed by non–work-related tasks and activities such as work area proximity, sex, age, education, or some personal characteristics. In some organizations membership in a grouping is a function of common professional identity. This is a common occurrence in high-technology organizations, such as hospitals or engineering firms.

Social groupings are a vital part of all organizations, and often the formation of social groups and an employee's entry into a group will have a positive effect on morale, attendance, and commitment to the organization. Many theorists suggest that without the formation and viability of social groupings, the work of the organization will not get done. Additionally, those who focus on the organization's culture suggest that management must not only be aware of these informal groups but must also manage them. From a psychoanalytic perspective the relationship between informal social groups and work is a complex issue. When consulting to dependency and autonomy issues, it is important to assess the nature of these informal groups and how they contribute to or detract from work-related activities. This analysis is conceptualized as the relationship between the task system (work-related activities) and the sentient system (informal grouping). (See Chapter 9 for further explanation of this concept.)

In groups, a person tends to seek those who think and feel as he/she does. The sharing of beliefs, values, and attitudes is a significant factor in creating the necessary homogeneity required for cohesion. These informal groups are defined as sentient groups, groups that provide the employee with friendship, social activities, and the support necessary to engage in the work activities of the organization. The employee's membership in a sentient group may be a sign of status, or it may be connected to joining a group that is opposed to some aspect of the organization's policy, rules, or regulations, or against a particular superior or class of superiors. The function of the sentient group is to allow the employee to psychically connect to others, to have his/her feelings confirmed and to allow the employee an opportunity to share his/her feelings. In this manner, the support provided by the sentient group has significant therapeutic value, and it can help reduce or mitigate an employee's fear of autonomy and rage at criticism by providing a secure and safe environment in what potentially can be a fearful workplace. Sentience is conceptualized as the affects associated with a psychic attachment to an object, where that object provides security and opportunities to gratify a set of wishes (including the wished-for self-image). In the group relations sense, sentience would be defined as an emotional bond with the group, where the group performs three functions: regulating the employees' impulsivity at work; providing for self-esteem regulation, and providing a psychological safety net.

THE PROBLEM WITH MERGING TASK AND SENTIENT SYSTEMS

The problem with satisfying sentient needs and wishes in an informal group is that they will take the employee away from work. If it is the group that provides the gratifications expected to be found in work-related activities, then work will be viewed as having little or no sentient value. This position is expressed repeatedly in the organization as its employees plan and engage in activities associated with nonwork (sports activities, parties, etc.). Management even colludes by sponsoring these activities, and in doing so communicates to the employees that sentient gratification cannot be obtained at work but only outside the boundaries of the task system.

Consider the following: A professor says to his students, "If you are really interested in this work you will run to the library after class, you will be 'on fire' and 'alive' with the desire to study, you will obtain gratification not from passing my exam but through spending long hours engaging in work." The students laugh and respond by saying, "We go to class and then hang out, we party on weekends and study only when you demand it, like when you test us." This description is an example of the separation of the task and sentient boundaries. This goes on at work and is responsible for the creation of situations in which work develops into a "political" endeavor where the objective is to "look good" or avoid "looking bad" and only to engage in activities that "impress" the people "who count." This is the equivalent of establishing a culture in an organization where the "false self" is valued.

When the sentient system is merged with the task system, the employee is related to his work. This relatedness is a psychic attachment to work and is measured as the employee's ability to utilize work to gratify conscious and unconscious wishes. If management understands the relationship between the sentient system and task system, they will most likely be able to develop an ideal arrangement where these systems are merged, and they can avoid situations where they collude with employees to escape from work. An ideal work situation, where the task and sentient systems are merged, occurs when employees are "ego involved" in work, where the employees' capacity to work is increased, they are focused, and work is de-sexualized and deaggressivised.

Consider an employee who once reported the mergence of the task and sentient systems during a week at work: "It occurred during tax audit time. We all pitched in and we worked till 12 A.M. or 2 A.M., I didn't know where I was, it didn't matter very much, and I remember we weren't tired. As a matter of fact we enjoyed it, it was a pleasant state of exhaustion, boy we were going strong." A student reports a similar phenomena: "The subject really excited me, like I've never been excited before, I wanted to read everything on the subject. One night, I forgot to go to a dance, I stayed in the library. I really surprised myself with that one." In the first instance the task and sentient systems are merged within a work group.[4] In the second, the student in isolation has merged the systems.

There is a regressive aspect to this phenomenon. When the systems are merged, both employees seem to be describing particular "moments" where they are fully immersed in their work, as though they are swallowed up in the activities, unaware of their sur-roundings, or "lost in work." This description is similar to one of a child fully engrossed in play, and fits White's (1960), suggestion that when this occurs, the child is using "independent ego energies," energies not derived from the neutralization of drive energies but energies inherent in one's personality and used for the functioning of motor, perceptual, and cognitive apparatuses. The feelings of eu-phoria derived from engagement in this work are a functioning of the feelings of competence, attunement to reality, and enhancement of self-esteem obtained immediately following the end of work. As with the child's experience, the employee is away from the world, function-ing autonomously, unaware of the conflicts within his/her mind and with his/her environment. The employee has found safety in work.

It often happens that employees who have captured this experi-ence continally attempt to replicate it. This may become an obsession or lead to an internal sense of disappointment and depression when they fail.

[4]When the task and sentient systems are merged in groups at work, the pleasure associated with this experience is often reported as euphoric. Many employees report such experiences when they contrast the past to the future: "In the good old days, everyone worked late, now they all go home at 5." In addition, the power of the joined task and sentient systems is so great that some organizations attempt to create events, and even crisis, in the hope that they can capture the experience associated with the merged systems. Depression and a sense of hopelessness emerge when employees fail to capture this euphoric experience. The response to this failure may further increase a separation of the task and sentient systems.

In organizations the mergence of task and sentient systems as described above rarely occurs. Most often what employees experience is a splitting of the task and sentient systems. When these systems are split, not merged, the task system suffers. This accounts for lowered productivity, disinterest in work, and the experience of work as a heavy burden.

THE RELATIONSHIP BETWEEN DEPENDENCY AND AUTONOMY AND TASK–SENTIENT SYSTEM MERGENCE

It has been repeatedly suggested that the structure of the organization influences the ability of employees to engage in the task requirements of the organization and the ability of individuals and groups to obtain gratifications from work. Of these structural issues, the organization's dependent and autonomous structures have the greatest influence. The dependent structure influences superior–subordinate relations and policies and regulations that control work activities and behavior. Autonomous structures give employees opportunities to increase discretion, creative efforts, and work in isolation of superior supervision.

Subsystem dependency–autonomy has an important relationship to task–sentient system mergence. An urban police department, for example, represents the importance of task–sentient system mergence, but also the fragility of this mergence and how issues of dependency–autonomy have an effect. Police officers are members of two systems: the local precinct and a pairing system, with their partner. In order for the work of policing to get done and to ward off the anxiety associated with their work, task–sentient mergence must exist within the precinct and partnership. Management prevents mergence of the task–sentient system when they fail to consider properly the membership of this pairing by aligning employees in conflicting relationships; by not permitting autonomous functioning by intruding into the sentient–task relationship through shifting work schedules and rotating members arbitrarily from one group to another; or by failing to protect the boundaries around the local precinct and the department in general from intrusions by politicians, community groups, civilian review boards, and so on. When the task–sentient systems are not merged, the work of patrolling , arresting, mediating conflicts, and so on, which precipitates considerable anxiety, requires the use of pathological defenses. Employees respond either by increasing dependency on the precinct subsystem and its leadership or through schizoid withdrawal, which takes the form of detachment from duties or an overaggressive response to work, similar to the "we–they" response described earlier.

A structure that supports task–sentient system mergence promotes autonomous functioning. Such a structure allows employees to move into teams that will work productively with a high potential for satisfaction and better equips employees to deal with conflict and ambiguity.

In order for management to create a structure to support task–sentient system mergence, management must intentionally design structural relationships that are consistent with their decision to place the organization on a dependency–autonomy continuum. This decision requires an analysis of the nature of the work as well as the sociocultural characteristics of the organization. Experience suggests that if management cannot assess the relationship between subsystems, employees will abandon the given structure and work toward creating a new one that they find more gratifying. An extreme example of such a reaction is the motivation of citizens to destroy a given political structure through revolution. In organizations, revolutions are rarely experienced, but pressures are often apparent that alter structures at a much slower pace. As mentioned earlier, management must continuously work to merge task and sentient boundaries. This is the task of the number two[5] person in the executive constellation. It is important to understand why management might fail to promote autonomy.

MOTIVATIONS FOR PROMOTING
AUTONOMOUS FUNCTIONING

Often managers use their followers to fill narcissistic voids or to repair fragmented self systems. When managers promote dependency, they are reacting to the fear of autonomy; they may fear that employees will leave them, or that they will be devalued in some manner. Con-

---

[5]The ideal executive constellation functions in the same manner as the stereotypical traditional family. This CEO is responsible for management of the external boundaries of the organization, spending most of his/her time outside in the environment creating a continuous supply of resources entering the organization, keeping out noxious stimuli, and increasing certainty that outputs are of acceptable quality. The internal manager, the vice president, stays home and manages the internal life of the organization. This arrangement is carefully followed in Japanese corporations where the CEO spends 80% of his time outside the organization. In U.S. companies, the percentage is reversed. This may account for differences in success between the companies.

sequently, dependency relations are created out of fear and anxiety. As stated before, employees may unconsciously wish for dependency relations, and these wishes may be projected onto the organization's leadership. These projections may coincide with a manager's fantasy to be a savior. To obtain a gratification of this fantasy, the manager will unconsciously undermine the employees' attempts at autonomy and create situations in which he/she can function as a savior. This manager will use an employee's vulnerability as an opportunity for self-aggrandizement. Additionally, this manager may see an employee's wish for autonomy as a rejection, which may precipitate a depressive response, bringing about withdrawal. The manager may also respond with rage to the experience of being hurt, resulting in negative evaluations and devaluation.

The degree to which a manager uses or needs his/her employees to fill some psychic deficits or to contain some intrapsychic conflicts will be directly related to the degree to which the manager promotes dependency and fears autonomy. The greater the degree of psychopathology in the manager, the more profound will be the nature of the dependency relations. Even a manager who, on the surface, is viewed by subordinates as depressed, detached, not involved in his/her work, and incapable of creating dependency relations, may in actuality promote dependency by creating an environment of empathy and concern, or an environment of hatred of disgust, or may seek employment in an organization in which the structure of the organization (its rules, regulations, etc.) demands dependency. The same may be true for a gregarious boss, who loves challenges, rewards risks and appears to promote autonomy. This superior may structure these relationships in such a manner that information is never given to the degree that the employees can completely function on their own; the employees must always return for more information, thereby promoting dependency. Or the superior may unconsciously give erroneous or ambiguous information and subtly undermine the employees' autonomous functioning. The superior is then required to "ride in on his white horse" to save the day, which further increases the idea that employees cannot function on their own, that they need their superior.

Now let us return to the task–sentient merger and the way it reduces autonomous functioning. Often superiors respond to the mergence of the task–sentient systems by offering an activity that essentially splits the merged systems. For example, a superior, responding to his department for engaging in what he describes as a "helluva job," offers to take his employees out for dinner and drinks, as a reward. This offer produces two negative responses. First, it increases the visibility of the superior's authority and creates a situation in which the employees now experience coercion; they have to go out with the boss. In addition, the invitation politicizes the work environment, and several employees feel that they now have to be entertained by the boss. Second, and more important, the invitation splits the task–sentient system, which the employees had just experienced as merged. The employees had just completed a task and they experienced euphoria; the reward the employees experienced was inherent in the work. When the boss takes the employees away from work for a "reward," he unconsciously communicates to them his belief that the work does not offer the reward. It would have been far better for the boss to thank his employees for helping him look good and doing a good job. Instead, his act, the equivalent of saying "now let's go have some fun," suggests that joy cannot be obtained within the task system. Often superiors unconsciously create a split in the task–sentient systems because they seek to be in control. The work offers such a high degree of gratification that it increases the possibility that the employees will continue to work with a high degree of autonomy, and the superior is threatened by their move away from him/her.

The task–sentient system mergence is a delicate psychic collaboration. Most employees are more comfortable with a split and would rather devote their energies to dealing with the dynamics that result from a split. Management can easily rupture the merger, and they often tamper with this delicate balance. The following case is an example of how management destroyed the task–sentient mergence and the consequences that required a consultation to correct.

CASE ANALYSIS

This case is a consultation to a college, an organization that has traditionally valued subsystem autonomy which is firmly embedded in its academic culture. It is a highly technical organization, where employees have undergone lengthy socialization in their respective professions. The employees—the faculty—demonstrate allegiance to their discipline and professional associations and department. Because of the highly technical nature of their discipline, research is performed autonomously, with some exceptions where disciplines collaborate and research mentees engage in collective work. The task of teaching requires autonomous functioning, and it is common for a faculty member to teach a course for decades without supervision or administrative intrusion.

Autonomy is protected by the tenure system and by unions or professional associations. The sentient system is perhaps stronger than in most professional groups. In addition, due to the strong socialization process, namely, graduate school, the faculty members are emotionally identified with the work of their respective profession. This bond is established early on in the career and matures over time as the employee seeks status within his discipline. The faculty member is generally a member of two strong sentient groups, his/her department and profession, and sentient gratifications are generally obtained from activities within these two groups. As stated earlier, if a strong sentient life is found within the boundaries of the task system, it will produce a productive faculty employee in the areas of scholarship and teaching. If the sentient system is split from the task system, the work of the task system will suffer and scholarship productivity will be lowered.

This case points to how a management group, while publicly stating that they wished to maintain autonomy among departments within the college, unconsciously created the opposite. The case explores how policy changes promoted dependency and how policy shifts played havoc with the sentient life of the faculty.

Description of the Problem

The consultation was to the graduate school at a small but well-established private university. The provost of the professional school made initial contact with the consultant, and said that the budgeting process had "broken down and help was needed in the design of a better budgeting process." The consultant arranged a meeting with the provost and the vice president of administrative affairs. Collectively they described the present budget process.

The budget for each school was created by the executive constellation of the university: the president, the vice president for administrative affairs and academic officers, which included all the deans and the provost. The annual budget was based on income from tuition, grants, gifts, and a small endowment. Expenditures included faculty salaries, administrative costs, and operational costs. In the past, the deans of the respective schools would submit an annual budget to the executive constellation, who would assume the title of budget committee during the budget-creating process. These budgets were originally created as a result of a series of meetings between a dean and his/her department chairs.

Department Budget Meetings—Preparing for Battle

The dean's budgetary meetings were sessions in which each department head presented the department's needs, a wish list along with a rationale for funds. The intention of these meetings was to promote openness and equity among the various departments. However, because there was little relationship between the outcomes of these meetings and the actual budget created by the executive constellation, these meetings were viewed by department heads as nothing but a plea for money and the development of a competitive strategy to increase allocation of funds by taking from other departments or schools. The department heads discussed the history of budget allocation process and described its results in terms of inequity and envy. The meetings also were also viewed as attempts to enlist the dean in a battle for increased funds, or at least for more than other schools received. The dean was prepped to go into battle to get more for his/her troops. If the dean failed, then the dean was accused of not being "tough enough." In their own defense, the deans described the process as political and they shifted the blame onto the higher-level officers. Thus, meetings took the form of preparation for battle, the battle of the budget, where members discussed strategies in light of past victories and successes.

The perception of inequity and the feeling that the process was one of a political nature had to do with the manner in which the executive constellation distributed funds. The distribution often had little or no relationship to the budgets outlined by the departments and presented by the deans. One example of this has to do with the relationship between income produced and expenditures. Those schools with a large number of students felt that the "full-time equivalent" (FTE) approach was necessary, where the budget ought to bear on the numbers of full-time students enrolled. These schools believed that the quality of their work was reflected in their ability to attract students and that they ought to be rewarded for this effort. Another school maintained that the FTE approach was valid, but the formula for a budget must include the amount of grant money received and scholarly output. The rationale was that the amount of grant money received contributed to the prestige of the institution and ought to be rewarded. The school of arts believed that although its FTE students had dwindled over the years, and its ability to bring in grant money was limited because of the nature of the profession, it was a vital part of the institution and must grow to maintain the intellectual and scholarly atmosphere. To grow was in keeping with the cultural values of the academy. In effect, this school maintained a critical view of the professional schools, calling them "nothing but vocational schools, which come and go."

Each school articulated its rationale and sent its deans off to bring back a victory. This resulted in a year-end war, which culminated at a general faculty meeting with the provost after the budgets were announced. The meeting turned into a heated, violent confrontation over the budget, where yelling and rage resulted in punches being thrown. The consultant was called in after the event.

Two major problems were isolated. The first concerned the process of distributing funds. While the president had hoped that the budgetary process would increase participation, the process of shifting decision making downward in the hierarchy resulted in the opposite effect. It failed because the president failed to give up authority, the delegation was a mirage, and the lack of clarity led to perceptions among lower-order participants that the budgeting system was inequitable. In addition, while hoping for autonomy, the president had actually increased dependency.

The second problem was the process of inviting faculty into the budgetary process, which had a negative impact on the task–sentient system mergence. The delicate balance of this merger was upset when faculty began to feel that the budget had no relationship to their work, that the process was political, and that faculty output, which had previously been within the domain of the task–sentient system, was now outside this system and moved within the budgetary process. In effect, increasing faculty involvement in the budgetary process, created the illusion that monetary rewards would be merged within the task–sentient system. Failure to then reward task effort created a split. The following exemplifies this situation.

The school of education had experienced a significant drop in enrollment. The school had not made or been awarded any grant applications, and had a complacent faculty, all of whom were tenured and aloof from the institution. In spite of this, the school was given an ample supply of funds. The executive constellation concluded that even though this school was near death and had been in this situation for quite some time, it needed additional funds not only to keep it alive but to bolster its efforts and image. They believed this would get the school of education out of its doldrums. However, the faculty in the productive schools of science, business, and human service could not fathom a reasonable explanation for this decision and assumed that because the provost was a member of the school of education the decision was made for political reasons. Also, the decision seemed to be made in a manner that excluded productivity; if productivity was included, then the process in effect rewarded low productivity. As one faculty member stated, "It's good to be unproductive here, and god help you if you are productive, you get treated as an orphan."

Diagnosis

A major problem for any organization that wishes to promote autonomous functioning occurs when delegated decision making is either unclear or deceptive. In this university, the culture historically valued autonomous functioning. Because of the uncertainty concerning the delegation of the budgetary process, the process itself promoted dependency. This process of having schools and the provost prepare a budget and a rationale, and then having the executive constellation hand out funds in the form of "allowances," was in opposition to the organization's intention. The process promoted dependency by placing faculty into the role of children, dependent on the parents to "give allowances." The experience was further compounded by the faculty's view that the decision-making process was a function of backroom bargaining, a room they were not permitted to enter.

As stated earlier, to maintain task–sentient mergence requires that the institution be clear about where it wishes to place its organization on a hypothetical continuum of autonomy to dependency. At the university, the task–sentient mergence was founded on and supported by an autonomous structure, which was supported by the institution's long-standing culture. The failure of the budgetary process and of the executive constellation to adequately delegate authority tampered with the autonomous structure. This failure resulted in a break in the task–sentient merger. Evidence of the break was found in the absence of interdisciplinary collaboration in research, no joint teaching, and a lowering of scholarly output in all departments. Faculty found themselves joining new subgroups that were against the administration and its policies in varying degrees. Old friendships and working alliances were strained and colleagues found themselves on opposite sides of budgetary issues.

After carefully assessing the situation, the consultant decided that a total system intervention was required. Merely suggesting to the executive constellation that they change the budgetary process would not work because of the damage that existed, primarily damage to the faculty's valued autonomy. Focusing on the executive constellation would not have contributed to autonomy. Consequently, the nature of the intervention was to restore the experience of autonomy among the faculty.

Intervention

The aim of the intervention was to move the institution from its dependency structure back to an autonomous structure. The intervention focused on the faculty's rage at the administration, and an attempt was made to utilize this rage to move toward autonomy. According to Bennis and Shepard (1956), "for a group to move from dependency to autonomy a revolt is a necessary requirement" (p. 4). The revolt usually takes the form of aggressive projections onto the organization's leadership. A revolt usually has unifying results in that it will bring the faculty together in an activity that has a powerful emotional base. In addition, a revolt has an organizing influence because it stimulates social interaction and requires the creation of rules and structure. The leadership of an organization generally sees any form of employee revolt as negative. Leadership usually reacts to revolt with fear and anxiety and will attempt to extinguish it by increasing rules and regulations and tightening control. Therefore, the second aspect of this intervention was to minimize the leadership's reaction to the revolt and to minimize the expected response, an aggressive and harsh reaction. This was accomplished by pointing out to the executive constellation that if they attempted to stifle the revolt, it would lead to greater conflict.

The faculty revolt was characterized by paranoid ideation where the faculty engaged in a "splitting" process whereby they projected "bad" parts of their experience onto the leadership. This occurred at a general faculty meeting where the executive constellation was openly condemned. Unity was created among all faculty members, except for a few, and they agreed that they must "take over" the budgetary process. A committee was formed and after a series of meetings with the executive constellation, the faculty had convinced the executive constellation that the faculty had the right to demand a restructuring of the budget committee. This restructuring increased the total membership in favor of the faculty and created the perception among the faculty that the executive constellation had their power significantly reduced.

From a psychoanalytic perspective, the consultant conceptualized the revolt as moving the faculty from a preoedipal to an oedipal position, and this allowed the emergence of an actual struggle for power. If the conflict had remained as a preoedipal conflict, the faculty would have remained in a depressive position and dependency would have increased. Also, given the passivity and the enduring frustrations at the hands of the executive constellation, it is quite likely the faculty would have eventually identified with the frustrator and promoted what Anna Freud (1936) called an "identification with the aggressor." This would have increased the task–sentient split because it would have reduced the faculty's "assimilative capacities." Aggression would eventually be displaced onto the student population.

Conceptually, the revolt is considered an oedipal manifestation. Over time, the conflict matured and in doing so allowed the faculty to developmentally advance as a group. The conflict, as an oedipal conflict, was not seen as defensive: It was viewed as a joyous growth experience. This is common in group conflicts of this nature. It allowed the faculty to return to their experience of autonomy. Maturationally the conflict allowed the faculty to experience themselves "as being in the adult world," as opposed to being in a passive, dependent, "childlike" position. Being in a childlike position results in shame and humiliation and the ultimate loss of self-esteem, which hampers the experience associated with the ego ideal. When this ideal is harmed, the individual finds it impossible to devote the necessary psychic energy to activate talents and skills, and the task and sentient systems are split.

Management and Change

Through its [the corporation's] primary concern for increased effectiveness, economic growth, rationalization, automation and world wide competition this seems to be devoted exclusively to the principles of the Olympic games: faster, higher, wider!
—BURKARD SIEVERS (1990, p. 89).

Considering the power of psychoanalysis to comprehend what goes on in the organization, this book has merely scratched the surface. The areas in which psychoanalysis can be intelligently applied to work and organizations are endless. For example, additional areas include decision making, work group or committees, communications, creativity and innovation, strategy and planning, leadership, ethics, conformity and rebellion, security and safety, ambition and motivation, career choice, retirement, performance, cooperation and conflict, corporate culture and identity, failure at work, corporate crisis, organizational expansion, growth and change, male–female relations, race and ethnicity, loyalty and commitment, the informal structure, power and politics, rewards and punishment, learning, termination and retirement, satisfaction, and the impact the organization and its exigencies has on the mental health of the employee.

Of all of the possible areas in which psychoanalysis can be applied, the following six guideposts—boundary maintenance and regulation, task analysis, authority, role acquisition, interorganizational relations, and dependent and autonomous structures—were chosen because they capture the broad-based areas of organizational, interpersonal, and intrapersonal dysfunctioning and they are amenable to psychoanalytic application. However, they are not conclusive; that is, it would be foolish to suggest that all a consultant needs to do is to focus on one of these guideposts and the intervention will succeed. They are merely conceived of as a help to the psychoanalytic thinker in providing a framework within which to think psychoanalytically about the problem(s) at hand.

It is also apparent that the cases used to support and clarify each guidepost are time-bounded consultations; that is, they are vignettes of relatively brief interventions. Unfortunately, they do not have a developmental or long-term analytic focus. A psychoanalytic consultation over a period of years would contribute greatly to our understanding of how organizations evolve and how they make crucial decisions that affect their life course. It is reasonable to assume that such a consultation would alter the nature of any intervention and would most certainly add to our understanding of the psychodynamic processes involved at work.

In addition, if the organization were viewed in a manner that resembles society, a long-term consultation would contribute to our understanding of the factors that influence the development of the organization's culture, which is considered the most significant factor in contributing to dysfunction and to how the organization perceives the dysfunction and goes about dealing with it.

EXPLAINING PSYCHOANALYSIS

How psychoanalysis can function as a method to understand work and the organization is of interest primarily to two audiences: the business student and the psychoanalyst. The business student needs the highly technical psychoanalytic concepts explained with clarity, and the psychoanalyst needs to understand the relevancy of the major conceptual leaps that are made between clinical theory and organizational theory. For example, a topic in which both business students and psychoanalysts show a considerable amount of interest is: Why does an employee who has achieved success, and is the envy of others, go into a sudden depression, start drinking excessively, or act in ways that hurt the corporation and ruin his/her career? We know that the unconscious influences these actions. But just what triggers the spiraling, inappropriate behaviors is unclear.

The tragedy associated with success is not a recent phenomenon; for example, Kubie (1961) refers to it as an ancient tragedy of human nature and he deplores the frequency with which it occurs among scientists and business leaders. It may very well be that everyone has unconscious goals, and it may be that the fantasies that bring these goals to life are buried in our unconscious. We also know that it is part of human nature to be self destructive and that a number of unconscious patterns and ideas buried within are associated with the wish to bring ruination upon us.

It is a rare employee, but nonetheless one whom we hold in high esteem, who says no to a promotion or a chance at "success." Some may find this employee cowardly, but most would say he is indeed a reasonable person for he knows his limitations, he knows what makes him happy, he knows he doesn't need the stress, albeit, he knows himself. On the other hand, we also know those employees who dream of success and possess what is referred to as "blind ambition." They are going somewhere; they seek the "fast track." It is this motivation, called "winning," that takes on pathological proportions and functions as a "driven" quality. These driven ambitions are thought to be nothing more than unconscious defensive styles or characterological styles, which are utilized to protect the self system from fears. Just what these fears are is difficult to determine. It would be foolish to suggest that they are simply fear of failure, fear of poverty, or fear of feeling inadequate. These problems lie much deeper in the employee's psyche. Just as the employee who has achieved success then begins to "fall apart," the employee who defends against failure may very well be suffering from the same fears.

Psychoanalytic theory has established that what lies at the basis of these fears is the fear of loneliness and abandonment. Just as the employee will avoid success because it unconsciously brings forth the fear of loneliness, the ambitious employee may be motivated by the same fear. Psychoanalytic theory has established that the fears associated with loneliness and isolation from other people have dire consequences for both physical and psychological health. In the famous infant studies by Spitz (1945), he showed that infants who were hospitalized and left unattended, not handled or stimulated by caretakers, developed "marasmus," an apathetic state, and many of the infants died. This study pointed to the power of being connected to others.

The executive who falls apart in the face of success is responding to the unconscious fear that success will elicit alienation, rejection, or hatred from friends and family. The work of seeking success is motivated by the unconscious wish that the effort will bring love. The more lofty the goal, the more an idealized love will be obtained. The attainment of love is connected to the effort, not to the actual success. Consider often-heard comments at cocktail parties by executives who have achieved success. They seem to have a need to discuss the "good old days," where they describe their struggles to "climb the ladder";

often, they turn to their spouse and say with a sense of pride, "Remember when we were struggling to make it and we didn't have a pot." The often-heard comment from Ivy Leaguers, "fight the good fight," is essentially a glorification of the effort. They do not say "win the good fight" because this way of thinking expresses the shame associated with winning and the underlying fear that one will be hated for doing so. These and other unconscious motivations form the basic substance of one's connection with work and the ill-fated consequences associated with both success and failure.

The expectation associated with a book of this nature is that through illumination of these "dark" forces, management and labor theorists, and those who consult to work and the organization, can increase their chances of improving conditions at work. The premise here is that improving conditions at work will only come through increasing self-knowledge. Techniques, educational programs, and interventions will fail if they do not consider this position. Only through self-knowledge can one understand why one works, why one chooses a specific occupation, why one "turns red" with rage when a certain employee speaks, why one hates to get up each morning to go to work, or why one cannot agree with another. Furthermore, only through a psychoanalytic understanding can one obtain a deeper, more comprehensive knowledge of the dynamic processes involved in work. Acquiring this knowledge gives the employee an opportunity to overcome the pathology that comes with the "darkness" of the absence of knowledge, and the misdirection that come from a lack of insight. More important, psychoanalytic knowledge stimulates an appreciation of the complexities associated with work and gives the theorist, student, and employee a greater capacity to tolerate its ambiguities.

AMBIGUITY AND WORK

The major problem that graduate students face when they enter the job market is that what they learned in school, all the answers and applications, does not seem to work. They become impatient with corporate life and they personalize it in the form of job dissatisfaction and a pattern of frequent job changes. The reason for this is that in school, they are not taught how to tolerate the ambiguities associated with work and organizational life. They do not have a sense of what it is to be patient at work and they have not yet acquired an appreciation for that which they do not know. They do not study organizational phenomena to the point where they can think about the nature of the questions asked. They become solution oriented, and they soon realize that their solutions do not work because they have not taken the time to ask the right questions. The question *why* is avoided with a constant refrain, fix it.

To tolerate ambiguity one requires understanding. Psychoanalysis as a depth psychology reaches into the complex nature of the human psyche, and at work this complexity dramatically increases. It is the very nature of psychoanalysis that requires an appreciation of the defenses that stifle learning and limit awareness. Consequently, psychoanalytic understanding requires an appreciation of complexity. As such, it is required to be a slow, deliberate, cautious, and at times cumbersome process. Consider a student who says, "I hate my boss." It marks the beginning of a journey into an analysis of the situation and of the student's experience. This is exceedingly difficult and typically the student will utilize defenses to avoid analyzing that which feels uncomfortable. If the student has been exposed to psychoanalytic theory he/she may experience the task of conducting an analysis with less anxiety. Having less anxiety will ultimately increase the student's capacity to engage in the type of learned intuitive efforts necessary to conduct an analysis. Consequently, the student will appreciate ambiguity and not run from it, he/she will find complexity engaging and not frightening, and will tolerate unique, strange, and difficult situations.

This is in direct contrast to how business schools conceive of the learning process. Here the student is generally expected to understand organizational functioning as having a "correct," as opposed to an "incorrect," way. The focus is on solutions and the correct answers. This type of teaching leads to nothing more than a superficial understanding of the organization and work. It is folly to believe that if the student learns 14 points, 10 methods, 6 factors, etc., he/she will be able to understand why some things do not work. The closest business schools come to conducting an in-depth analysis are in two types of courses: those devoted to case analysis and self-management/leadership types of courses.

In case analysis courses, students cover a number of cases and present solutions within a limited period of time. The efficacy of this method of teaching is in the suitability of the students' solutions to a particular problem. Typically, students present an array of solutions and the professor comments on or criticizes each solution. The professor then proposes the "correct one." The focus is on answers; the questions, or at least groping for the right question, are rarely explored. Sometimes the questions are given by the professor, with help from the textbook. This process is typically replicated in the "real world," in the organization, where little thought is given to the question(s) and instead employees charge ahead, seeking solutions. When they fail to find an adequate solution, rarely do they say, "Well maybe we asked the wrong question." Instead, they ask the same question over and over again, and each time the solution fails. In psychoanalytic terms this is referred to as the compulsion to repeat. These predictable, consistent and repetitious patterns can be changed only if different and perhaps uncomfortable questions are asked. However, these types of questions increase anxiety; consequently they are avoided.

Psychoanalysis is a field in which one is expected to grapple with questions. Its propensity for insight and "going deep" implies that the questions one initially asks should change if the analysis is being done correctly. Asking only one question and then seeking a solution invariably brings a false solution. The answer to the initial question is less important as a vehicle to a specific answer than it is as a vehicle to raise other, more sophisticated and anxiety-producing questions. In psychoanalytic thinking, the complexity of the search increases as the analyst seeks answers to interconnecting questions, which lead to more and more interconnecting questions, which then may lead to the final or end point, a point where there is no correct question and no correct answer. It is the exercise itself, the insight itself, and the illumination itself, that will bring about the change and a reduction in the symptoms that once were perceived as bothersome. If business schools were to explore cases in this manner, they would increase appreciation of the complexities of organizational life and bring joy to the processes of exploration and insight, instead of fear and intimidation.

In the more personal courses, where self-knowledge is promoted, students are taught self-management, or "stress management," techniques. This is sometimes referred to as self-control and is defined by Thorensen and Mahoney (1974) as that which an employee displays when "in the relative absence of immediate external constraints, he engages in behavior whose previous probability has been less than that of alternatively available behaviors" (p. 83). Manz and Sims (1980) use Mischel's (1973) description of self-control as a behavior that "may include personal goals, self-instructions towards achieving goals, self-administered consequences, and plans for one's behavior patterns" (Manz & Sims, p. 87).

As in case analysis courses, self-management courses invariably defeat any attempt on the students' part to engage in an analysis.

These courses are solution oriented; they focus on everything from breathing techniques to reduce stress to how to calm down an angry boss. In short, they are nothing more than a convoluted shortcut toward nirvana. As a consequence, they diminish the student's appreciation for complexity and the ambiguity associated with work. Also, they fail to introduce the student to the possibility that things can get better through the process of insight and knowledge.

UNDERSTANDING CHANGE FROM A PSYCHOANALYTIC PERSPECTIVE

In the early 1970s, criticism began to mount of U.S. management methods. Management methods were deemed incapable of success in a changing international environment that required innovation, entrepreneurialship, and the management of complexity in increasingly large organizations. Since then, these once valued methods of managing corporations have given way to styles promoted largely by the Japanese and secondarily by the Europeans.

In the face of demands to adopt "new" management styles, U.S. managers have been accused of overmanaging, conservativism, inflexibility, and bureaucratic languor (Burgelman & Sayles, 1986). Managers have been accused of exerting too much control in the workplace. In the literature on organizations, the current trends are minimizing control, making the structure more horizontal, and promoting autonomous functioning, which are supposed to create a more innovative and cooperative work environment. These trends have inspired the emergence of writers who offer "quick fix" solutions. Writers such as Peters and Waterman (1982), Ouchi (1981), Kanter (1983), Deal and Kennedy (1984), and Kilman et al. (1988), have offered broad-stroke approaches and theoretical frameworks. By suggesting change without a careful analysis of internal dynamics, they are creating the same problems that typically plague managers. Internal dynamics require careful analysis because not only do they contribute to the dysfunction, they ultimately add to or detract from any efforts to change the organization. Furthermore, the ideas of these writers are based on an ideal, and the work necessary to understand and explain how to overcome the resistance necessary to achieve their ideal is unclear. In short, their ideal appears to be an organization in which control is dismantled, and replaced by a cooperative, supportive, quality-oriented, proud team of employees. Getting to that point or to any innovative ideal ought to be the scope of their efforts, not merely the description of an ideal state.

The psychoanalytic position maintains that reaching any ideal is exceedingly problematic. This is consistent with the dim view psychoanalysts have of the notion that an ideal state of mental health can be attained. Psychoanalysts assumes that any effort to bring about change must first focus on an understanding of the nature of the phenomena that are to be changed. This is a vital exercise before change can occur. It requires an understanding of the forces that prohibit change and leads to apathy, conservativism, inflexibility, and increased bureaucracy. Typically, employees adhere to a particular mode of operation, even though it may be counterproductive, because it serves some unconscious motivations. This view is especially relevant when we consider the type of change current theorists favor. In essence, they suggest a second-order change, a change in the basic structure of an employee's values and beliefs and the way they perceive the workplace and obtain gratifications. Without insight into, or an appreciation of, the complexities associated with both conscious and unconscious motivations, it is doubtful whether this type of change will succeed.

Consider the following example: Organizational theorists typically define power as having something to do with controlling the work environment. For example, Pfeffer and Salancik (1978) suggest that if employees can organize and control the allocation of resources, they have power. Power is synonymous with getting things done, and it is also defined as controlling such resources as money, time, staffing, and information. The preoccupation, almost the obsession, with control in the modern workplace has shifted in recent years away from its more human interactional aspects toward "colder" and more remote forms of control such as electronic computational monitoring. Control is now deemed to be a necessary ingredient for the outcome of efficiency and effectiveness. Quality consultants now emphasize technical/statistical control rather than interpersonal control. They claim this new form of control is more desirable. However, whether the desire for control is interpersonal or statistical, the unconscious motivations are the same, essentially a defensive process.

For example, the motivation for the control of information may be a function of the desire for power, but it is also a function of the wish to keep information that is potentially destructive away from others. In this instance, enhancing control is an attempt to manage secrets, to hide information, or to keep information from leaking out. One sees ample evidence of this attempt within the political arena, where elected officials are more interested in protecting the boundaries around information than they are in understanding or analyzing the information. An analysis of the events that lead to these motivations would suggest that they are paranoid responses and are typical in contemporary workplaces. Control, namely, monitoring and evaluating, typically displaces fear and anxiety in management on to their employees. Now contemporary theorists suggest that employees give up the competition for scarce resources and cease in their desire to manifest control. These statistical control consultants also claim that each individual worker controls his own quality-related work activities. This requires a higher level of ego functioning, not only from management, but from all employees. They suggest a radical shift away from the current legalistic–paternalistic structure toward a cooperative structure. But one cannot make such a shift without first answering the question: What about the issue of scarcity of resources?

As Freud says, the struggles and conflicts experienced in adult life center around scarcity. Mastery of these struggles begins in childhood, as one learns how to "get," how to "share," and how to accept "not getting." It is folly even to propose the creation of a cooperative organizational structure without an examination of the modal characterological styles we as a society value, and hold as we participate in the struggle for scarce resources. Engaging successfully in all structures requires certain types of ego capacities. At this point, we do not know what types of ego capacities would work within what types of structures. Until we do know, suggesting an ideal structure is futile. While it is enviable to propose a cooperative organization as an ideal, it will not work as long as those who occupy superior positions "get more" than those who occupy subordinate positions. The fact that American CEOs receive more than 160 to 250 times the salary of their lowest-level subordinate suggests that we have a long way to go before we can hope to reach an equitable, cooperative, self-controlling workplace.

To varying degrees, all organizations seek control. Asking management to reduce or give up control would be met with heightened resistance. Many theorists suggest that factors such as environmental events, the organization's technology, and job satisfaction are major contributors to the motivation to increase control. This book suggests that these factors and others are merely symptoms associated with control and are not sufficient to explain this motivation.

The psychodynamic explanation for manifesting increased control has focused on three possible factors. From the Freudian perspective, control is used to thwart or renounce the instincts. The object relation school suggests that control is used to reduce the anxiety associated with paranoid and depressive affects which arise when people work closely in hierarchical systems. And the self psychology position suggests that control is used to maintain narcissistic equilibrium under potentially injurious conditions.

All these approaches suggest that the environment and its failure to promote an optimal gratifying environment will activate the wish for increased control. It would seem that given the hierarchical nature of organizations and their propensity for passing judgment on those who occupy subordinate positions, control would naturally increase over time; that is, there is a natural propensity for control in the hierarchical organization. In these organizations, Gouldner's position holds up rather well: that employees attempt to evade control by using self-protective devices to thwart their superior's attempts to keep them (subordinates) in childlike, dependent, and powerless positions. This precipitates the following type of conflicts: Employees will attempt to overcome the subordination process by actively seeking and pushing to enter into management positions. Given the organization's hierarchical nature and scarce resources, this attempt creates a Darwinian contest in which the organization and many employees will ultimately lose.

THE WORK OF MANAGEMENT AND ITS IMPACT ON THE TECHNOLOGICAL CORE

Consider the following observation: Over the past several years, large numbers of engineering students seek to leave the engineering field for management positions. When asked why they are pursuing an MBA degree, they typically respond by saying that they see no future as an engineer. They claim that the managers have the big offices, big salaries, perks, and status. That is what they want. Can one blame them? Many suggest that in spite of the fact that they truly love engineering, they feel they must advance into management to "make it." Why is this the case? Why are thousands of educated and competent engineers and scientists enrolled in MBA programs?

Engineering or high-technology organizations are typical of U.S. companies in that they establish hierarchical structures that are heavily management oriented. While management structures provide ample opportunity for advancement, the technological core is structurally flat and provides little opportunity for advancement. Managerial and support structures are vertical. This means that promotions and rewards are more readily apparent within the managerial/support structures. These managerial jobs are the jobs that control the organization's information and have a greater share of the organization's resources. Because of their manifest authority and perceived power, management as it presently exists devalues the technological core. Consequently, those who work within the core, the engineers, will seek escape. The problem lies not just with management but with the ancillary or support services. Ideally, one would expect both management and support services to support and devote their energies to making work within the technological core easy and gratifying (task–sentient fusion), but this is rarely the case. Hundreds of examples can be offered where these nontechnological/managerial offices take on importance, status, and a life of their own, and in doing so actually constrain and stifle the efforts of those who work in the technological core.

Thus, engineers seek to escape the technological core and become management because they experience a devaluation.

An informal analysis of 20 organizations suggests that the violation of an employee's capacity to work within the technological core is quite common. The results suggest that 80% of those who report that their capacity to work has been violated are located within the technological core. The consequences of this violation create the experience of a general degradation and devaluation of one's work. How and why does this occur?

MOTIVATIONS FOR VIOLATING THE WORK WITHIN THE TECHNOLOGICAL CORE

When employees in the technological core see administration/management "get more" (e.g., status, perks, and salary), they feel devalued. They know they achieved a lot by studying engineering or the given technology in which they work. They also believe that their work is important for the life of the company; it is the company's heart and soul. The belief that work in the technological core is important and vital begins in college. Typically technologists such as engineers and computer scientists, for example, look down at the business school students. They see them as taking easy courses and as not being as "smart." But when these business students graduate and enter the business world, the technologists face hard realities. They see these same students as "getting more." A placard exhibited during the graduation ceremony of business school students and directed toward engineering students read, "Someday we will be your boss."

This conflict between management and technologists begins long before one joins an organization, and it is most likely a function of the long history of business in this country. For example, these attitudes and conflicts may be a function of class distinctions that are a holdover from the industrial revolution, and are described in metaphors such as "blue-collar worker" and "white-collar worker," or of the idea that management "thinks" and the worker "labors." In today's workplace this distinction is blurred because the nature of work has dramatically changed. Work has increasingly required thinking, as opposed to physical effort. Work relies more on machines to take care of physical toil. This has freed all workers to engage in thinking work. Management no longer has the exclusive responsibility for doing all the thinking. This is especially apparent in today's high-tech organizations, which require innovation and risk taking in product design and venture.

The psychoanalyst views management's responses to this changing technological workplace as motivated by the wish to hold on to their status and positions. This wish is fraught with problems and potential conflict. Essentially, management is attempting to hold on to an old, outmoded structure. But why is this the case? Why is management driven to hold on to an outmoded structure and unable to give up their positions in favor of a less hierarchical structure? In U.S. business, management makes decisions and holds on to an inequitable share of the organization's scarce resources. To entertain an alternative, until recently, has been unthinkable.

BUREAUCRATIZATION OF HEALTH CARE

An ongoing debate continues between those who believe managers ought to be knowledgeable about the organization's technology and those who believe that professional managers are sufficient. It appears that the professional managers are winning the debate. An example of this is manifested in the health care field. In the 1960s, professional managers with no medical training moved into management positions. Today, most health care administrators do not have medical training. As nonmedical managers and those with financial training have accumulated more and more authority, physicians, unlike engineers, have responded by seeking more resources. Physicians have demanded an increase in fees for service and have further increased their technological domain. The physicians are responding to a loss of status and a threat from professional managers. Conflict has resulted and the physicians are responding by seeking greater control over that which they know about, and management does not, technology. This has had a spiraling effect. The spiraling effect has caused a dramatic increase in health care costs, which has led to more management controls, now referred to as "managed health care." A vicious cycle has evolved where physicians seek increased status and greater areas of domain and management responds by seeking greater control. Management uses metaphors such as "cost containment," and physicians respond with their own metaphors such as "freedom to choose a physician" and "quality care." Physicians respond to management's attempts to increase management's status by promoting their own professionalism and professional autonomy.

According to Braverman (1984), when professional managers gain control they "assume the burden of gathering together all of the technological knowledge which in the past was processed by the worker [in this case physician] and then of classifying, tabulating, and reducing this knowledge to rules, laws and formulae . . ." (p. 80). This process of dissociating the labor process from the skills of the technical worker amounts to deprofessionalizing the worker. This is the chief aim of cost containment. As physicians are brought into "managed care" organizations (organizations run by professional managers), they complain that being employed in these organizations has lowered not only their economic status but their social status as well (Karmon, 1988). One would expect a lowering of income because this is the stated reason for organizing, but why are the physicians reporting lowered social status? They claim that they have lost their authority and independence to government officials, insurers, corporation managers, and hospital administrators. According to Roper (1987), a head of a Medicare program, "Physicians are pulling their hair out when bureaucrats like me tell them how to practice medicine" (p. 61). He goes on to say, "[I]n the future there will be even more regulations" (p. 6).

The bureaucratization of health care has destroyed the collegial environment to which physicians are accustomed and it has brought with it a centralization of authority where all the information flows upward. Management controls the efforts of the technologists in a variety of ways, all under the banner of cost containment. The collegial environment or team approach that physicians value threatens professional managers. Managers value the centralization of authority, and they see the team approach as inefficient, costly, and having the potential to increase ideological and political conflict.[1] Covertly

---

[1]In the United States, conflict between management and professional workers has rarely moved beyond being garrulous. Professionals fail to organize in spite of their collective roots because of memberships in professional societies, which Zwerling (1976) calls the foundation for elitism. Also, the inherent properties of bureaucratic control with its stratifications and redivision of workers make it difficult to organize (Edwards, 1984).

these managers see collegialism as a threat because it tends to bring workers together, and they fear the consequences of a strong team capable of exercising authority and power. Professional managers respond by seeking centralized authority, and they call it the most cost-efficient method of operating.

The centralization of authority also allows professional managers to keep their work secret from those who work within the technological core. Professional managers claim that they have knowledge that only they can understand. This knowledge is generally referred to by such names as "managerial technical expertise" or "operations research." These names are nothing more than an enlargement or increased sophistication of the intelligence function that goes with rapid information processing and planning as well as the development of appropriate technology to facilitate these functions (Burris & Heydebrand, 1984). Managers hide behind their flowcharts, computer data printouts, and classy presentations, and they seek to impress the technologists with the mysticism of this management technology. However, while this management technology can be impressive and organizationally useful, it is often unreliable and sometimes self-serving. Thus the conflict centers around that which each group values. This is a repetition of the management–labor conflict that has existed since the industrial revolution, but it has taken a different form.

If the physicians had not responded or engaged in conflict with the professional managers, to preserve their dignity and status, they would be in the same position that the engineers are now in, depressed and desirous of getting out of their chosen profession.

VALUING THE TECHNOLOGICAL CORE

Drucker, Zalesnik, and others call for a new type of corporate leader who is capable of motivating employees and getting highly trained professionals to work together in harmony. Consider Drucker's metaphor of the corporate leader as a "symphony conductor." He says that the leader who conceptualizes his/her role in this manner is in an optimal position to lead today's organizations. Drucker says that the corporate leader does not play the music but leads the musicians, the highly skilled experts. But, he/she must also know music. The corporate leader's knowledge of the technology not only wins the respect of his/her followers (technologists) but adds value to their profession.

If an employee from the technological core rises to the top, the likelihood increases that the core will be valued. Also, having one of them make it will instill a sense of hope in the others. It is this hope that is perhaps the most significant factor in determining motivation. When this hope is taken away, as with the example of the engineers, motivation is destroyed.

In addition, when the corporate leader does not know or cannot comprehend the organization's technology, he/she is wrought with anxiety and assumes a defensive position. The leader will respond to this experience of anxiety and powerlessness by seeking accoutrements. The corporate leader will seek to inflate his/her own sense of power with symbols, and most dramatically he/she will intrude into the technological core by imposing greater degrees of control and constraints on the technologists' capacity to work competently and autonomously. In other words, out of the experience of powerlessness, the corporate leader will undermine the technologists' work and devalue it.

Consider the following example: In a small engineering firm the founding father, himself an engineer, retired. He had built the company into a highly technological corporation with a considerable amount of respect from colleagues. The retiring CEO appointed his son as his replacement. Such a shift in authority is generally fraught with complexities; here it was compounded by the fact that the son knew little about the technology. He had flunked out of engineering school and transferred into a business school. With an undergraduate degree in business and an MBA, he was ill equipped to meet with the engineers and intelligently discuss their concerns, inventions, and product designs. He was lost and his subordinates knew it. This situation is common in today's corporations. CEOs and top-level managers are appointed to a position without knowledge of the technology. It is Drucker's equivalent of conducting a symphony while being unable to read a music score.

When one envisions the ideal leader, one assumes that he/she has technical knowledge. A CEO who knows the technology of the task is not only capable of loving the work but less prone to demonstrating narcissistic preoccupation with perceptions of threats and anxiety that come from not knowing. When the CEO does not know the technology, narcissistic concerns come to the fore, which in turn facilitates an atmosphere of stress. It significantly reduces the cooperation necessary to complete the task, which requires creativity, risk, and innovation.

In Japanese corporations the CEOs are often men who not only know the technology but began their career "in the trenches," building the company from a series of technological innovations. The opposite is true of U.S. companies, which rely on financial and marketing personnel to assume leadership roles.

If a CEO is knowledgeable of the complex technology, he/she is then capable of putting the interests of the task ahead of his/her own self-interests. When the CEO places the interests of the task above his/her own self interests he/she is perceived by personnel as having feelings for his/her followers and their work, of being empathic and concerned with what they are saying, doing, and feeling. As an engineer responded when visited by a CEO who was also an engineer, "He understands me, he knows what I'm going through."

We see ample evidence of professional managers assuming leadership positions in educational institutions. This began with our public school systems and it still continues today. As public educational systems grew, business leaders entered the business of educating on the local community level and then in the universities, and with them they brought general business practice and methods. It did not matter what type of businesses these managers were in, it was assumed that if they had been successful in one type of business they could apply this success to any other business. Therefore, bankers, manufacturing leaders, doctors, lawyers, and other business leaders were considered capable of leading educational institutions. After all, they believed that what counted were leadership talents and knowledge of basic business practice. In almost all cases where these business leaders assumed managerial authority over educational systems, they brought with them the management skills laid down by F. W. Taylor and others from the school of scientific management. The aim of this school was twofold: (1) to increase production through rountinization of the technology, and (2) to create an executive constellation who were responsible for defining roles, responsibilities, and duties. Burris and Heydebrand (1984) describe the impact of bringing professional management, or what they refer to as Taylorism, to our educational institutions:

> Early attempts to professionalize administration drew upon Taylorism and its rudimentary science of management. However, the crudity of Taylorism attempts to objectify educational outcomes and the compulsiveness with which Taylorism reformers tried to compensate for their lack of expertise aroused substantial faculty opposition and led to complaints that the university cannot follow the definite precise methods employed by the manufacturer. (p. 198)

Appointing professional managers who then apply business methods without knowledge of the technology leads to a deprofessionalization of those within the technological core. These professional managers exert control over the work force, reduce labor cost, increase consumer costs, and increase production. Their appointment has the iatrogenic consequences of de-skilling the work force, creating a demoralizing atmosphere and a situation where working within the technological core becomes a demeaning experience. As Morgan (1988) has pointed out, these scientific managers have "produced vast numbers of jobs of very uniform skill levels, the special characteristics of which can be quickly learned. One recent estimate suggests, that in some modern organizations, 87% of . . . workers exercise less skill in their jobs than they use driving to work" (p. 283).

FINDING A SOLUTION

We now reach the point of answering the difficult question: What can be done to return the organization to the technologists? As with many difficult questions, the answer may not be a satisfying one, especially to those who have the most to lose, those who occupy positions of authority. It seems evident that if we are to return U.S. industry to the forefront, we must restructure our organizations to a point where the technological core is valued. This restructuring is not so simple; it requires changing the basic attitudes and values of our society, especially among those who lead corporations. The following example demonstrates how difficult it will be to implement these ideas.

Several years ago I, consulted to a large state mental institution. The new CEO, a retired Army colonel, asked me to come in and discuss some management training programs. He felt that the staff was severely lacking in managerial skills. On a tour of the facilities we passed a man who appeared to be a patient, the CEO leaned toward me and whispered, "You won't believe this, but he is the chief psychiatrist." The man was shuffling down the hall, with old baggy pants, his front fly was half undone, his shirt was wrinkled, his tie undone, and his hair quite unruly. Later on, I discovered that this same man drove an old volkswagen with a fender missing and worked out of an office on the ward, which was the size of a large closet. Back at the CEO's ample office, the CEO reported that he was not only disgusted with the chief psychiatrist but with the staff in general. He wanted the chief psychiatrist out and he needed my help in shaping up the staff.

As I left the CEO, I made the following observations: The CEO was a likable, handsome man, well groomed, who had an exceptionally large office that was "spit and polished." But I was fascinated by this chief psychiatrist, and considering that the first official act of this new CEO would be to fire this man, I made an effort to find out more about this man. It was unanimously reported to me that the chief psychiatrist was a gifted clinician, that he was the only staff member who could break through to schizophrenics with ease, and he actually had a good record of successfully treating patients and sending them back home. This was unheard of in state institutions, where the most unskilled clinicians tend to congregate. The CEO was reported to be a man "obsessed" with order and discipline; he was given his position because he had a reputation of "straightening things out."

This example illustrates the folly of managing without knowledge of the technology. Without knowledge of the technology, management typically responds to the job with vulnerability and fear. They seek control as a desperate way of obtaining a psychological sense of security.

The CEO was determined to implement his ideas concerning the correct way to run an organization. In his zeal to "shape up" the staff, by terminating the most threatening figure, he established fear in others. This was a direct response to his own fear. The CEO knew nothing of clinical work; he was a retired military man. The technology threatened the CEO, the patients terrified him, and the psychiatrist symbolized this threat. All the psychiatrist wished to do was be left alone to do his work, that which he was good at and loved to do. But the CEO could not accommodate him; the psychiatrist, as with other staff, had to be "brought into line," which meant under the control of an insecure and threatened CEO.

The CEO wanted to fire the psychiatrist as a symbol of his toughness. However, this was not toughness at all; it was a representation of the fear that he would collapse and become a patient himself and would end up under the care or control of the chief psychiatrist.

This brief vignette demonstrates the anxiety and responses management experience when they are not knowledgeable of the work within the technological core. It also emphasizes the importance of valuing those who work within the technological core. In this case the chief psychiatrist should have had the big office; he was the valued employee in the organization, he knew the technology better than anyone. The role of the CEO should have been to serve this man, not the other way around. According to Fromm (1970), the assumption that management knows what to do to enhance a given technology in an organization is prevalent in the field of industrial management: "[W]hat is good for management is good for man, and what is good for man is good for managed institutions" (p. 166). Fromm (1970) goes on to say that there is an assumption of preestablished harmony between labor and management that is incorrect. He states that the "interests of management and that of man is [are] not harmonious" (p. 166), and he suggests that the interests of management will, consciously or unconsciously, stifle employees' self-expression, spontaneity, and the capacity to reach a potential in the interests of production, profit, expansion, and efficiency. This is not new. Sutherland (1990), in his analysis of organizational tasks, along with organizational theorists such as Trist and Rice, and others from the Tavistock Centre in England, as far back as the 1950s, found considerable flaws in the traditional organizational structures of hierarchical layers, with a leader at the top and levels of command. These theorists claim that these types of militaristic structures actually decreased opportunities for knowledge of the organization's technological task(s) and limited the organization's capacity to function as an adaptive learning system. They claim that these structures reduce the knowledge and skills required to do the work, as well as the required degrees of confidences and capacities to maintain satisfactory relations with their customers and publics. According to this group, the managerial-based organization does not lend itself to the creation of a permanently dynamic organization. On the contrary, it deadens the organization.

The CEO of the mental institution had an opportunity to build the institution by servicing and valuing those who worked within the technological core. His efforts could have gone toward increasing their status. He could have increased coordination and training of the ancillary subsystems to work for those within the technological core. Had he done so, the patients might have been helped and the organization might have flourished and he would have gained the respect of his employees.

References

Alderfer, C. (1972). *Change process in organizations.* Unpublished manuscript, Yale University, New Haven, CT.

Aldrich, H. (1971). Organizational boundaries and interorganizational conflict. *Human Relationns, 24,* 279–293.

Alinsky, S. (1959). *Reveille for radicals.* New York: Random House.

Anthony, E. (1970). Folie a deux. In E. Anthony & T. Benedeke (Eds.), *Parenthood: Its psychology and psychopathology* (pp. 571–595). Boston: Little, Brown.

Appelbaum, S. A. (1963). The pleasure and reality principles in group process teaching. *British Journal of Medical Psychology, 36,* 49–56.

Argyris, C. (1964). *Integrating the individual and the organization.* New York: Wiley.

Argyris, C. (1970). *Intervention theory and method.* Reading, MA: Addison-Wesley.

Arlow, J. (1969). Unconscious fantasy and disturbances of conscious experience. *Psychoanalytic Quarterly, 1,* 1–25.

Ashbach, C., & Schermer, V. L. (1987). *Object relations, the self, and the group.* New York: Routledge & Kegan Paul.

Astrachan, B. M., & Flynn, H. R. (1976). The intergroup excercise: A paradigm for learning about the development of organizational structure. In E. Miller (Ed.), *Task and organization* (pp. 47–68). New York: Wiley.

Baker, F. (1969). Open systems approach to the study of mental hospitals in transition. *Community Mental Health Journal, 5,* 403–412.

Balint, E. (1937). Early developmental states of the ego. *International Journal of Psychoanalysis, 30,* 265–273.

Bechland, H. (1971). Assessment of organizational development consulting. *Journal of Applied Behavioral Science, 7*(5), 557–567.

Beer, M., & Huse, E. F. (1972). A systems approach to organizational development. *Journal of Applied Behavioral Science, 8,*(1), 79–101.

Bendix, R. (1956). *Work and authority in industry.* New York: Wiley.

Bennis, W. (1962). *Organizational development: Its nature, origins and prospects.* Reading, MA: Addison-Wesley.

Bennis, W. (1965). Beyond bureaucracy. *Trans-Action, 2,* 31–35.

Bennis, W., & Shepard, H. (1956). A theory of group development. *Human Relations, 9*(4), 415-437

Bensman, J., & Lilienfeld, R. (1979). *Between public and private.* New York: Free Press.

Bergmann, M. S. (1982). Platonic love, transference love and love in real life. *Journal of the American Psychoanalytic Association, 30*, 87–98.

Bieber, I. (1970). Disorder of the work function: An overview. In J. H. Masserman (Ed.), *The dynamics of work and marriage* (pp. 92–98). New York: Grune & Stratton.

Bion, W. (1961). *Experiences in groups.* London: Tavistock. (Original work published 1948)

Bion, W. (1970). Attention and intrepretation. New York: Basic Books.

Blake, R. R., & Mouton, J. S. (1964). *The managerial grid.* Houston, TX: Gulf.

Blake, R. R., & Mouton, J. S. (1976). *Consultation.* Reading, MA: Addison-Wesley.

Blanck, G., & Blanck, R. (1974). *Ego psychology: Theory and practice.* New York: Columbia University Press.

Blos, P. (1974). The genealogy of the ego ideal. *Psychoanalytic Study of the Child, 20*, 43–88.

Blum, H. P. (1988). Shared fantasies and reciprocal identifications and their role in gender disorders. In H. Blum , Y. Kramer, A. Richards, & A. Richards (Eds.), *Fantasy, myth and reality* (pp. 323–338). New York: International Universities Press.

Boulding, K. E. (1953). *The organizational revolution.* New York: Harper & Row.

Bowers, K. S. (1984). *The unconscious reconsidered.* New York: John Wiley.

Bowlby, J. (1961). Processes of mourning. *International Journal of Psychoanalysis, 42*, 317–340.

Bowlby, J. (1973). *Separation: Anxiety and anger: Vol. 2. Attachment and loss.* New York: Basic Books.

Bowles, S., Gordon, D. M., & Weisskopf, T. E. (1983). *Beyond the waste-land: A democratic alternative to economic decline.* New York: Doubleday.

Braverman, H. (1984). The real meaning of Taylorism. In F. Fisher & C. Sirianni (Eds.), *Organization and bureacuracy* (pp. 79–85). Philadelphia: Temple University Press.

Brenner, C. (1982). *The mind in conflict.* New York: International Universities Press.

Brockner, J. (1988). *Self esteem at work.* Lexington, MA: Lexington Books.

Brochek, F. (1979). Computer, technological order and psychoanalysis. *Psychoanalytic Review, 71*(2), 263–277.

Brodsky, C. (1977). Suicide attributed to work. *Suicide and Life-Threatening Behavior, 7*(4), 216–229.

Burgelman, R. A., & Sayles, L. R. (1986). *Inside corporate innovation.* New York: Free Press.

Burris, B. H., & Heydebrand, W. U. (1984). Technocratic administration and educational control. In F. Fisher & C. Sirianni (Eds.), *Organization and bureaucracy* (pp. 191–210). Philadelphia: Temple University Press.

Bursten, B. (1978). *The manipulator.* New Haven, CT: Yale University Press.

Caplan, G. (1964). *Principles of preventive psychiatry.* New York: Basic Books.

Caplan, G. (1970). *The theory and practice of mental health consultation.* New York: Basic Books.

Chein, I. (1946). Personality & typology. In P. L. Harrison (Ed.), *Twentieth century psychology* (pp. 37–56).

Chein, I. (1947). The genetic factor in a historical psychology. *Journal of General Psychology, 36,* 151–172.

Chein, I. (1972). *The science of behavior and the image of man.* New York: Basic Books.

Chin, R. (1961). The planning of change. In W. Bennis, K. Benne, & R. Chin (Eds.), *Readings in applied behavioral sciences* (pp. 110–131). New York: Holt, Rinehart & Winston.

Chisholm, R. M. (1967). Intentionality. In P. Edwards (Ed.), *The encyclopedia of philosophy* (Vol. 1, pp. 365–368). New York: Macmillan/Free Press. (Original work published 1946)

Cooper, G. L., & Davidson, M. J. (1982). The high cost of stress on women managers. *Organizational Dynamics, 10* (Winter), 44–53.

Cox, R., & Walderson, W. (Eds.). (1949). *Theory in marketing.* Homewood, IL: Richard Irwin.

Crosby, P. B. (1984). *Quality without tears.* New York: McGraw-Hill

Crozier, M. (1964). *The bureaucractic phenomenon.* London: Tavistock.

Czander, W. (1983). Improving recuperative tendencies of organizations. *Consultants' Communique, 11*(3), 1–10.

Czander, W. (1985). *The application of social systems thinking to organizational consulting.* Washington, DC: University Press.

Czander, W. (1990). *The absence of intrapsychic life in organizational psychology textbooks.* Unpublished manuscript.

Dalton, G. W., & Lawrence, P. R. (1970). *Organizational change and development.* Homewood, IL: Richard Irwin.

Deal, T. E., & Kennedy, A. A. (1982). *Corporate cultures.* Reading, MA: Addison-Wesley.

Deal, T. E., & Kennedy, A. A. (1984, Jan./Feb.). How to create an outstanding hospital culture. *Hospital Forum,* pp. 21–34.

de Charm, R. (1968). *Personal causation.* New York: Academic Press

Deutscher, M. (1968). Adult work and developmental models. *American Journal of Orthopsychiatry, 18,* 882–892.

DiTomasi, N. (1984). Class and politics in the organization of public administration: The U.S. Department of Labor. In F. Fischer & C. Sirianni (Eds.), *Critical studies in organization and bureaucracy* (pp. 335–355). Philadelphia: Temple University Press.

Dolgoff, T. (1972). Organizations as socio-technical systems. *Bulletin of the Menninger Clinic, 37,* 232–257.

Doroff, D. (1974). Developing and mastery of a therapeutic alliance with the narcissistic personality. *American Academy of Psychoanalysis, 4*(2), 137–160.

Durkin, H. (1964). *The group in depth.* New York: International Universities Press.

Dyer, W. G. (1982). *Culture in organizations: A case study and analysis* (Working paper 1279-82). Cambridge, MA: Sloan School of Management, MIT.

Eagle, M. (1981). Interests as object relations. *Psychoanalysis and Contemporary Thought, 4*(4), 527–565

Eagle, M. (1990). The concept of need and wish in self psychology. *Psychoanalytic Psychology, 7,* 71–88.

Edelman, M. (1977). *Political language.* New York: Academic Press.

Edelson, M. (1984). *Hypothesis and evidence in psychoanalysis.* Chicago: University of Chicago Press.

Edwards, R. C. (1984). Forms of control in the labor process. In F. Fischer & C. Sirianni (Eds.), *Organizational and bureaucracy* (pp. 109–142). Philadelphia: Temple University Press.

Ellul, J. (1964). *The technological society* (J. Wilkinson, Trans.). New York: Knopf.

Emde, R. N., & Harmon, R. J. (Eds.). (1991) *Development of attachment and affiliated systems.* New York: Plenum Press.

Emery, F. E., & Trist, E. L. (1960). Socio-technical systems. In C. W. Churchman & M. Verkulat (Eds.), *Management science* (pp. 214–232). London: Pergamon Press.

Emery, F. E., & Trist, E. L. (1965). The causal texture of organizational environments. *Human Relations, 18,* 21–32.

Erikson, E. (1950). *Childhood and society.* New York: W. W. Norton.

Evan, W. (1966). The organization set: Toward a theory of interorganizational relations. In J. D. Thompson (Ed.), *Approaches to organizational design* (pp. 171–191). Pittsburgh, PA: University of Pittsburgh Press.

Faigel, H. C. (1968). The wandering womb: Mass hysteria in schoolgirls. *Clinical Pediatrics, 7,* 377–383.

Fairbairn, W. R. D. (1952). *An object relations theory of personality.* New York: Basic Books.

Farber, L. (1976). *Lying, despair, jealously, envy, sex, suicide, drugs, and the good life.* New York: Basic Books.

Ferber, L., & Kent, J. (1976). Forum: Role of psychoanalysis in a changing society. *International Journal of Psychoanalysis, 57,* 441–474.

Ferenczi, S. (1950). On Sunday neurosis. In *Further contributions to the theory and technique of psychoanalysis* (2nd ed., pp. 174–177). New York: Basic Books. (Original work published 1918)

Ferguson, C. K. (1968, April–June). Concerning the nature of human systems and the consultant's role. *Journal of Applied Behavioral Science, 4,* 179–193.

Field, G. (1974). The unconscious organization. *Psychoanalytic Review, 61*(3), 327–354.

Fine, M., & Wolf, E.S. (1987). Career choice: The dynamics of self-expression. *Psychoanalytic Inquiry, 7*(1), 39–57.

Foulkes, S. H. (1948). *Introduction to group-analytic psychotherapy.* London: Maresfield Reprints.

Foulkes, S. H. (1964). *Therapeutic group analysis.* New York: International Universities Press.

Freud, A. (1966). *The ego and the mechanisms of defense.* New York: International Universities Press.

Freud, A. (1967). About losing and being lost. In *Problems in psychoanalytic training, diagnosis and the technique of therapy* (pp. 9–19). New York: International Universities Press.

Freud, S. (1953). The interpretation of dreams. In J. Strachey (Ed. and Trans.), *The standard edition of the complete psychological works of Sigmund Freud* (Vols. 4 & 5, pp. 1–723). London: Hogarth Press. (Original work published 1900)

Freud, S. (1953). Three essays on the theory of sexuality. In J. Strachey (Ed. and Trans.), *The standard edition of the complete psychological works of Sigmund Freud* (Vol. 7, pp. 125–245). London: Hogarth Press. (Original work published 1905)

Freud, S. (1953). Totem and taboo. In J. Strachey (Ed. and Trans.), *The standard edition of the complete psychological works of Sigmund Freud* (Vol. 13, pp. 1–162). London: Hogarth Press. (Original work published 1912–1913)

Freud, S. (1955). Beyond the pleasure principle. In J. Strachey (Ed. and Trans.), *The standard edition of the complete psychological works of Sigmund Freud* (Vol. 18, pp. 3–64). London: Hogarth Press. (Original work published 1920)

Freud, S. (1955). Group psychology and the analysis of the ego. In J. Strachey (Ed. and Trans.), *The standard edition of the complete psychological works of Sigmund Freud* (Vol. 18, pp. 67–143). London: Hogarth Press. (Original work published 1921)

Freud, S. (1957). Instincts and their vicissitudes. In J. Strachey (Ed. and Trans.), *The standard edition of the complete psychological works of Sigmund Freud* (Vol. 14, pp. 117–140). London: Hogarth Press. (Original work published 1915)

Freud, S. (1957). Mourning and melancholia. In J. Strachey (Ed. and Trans.), *The standard edition of the complete psychological works of Sigmund Freud* (Vol. 14, pp. 237–258). London: Hogarth Press. (Original work published 1917)

Freud, S. (1957). On narcissism: An introduction. In J. Strachey (Ed. and Trans.), *The standard edition of the complete psychological works of Sigmund Freud* (Vol. 14, pp. 67–102). London: Hogarth Press. (Original work published 1914)

Freud, S. (1958). The dynamics of transference. In J. Strachey (Ed. and Trans.), *The standard edition of the complete psychological works of Sigmund Freud* (Vol. 12, pp. 97–108). London: Hogarth Press. (Original work published 1912)

Freud, S. (1959). Inhibitions, symptoms and anxiety. In J. Strachey (Ed. and Trans.), *The standard edition of the complete psychological works of Sigmund Freud* (Vol. 20, pp. 75–175). London: Hogarth Press. (Original work published 1926)

Freud, S. (1961). Civilization and its discontents. In J. Strachey (Ed. and Trans.), *The standard edition of the complete psychological works of Sigmund Freud* (Vol. 21, pp. 59–145). London: Hogarth Press. (Original work published 1930)

Freud, S. (1961). The dissolution of the Oedipus complex. In J. Strachey (Ed. and Trans.), *The standard edition of the complete psychological works of Sigmund Freud* (Vol. 19, pp. 173–179). London: Hogarth Press. (Original work published 1924)

Freud, S. (1961). The ego and the id. In J. Strachey (Ed. and Trans.), *The standard edition of the complete psychological works of Sigmund Freud* (Vol. 19, pp. 1–66). London: Hogarth Press. (Original work published 1923)

Freud, S. (1964). Introductory lectures. In J. Strachey (Ed. and Trans.), *The standard edition of the complete psychological works of Sigmund Freud* (Vol. 15, pp. 1–283). London: Hogarth Press. (Original work published 1916–1917)

Freud, S. (1964). Moses and monotheism. In J. Strachey (Ed. and Trans.), *The standard edition of the complete psychological works of Sigmund Freud* (Vol. 23, pp. 1–137). London: Hogarth Press. (Original work published 1937–1939)

Freud, S. (1964). Libidinal types. In J. Stroeber (Ed. and Trans.), *The standard edition of the complete psychology of Sigmund Freud* (Vol. 22, pp. 215–222). London: Hogarth Press. (Original work published 1931)

Freud, S. (1964). An outline of psychoanalysis. In J. Strachey (Ed. and Trans.), *The standard edition of the complete psychological works of Sigmund Freud* (Vol. 23, pp. 139–207). London: Hogarth Press. (Original work published 1940)

Friedman, T. (1967). Methodological considerations and research need in the study of epidemic hysteria. *American Journal of Public Health, 57,* 2009–2011.

Fromm, E. (1941). *Escape from freedom.* New York: Holt, Rinehart & Winston.

Fromm, E. (1970). Thoughts on bureaucracy. *Management Science, 16*(12), B699–B705.

Gabriel, Y. (1982). Freud, Rieff and the critique of American culture. *Psychoanalytic Review, 69*(3) 341–366.

Garvey (1984). *Childrens talk.* Cambridge, MA: Harvard University Press.

Garvey, C., & Berndt, C. (1977). *Play.* Cambridge, MA: Harvard University Press.

Gay, P. (1988). *Freud: A life for our times.* New York: W. W. Norton.

Gerard, R. W. (1968). Units and concepts of biology. In W. Buckley (Ed.), *Modern systems research for the behavioral scientist* (pp. 51–58). Chicago, IL: Aldine.

Gibbard, G. (1974). Individuation, fusion, and role specialization. In G. Gibbard, H. Hartman, & G. Mann (Eds.), *Analysis of groups* (pp. 115–126). San Francisico: Jossey-Bass.

Gill, M. (1976). Metapsychology is not psychology. In M. Gill & P. Holzman (Eds.), *Psychology versus metapsychology: Psychoanalytic essays in memory of George S. Klein (Psychological Issues,* Monograph 36). New York: International Universities Press.

Ginsberg, E., et al. (1951). *Occupational choice.* New York: Columbia University Press.

Ginsburg, S. W. (1956). Work and its satisfactions. *Journal of the Hillside Hospital, 5,*(3–4), 301–311.

Globus, G. G. (1974). The problem of consciousness. In L. Goldberger & V. H. Rosen (Eds.), *Psychoanalysis and contemporary science,* (Vol 3, pp. 40–69). New York: International Universities Press.

Goldberg, A. (Ed.). (1980). *Advances in self psychology.* New York: International Universities Press.

Gordon, J. (1987). *Organizational behavior.* Boston: Allyn & Bacon.

Gouldner, A. (1954). *Patterns of industrial bureaucracy.* Chicago: Free Press.

Greenacre, P. (1959). On focal symbiosis. In L. Jessuh & E. Pavenstedt (Eds.), *Dynamic psychopathology in childhood* (pp. 243–256). New York: Grune & Statton.

Greenberg, J. R., & Mitchell, S. A. (1983). *Object relations in psychoanalytic theory.* Cambridge, MA: Havard University Press.

Greenson, R. (1967). The technique and practice of psychoanalysis. New York: International Universities Press.

Grey, A. (1988). Work role and private self. *Contemporary Psychoanalysis, 24*(3), 484-497.

Grotstein, J. S. (1983). Some perspectives on self psychology. In A. Goldberg (Ed.), *The future of psychoanalysis* (pp. 165–202). New York: International Universities Press.

Grunbaum, A. (1953). Causality and the science of human behavior. In H. Feigl & M. Brodbeck (Eds.), *The philosophy of science* (pp. 110–124). New York: Appleton-Century.

Grunberger, B. (1971). *Narcissism.* New York: International Universities Press.

Grunberger, B. (1966). Narcissism and the Oedipus complex. In B. Grunberger (Ed.), *Narcissism: Psychoanalytic essays* (pp. 265–281). New York: International Universities Press

Grunbaum, A. (1977). How scientific is psychoanalysis? In R. Stern, L. Horowitz, & J. Lynes (Eds.), *Science and psychotherapy* (pp. 219–254). New York: Haven Press.

Grunebaum, H. (1989). [review of *Restoration of self*]. *Bulletin of the Menninger Clinic, 11,* 561–567.

Grunebaum, H., & Kates, W. (1977). Whom to refer for group psychotherapy. *American Journal of Psychiatry, 134,* 130–133.

Guntrip, H., (1969). *Schizoid phenomena, object relations and the self.* New York: International Universities Press.

Gutmann, D. (1965). Woman and the conception of ego strength. *Merrill-Palmer Quarterly, 11,* 229–240.

Hall, C. (1954). *A primer in Freudian psychology.* New York: Mentor Books.

Halpern, H., and Halpern, T. (1966). Psychological perspectives on anti-achievement. *Psychoanalytic Review, 53*(3), 407–417.

Halpern, J., & Halpern, I. (1983). *Projections.* New York: Seaview/Putnam Press.

Hanlon, J. (1990). Modes of internalizing the supervisor. *Psychoanalysis and Psychotherapy*, 8(1), 5–11.

Harlow, H. F. (1972). The language of love. In T. Alloway, L. Krames, & P. Pliner (Eds.), *Communication and affect* (pp. 1–18). New York: Academic Press.

Hartmann, H. (1958). *Ego psychology and the problem of adaptation.* International Universities Press.

Hartmann, H. (1984). *Essays on ego psychology.* New York: International Universities Press.

Hartmann, H., & Lowenstein, R.M. (1962). The development of the ego content in Freud's work. *Psychoanalytic Study of the Child, 17,* 42–81.

Harvey, J. B. (1988). *The Abilene paradox and other meditations on management.* Lexington, MA: Lexington Books.

Harvey, J. B., & Albertson, R. (1971). Neurotic organizations: Symptoms, causes and treatment:Part 1. *Personnel Journal, 20,* 27–62.

Harvey, J. B., & Albertson, R. (1977). Neurotic organizations: Symptoms, causes and treatment:Pt. 2. *Personnel Journal, 20,* 1–17.

Hayes, R. H., & Abernathy, W. J. (1980, July–August). Managing our way to ecomonic decline. *Harvard Business Review,* pp. 67–77.

Hendrik I. (1943a). Discussion of the instinct to master. *Psychoanalytic Quarterly, 12,* 516–565.

Heller, J. (1974). *Something happened.* New York: Knopf.

Hendrik I. (1943b). Work and the pleasure principle. *Psychoanalytic Quarterly, 12,* 311–329.

Herzberg, F. (1966). *Work and human nature.* Cleveland, OH: World.

Herzberg, F., Mauser, F., & Snyderman, B. B. (1959). *The motivation to work* (2nd ed.). New York: Wiley.

Hirsch, P. (1984). Ambushes, shootouts, and Knights of the Roundtable: The language of corporate takeovers. In J. G. Hunt, D. M. Hosking, C. A. Schriesheim, & R. Stewart (Eds.), *Leaders and managers* (pp. 228). New York: Pergamon Press. (Original work presented 1980)

Hirschhorn, H. (1988). *The workplace within.* Cambridge, MA: MIT Press.

Hodgson, R. C. (1965). *The executive role constellation: An analysis of personality and role relations in management.* Cambridge, MA: Harvard Business School.

Holt, R. (1967). The development of the primary process: A structural view. In R. Holt (Ed.), *Motives and thought: Essays in the honor of David Rapaport* (pp. 344–384). New York: International Universities Press.

Holt, R. (1976). Drive or wish?: A reconsideration of the psychoanalysis theory of motivation. In M. Gill & P. Holzman (Eds.), *Psychology vs. metapychology* (pp. 158–197). New York: International Universities Press.

Holmes, D. (1965). A contribution to the psychoanalytic theory of work. *Psychoanalytic Study of the Child, 20,* 384–291.

Homans, G. C. (1950). *The human group.* New York: Harcourt Brace.

Horkheimer, M. (1949). Authoritarianism and the family today. In R. Anshen (Ed.), *The family: Its function and destiny* (pp. 381–398). New York: Harper.

Horney, K. (1937). *The neurotic personality of our time.* New York: W. W. Norton.

Hornstein, H. A., Bunker, D. B., Burke, W. W., Gindes, M., & Lewicki, R. J. (1971). *Social intervention.* New York: Free Press.

Howenstein, R. (1975). *Consulting to a youth center.* Unpublished manuscript, Yale University, New Haven, CT.

Husserl, E. (1965). Philosophy as rigorous science. In Q. Lauer (Ed.), Edmund Husserl: *Phenomenology and the crisis of philosophy* (pp. 69–147). New York: Harper. (Original work published 1910–1911)

Ilan, E. (1963). The problem of motivation in the educators' vocational choice, *Psychoanalytic Study of the Child, 28,* 266–285.

Ingber, D. (1981). Computer addicts. *Science Digest,* July, 114–121.

Ingram, D. H. (1986). Remarks on intimacy and the fear of commitment. *American Journal of Psychoanalysis, 46*(1), 76–79.

Ivancevich, J. M., & Mattesen, M. T. (1987). Employee claims for damages add to the high cost of job stress. In J. Gordon (Ed.), *Organizational behavior* (pp. 193–198). Boston: Allyn & Bacon.

Jacobs, N. (1965). The phantom slashes of Taipei: Mass hysteria in a non-Western society. *Social Problems, 12,* 318–322.

Jacobson, E. (1954). The self and the object world. *Psychoanalytic Study of the Child, 9,* 75–127.

Jacobson, E. (1964). *The self and the object world.* New York: International Universities Press.

Jahoda, M. (1966). Notes on work. In R. Loewenstein (Ed.), *Psychoanalysis: A general psychology* (pp. 622–633). New York: International Universities Press.

Jahoda, M. (1982). *Employment and unemployment.* Cambridge, England: Cambridge University Press.

Jaques, E. (1951). *The changing culture of the factory.* London: Tavistock.

Jaques, E. (1971). Social systems as defense against persecutory and depressive anxiety. In M. Klein, P. Heinium, & R. E. Money-Kyrle (Eds.), *New directions in psychoanalysis* (pp. 478–498). New York: Basic Books.

Kahn, R. L., Wolfe, D. M., Quinn, R. P., & Snock, J. D. (1964). *Organizational stress studies in role conflict and ambiguity.* New York: Wiley.

Kanter, R. M. (1977). *Men and women of the corporation.* New York: Basic Books.

Kanter, R. M. (1983). *The change masters.* New York: Simon & Schuster.

Kaplan, S. R. (1967). Therapy groups and training groups: Similarities and differences. *International Journal of Group Psychotherapy, 17,* 437–504.

Karmon, G. (1988, June 14). "Managed care": It's time to plan now. *New York Times,* p. D. 2.

Katz, D., & Kahn, R. L. (1966). *The social psychology of organizations.* New York: Wiley.

Kaufman, C. B. (1967). *Man incorporate.* New York: Doubleday.

Kerckhoff, A. C., & Bach, K. W. (1968). *The June bug: A study of hysterical contagion.* New York: Appleton-Century-Crofts.

Kernberg, O. (1971). The couch at sea: Psychoanalytic study of group and organizational leadership. *International Journal of Group Psychotherapy, 34*(1), 5–23.

Kernberg, O. (1975). *Borderline conditions and pathological narcissism.* New York: Aronson.

Kernberg, O. (1976). *Object relations and clinical psychoanalysis.* New York: Aronson.

Kernberg, O. (1978). Leadership and organizational functioning: Organizational regression. *International Journal of Group Psychotherapy, 21,* 3–25.

Kernberg, O. (1980). *Internal world and external reality.* New York: Aronson.

Kernberg, O. (1984). The couch at sea: Psychoanalytic studies of group and organizational leadership. *International Journal of Group Psychotherapy, 34*(1), 5–23.

Kets de Vries, M. F. (1978). Defective adaptation to work. *Bulletin of the Menninger Clinic, 42*(1), 35–50.

Kets de Vries, M. F. (1980). *Organizational paradoxes.* London: Tavistock.

Kets de Vries, M. F., & Miller, D. (1984). *The neurotic organization.* San Francisco: Jossey-Bass.

Kets de Vries, M. F. (Ed.). (1984). *The irrational executive.* New York: International Universities Press.

Kilman, R. H., & Covin, T. J. (1988). *Corporate transformation.* San Francisco: Jossey-Bass.

Kirkpatrick, R. G. (1975). Collective consciousness and mass hysteria: Collective behavior and anti-pornography crusades in Durkeimian perspective. *Human Relations, 28,* 63–84.

Kipling, R. (1925). In the house of Suddhoo. In *The malady and other works of Rudyard Kipling* (p. 131). Garden City, NY: Doubleday.

Klein, E. B. & Gould, L. T. (1973). Bondary issues and organizational dynamics: A case study. *Social Psychiatry, 4,* 204–211.

Klein, G. (1976). *Psychoanalytic theory: An explanation of essentials.* New York: International Universities Press.

Klein, M. (1964). *Contributions to psychoanalysis, 1921–1945.* New York: McGraw-Hill.

Klein, M. (194e0. Mourning and its relation to manic-depressive states. *International Journal of Psychoanalysis, 21,* 76–95.

Klein, M. (1975). *Envy and gratitude and other works, 1946–1963.* New York: Delacorte Press.

Klein, M. (1975). *Love, guilt and reparation and other work: 1921–1945.* New York: Delta Press.

Klingerman, C. (1980). Art and the self of the artist. In A. Goldberg (Ed.), *Advances in self psychology* (pp. 212–232). New York: International Universities Press.

Knapp, H. (1989). Projective identification: Whose projection—whose identity. *Psychoanalytic Psychology, 6*(1), 47–59.

Knight, J. A., Friedman, T. I., & Sulianti, J. (1965). Epidemic hysteria: A field study. *American Journal of Public Health, 55,* 858–865.

Kohn, M. L., & Schooler, L. C. (1983). *Work and personality.* Norwood, NJ: Ablex.

Kohut, H. (1971). *The analysis of self.* New York: International Universities Press.

Kohut, H. (1977). *The restoration of self.* New York: International Universities Press.

Kohut, H. (1980). Summarizing reflections In A. Goldberg (Ed.), *Advances in self psychology* (pp. 473–553). New York: International Universities Press.

Kohut, H. (1985). *Self psychology and the humanities.* New York: W. W. Norton.

Kohut, H., & Wolf, E. (1978). Disorders of the self and their treatment. *International Journal of Psychoanalysis, 59,* 413–425.

Kramer, Y. (1977). Work compulsion—A psychoanalytic study. *Psychoanalytic Quarterly, 46,* 361–377.

Kris, E. (1956). The personal myth. *Journal of the American Psychoanalytic Association, 4,* 653–681.

Kubie, L. S. (1961). *Neurotic distortion of the creative process.* Lawrence, KS: University of Kansas Press.

Kuhn, T. S. (1965). *The structure of scientific revolution.* Chicago: University of Chicago Press.

Kuhn, T. S. (1974). Second thoughts on paradigms. In *The essential tension: Selected studies in scientific tradition and change* (pp. 293–319). Chicago: University of Chicago Press.

Lakoff, G., & Johnson, M. (1980). *Metaphors we live by.* Chicago, University of Chicago Press.

Lang, J. A. (1984). Notes toward a psychology of the feminine self. In P. E. Stepansky & A. Goldberg (Eds.), *Kohut's legacy.* Hillsdale, NJ: Analytic Press.

Langs, R. (1980). *Interactions.* New York: Aronson.

Lampl-de Groot, J. (1962). The ego ideal and superego. *Psychoanalytic Study of the Child, 27,* 94–106.

Lantos, B. (1943). Work and the instincts. *International Journal of Psychoanalysis, 24,* 114–119.

Lantos, B. (1952). Metapsychological considerations on the concept of work. *International Journal of Psychoanalysis, 33,* 439–444.

Lawrence, P. R., & Lorsch, J. W. (1969). *Developing organizations: Diagnosis and actions.* Reading, MA: Addison-Wesley.

Lawrence, P. R., & Lorsch, J. W. (1970). *Studies in organizational design.* Homewood, IL: Richard Irwin.

Levine, S., & White, P. E. (1961). Exchange as a conceptual framework for the study of inter-organizational relations. *Administrative Science Quarterly, 5,* 5883–6601.

Levinson, H. (1984). Management by guilt. In M. Kets de Vries (Ed.), *The irrational executive* (pp. 132–151). New York: International Universities Press.

Levy-Leboyer, C. (1988). Success and failure in applying psychology. *American Psychologist, 10,* 779–784.

Lewin, K. (1947). Frontiers in group dynamics. *Human Relations, 1,* 5–41.

Lieberman, M. A., Yalom, I. D., & Miles, M. B. (1973). *Encounter groups: First facts*. New York: Basic Books.

Lifton, R. J. (1968, Winter). Protean man. *Partisan Review*, pp. 13–27.

Lincoln, J. R., Hanada, M., & McBride, K. (1986). Organizational structures in Japanese and U.S. manufacturing. *Administrative Science Quarterly, 31*, 338–364.

Lippitt, G. L. & Swartz, D. (1975). Evaluating the consulting process. *Journal of European Training, 4*(5), 301–310.

Lippitt, R. (1959). Dimensions of the consultant's job. *Journal of Social Issues, 15*(2), 5–12.

Loewald, H. (1960a). Internalization, separation, mourning, and the super-ego. In H. Loewald (Ed.), *Papers on psychoanalysis* (pp. 457–476). New Haven, CT: Yale University Press.

Loewald, H. (1960). On the therapeutic action of psychoanalysis. *International Journal of Psychoanalysis, 58*, 463–472.

Loewald, H. (1960b). Primary process, secondary process and language. In *Papers on psychoanalysis* (pp. 178–206). New Haven, CT: Yale University Press.

Loewald, H. (1971). On motivation and instinct theory. *Psychoanalytic Study of the Child, 26*, 91–128.

Loewald, H. (1980). *Papers on psychoanalysis*. New Haven, CT: Yale University Press.

Maccoby, M. (1976). *The gamesman*. New York: Simon & Schuster.

Mahler, M. (1965). On the significance of the normal separation-individuation phase. In M. Schur (Ed.), *Drives, affects and behavior* (pp. 161–169). New York: International Universities Press.

Mahler, M. (1972). Reapproachment sub-phase of the separation–individuation process. *Psychoanalytic Quarterly, 41*, 487–506.

Mahler, M., Pine, F., & Bergman, A. (1975). *The psychological birth of the human infant*. New York: Basic Books.

Mann, F. & Hoffman, R. (1960). *Automation and the worker*. New York: Holt & Dryden.

Mann, R. D. (1967). *Interpersonal styles and group development*. New York: Wiley.

Manz, C. C., & Sims, H. P. (1980). Self-management as a substitute for leadership: A social learning theory perspective. In D. D. White (Ed.), *Contemporary perspectives in organizational behavior* (pp. 84–93). New York: Allyn & Bacon.

March, J. G., & Simon, H. (1958). *Organizations*. New York: Wiley.

Marcuse, H. (1955). *Eros and civilization*. Boston: Beacon Press.

Marcus, S. (1978). There brother's keeper. In W. Gaylin, I. Glasser, S. Marcus, & D. Rothman (Eds.), *Doing good* (pp. 49–66). New York: Pantheon.

Markus, M. L. (1984). *Systems in organizations*. Boston, MA: Pitman.

Martin, J., Feldman, M. S., Hatch, M. J., & Sitkin, S. B. (1983). The uniqueness paradox in organizational stories. *Administrative Science Quaterly, 28*, 438–453.

Martin, J., and Siehl, C. (1983, Autumn). Organizational culture and counter-culture. *Organization Dynamics*. pp. 52–64.

Maslow, A. (1954). *Motivation and personality.* New York: Harper and Row.

Masson, J. M. (Ed.). (1985). *The complete letters of Sigmund Freud to Wilhelm Fliess: 1897 to 1904.* Cambridge, MA: Harvard University Press. (Original work published 1950)

Masterson, J. (1981) *The narcissistic and borderline disorder.* New York: Brunner/Mazel.

May, R. (1975). *The courage to create.* New York: W. W. Norton.

McDougall, J. (1980). *Plea for a measure of abnormality.* New York: International Universities Press.

McDougall, W. (1973). *The group mind.* California: Ayer. (Original work published in 1920)

McNamara, R. S. (1968). *The essence of security,* New York: Harper & Row (pp. 109–110).

Mead, G. H. (1934). *Mind, self and society.* Chicago: University of Chicago Press.

Medalia, N., & Larsen, O. (1958). Diffusion and belief in a collective delusion: The Seattle windshield pitting epidemic. *American Sociological Review, 23,* 180–186.

Meissner, W. (1972). Notes on identification. *Psychoanalytic Quarterly, 41,* 224–266.

Meissner, W. (1975). A note on internalization as process. *Psychoanalytic Quarterly, 45,* 374–393.

Meissner, W. (1984). The cult phenomenon: A psychoanalytic perspective. In W. Muensterberg, L. B. Boyer, & S. A. Grolnick (Ed.), *The psychoanalytic study of society* (Vol. 10, pp. 91–112). Hillside, NJ: Analytic Press.

Menninger, K. (1942). Work as sublimation. *Bulletin of the Menninger Clinic, 6,* 170–182.

Menzies, I. E. P. (1960). A case study in the functioning of social systems as a defense against anxiety. *Human Relations, 13,* 95–121.

Merry, V. & Brown, G. L. (1987). *The neurotic behavior of organizations.* New York: Gardner Press.

Miller, D., Kets de Vries, M. F., & Toulouse, J. M. (1988). Top executives focus of control and its relationship to strategy-making structure, and environment. *Academy of Management Journal, 25,* 237–253.

Miller, E. (1973). Technology, territory and time: The internal differentiation. In F. Baker (Ed.), *Organizational systems* (pp. 261–294). Homewood, IL: Richard Irwin.

Miller, E. J., & Rice, A. K. (1967). *Systems of organization.* London, England: Tavistock.

Miller, E. J., & Rice, A. K. (1975). Selection from systems of organization. In A. D. Coleman (Ed.), *Group relations reader* (pp. 43–68). Sausalito, CA: Grex

Miller, J. C. (1965). Living systems: Basic concepts. *Behavioral Science, 10,* 193–237.

Milrod, D. (1982). The wished-for self image. *Psychoanalytic Study of the Child, 37,* 95–115.

Mintzberg, H. (1988). The structuring of organizations. In H. Mintzberg & J.

B. Quinn (Eds.), *The strategy process* (pp. 330–350). Englewood Cliffs, NJ: Prentice Hall.

Mirvis, P. H., & Berg, D. N. (1977). *Failures in organizational development and change*. New York: Wiley.

Mischel, W. (1973). Toward a cognitive social learning reconceptualization of personality. *Psychological Review, 80,* 252–283.

Mitchell, S. (1988). *Relational concepts in psychoanalysis*. Cambridge, MA: Harvard University Press.

Moscovici, S. (1985). *The age of the crowd*. Cambridge, MA: Cambridge University Press.

Morgan, G. (1988). *Images of organizations*. Beverly Hills, CA: Sage.

Morrison, A. (1984). Shame and the psychology of self. In P. E. Stepansky & A. Goldberg (Eds.), *Kohut's legacy* (pp. 71–92). New York: International Universities Press.

Neff, W. S. (1977). *Work and human behavior*. Chicago: Aldine.

Neisser, U. (1967). *Cognitive psychology*. New York: Appleton-Century-Crofts.

Nelson, D. L., & Quick, J. C. (1985). Professional women: Are distress to disease inevitable? *Academy of Management Review, 10,* 206–218.

Newton, P. (1974). Social structure and process in psychotherapy: A sociopsychological analysis of transference, resistance and change. *International Journal of Psychiatry, 22,* 480–552.

Novey, S. (1955). The role of the superego and the ego ideal in character formation. *International Journal of Psychoanalysis, 24,* 28–42.

Noy, P. (1968). A theory of art and aesthetic experience. *Psychoanalytic Review, 55,* 623–645.

Nunberg, H. (1933). *Principles of psychoanalysis*. New York: International Universities Press.

Oberndorf, C. (1951). The psychopathology of work. *Bulletin of the Menninger Clinic, 13,* 77–84.

Ogden, T. (1982). *Projective identification and therapeutic technique*. New York: Aronson.

Orgel, S. (1990). The future of psychoanalysis. *Psychoanalytic Quarterly, 59,* 1–21.

Ouchi, W. G. (1981a). *How American business can meet the Japanese challenge*. Reading, MA: Addison-Wesley.

Ouchi, W. G. (1981b). Going from A to Z: Thirteen steps to a theory Z organization. *Management Review, 2,* 6–16.

Peterfreund, E. (in collaboration with Schwartz, J. T.) (1971). *Information, systems, and psychoanalysis* (*Psychological Issues,* Monograph 25/26). New York: International Universities Press.

Pederson-Krag, G. (1955). *Personality factors in work and employment*. New York: Funk & Wagnalls.

Peters, T. J., & Austin, N. K. (1985). *A passion for excellence*. New York: Random House.

Peters, T. J., & Waterman, R. H. (1982). *In search of excellence*. New York: Harper & Row.

Piers, G. O., & Singer, M. B. (1952). *Shame and guilt*. Springfield, IL: Thomas.

Pine, F. (1985). *Developmental theory and clinical process.* New Haven, CT: Yale University Press.

Pines, M. (1982). *On mirroring in group psychotherapy* (Group Therapy Monograph No. 9) New York: Washington Square Institute.

Pines, M. (1983). Psychoanalysis and group analysis. *International Journal of Group Psychotherapy, 33*(2), 155–170.

Pines, M. (1984). Reflections on mirroring. *International Review of Psychoanalysis, 11*, 37–42.

Polanyi, M. (1958). *Personal knowledge.* Chicago: University of Chicago Press.

Pondy, L. R. (1978). Leadership is a language game. In M. McCall & M. Lombardo (Eds.), *Leadership: Where else can we go?* (pp. 88–105). Durham, NC: Duke University Press.

Polk, L. D. (1974). Mass hysteria in an elementry school. *Clinical Pediatrics, 13*, 1013–1014.

Prien, E. P., Jones, M. A., Miller, L. M., Gulkin, R., & Sutherland, M. (1979). *Mental health in organizations.* Chicago: Nelson-Hall.

Prigogine, I., & Stengers, I. (1984). *Order out of chaos.* New York: Bantam Books.

Pruyser, P. W. (1980). Work: A curse or blessing. *Bulletin of the Menninger Clinic, 44*(1), 59–73.

Rangell, C. (1955). On the psychoanalytic theory of anxiety: A statement of a unitary theory. *Journal of American Psychoanalytic Association, 3*, 389–414.

Rapaport, D., & Gill, M. (1959). The points of view and assumptions of metapsychology. In M. Gill (Ed.), *The collected papers of David Rapaport* (pp. 327–388). New York: Basic Books.

Reich, A. (1954). Early identifications as archaic elements in the superego. *Journal of the American Psychoanalytic Association, 2*, 218–234.

Reich, A. (1960). Pathological forms of self-esteem regulation. *Psychoanalytic Study of the Child, 15*, 215–231.

Reich, W. (1928). On character analysis. In R. Fliess (Ed.), *The psychoanalytic reader* (pp. 121–147). New York: International Universities Press.

Reider, N. (1953). A type of transference to an institution. *Bulletin of the Menninger Clinic, 7*, 58–63.

Reider, N. (1957). Transference psychosis. *Journal of Hillside Hospital, 6*, 131–149.

Reisman, D., Glazer, D., & Denney, R. (1950). *The lonely crowd.* New Haven, CT: Yale University Press.

Redl, F. (1942). Group emotion and leadership. *Psychiatry, 5*, 573–596.

Rice, A. K. (1952). The relative independence of sub-institutions as illustrated by Department of Labor turnover. *Human Relations, 5*, 83–98.

Rice, A. K. (1963). *The enterprise and its environment.* London: Tavistock.

Rice, A. K. (1969). Individual, group and intergroup processes. *Human Relations, 22*, 565–584.

Rieman, D. (1963). Group mental health consultation with public health nurses. In L. Rapaport, (Ed.), *Consultation in social work practice* (pp. 85–95). New York: National Association of Social Workers.

Ringwald, J. (1974). An investigation of group reaction to central figures. In

G. S. Gibbard, J. J. Hartman, and R. D. Mann (Eds.), *Analysis of groups* (pp. 220–248). San Francisico: Jossey-Bass.

Rogers, R. (1980). Pschoanalysis and cybernetic models of mentation. *Psychoanalysis and Contemporary Thought, 3*(1), 21–55.

Roheim, G. (1943). *Origins and functions of culture.* New York: Doubleday.

Rohrlich, J. B. (1980). *Work and love.* New York: Harmony Books.

Roper, W. (1987, October 13). Managed care, medicine and health. *New York Times,* Sec. I, pp. 1, 6.

Roszak, T. (1969). *The making of a counterculture.* New York: Doubleday.

Rosenblum, G. (1970). Social intervention: Consultations to organizations. *Mental Hygiene, 54,* 393–400.

Rothlisberger, F. J., & Dickson, W. J. (1939). *Management and the worker.* Cambridge, MA: Harvard University Press.

Rothstein, A. (1980). *The narcissistic pursuit of perfection.* New York: International Universities Press.

Rycroft, C. (1956). Symbolism and its relationship to primary and secondary processes. *International Journal of Psychoanalysis, 37,* 137–146.

Sachs, H. (1933). The delay of the machine age. *Psychoanalytic Quarterly, 2,* 404–411.

Samberg, E., & Frances, E. (1987). Models of change in psychoanalysis and psychotherapy. In P. Buirski (Eds.), *Frontiers of dynamic psychotherapy* (pp. 3–20). New York: Brunner/Mazel.

Sampson, E. E. (1971). *Social psychology and contemporary society.* New York: Wiley.

Sandler, J. (1981). Unconscious wishes and human relationships. *Contemporary Psychoanalysis, 17,* 180–196.

Sandler, J., Holder, A., & Meers, D. (1963). The ego ideal and the ideal self. *Psychoanalytic Study of the Child, 28,* 139–158.

Santostefano, S. (1977). Action, fantasy and language: Developmental levels of ego organization in communicating drives and affects. In N. Freedman & S. Grand (Eds.), *Communicative structures and psychic structures* (pp. 131–154). New York: Plenum Press.

Saravay, S. (1978). A psychoanalytic theory of group development. *International Journal of Group Psychotherapy, 28*(4), 481–507.

Schafer, R. (1960). The loving and beloved superego in Freud's structural theory. *Psychoanalytic Study of the Child, 15,* 163–190.

Schafer, R. (1968). *Aspects of internalization.* New York: International Universities Press.

Schafer, R. (1972). Internalization: Process or fantasy? *Psychoanalytic Study of the Child, 27,* 411–436.

Schafer, R. (1976). *A new language for psychoanalysis.* New Haven, CT: Yale University Press.

Schecter, D. (1979). The loving and persecuting superego. *Contemporary Psychoanalysis, 15,* 361–379.

Schein, E. H. (1969). *Process consultation.* Reading, MA: Addison-Wesley.

Schwartz, B. (1981). *Queuing and waiting.* Chicago: Univerity of Chicago Press.

Schwartz, H. (1989). The psychodynamics of organizational totalitarianism. *Journal of General Management, 13*(1), 41–54.

Segal, H. (1967). *Introduction to the work of Melanie Klein*. New York: Basic Books.

Selznick, P. (1988). Leadership in Administration. In J. Quinn (Ed.), *The strategic process* (pp. 38–43). Englewood Cliffs, NJ: Prentice Hall.

Semrad, E. V., Kanter, S., Shapiro, D., & Assenian, J. (1963). The field of group psychotherapy. *International Journal of Group Psychotherapy, 13*, 452–475.

Sharpe, E. (1950). Psychological problems revealed in language: An examination of metaphor. In *Collected papers on psychoanalysis* (pp. 163–188). London: Hogarth Press.

Sherif, M. (1966). *In common predicament*. Boston: Houghton Mifflin.

Sherman, M. H. (1972). Role titles, vocations and psychotherapy. *Psychoanalytic Review, 58*(4), 511–527.

Sherwood, M. (1969). *The logic of explanation in psychoanalysis*. New York: Academic Press.

Siehl, C., & Martin, J. (1984). The role of symbolic management: How can managers effectively transmit organizational culture? In J. G. Hunt, D. Hoskins, & R. Stewart (Eds.), *Managerial work and leadership: International perspectives* (pp. 122–138). Elmsford, NY: Pergamon Press

Sievers, B. (1990). Zombies or people-What is the product of work? In B. A. Turner (Ed.), *Organizational symbolism* (pp. 83–94). New York: de Gruyter.

Slater, P. (1966). Microcosms. New York: Wiley.

Smelser, N. (1962). *The theory of collective behavior*. New York: Free Press.

Smith, S. (1977). The golden fantasy: A regressive reaction to separation anxiety. *International Journal of Psychoanalysis, 58*(3), 311–324.

Sofer, C. (1961). *The organization from within*. London: Tavistock.

Solomon, L. N. (1971). Humanism and the training of applied berhavioral scientists. *Journal of Applied Behavorial Sciences, 7*(5) 531–547.

Spieberger, C. D. (1966). *Anxiety and behavior*. New York: Academic Press.

Spitz, R. (1945). Hospitalism. *Psychoanalytic Study of the Child, 1*, 113–117.

Stahl, S. N., & Lebedum, M. (1974). Mysterious gas: An analysis of mass hysteria. *Journal of Health and Social Behavior, 15*, 434–50.

Stark, M. (1989). Work inhibition. *Contemporary Psychoanalysis, 21*(1), 135–158.

Steele, F. (1969b). Consultants and detectives. *Journal of Applied Behavior Science, 5*(2), 187–202.

Steele, F. (1969a). *Consulting for organizational change*. Amherst, MA: Amherst University Press.

Stern, D. (1985). *The interpersonal world of the infant*. New York: Basic Books.

Stolorow, R. D., & Lachmann, F. L. (1985–1986). Transference: The future of an illusion. In Chicago Institute of Psychoanalysis Staff (Ed.), *The annual of psychoanalysis* (Vols. 12/13, pp. 19–38). New York: International Universities Press.

Strean, H. S. (1968). Role theory: Its implications for social casework treatment. In M. C. Nelson (Ed.), *Roles and paradigms in psychotherapy* (pp. 274–288). New York: Grune & Stratton.

Sutherland, J. (1990). [An interview with Dr. John Sutherland]. *Austen Riggs Center Review, 2*(2), 7–12.

Swartz, W. (1958). Using the outside expert. *Management Review, 47,* 4–8.

Tannenbaum, A. S., Kavcic, B., Rosner, M., Vianello, M., & Wiesner, G. (1968). *Hierarchy in organizations.* San Fransisco: Jossey-Bass.

Tannenbaum, A. S. (1955). Change as a result of an experimental change in environmental conditions. *Journal of Administration and Social Psychology, 55,* 404–406.

Taylor, F. W. (1939). Scientific management. In F. Fischer & C. Sirianni (Eds.), *Organization and bureaucracy* (pp. 68–68). Philadelphia: Temple University Press.

Thorenson, E. E., & Mahoney, M. J. (1974). *Behavioral self-control.* New York: Holt, Rinehart & Winston.

Tiger, L. (1989). *Men in groups.* New York: Boyars.

Tolpin, M. (1971). On the beginnings of a cohesive self. *Psychoanalytic Study of the Child, 26,* 316–352.

Tomkins, S. S. (1965). *Affect, imagery, consciousness* (Vol. I). New York: Springer.

Travelbee, J. (1974). *Interpersonal aspects of nursing* (2nd ed.). Philadelphia: F. A. Davis.

Trice, H. M., & Beyer, J. M. (1984). Studying organizational cultures through rites and rituals. *Academy of Management Review, 9,* 653–669.

Turquet, P. (1975). Threats to identity in a large group. In L. Kreeger (Ed.), *The large group: Dynamics and therapy* (pp. 87–144). London: Constable.

von Bertalanffy, L. (1950). The theory of open systems in physics and biology. *Science, 3,* 23–29.

Waelder, R. (1936). The principle of multiple functioning. *Psychoanalytic Quarterly, 5,* 45–62.

Waelder, R. (1951). The structure of paranoid ideas. *International Journal of Psychoanalysis, 32,* 167–177.

Wangh, M. (1962). The evocation of a proxy. *Psychoanalytic Study of the Child, 17,* 451–472.

Watkins, M. (1986). *Invisible guests.* Hillsdale, NJ: Analytic Press.

Watson, T. (1984). *A business and its belief: The ideas that helped build IBM.* New York: McGraw-Hill.

Weil, E. (1959). Work block: The role of work in mental health. *Psychoanalysis and Psychoanalytic Review, 46*(2), 99–125.

Wheeler, L. (1966). Toward a theory of behavior contagion. *Psychological Review, 73,* 179–192.

White, R. W. (1960). Competence and psychosexual stages of development. In M. R. Jones (Ed.), *Nebraska Symposium on Motivation* (Vol. 8, pp. 28). Lincoln, NB: University of Nebraska Press.

Whyte, W. H. (1956). *The organizational man.* New York: Simon & Schuster.

Wilson, A., & Weinstein, L. (in press). Language, Vygotskian psychology, and the psychoanalytic process. *Journal of the American Psychoanalytic Association.*

Winnicott, D. W. (1958). *Through pediatrics to psychoanalysis.* London: Hogarth Press.

Winnicott, D. W. (1965). Ego distortion in terms of true and false self. In *Maturational processess and the facilitating environment* (pp. 140–154). New York: International Universities Press.

Wolberg, A. (1975). The leader and society. In Z. Liff (Ed.), *The leader in the group* (pp. 247–250). New York: Aronson.

Wolf, A. (1950). The psychoanalysis of groups. *American Journal of Psychotherapy, 3*(4), 16–50.

Wolhiem, R. (1974). Identification and imagination. In R. Wolhiem (Ed.), *Freud: A collection of critical essays* (pp. 172–195). Garden City, NY: Anchor.

Zaleznik, A. (1970). Power and politics of organizational life. *Harvard Business Review, 48,* 47–60.

Zaleznik, A., & Kets de Vries, M. F. (1984). Leadership and executive action. In M. F. Kets de Vries (Ed.), *The irrational executive* (pp. 286–314). New York: International Universities Press.

Zwerling, I. (1976). *Racism, elitism and professionalism.* New York: Aronson.

Index